Cultural Products and the World Trade Organization

Debate about trade and culture has a long history, but the application of WTO rules to cultural products such as films, radio, and books remains one of the most divisive issues in the organisation. After assessing the economic and social arguments for treating cultural products differently from things like steel or wheat, this book explains how the vastly different views of WTO Members in earlier negotiations led to an outcome that is disappointing for all. It goes on to provide a comprehensive evaluation of possible solutions, including evolution of the law through WTO dispute settlement, a new agreement outside the WTO, and reforms to improve the balance between trade liberalisation and cultural policy objectives. As UNESCO's new convention affecting trade and cultural diversity is due to enter into force in 2007 and the WTO's Doha Round of negotiations is stumbling, the need for such an evaluation is all the more pressing.

TANIA VOON is Senior Lecturer in Law at the University of Melbourne. From 2003 to 2005, she was Legal Officer in the Appellate Body Secretariat of the WTO. Tania studied law at the University of Cambridge (Ph.D.), Harvard Law School (LL.M.), and the University of Melbourne (LL.B. (Hons), Grad. Dip. Intl. L.). She has taught WTO law in Canada and Australia and published extensively in leading journals.

Cultural Products and the World Trade Organization

Tania Voon

CAMBRIDGE UNIVERSITY PRESS
Cambridge, New York, Melbourne, Madrid, Cape Town, Singapore,
São Paulo, Delhi, Dubai, Tokyo, Mexico City

Cambridge University Press
The Edinburgh Building, Cambridge CB2 8RU, UK

Published in the United States of America by Cambridge University Press, New York

www.cambridge.org
Information on this title: www.cambridge.org/9780521184052

© Tania Voon 2007

This publication is in copyright. Subject to statutory exception
and to the provisions of relevant collective licensing agreements,
no reproduction of any part may take place without the written
permission of Cambridge University Press.

First published 2007
Reprinted 2008
First paperback edition 2010

A catalogue record for this publication is available from the British Library

ISBN 978-0-521-87327-7 Hardback
ISBN 978-0-521-18405-2 Paperback

Cambridge University Press has no responsibility for the persistence or
accuracy of URLs for external or third-party internet websites referred to in
this publication, and does not guarantee that any content on such websites is,
or will remain, accurate or appropriate.

For Chester

Contents

Detailed chapter outline	page ix
Table of GATT/WTO agreements	xiii
Table of GATT/WTO cases	xiv
Table of abbreviations	xvii
GATT/WTO agreements	xvii
GATT/WTO cases	xviii
Other abbreviations	xxvi
Foreword	xxxi
Acknowledgements	xxxiv
Part I Stalemate and its ideological origins	1
1 Trade and culture	3
2 A case study of cultural products: protectionism vs cultural policy	37
3 What's wrong with the current treatment of cultural products?	69
Part II Options for the future	121
4 Resolution through dispute settlement and international law	123
5 Constructing a new agreement outside the WTO	173
6 Improving the existing WTO agreements	217
7 Conclusion	248
Bibliography	257
Non-WTO agreements, cases, statutes, and treaties	257
Other official documents and reports	259
Articles, books, chapters, and papers	271
Index	295

Detailed chapter outline

1 Trade and culture	page 3
1.1 'Trade and ...' problems	3
1.2 Cultural implications of WTO rules	11
1.3 Cultural industries, cultural products, and cultural policy measures	18
1.3.1 Definitions	18
1.3.2 Common cultural policy measures	19
1.3.3 Significance in the WTO	23
1.3.4 Significance in other international contexts	29
1.4 Towards a solution	33
2 A case study of cultural products: protectionism vs cultural policy	37
2.1 Introduction	37
2.2 Legitimacy of State support for cultural products	39
2.2.1 The nature of cultural products	39
2.2.2 Promoting or preserving culture through cultural products	41
2.3 Justification for discriminatory cultural policy measures	43
2.3.1 The market for cultural products	43
A. US dominance	44
B. Positive externalities of cultural products	50
2.3.2 The need for discrimination	54
A. Against foreign cultural products	54
B. Between foreign cultural products	59
2.4 Evaluating cultural policy measures in the WTO	60
2.4.1 Motives for cultural policy measures	60
2.4.2 Effectiveness of cultural policy measures	61
2.4.3 Minimising trade restrictions	64
2.5 Conclusion	67

3 What's wrong with the current treatment of
cultural products? 69
 3.1 Introduction 69
 3.2 Cultural products as goods and services 70
  3.2.1 Basic definitions and classifications 70
  3.2.2 Digital products 73
 3.3 Presumed 'likeness' of cultural products 75
  3.3.1 Likeness under GATT 1994 76
   A. Like products 76
   B. Directly competitive or substitutable products 80
   C. Aims-and-effects test 82
  3.3.2 Like services and service suppliers under GATS 85
 3.4 Unbalanced and uncertain exceptions 89
  3.4.1 Government-supplied services 90
  3.4.2 Screen quotas 92
  3.4.3 Subsidies 96
   A. GATT Articles III:8(b) and XVI and the SCM Agreement 96
   B. GATS Article XV 98
  3.4.4 General exceptions (GATT Article XX, GATS Article XIV) 100
   A. Structure and *chapeau* 100
   B. National treasures 104
   C. Public morals and public order 105
 3.5 The GATS outcome 109
  3.5.1 Limited national treatment and market access commitments 109
  3.5.2 Excessive MFN exemptions 113
 3.6 Conclusion 117

4 Resolution through dispute settlement and international law 123
 4.1 Introduction 123
 4.2 The role of international law in interpreting WTO law 124
  4.2.1 Relevant provisions 125
   A. Article 3.2 of the DSU 125
   B. Article 31 of the VCLT 126

		4.2.2	Use of international law by the Appellate Body	128
			A. Significance of past Appellate Body Reports	128
			B. Ordinary meaning (VCLT Article 31(1))	130
			C. International law between the parties (VCLT Article 31(3)(c))	137
	4.3	Using international law to interpret WTO law on cultural products		142
		4.3.1	National treasures	143
		4.3.2	A human rights approach to cultural products	149
		4.3.3	Public morals and public order	156
		4.3.4	Screen quotas	159
		4.3.5	Protecting human life or health	162
		4.3.6	Securing compliance with other laws or regulations	166
	4.4	Conclusion		171
5	Constructing a new agreement outside the WTO			173
	5.1	Introduction		173
	5.2	National and non-governmental initiatives		175
		5.2.1	Canadian Department of Foreign Affairs and International Trade	175
		5.2.2	International Network on Cultural Policy	178
		5.2.3	International Network for Cultural Diversity	181
	5.3	UNESCO Convention on the Protection of the Diversity of Cultural Contents and Artistic Expressions		183
		5.3.1	Background	183
		5.3.2	Key features of the UNESCO Convention	185
		5.3.3	Implications for the WTO	189
			A. WTO Members' views on the UNESCO Convention	189
			B. Conduct of UNESCO Convention parties in the WTO	194
			C. Complaints relating to the UNESCO Convention	199
			D. The UNESCO Convention as a defence to a WTO violation	202
	5.4	Conclusion		216

6 Improving the existing WTO agreements 217
  6.1 Introduction 217
  6.2 Improving treatment of cultural products under GATT 1994 219
    6.2.1 Screen quotas: remove or modify 219
    6.2.2 A new general exception? 220
  6.3 Improving treatment of cultural products under GATS 223
    6.3.1 Digital cultural products as services 223
    6.3.2 Mandated national treatment, market access, and MFN 225
    6.3.3 Escape routes 227
      A. Discriminatory subsidies 227
      B. Developing country Members 232
      C. Screen quotas 233
  6.4 Effecting changes 234
  6.5 Other proposals 236
    6.5.1 Anti-dumping measures against audiovisual services 237
    6.5.2 Cultural diversity safeguards 239
    6.5.3 Intellectual property rights and anti-competitive conduct 243
  6.6 Conclusion 246

7 Conclusion 248

Bibliography 257
Index 295

Table of GATT/WTO agreements

Agreement on Agriculture 231, 232
Agreement on Government Procurement 235
Agreement on Trade in Civil Aircraft 235
Anti-Dumping Agreement 8, 125, 237, 239
DSU 9, 123, 124, 125, 126, 128, 129, 130, 134, 140, 142, 148, 170, 171, 180, 183, 195, 196, 197, 198, 199, 201, 203, 204, 205, 206, 207, 208, 209, 214, 251
Enabling Clause 8, 132, 133, 137, 222
GATS 8, 22, 23, 24, 25, 26, 28, 34, 35, 42, 51, 54, 62, 66, 69, 70, 71, 72, 73, 74, 75, 85, 86, 87, 88, 89, 90, 91, 92, 95, 96, 98, 99, 100, 104, 105, 107, 108, 109, 110, 111, 112, 113, 114, 116, 117, 118, 119, 132, 142, 143, 149, 156, 157, 158, 159, 162, 163, 165, 166, 167, 171, 172, 173, 182, 186, 194, 195, 199, 200, 201, 203, 210, 212, 216, 217, 218, 219, 223, 224, 225, 226, 227, 228, 229, 230, 231, 233, 234, 235, 236, 238, 239, 240, 241, 242, 243, 244, 246, 247, 248, 250, 251, 252, 253, 254, 256
GATT 1947 3, 4, 5, 13, 23, 80, 82, 92, 94, 95, 136, 200
GATT 1994 5, 6, 7, 8, 9, 15, 23, 26, 27, 34, 35, 67, 69, 70, 71, 73, 74, 75, 76, 78, 79, 80, 83, 86, 87, 88, 89, 90, 92, 93, 96, 98, 100, 101, 103, 104, 106, 107, 109, 110, 113, 114, 117, 118, 119, 127, 130, 132, 136, 139, 142, 143, 145, 147, 149, 150, 159, 161, 162, 163, 164, 165, 167, 171, 172, 173, 177, 182, 186, 200, 201, 210, 212, 218, 219, 220, 221, 222, 223, 224, 225, 228, 230, 231, 233, 234, 236, 237, 239, 240, 243, 244, 246, 247, 250, 251, 253
Marrakesh Agreement 4, 6, 10, 16, 28, 42, 71, 99, 117, 163, 195, 218, 234, 235, 236
Safeguards Agreement 141, 210, 240, 242
SCM Agreement 8, 67, 96, 100, 229, 230, 231, 232
SPS Agreement 7, 9, 10, 14, 15, 42, 66, 206
Textiles Agreement 141
TRIPS Agreement 10, 15, 16, 17, 70, 186, 234, 236, 243, 244, 245

Table of GATT/WTO cases

Argentina – Footwear 130, 210
Argentina – Hides and Leather 102
Argentina – Poultry Anti-Dumping Duties 142, 207
Argentina – Preserved Peaches 129
Argentina – Textiles and Apparel 206
Australia – Salmon 7
Border Tax Adjustments 76
Brazil – Aircraft 129, 209
Brazil – Desiccated Coconut 139
Canada – Autos 6, 79, 80, 86, 88
Canada – Patent Term 139
Canada – Periodicals 26, 27, 40, 55, 56, 71, 73, 76, 77, 81, 82, 84, 85, 88, 96, 97, 98, 124, 129, 167, 248
Canada – Wheat Exports and Grain Imports 209
Chile – Alcoholic Beverages 82, 84, 125
Chile – Price Band System 240
Dominican Republic – Import and Sale of Cigarettes 4, 76, 104, 107, 167
EC – Asbestos 3, 76, 78, 79, 81, 103, 107, 162, 163, 200, 201, 211
EC – Bananas III 71, 78, 80, 84, 86, 87, 88, 139, 196, 209
EC – Bed Linen 130, 137
EC – Biotech 15, 131, 138, 142, 206
EC – Chicken Cuts 137
EC – Computer Equipment 126
EC – Export Subsidies on Sugar 207, 208, 210, 231
EC – Hormones 3, 14, 205, 206, 209, 215
EC – Poultry 6, 206
EC – Sardines 126, 140, 206

EC – *Tariff Preferences* 6, 8, 102, 130, 132, 133, 137, 164, 165, 171, 211, 222
EC – *Trade Marks and Geographical Indications* 15
EC – *Tube or Pipe Fittings* 237
EEC – *Oilseeds I* 97
Greece – *Import Taxes* 82
India – *Patents (US)* 126
Indonesia – *Autos* 76, 87, 97, 212
Japan – *Alcoholic Beverages* 13, 14, 76, 77, 78, 81, 82, 83, 84, 103, 126, 128
Japan – *Film* 201
Japan – *Leather II (US)* 13
Korea – *Alcoholic Beverages* 82
Korea – *Beef* 107, 167, 168
Korea – *Dairy* 240
Korea – *Procurement* 204, 207, 208
Mexico – *Taxes on Soft Drinks* 167, 168, 169, 170, 171, 205, 208, 209
Mexico – *Telecoms* 86, 234, 235
Thailand – *Cigarettes* 4, 107
Thailand – *H-Beams* 237
Turkey – *Textiles* 215
US – *Carbon Steel* 126, 209
US – *Certain EC Products* 196
US – *Corrosion-Resistant Steel Sunset Review* 130, 135, 199, 200, 237
US – *Cotton Yarn* 140, 141, 171
US – *FSC* 139
US – *Gambling* 4, 72, 74, 88, 99, 100, 104, 107, 108, 109, 132, 156, 158
US – *Gasoline* 10, 42, 78, 101, 102, 103, 106, 126, 127, 162
US – *Hot-Rolled Steel* 125, 139, 237
US – *Lamb* 240
US – *Line Pipe* 141, 210, 240
US – *Malt Beverages* 82
US – *Offset Act (Byrd Amendment)* 207
US – *Oil Country Tubular Goods Sunset Reviews* 129
US – *Section 211 Appropriations Act* 6, 130
US – *Section 301 Trade Act* 135, 200
US – *Shrimp* 3, 9, 10, 42, 101, 102, 105, 128, 130, 131, 132, 133, 135, 136, 137, 139, 148, 163, 171, 222
US – *Softwood Lumber V* 129, 130
US – *Steel Safeguards* 130, 137, 210, 211, 240
US – *Superfund* 82
US – *Taxes on Automobiles* 82

US – Tuna (Mexico) 3
US – Underwear 209
US – Upland Cotton 129, 211, 231
US – Wheat Gluten 211, 240
US – Wool Shirts and Blouses 209
US – Zeroing (Japan) 129

Table of abbreviations

GATT/WTO agreements

Short title	Full citation
Agreement on Agriculture	*Agreement on Agriculture*, LT/UR/A-1A/2 (signed 15 April 1994)
Agreement on Government Procurement	*Agreement on Government Procurement*, LT/UR/A-4/PLURI/2 (signed 15 April 1994)
Agreement on Trade in Civil Aircraft	*Agreement on Trade in Civil Aircraft*, LT/UR/A-4/PLURI/1 (signed 15 April 1994)
Anti-Dumping Agreement	*Agreement on Implementation of Article VI of the General Agreement on Tariffs and Trade 1994*, LT/UR/A-1A/3 (signed 15 April 1994)
DSU	*Understanding on Rules and Procedures Governing the Settlement of Disputes*, LT/UR/A-2/DS/U/1 (signed 15 April 1994)
Enabling Clause	*Decision on Differential and More Favourable Treatment, Reciprocity, and Fuller Participation of Developing Countries*, L/4903, BISD 26S/203 (28 November 1979)
GATS	*General Agreement on Trade in Services*, LT/UR/A-1B/S/1 (signed 15 April 1994)
GATT 1947	*General Agreement on Tariffs and Trade*, LT/UR/A-1A/1/GATT/2 (signed 30 October 1947)
GATT 1994	*General Agreement on Tariffs and Trade*, LT/UR/A-1A/1/GATT/1 (signed 15 April 1994)
Marrakesh Agreement	*Marrakesh Agreement Establishing the World Trade Organization*, LT/UR/A/2 (signed 15 April 1994)
Safeguards Agreement	*Agreement on Safeguards*, LT/UR/A-1A/8 (signed 15 April 1994)
SCM Agreement	*Agreement on Subsidies and Countervailing Measures*, LT/UR/A-1A/9 (signed 15 April 1994)
SPS Agreement	*Agreement on the Application of Sanitary and Phytosanitary Measures*, LT/UR/A-1A/12 (signed 15 April 1994)

Short title	Full citation
Textiles Agreement	*Agreement on Textiles and Clothing*, LT/UR/A-1A/11 (signed 15 April 1994) (now expired)
TRIPS Agreement	*Agreement on Trade-Related Aspects of Intellectual Property Rights*, LT/UR/A-1C/IP/1 (signed 15 April 1994)
WTO agreements	The Marrakesh Agreement and the documents contained in its four annexes

GATT/WTO cases

Short title	Full citation
Argentina – Footwear (EC)	Appellate Body Report, *Argentina – Safeguard Measures on Imports of Footwear*, WT/DS121/AB/R (circulated 14 December 1999)
Argentina – Hides and Leather	Panel Report, *Argentina – Measures Affecting the Export of Bovine Hides and the Import of Finished Leather*, WT/DS155/R (circulated 19 December 2000)
Argentina – Poultry Anti-Dumping Duties	Panel Report, *Argentina – Definitive Anti-Dumping Duties on Poultry from Brazil*, WT/DS241/R (circulated 22 April 2003)
Argentina – Preserved Peaches	Panel Report, *Argentina – Definitive Safeguard Measure on Imports of Preserved Peaches*, WT/DS238/R (circulated 14 February 2003)
Argentina – Textiles and Apparel	Appellate Body Report, *Argentina – Measures Affecting Imports of Footwear, Textiles, Apparel and Other Items*, WT/DS56/AB/R and Corr.1 (circulated 27 March 1998)
Australia – Salmon	Appellate Body Report, *Australia – Measures Affecting Importation of Salmon*, WT/DS18/AB/R (circulated 20 October 1998)
Brazil – Aircraft	Appellate Body Report, *Brazil – Export Financing Programme for Aircraft*, WT/DS46/AB/R (circulated 2 August 1999)
Brazil – Aircraft (Article 21.5 – Canada II)	Panel Report, *Brazil – Export Financing Programme for Aircraft, Second Recourse by Canada to Article 21.5 of the DSU*, WT/DS46/RW/2 (circulated 26 July 2001)
Brazil – Desiccated Coconut	Appellate Body Report, *Brazil – Measures Affecting Desiccated Coconut*, WT/DS22/AB/R (circulated 21 February 1997)

Short title	Full citation
Border Tax Adjustments	GATT Working Party Report, *Border Tax Adjustments*, L/3464, BISD 18S/97 (adopted 2 December 1970)
Canada – Autos	Appellate Body Report, *Canada – Certain Measures Affecting the Automotive Industry*, WT/DS139/AB/R, WT/DS142/AB/R (circulated 31 May 2000)
	Panel Report, *Canada – Certain Measures Affecting the Automotive Industry*, WT/DS139/R, WT/DS142/R (circulated 11 February 2000)
Canada – Patent Term	Appellate Body Report, *Canada – Term of Patent Protection*, WT/DS170/AB/R (18 September 2000)
Canada – Periodicals	Appellate Body Report, *Canada – Certain Measures Concerning Periodicals*, WT/DS31/AB/R (circulated 30 June 1997)
	Panel Report, *Canada – Certain Measures Concerning Periodicals*, WT/DS31/R and Corr.1 (circulated 14 March 1997)
Canada – Wheat Exports and Grain Imports	Appellate Body Report, *Canada – Measures Relating to Exports of Wheat and Treatment of Imported Grain*, WT/DS276/AB/R (30 August 2004)
Chile – Alcoholic Beverages	Appellate Body Report, *Chile – Taxes on Alcoholic Beverages*, WT/DS87/AB/R, WT/DS110/AB/R (circulated 13 December 1999)
	Panel Report, *Chile – Taxes on Alcoholic Beverages*, WT/DS87/R, WT/DS110/R (circulated 15 June 1999)
Chile – Price Band System	Appellate Body Report, *Chile – Price Band System and Safeguard Measures Relating to Certain Agricultural Products*, WT/DS207/AB/R (circulated 23 September 2002)
Dominican Republic – Import and Sale of Cigarettes	Appellate Body Report, *Dominican Republic – Measures Affecting the Importation and Internal Sale of Cigarettes*, WT/DS302/AB/R (circulated 25 April 2005)
	Panel Report, *Dominican Republic – Measures Affecting the Importation and Internal Sale of Cigarettes*, WT/DS302/R (circulated 26 November 2004)
EC – Asbestos	Appellate Body Report, *European Communities – Measures Affecting Asbestos and Asbestos-Containing Products*, WT/DS135/AB/R (circulated 12 March 2001)
	Panel Report, *European Communities – Measures Affecting Asbestos and Asbestos-Containing Products*, WT/DS135/R and Add.1 (circulated 18 September 2000)

Short title	Full citation
EC – Bananas III	Appellate Body Report, *European Communities – Regime for the Importation, Sale and Distribution of Bananas*, WT/DS27/AB/R (circulated 9 September 1997)
EC – Bananas III (Article 21.5 – EC)	Panel Report, *European Communities – Regime for the Importation, Sale and Distribution of Bananas, Recourse to Article 21.5 of the DSU by the European Communities*, WT/DS27/RW/EEC and Corr.1 (circulated 12 April 1999)
EC – Bananas III (Ecuador)	Panel Report, *European Communities – Regime for the Importation, Sale and Distribution of Bananas, Complaint by Ecuador*, WT/DS27/R/ECU (circulated 22 May 1997)
EC – Bed Linen	Appellate Body Report, *European Communities – Anti-Dumping Duties on Imports of Cotton-Type Bed Linen from India*, WT/DS141/AB/R (circulated 1 March 2001)
EC – Biotech	Panel Report, *European Communities – Measures Affecting the Approval and Marketing of Biotech Products*, WT/DS291/R, WT/DS292/R, WT/DS293/R (circulated 29 September 2006)
EC – Chicken Cuts	Appellate Body Report, *European Communities – Customs Classification of Frozen Boneless Chicken Cuts*, WT/DS269/AB/R, WT/DS286/AB/R (circulated 12 September 2005)
	Panel Report, *European Communities – Customs Classification of Frozen Boneless Chicken Cuts, Complaint by Brazil*, WT/DS269/R (circulated 30 May 2005)
	Panel Report, *European Communities – Customs Classification of Frozen Boneless Chicken Cuts, Complaint by Thailand*, WT/DS286/R (circulated 30 May 2005)
EC – Computer Equipment	Appellate Body Report, *European Communities – Customs Classification of Certain Computer Equipment*, WT/DS62/AB/R, WT/DS67/AB/R, WT/DS68/AB/R (circulated 5 June 1998)
EC – Export Subsidies on Sugar	Appellate Body Report, *European Communities – Export Subsidies on Sugar*, WT/DS265/AB/R, WT/DS266/AB/R, WT/DS283/AB/R (circulated 28 April 2005)
EC – Hormones	Appellate Body Report, *EC Measures Concerning Meat and Meat Products (Hormones)*, WT/DS26/AB/R, WT/DS48/AB/R (circulated 16 January 1998)

Short title	Full citation
EC – Hormones (Canada)	Panel Report, *EC Measures Concerning Meat and Meat Products (Hormones), Complaint by Canada*, WT/DS48/R/CAN (circulated 18 August 1997)
EC – Hormones (US)	Panel Report, *EC Measures Concerning Meat and Meat Products (Hormones), Complaint by the United States*, WT/DS26/R/USA (circulated 18 August 1997)
EC – Hormones (US) (Article 22.6 – EC)	Decision by the Arbitrators, *European Communities Measures Concerning Meat and Meat Products (Hormones), Original Complaint by the United States – Recourse to Arbitration by the European Communities under Article 22.6 of the DSU*, WT/DS26/ARB (circulated 12 July 1999)
EC – Poultry	Appellate Body Report, *European Communities – Measures Affecting the Importation of Certain Poultry Products*, WT/DS69/AB/R (circulated 13 July 1998)
	Panel Report, *European Communities – Measures Affecting the Importation of Certain Poultry Products*, WT/DS69/R (circulated 12 March 1998)
EC – Sardines	Appellate Body Report, *European Communities – Trade Description of Sardines*, WT/DS231/AB/R (circulated 26 September 2002)
EC – Tariff Preferences	Award of the Arbitrator, *European Communities – Conditions for the Granting of Tariff Preferences to Developing Countries*, WT/DS246/14 (circulated 20 September 2004)
	Appellate Body Report, *European Communities – Conditions for the Granting of Tariff Preferences to Developing Countries*, WT/DS246/AB/R (circulated 7 April 2004)
	Panel Report, *European Communities – Conditions for the Granting of Tariff Preferences to Developing Countries*, WT/DS246/R (circulated 1 December 2003)
EC – Trade Marks and Geographical Indications	Panel Reports, *European Communities – Protection of Trademarks and Geographical Indications for Agricultural Products and Foodstuffs*, WT/DS290/R (Australia), WT/DS174/R (US) (circulated 15 March 2005)
EC – Tube or Pipe Fittings	Appellate Body Report, *European Communities – Anti-Dumping Duties on Malleable Cast Iron Tube or Pipe Fittings from Brazil*, WT/DS219/AB/R (circulated 22 July 2003)

Short title	Full citation
EEC – Oilseeds I	GATT Panel Report, *European Economic Community – Payments and Subsidies Paid to Processors and Producers of Oilseeds and Related Animal-Feed Proteins*, L/6627, BISD 37S/86 (adopted 25 January 1990)
Greece – Import Taxes	GATT Panel Report, *Special Import Taxes Instituted by Greece*, G/25, BISD 1S/48 (adopted 3 November 1952)
India – Patents (US)	Appellate Body Report, *India – Patent Protection for Pharmaceutical and Agricultural Chemical Products*, WT/DS50/AB/R (circulated 19 December 1997)
Indonesia – Autos	Panel Report, *Indonesia – Certain Measures Affecting the Automobile Industry*, WT/DS54/R, WT/DS55/R, WT/DS59/R, WT/DS64/R and Corr.1, 2, 3, 4 (circulated 2 July 1998)
Japan – Alcoholic Beverages I	GATT Panel Report, *Japan Customs Duties, Taxes and Labelling Practices on Imported Wines and Alcoholic Beverages*, L/6216, BISD 34S/83 (adopted 10 November 1987)
Japan – Alcoholic Beverages II	Appellate Body Report, *Japan – Taxes on Alcoholic Beverages*, WT/DS8/AB/R, WT/DS10/AB/R, WT/DS11/AB/R (circulated 4 October 1996)
	Panel Report, *Japan – Taxes on Alcoholic Beverages*, WT/DS8/R, WT/DS10/R, WT/DS11/R (circulated 11 July 1996)
Japan – Film	Panel Report, *Japan – Measures Affecting Consumer Photographic Film and Paper*, WT/DS44/R (circulated 31 March 1998)
Japan – Leather II (US)	GATT Panel Report, *Japanese Measures on Imports of Leather*, L/5623, BISD 31S/94 (adopted 15 May 1984)
Korea – Alcoholic Beverages	Appellate Body Report, *Korea – Taxes on Alcoholic Beverages*, WT/DS75/AB/R, WT/DS84/AB/R (circulated 18 January 1999)
	Panel Report, *Korea – Taxes on Alcoholic Beverages*, WT/DS75/R, WT/DS84/R (circulated 17 September 1998)
Korea – Beef	Appellate Body Report, *Korea – Measures Affecting Imports of Fresh, Chilled and Frozen Beef*, WT/DS161/AB/R, WT/DS169/AB/R (circulated 11 December 2000)
Korea – Dairy	Appellate Body Report, *Korea – Definitive Safeguard Measure on Imports of Certain Dairy Products*, WT/DS98/AB/R (circulated 14 December 1999)
Korea – Procurement	Panel Report, *Korea – Measures Affecting Government Procurement*, WT/DS163/R (circulated 1 May 2000)

Short title	Full citation
Mexico – Taxes on Soft Drinks	Appellate Body Report, Mexico – Tax Measures on Soft Drinks and Other Beverages, WT/DS308/AB/R (circulated 6 March 2006) Panel Report, Mexico – Tax Measures on Soft Drinks and Other Beverages, WT/DS308/R (circulated 7 October 2005)
Mexico – Telecoms	Panel Report, Mexico – Measures Affecting Telecommunications Services, WT/DS204/R (circulated 2 April 2004)
Thailand – Cigarettes	GATT Panel Report, Thailand – Restriction on Importation of and Internal Taxes on Cigarettes, DS10/R, BISD 37S/200 (adopted 7 November 1990)
Thailand – H-Beams	Appellate Body Report, Thailand – Anti-Dumping Duties on Angles, Shapes and Sections of Iron or Non-Alloy Steel and H-Beams from Poland, WT/DS122/AB/R (circulated 12 March 2001)
Turkey – Textiles	Appellate Body Report, Turkey – Restrictions on Imports of Textile and Clothing Products, WT/DS34/AB/R (circulated 22 October 1999) Panel Report, Turkey – Restrictions on Imports of Textile and Clothing Products, WT/DS34/R (circulated 31 May 1999)
US – Carbon Steel	Appellate Body Report, United States – Countervailing Duties on Certain Corrosion-Resistant Carbon Steel Flat Products from Germany, WT/DS213/AB/R and Corr.1 (circulated 28 November 2002)
US – Certain EC Products	Panel Report, United States – Import Measures on Certain Products from the European Communities, WT/DS165/R and Add.1 (circulated 17 July 2000)
US – Corrosion-Resistant Steel Sunset Review	Appellate Body Report, United States – Sunset Review of Anti-Dumping Duties on Corrosion-Resistant Carbon Steel Flat Products from Japan, WT/DS244/AB/R (circulated 15 December 2003) Panel Report, United States – Sunset Review of Anti-Dumping Duties on Corrosion-Resistant Carbon Steel Flat Products from Japan, WT/DS244/R (circulated 14 August 2003)
US – Cotton Yarn	Appellate Body Report, United States – Transitional Safeguard Measure on Combed Cotton Yarn from Pakistan, WT/DS192/AB/R (circulated 8 October 2001)
US – FSC	Appellate Body Report, United States – Tax Treatment for 'Foreign Sales Corporations', WT/DS108/AB/R (circulated 24 February 2000)
US – Gambling	Appellate Body Report, United States – Measures Affecting the Cross-Border Supply of Gambling and

Short title	Full citation
	Betting Services, WT/DS285/AB/R (circulated 7 April 2005)
	Panel Report, *United States – Measures Affecting the Cross-Border Supply of Gambling and Betting Services*, WT/DS285/R (circulated 10 November 2004)
US – Gasoline	Appellate Body Report, *United States – Standards for Reformulated and Conventional Gasoline*, WT/DS2/AB/R (circulated 29 April 1996)
	Panel Report, *United States – Standards for Reformulated and Conventional Gasoline*, WT/DS2/R (circulated 29 January 1996)
US – Hot-Rolled Steel	Appellate Body Report, *United States – Anti-Dumping Measures on Certain Hot-Rolled Steel Products from Japan*, WT/DS184/AB/R (circulated 24 July 2001)
US – Lamb	Appellate Body Report, *United States – Safeguard Measures on Imports of Fresh, Chilled or Frozen Lamb Meat from New Zealand and Australia*, WT/DS177/AB/R, WT/DS178/AB/R (circulated 1 May 2001)
US – Line Pipe	Appellate Body Report, *United States – Definitive Safeguard Measures on Imports of Circular Welded Carbon Quality Line Pipe from Korea*, WT/DS202/AB/R (circulated 15 February 2002)
	Panel Report, *United States – Definitive Safeguard Measures on Imports of Circular Welded Carbon Quality Line Pipe from Korea*, WT/DS202/R (circulated 29 October 2001)
US – Malt Beverages	GATT Panel Report, *United States – Measures Affecting Alcoholic and Malt Beverages*, DS23/R, BISD 39S/206 (adopted 19 June 1992)
US – Offset Act (Byrd Amendment)	Appellate Body Report, *United States – Continued Dumping and Subsidy Offset Act of 2000*, WT/DS217/AB/R, WT/DS234/AB/R (circulated 16 January 2003)
US – Oil Country Tubular Goods Sunset Reviews	Appellate Body Report, *United States – Sunset Reviews of Anti-Dumping Measures on Oil Country Tubular Goods from Argentina*, WT/DS268/AB/R (circulated 29 November 2004)
US – Section 211 Appropriations Act	Appellate Body Report, *United States – Section 211 Omnibus Appropriations Act of 1998*, WT/DS176/AB/R (circulated 2 January 2002)
US – Section 301 Trade Act	Panel Report, *United States – Sections 301–310 of the Trade Act of 1974*, WT/DS152/R (circulated 22 December 1999)
US – Shrimp	Appellate Body Report, *United States – Import Prohibition of Certain Shrimp and Shrimp Products*, WT/DS58/AB/R (circulated 12 October 1998)

Short title	Full citation
US – Shrimp (Article 21.5 – Malaysia)	Appellate Body Report, *United States – Import Prohibition of Certain Shrimp and Shrimp Products, Recourse to Article 21.5 of the DSU by Malaysia*, WT/DS58/AB/RW (circulated 22 October 2001)
US – Softwood Lumber V	Appellate Body Report, *United States – Final Dumping Determination on Softwood Lumber from Canada*, WT/DS264/AB/R (circulated 11 August 2004)
US – Steel Safeguards	Appellate Body Report, *United States – Definitive Safeguard Measures on Imports of Certain Steel Products*, WT/DS248/AB/R, WT/DS249/AB/R, WT/DS251/AB/R, WT/DS252/AB/R, WT/DS253/AB/R, WT/DS254/AB/R, WT/DS258/AB/R, WT/DS259/AB/R (circulated 10 November 2003)
US – Superfund	GATT Panel Report, *United States – Taxes on Petroleum and Certain Imported Substances*, L/6175, BISD 34S/136 (adopted 17 June 1987)
US – Taxes on Automobiles	GATT Panel Report, *United States – Taxes on Automobiles*, DS31/R (11 October 1994, unadopted)
US – Tuna (Mexico)	GATT Panel Report, *United States – Restrictions on Imports of Tuna*, DS21/R, BISD 39S/155 (3 September 1991, unadopted)
US – Underwear	Appellate Body Report, *United States – Restrictions on Imports of Cotton and Man-made Fibre Underwear*, WT/DS24/AB/R (circulated 10 February 1997)
US – Upland Cotton	Appellate Body Report, *United States – Subsidies on Upland Cotton*, WT/DS267/AB/R (circulated 3 March 2005)
	Panel Report, *United States – Subsidies on Upland Cotton*, WT/DS267/R, Add.1–3, and Corr.1 (circulated 8 September 2004)
US – Wheat Gluten	Appellate Body Report, *United States – Definitive Safeguard Measures on Imports of Wheat Gluten from the European Communities*, WT/DS166/AB/R (circulated 22 December 2000)
US – Wool Shirts and Blouses	Appellate Body Report, *United States – Measure Affecting Imports of Woven Wool Shirts and Blouses from India*, WT/DS33/AB/R and Corr.1 (circulated 25 April 1997)
US – Zeroing (Japan)	Panel Report, *United States – Measures Relating to Zeroing and Sunset Reviews*, WT/DS322/R (circulated 20 September 2006)

Other abbreviations

Short name	Long name
1993 Scheduling Guidelines	Uruguay Round Group of Negotiations on Services, GATT, *Scheduling of Initial Commitments in Trade in Services: Explanatory Note*, MTN.GNS/W/164 (3 September 1993)
2001 Scheduling Guidelines	Council for Trade in Services, WTO, *Guidelines for the Scheduling of Specific Commitments under the General Agreement on Trade in Services (GATS): Adopted by the Council for Trade in Services on 23 March 2001*, S/L/92 (28 March 2001)
ACUNS	Academic Council on the United Nations System
ASIL	American Society of International Law
Beirut Agreement	*Agreement for Facilitating the International Circulation of Visual and Auditory Materials of an Educational, Scientific and Cultural Character*, 197 UNTS 3 (adopted 10 December 1948)
Cartagena Protocol	*Cartagena Protocol on Biosafety to the Convention on Biological Diversity*, 39 ILM 1027 (adopted 29 January 2000)
Convention for the Protection of Cultural Heritage	*Convention for the Protection of the World Cultural and Natural Heritage*, 1037 UNTS 151 (adopted 16 November 1972)
Convention on Biological Diversity	*Convention on Biological Diversity*, 1760 UNTS 79; 31 ILM 818 (adopted 5 June 1992)
Convention on Cultural Property in Armed Conflict	*Convention for the Protection of Cultural Property in the Event of Armed Conflict*, 249 UNTS 240 (adopted 14 May 1954)
Convention on Migratory Species	*Convention on the Conservation of Migratory Species of Wild Animals*, 1651 UNTS 333; 19 ILM 11 (adopted 23 June 1979)
CPC	Central Product Classification
CRTC	Canadian Radio-Television and Telecommunications Commission
CUSFTA	*Canada United States Free Trade Agreement*, 27 ILM 281; 2 BDIEL 359 (signed 2 January 1988)

Short name	Long name
Document W/120	Uruguay Round Group of Negotiations on Services, GATT, *Services Sectoral Classification List – Note by the Secretariat*, MTN.GNS/W/120 (10 July 1991)
Doha Declaration	Ministerial Conference, WTO, *Ministerial Declaration adopted on 14 November 2001*, WT/MIN(01)/DEC/1 (20 November 2001)
DSB	Dispute Settlement Body
EC	European Communities
EC Treaty	*Treaty establishing the European Community*, OJ C340, 173; 37 ILM 79 (signed 25 March 1957), consolidated version OJ C325, 33 (24 December 2002)
ELSA	European Law Students' Association
European Convention on Human Rights	*Convention for the Protection of Human Rights and Fundamental Freedoms*, 213 UNTS 221; ETS 5 (signed 4 November 1950), as amended by Protocol No. 11 (ETS 155)
Florence Agreement	*Agreement on the Importation of Educational, Scientific and Cultural Materials*, 131 UNTS 25 (adopted 17 June 1950)
GSP	Generalised System of Preferences
Harmonized System	Nomenclature set out in *International Convention on the Harmonized Commodity Description and Coding System*, 1503 UNTS 167 (signed 14 June 1983), annex
Hong Kong Declaration	Ministerial Conference, WTO, *Doha Work Programme: Ministerial Declaration Adopted on 18 December 2005*, WT/MIN(05)/DEC (22 December 2005)
ICCPR	*International Covenant on Civil and Political Rights*, 999 UNTS 171 (adopted 16 December 1966)
ICESCR	*International Covenant on Economic, Social and Cultural Rights*, 999 UNTS 3 (adopted 16 December 1966)
ICJ	International Court of Justice
ILC	International Law Commission
INCD	International Network for Cultural Diversity
INCP	International Network on Cultural Policy
Indigenous and Tribal Peoples Convention	*Indigenous and Tribal Peoples Convention*, ILO Convention 169 (adopted 27 June 1989)

Short name	Long name
July Package	General Council, WTO, *Decision Adopted by the General Council on 1 August 2004*, WT/L/579 (2 August 2004)
MAI	Multilateral Agreement on Investment
MFN	Most-favoured nation
NAFTA	*North American Free Trade Agreement*, 32 ILM 289 and 605 (signed 17 December 1992)
Nairobi Protocol	*Protocol to the Agreement on the Importation of Educational, Scientific and Cultural Materials*, 1259 UNTS 3 (adopted 26 November 1976)
NGO	Non-governmental organisation
OECD	Organisation for Economic Co-operation and Development
SAGIT	Sectoral Advisory Group on International Trade
Television Without Frontiers Directive	Council of the European Communities, EC, *Council Directive 89/552/EEC of 3 October 1989 on the coordination of certain provisions laid down by Law, Regulation or Administrative Action in Member States concerning the pursuit of television broadcasting activities*, OJ L298, 23 (17 October 1989) as amended by European Parliament and Council of the European Union, *Directive 97/36/EC of the European Parliament and of the Council of 30 June 1997 amending Council Directive 89/552/EEC on the coordination of certain provisions laid down by law, regulation or administrative action in Member States concerning the pursuit of television broadcasting activities*, OJ L202, 60 (30 July 1997)
TPRB	Trade Policy Review Body
UDHR	UN, *Universal Declaration of Human Rights*, GA Res. 217A(III) (10 December 1948)
UK	United Kingdom
UN	United Nations
UNCTAD	United Nations Conference on Trade and Development
UN Declaration on Minorities	General Assembly, UN, *Declaration on the Rights of Persons Belonging to National or Ethnic, Religious and Linguistic Minorities*, A/RES/47/135 (18 December 1992)
UNESCO	United Nations Educational, Scientific and Cultural Organization

Short name	Long name
UNESCO Convention	UNESCO, *Convention on the Protection and Promotion of the Diversity of Cultural Expressions*, CLT-2005/CONVENTION DIVERSITE-CULT REV (adopted 20 October 2005, entering into force 18 March 2007)
UNESCO Convention on Cultural Property	*Convention on the Means of Prohibiting and Preventing the Illicit Import, Export and Transfer of Ownership of Cultural Property*, [1972] UNTS 230 (adopted 14 November 1970)
UNESCO Recommendation on Participation in Cultural Life	UNESCO, *Recommendation on Participation by the People at Large in Cultural Life and their Contribution to It*, 19 C/Resolutions, annex I, 29 (26 November 1976)
UNIDROIT Convention on Cultural Objects	*UNIDROIT Convention on Stolen or Illegally Exported Cultural Objects*, Diplomatic Conference for the Adoption of the Draft UNIDROIT Convention on the International Return of Stolen or Illegally Exported Cultural Objects, Rome – Acts and Proceedings 1996 (adopted 24 June 1995)
Universal Declaration on Cultural Diversity	UNESCO, *Records of the General Conference, 31st Session, vol. I: Resolutions* (15 October to 3 November 2001) 61, Resolution 25.
US or USA	United States of America
USTR	United States Trade Representative
VCLT	*Vienna Convention on the Law of Treaties*, 1155 UNTS 331 (adopted 22 May 1969)
WTO	World Trade Organization

Foreword

Whether you stand closer to the trade side or the culture side in the trade and culture debate, or if you have not yet decided where your sympathies lie, you would do well to read Dr Voon's informative and insightful book on *Cultural Products and the World Trade Organization*. The trade and culture dilemma is not new, but Dr Voon's proposed solution is.

'Trade and ...' questions tend to pit one side against the other, and the literature so often promotes only one view, while undermining conflicting approaches. The virtue of Dr Voon's study is that it avoids this tendency and instead provides a balanced and thoughtful view of the highly complex issues surrounding the challenge of protecting and promoting culture and cultural diversity, while at the same time pursuing the goal of further trade liberalisation among States. The key to addressing this debate is to acknowledge, as Dr Voon does, that cultural products have cultural as well as commercial value, and to understand, as Dr Voon so clearly explains, that cultural value is highly prized, just as is the multi-billion-dollar industry that produces cultural products.

Dr Voon explores what she describes as 'a particular notion of culture' as it relates to defined cultural products – film, video, radio, television, sound recordings, books, magazines, and periodicals – that are created or provided by cultural industries – audiovisual, printing, and publishing. The highly readable review of the current treatment of cultural products in the WTO demonstrates that the trade and culture stalemate in the WTO is no longer tenable and that, unless the WTO addresses the problem soon, it will effectively abdicate to other organisations that have no interest in the trade side of this issue. Indeed, while WTO Members have been satisfied with merely agreeing to disagree, UNESCO adopted in 2005 a *Convention on the Protection and Promotion of* the *Diversity of Cultural Expressions*, which could have a profound and unpredicted influence on WTO Members that are also members of UNESCO in their WTO negotiating positions and in resolving trade disputes about cultural products. Dr Voon's discussion of this new Convention as well as other international and domestic initiatives for promoting and protecting cultural products is highly instructive in this regard.

Dr Voon opines that promotion and preservation of culture are legitimate regulatory objectives of WTO Members and that cultural policy measures can achieve their cultural goals without unduly restricting trade. She maintains, however, that existing WTO rules do not promote or ensure a balance between Members' cultural objectives and trade liberalisation. She points to the lack of clarity and predictability in the rules, due in part to the stark differences in treatment between the GATT 1994 and the GATS and the fact that cultural products, often having both goods and services features, may be subject to diverging rules. Another problem with the current rules is the uncertainty about 'safety valves' or exceptions currently available in respect of cultural policy measures. Moreover, the GATS 'bottom-up' approach serves as an effective bar to further trade liberalisation in cultural products because Members are free to refrain from making commitments, a course most Members have chosen in respect of cultural products. As Dr Voon explains, this not only undermines trade liberalisation in cultural products, but could also lead to cultural isolation rather than cultural diversity.

The WTO's dispute settlement system has played a central role in addressing a number of issues that, like the trade and culture conundrum, have been left unresolved in the various WTO agreements. A significant body of case law has been developed that clarifies Members' rights and obligations in a number of areas. However, it provides little guidance for those seeking solutions to the trade and culture issue and it is unlikely to prove effective in the future in improving the treatment of cultural products in the WTO. This is because dispute settlement cannot solve the problem of the GATT/GATS incompatibility, as this is possible only through an amendment of the current rules. And although Dr Voon points to the vast array of international law applicable to cultural products and cultural rights and provides thoughtful ideas as to where helpful approaches might be found, she acknowledges that its utility in WTO dispute settlement is likely to be limited. The fiercely debated and as yet unresolved issue of the role of international law generally in WTO dispute settlement and the WTO Appellate Body's reluctance thus far to look very far afield – such as in multilateral conventions – to determine the extent of Members' rights and obligations under WTO agreements means that international law governing cultural products will not play a significant role in resolving trade and culture disputes in the WTO. Thus, as Dr Voon correctly concludes, the trade/culture problem is unlikely to be resolved through recourse to the WTO dispute settlement system.

Dr Voon's analysis makes clear that the best choice for resolving legal aspects of trade in cultural products is through improvements to existing WTO agreements. Negotiating a reconciliation between trade and culture will no doubt be extremely difficult; indeed, it has eluded trade diplomats for many years. But finding a diplomatic solution will be preferable to leaving the controversy to be resolved in other forums where the objective of trade liberalisation is beside the point, an outcome that is increasingly likely, given UNESCO's 2005 Convention.

As Dr Voon puts it, there is no need to portray the trade and culture impasse *à la* 'film noir', with gloomy lighting and fatalistic characters. For Dr Voon offers an optimistic script, which calls for harmonising the treatment of cultural products as goods and services and subjecting all cultural products to the requirements of MFN, national treatment and market access, tempered by clearly defined exceptions such as discriminatory subsidisation. She suggests that these changes could be effected through an annex on cultural products along the lines of the annexes on air transport services and financial services.

At this point, we do not know how the trade and culture story will end. Dr Voon offers some thoughtful and creative ideas on how this plot can move forward. In the meantime, I nominate Dr Voon's script for the Palme D'Or, and I am waiting for the sequel.

Valerie Hughes
Assistant Deputy Minister
Law Branch, Department of Finance
Ottawa, Canada
Former Director, WTO Appellate Body Secretariat
Geneva

Acknowledgements

I am indebted to my Ph.D. supervisor at the University of Cambridge, Roger O'Keefe, for his patience, encouragement, and valuable feedback on my work over the years. For insightful comments on and welcome criticism of earlier drafts, I thank Luca Castellani, Kaarlo Castren, Carmen Domínguez, Lothar Ehring, Justin Fung, Alison Lam, Katie Mitchell, Matthew Stilwell, Arun Venkataraman, Hannu Wager, and Alan Yanovich. I am also grateful for the wisdom shared in discussions with Rudolf Adlung, Guido Carducci, Dale Honeck, Clare Kelly, Jane Kelsey, Trevor Knight, Robert Ley, Nicolas Lockhart, Gabrielle Marceau, Aaditya Mattoo, Donald McRae, Peter Morrison, Julia Nielson, Maria Pereyra-Friedrichsen, and Werner Zdouc. In revising my original Ph.D. dissertation for publication, several anonymous referees offered detailed feedback, and Anne Kallies provided excellent research assistance, including helping me understand certain relevant texts in German. I thank also Cambridge University Press for their careful editing and indexing.

Daniel Bethlehem forced me to get a tighter grip on my topic through his probing questions in my first-year oral exam, and he and Mary Footer raised additional issues during the final viva voce for my Ph.D. The organisers and participants in the 2003 ACUNS/ASIL Summer Workshop on Human Rights at Yale, the 2006 ELSA Moot Court Competition at the Institute for International Economics, Business & Law in Adelaide, and the 2006 Symposium on WTO Issues and Law held in Sydney by the Gilbert & Tobin Centre of Public Law and the University of New South Wales made me get my thoughts together and keep thinking. Several other people, including Tomer Broude, Christophe Germann, Allegre Hadida, Michael Hahn, Joel Paul, Paul Stephan, Rolf Weber, and Sacha Wunsch-Vincent, kindly provided me with copies of their own work in this area and expressed an interest in my research. I also especially appreciate the help I received from certain members of the UNESCO Secretariat, including Abdulqawi Yusuf, in following developments there, as well as the librarians at the WTO, the Georgetown University Law Center, and the Universities of Cambridge and Melbourne.

I wish to recognise the generous financial assistance of Gonville & Caius College during my time as a WM Tapp Scholar and Ph.D. candidate at Cambridge, where Pippa Rogerson and Alison Hirst were always ready with assistance and advice. The Australian Federation of University Women (Queensland and Victorian branches), the Foundation for Young Australians, and the International Chapter PEO Sisterhood provided much-needed funding during my LL.M. at Harvard. I thank also Mallesons Stephen Jaques and Cheng Lim for supporting my decision to take leave for further study, and the University of Melbourne Law School for providing research support funds in the final stages of my work. The referees who helped me get into all this in the first place include Michael Bryan, Emma Henderson, Ian Malkin, Pene Mathew, Tim McCormack, Wayne Morgan, Kim Rubenstein, Cheryl Saunders, Anne-Marie Slaughter (who taught me how to write again), and Kris Walker. Martin Davies and Joseph Weiler deserve thanks for their inspiring classes, which first sparked my interest in WTO law. Thanks also to Valerie Hughes, who supported my efforts during the last few years.

Parts of Chapters 4 and 5 were first published by Oxford University Press in July 2006 as 'UNESCO and the WTO: A Clash of Cultures?' (2006) 55(3) *International & Comparative Law Quarterly* 635. Parts of Chapter 2 were first published by Cambridge University Press in December 2006 as 'State Support for Audiovisual Products in the WTO: Protectionism or Cultural Policy?' (2006) 13(2) *International Journal of Cultural Property* 129. Parts of Chapters 3 and 6 were first published in early 2007 as 'A New Approach to Audiovisual Products in the WTO: Rebalancing GATT and GATS' (2007) 14(1) *UCLA Entertainment Law Review* 1.

Lastly, I thank my parents and my husband Andrew, without whom I could never have done this.

PART I

Stalemate and its ideological origins

1 Trade and culture

1.1 'Trade and ...' problems

At the heart of a great many trade disputes lies a 'trade and ...' problem;[1] that is, a clash between the goal of trade liberalisation and some other goal. As Joel Trachtman has explained, these problems involve 'conflicts between trade values and other social values', such as 'environmental protection, labour rights or free competition'.[2] Indicative of such conflicts are clashes within the WTO (and its predecessor, GATT 1947) over EC import bans on asbestos[3] and meat treated with certain growth hormones,[4] US prohibitions on imports of shrimp harvested in a manner threatening sea turtles[5] and on the cross-border supply of

---

[1] I take this terminology from Joel Trachtman, 'Trade and ... Problems, Cost-Benefit Analysis and Subsidiarity' (1998) 9(1) *European Journal of International Law* 32.

[2] Trachtman, 'Trade and ... Problems', 33. See also, e.g., Steve Charnovitz, 'The World Trade Organization and Social Issues' (1994) 28(5) *Journal of World Trade* 17; Robert Howse, Brian Langille, and Julien Burda, 'The World Trade Organization and Labour Rights: Man Bites Dog' in Virginia Leary and Daniel Warner (eds.), *Social Issues, Globalisation and International Institutions: Labour Rights and the EU, ILO, OECD and WTO* (2006) 157; Matthew Stilwell and Jan Bohanes, 'Trade and the Environment' in Patrick Macrory, Arthur Appleton, and Michael Plummer (eds.), *The World Trade Organization: Legal, Economic and Political Analysis* (2005) (vol. II) 511; Tania Voon, 'Sizing Up the WTO: Trade-Environment Conflict and the Kyoto Protocol' (2000) 10(1) *Journal of Transnational Law & Policy* 71.

[3] Appellate Body Report, *EC – Asbestos*, [1]–[2].

[4] Appellate Body Report, *EC – Hormones*, [2]. See also WTO, DSB, *United States – Continued Suspension of Obligations in the EC – Hormones Dispute: Request for the Establishment of a Panel by the European Communities*, WT/DS320/6 (14 January 2005); WTO, DSB, *Canada – Continued Suspension of Obligations in the EC – Hormones Dispute: Request for the Establishment of a Panel by the European Communities*, WT/DS321/6 (14 January 2005) (Panel Reports not yet circulated at time of writing).

[5] Appellate Body Report, *US – Shrimp*, [1]–[6]; Appellate Body Report, *US – Shrimp (Article 21.5 – Malaysia)*, [3]–[7]. See also GATT Panel Report, *US – Tuna (Mexico)*, [2.3]–[2.12].

gambling and betting services,[6] and import restrictions and tax requirements imposed on cigarettes by Thailand[7] and the Dominican Republic.[8]

I do not propose to debate the virtues of trade liberalisation as a general matter. However, in a nutshell, the theory is that the removal of trade barriers (such as tariffs and import quotas), which distort international trade, will allow each country to specialise in producing goods or providing services in industries in which it has the greatest 'comparative advantage', and to import goods and services in industries in which it lacks this advantage. Although initially this may cause some adjustment problems (because, for instance, a steel worker cannot transform overnight into a computer programmer), in the longer term, national and global welfare will increase.[9] Of course, the underlying theory of comparative advantage has its limits. In some areas, such as national security, countries may want to retain all or some of their industrial and technical capabilities, regardless of their comparative advantage. In addition, even in industries to which the theory of comparative advantage applies easily, governments should not have to give up their right to regulate their territories as they see fit purely in the interests of trade liberalisation.

The WTO agreements reflect the goal of trade liberalisation, or at least its value as a means to achieve broader social and economic objectives. The WTO was established on 1 January 1995, following the eighth round of trade talks launched in Uruguay in 1986[10] under GATT 1947. In the preamble to the Marrakesh Agreement, WTO Members recognise 'that their relations in the field of trade and economic endeavour should be conducted with a view to raising standards of living, ensuring full employment and a large and steadily growing volume of real income and effective demand, and expanding the production of and trade in goods and services'. The preamble goes on to express the Members' desire

---

[6] Appellate Body Report, *US – Gambling*, [1]–[2].
[7] GATT Panel Report, *Thailand – Cigarettes*, [6]–[11].
[8] Panel Report, *Dominican Republic – Import and Sale of Cigarettes*, [2.1]–[2.6].
[9] See generally Douglas Irwin, *Against the Tide: an Intellectual History of Free Trade* (1996); Alan Sykes, 'Comparative Advantage and the Normative Economics of International Trade Policy' (1998) 1(1) *Journal of International Economic Law* 49. For a brief discussion of the history of the WTO, focusing on key disciplines and underlying trade theory, see Kym Anderson, 'Setting the Trade Policy Agenda: What Roles for Economists?' (2005) 39(2) *Journal of World Trade* 341, 342–54.
[10] GATT, *Ministerial Declaration to Launch the Uruguay Round of Multilateral Trade Negotiations* MIN.DEC (20 September 1986).

to 'contribut[e] to these objectives by entering into reciprocal and mutually advantageous arrangements directed to the substantial reduction of tariffs and other barriers to trade and to the elimination of discriminatory treatment in international trade relations'.

In simplified terms, the core obligations or disciplines imposed on WTO Members in connection with trade in goods (essentially unchanged since GATT 1947) are as follows.[11]

To reduce trade barriers and increase market access:

(a) A general *prohibition on quantitative restrictions* (such as quotas) and equivalent measures on imports or exports from or to other Members.[12] Pre-existing quantitative restrictions and equivalent measures on agricultural and industrial products were converted to tariffs (customs duties) during the Uruguay Round, in a process known as 'tariffication'. Various economic and policy reasons explain this preference for tariffs over quantitative restrictions as a form of protection.[13]

(b) *Tariff bindings*: the tariff that a Member applies to imported goods of other WTO Members must be no greater than the tariff that the importing Member has agreed or 'bound' for the relevant product in its 'schedule of concessions'.[14] These tariff bindings under GATT 1994 continue the process of negotiated tariff reductions that took place under GATT 1947.[15]

To eliminate discrimination:

(c) *National treatment*: Discrimination by WTO Members against products of other Members in favour of domestic products may distort trade, much like a tariff, artificially increasing the competitiveness of the

---

[11] For a more detailed explanation of the core WTO disciplines, see Michael Trebilcock and Robert Howse, *The Regulation of International Trade* (3rd edn, 2005) 27–32, 49–111, 177–93; Peter Van den Bossche, *The Law and Policy of the World Trade Organization: Text, Cases and Materials* (2005) chs. 4–5.

[12] GATT 1994, art. XI:1.

[13] In particular, tariffs provide greater transparency and economic certainty (e.g., for importers calculating transaction costs). In addition, tariffs generate revenue for the government imposing them, rather than simply for the domestic producers, who can charge higher prices when imports are restricted through either tariffs or quotas. See Bernard Hoekman and Michel Kostecki, *The Political Economy of the World Trading System: The WTO and Beyond* (2nd edn, 2001) 148; John Jackson, *The World Trading System: Law and Policy of International Economic Relations* (2nd edn, 1997) 140; Richard Posner, *Economic Analysis of Law* (2003) 315. See also UNCTAD and World Bank, *Liberalizing International Transactions in Services: A Handbook* (1994) 54.

[14] GATT 1994, art. II. See, e.g., Anwarul Hoda, *Tariff Negotiations and Renegotiations under the GATT and the WTO: Procedures and Practices* (2001) 19.

[15] See Jackson, *World Trading System*, 74.

domestic industry and reducing imports.[16] Therefore, under national treatment, each WTO Member must treat imported products, after they have crossed the border,[17] no less favourably than like products produced domestically. Specifically, internal taxes and charges, and laws and regulations affecting internal sale and distribution, 'should not be applied to imported or domestic products so as to afford protection to domestic production'.[18] Thus, national treatment precludes discrimination against imported products.

(d) *MFN treatment*: Discrimination by WTO Members in favour of imports from certain Member or non-Member countries (rather than imports from all WTO Members) may also distort trade.[19] According to the MFN obligation, described as a 'cornerstone' of the WTO[20] and 'the defining principle of the GATT',[21] where a Member grants an advantage (with respect to import, export, sale, purchase, transportation, distribution or use) to a product being imported from or exported to another country, it must also accord that advantage to all Members' like products.[22] Thus, MFN treatment precludes discrimination among imports of WTO Members or in favour of imports of non-WTO Members.

A recurrent difficulty in the global trading system (as well as regional and national counterparts)[23] involves distinguishing between trade-restrictive or discriminatory governmental measures that are imposed in the pursuit of a legitimate government objective from those imposed purely to protect domestic industries from foreign competition. Arguably, no 'trade and . . .' problem arises where the competing objective is mere protectionism, since trade liberalisation trumps protectionism in the absence of other considerations. However, numerous 'other' considerations exist, many of which the WTO agreements identify. The preamble to the Marrakesh Agreement itself recognises certain values

---

[16] See, e.g., John Jackson, *World Trade and the Law of the GATT (A Legal Analysis of the General Agreement on Tariffs and Trade)* (1969) 273.
[17] See Panel Report, *EC – Poultry*, [273]–[275].
[18] GATT 1994, art. III:1. See also GATT 1994, arts. III:2, III:4.
[19] On the trade effects of such measures, see Robert Hudec, 'Tiger Tiger, in the House: A Critical Appraisal of the Case Against Discriminatory Trade Measures' in Robert Hudec (ed.), *Essays on the Nature of International Trade Law* (1999) 281, 286.
[20] Appellate Body Report, *Canada – Autos*, [69]; Appellate Body Report, *EC – Tariff Preferences*, [104]; Appellate Body Report, *US – Section 211 Appropriations Act*, [297].
[21] WTO, Consultative Board, *The Future of the WTO: Addressing Institutional Challenges in the New Millennium* (2004) [59].
[22] GATT 1994, art. I:1.
[23] E.g., regional trade under NAFTA or the EC, and interstate trade in countries such as Australia or the USA.

or concerns other than trade liberalisation, such as development and the environment, noting that Members' trade should

allo[w] for the optimal use of the world's resources in accordance with the objective of sustainable development, seeking both to protect and preserve the environment and to enhance the means for doing so in a manner consistent with their respective needs and concerns at different levels of economic development,

Recognizing further that there is need for positive efforts designed to ensure that developing countries, and especially the least developed among them, secure a share in the growth in international trade commensurate with the needs of their economic development ...

As Trachtman has pointed out, a variety of 'trade-off devices' may assist in resolving 'trade and ...' problems.[24] GATT Article XX provides an example of such a device in connection with the problem of trade and environment. As the key exception clause in GATT 1994, Article XX lists certain '[g]eneral exceptions' to the usual trade-liberalising disciplines of the WTO, allowing Members to adopt or enforce measures 'necessary to protect human, animal or plant life or health'[25] or 'relating to the conservation of exhaustible natural resources'[26] (among other things) provided that certain other conditions are met.[27] Other WTO agreements besides GATT 1994 also recognise the trade and health problem. Consider a strict quarantine law on imported produce, which a WTO Member might impose on genuine health grounds or to protect its farmers or fisheries from competitors worldwide.[28] The WTO's SPS Agreement (which governs Members' 'sanitary or phytosanitary' measures that affect international trade)[29] captures the difference between these objectives by

[r]eaffirming that no Member should be prevented from adopting or enforcing measures necessary to protect human, animal or plant life or health, subject to the requirement that these measures are not applied in a manner which would constitute a means of arbitrary or unjustifiable discrimination between

---

[24] Trachtman, 'Trade and ... Problems', 35.   [25] GATT 1994, art. XX(b).
[26] Such measures must be 'made effective in conjunction with restrictions on domestic production or consumption': GATT 1994, art. XX(g).
[27] In particular, the *chapeau* to GATT 1994, art. XX, makes all the exceptions '[s]ubject to the requirement that such measures are not applied in a manner which would constitute a means of arbitrary or unjustifiable discrimination between countries where the same conditions prevail, or a disguised restriction on international trade'.
[28] Cf. Appellate Body Report, *Australia – Salmon*, [1]–[2].
[29] SPS Agreement, art. 1:1, annex A.

Members where the same conditions prevail or a disguised restriction on international trade.[30]

Similarly, the Enabling Clause allows some discrimination in favour of developing countries, contrary to the usual WTO rules, recognising the importance of development.[31] The WTO rules also recognise the potential problem of trade and security, providing that GATT 1994 is not to be construed to prevent a Member 'from taking any action which it considers necessary for the protection of its essential security interests' relating to traffic in arms, for example.[32]

Other 'exceptions'[33] to WTO disciplines are not necessarily or ordinarily characterised as such. For example, to counter injury to their domestic industries, Members are entitled to impose anti-dumping duties on dumped imports,[34] and countervailing duties on certain subsidised imports,[35] subject to compliance with detailed procedural and substantive requirements set out in the WTO agreements. That these kinds of 'trade remedies' involve exceptions to WTO disciplines is clear. They might otherwise violate the MFN obligation or tariff bindings. They are also examples of 'trade and ...' problems. Although their rationale is debatable,[36] some might describe anti-dumping and countervailing duties as reflecting the conflict between free trade and unfair trade.[37] This conflict is purportedly resolved by creating strict

---

[30] Ibid., preamble (see also art. 2.3). The wording of this passage is comparable to that in the *chapeau* of GATT 1994, art. XX.
[31] Enabling Clause, [1].
[32] GATT 1994, art. XXI. See also GATS, art. XIV *bis*.
[33] Although the point was disputed, the Appellate Body found that the Enabling Clause is an exception to MFN treatment in Appellate Body Report, *EC – Tariff Preferences*, [98]–[99].
[34] GATT 1994, art. VI:2; Anti-Dumping Agreement, art. 1. In the WTO, 'dumping' occurs where 'products of one country are introduced into the commerce of another country at less than the normal value of the products': GATT 1994, art. VI:1. See also Anti-Dumping Agreement, art. 2.
[35] GATT 1994, art. VI:3; SCM Agreement, art. 10. In the WTO, a 'subsidy' essentially involves conferring a benefit through either a 'financial contribution' by a government or public body or 'income or price support' that increases exports from or reduces imports to that country: GATT 1994, art. XVI:1; SCM Agreement, art. 1.1.
[36] See below, 237.
[37] GATT 1994, art. VI:1 reflects the alleged unfairness of dumping, stating that WTO Members 'recognize that dumping ... is to be condemned if it causes or threatens material injury to an established industry in the territory of a Member or materially retards the establishment of a domestic industry'. GATT 1994, art. XVI:2 provides an example of WTO Members' recognition of the alleged unfairness of certain subsidies, stating that WTO Members 'recognize that the granting by a Member of a subsidy on the export of any product may have harmful effects for other contracting parties, both

conditions on the imposition of these duties to prevent their use as protectionist measures, just as the SPS Agreement, '[i]n an effort to eliminate protectionist and unnecessary non-tariff barriers ... imposes strict scientific justification requirements'.[38]

According to the Appellate Body, Article XX of GATT 1994 describes 'measures that are recognized as exceptions to substantive obligations established in GATT 1994, because the domestic policies embodied in such measures have been recognized as important and legitimate in character'.[39] Petros Mavroidis has pointed out that 'one tenable reading' of this list of exceptions 'would be to exclude regulatory intervention on grounds not mentioned' therein.[40] However, although Article XX is restricted to certain domestic policies that WTO Members have identified as legitimate, this does not necessarily mean that all other domestic policies (including policies regarding cultural products) are illegitimate for the purposes of WTO law.[41] Leaving to one side the issue of whether it is appropriate for WTO Panels and the Appellate Body (which resolve disputes between WTO Members regarding trade-related measures)[42] to assess the legitimacy of particular domestic regulatory goals,[43] several factors suggest that WTO Members never intended to limit their regulatory objectives to those listed in Article XX (or explicitly specified

---

importing and exporting, may cause undue disturbance to their normal commercial interests, and may hinder the achievement of the objectives of this Agreement'.

[38] Catherine Button, *The Power to Protect: Trade, Health and Uncertainty in the WTO* (2004) 103.
[39] Appellate Body Report, *US – Shrimp*, [121]. See also [156].
[40] Petros Mavroidis, '"Like Products": Some Thoughts at the Positive and Normative Level' in Thomas Cottier and Petros Mavroidis (eds.), *Regulatory Barriers and the Principle of Non-Discrimination in World Trade Law* (2000) 125, 129.
[41] Cf. William Davey and Joost Pauwelyn, 'MFN Unconditionality: A Legal Analysis of the Concept in View of its Evolution in the GATT/WTO Jurisprudence with Particular Reference to the Issue of "Like Product"' in Cottier and Mavroidis, *Regulatory Barriers*, 13, 38.
[42] Disputes between WTO Members about compliance with WTO rules are settled by Panels (established on an *ad hoc* basis and generally comprising three individuals) and the Appellate Body (comprising seven individuals who serve four-year terms). Reports of Panels and the Appellate Body become effective only upon adoption by the DSB (comprising representatives of all WTO Members), but adoption is virtually automatic. The DSU is the WTO agreement that establishes the rules for resolving disputes. Although the DSB could in theory agree by consensus not to adopt a Panel or Appellate Body Report (DSU, arts. 16.4, 17.14), it has not done so to date. For more detailed commentary see generally Jeffrey Waincymer, *WTO Litigation: Procedural Aspects of Formal Dispute Settlement* (2002).
[43] Aaditya Mattoo and Arvind Subramanian, 'Regulatory Autonomy and Multilateral Disciplines: The Dilemma and a Possible Resolution' (1998) 1 *Journal of International Economic Law* 303, 321.

elsewhere in the WTO agreements), and that the Appellate Body would be loath to impose such a requirement.

First, this reading is inconsistent with the preamble to the Marrakesh Agreement, which appears to recognise other legitimate objectives of WTO Members, as already mentioned. Indeed, the Appellate Body itself has looked to the preamble in the course of interpreting GATT Article XX(g).[44] Second, it inexplicably excludes numerous goals of domestic policy that are both common and apparently non-protectionist, such as consumer protection,[45] 'competition policy, company law and investment-related matters', 'income distribution, revenue raising' and 'the environment *per se*'[46] (i.e. other than for measures 'relating to the conservation of exhaustible natural resources . . .', which are explicitly recognised in Article XX(g)).[47] Third, and most importantly, it is contrary to 'the notion of trade liberalization as consistent with deep regulatory diversity, accommodating a full range of noneconomic public values'.[48] This notion is supported by GATT contracting parties' refusal during the Uruguay Round to craft the WTO system 'as an autonomous level of governance' with regulatory powers.[49] Moreover, it is a key factor in maintaining support for and institutional legitimacy of the WTO. Although certain WTO agreements involve some harmonisation,[50] in general the WTO refuses to characterise the multilateral trading system as harmonising or deregulating.[51] Substantial freedom to regulate domestically according to any social or political agenda is essential to achieving agreement in the WTO among countries of vastly different backgrounds, values, and levels of development.[52]

---

[44] See, e.g., Appellate Body Report, *US – Shrimp*, [129].
[45] Mavroidis, 'Like Products', 129.
[46] Mattoo and Subramanian, 'Regulatory Autonomy', 308, 313–14.
[47] Other legitimate policies that might fall outside Article XX include those 'designed to harmonize technical standards, to avoid the accumulation of waste, or to tax the consumption of luxury goods': Frieder Roessler, 'Diverging Domestic Policies and Multilateral Trade Integration' in Jagdish Bhagwati and Robert Hudec (eds.), *Fair Trade and Harmonization: Prerequisites for Free Trade?* (1996) (vol. II) 21, 30.
[48] Robert Howse and Kalypso Nicolaïdis, 'Enhancing WTO Legitimacy: Constitutionalization or Global Subsidiarity?' (2003) 16(1) *Governance* 73, 79–80.
[49] Ibid., 84.
[50] E.g. TBT Agreement, art. 2.6; SPS Agreement, art. 3.1; TRIPS Agreement.
[51] See, e.g., Appellate Body Report, *US – Gasoline*, 30; WTO, Economic Research and Analysis Division, *Market Access: Unfinished Business – Post-Uruguay Round Inventory and Issues* (Special Study No. 6) 122; GATT, *Countdown for the Uruguay Round: Address by Peter Sutherland to the Forum de l'Expansion, Paris, 19 October 1993*, NUR 070 (20 October 1993) IV. See also Steve Charnovitz, 'Free Trade, Fair Trade, Green Trade: Defogging the Debate' (1994) 27 *Cornell International Law Journal* 459, 471; Mavroidis, 'Like Products', 129.
[52] See Howse and Nicolaïdis, 'Enhancing WTO Legitimacy', 86.

This assessment is consistent with the statement by Robert Howse and Kalypso Nicolaïdis that a 'large part of the membership of the WTO opposes the WTO having any social agenda'.[53]

Thus, an undefined list of legitimate regulatory objectives or social values may compete with the endorsement of trade liberalisation within the WTO. Promotion or preservation of culture is one of these.

1.2 Cultural implications of WTO rules

Individuals, non-governmental organisations and certain States have made clear their anxiety about increasing cultural homogenisation and a world swamped with burgers from McDonald's and films from Hollywood.[54] Few would dispute that Members should be allowed to retain their 'culture', whether or not they could be said to have a 'comparative advantage' in this area. However, as some traded goods and services have both economic and cultural value (in such forms as aesthetics, spirituality, history, symbolism, and authenticity),[55] a Member could impose trade-restrictive or discriminatory measures on imports of these items either to preserve and promote local culture or to protect its producers. The cultural value of a given product may be reflected not only in the nature of the product, or who produced it, but also in the way it is produced or consumed or the way it affects local identity.[56] Moreover, a desire to protect local culture, broadly defined, could undermine the wisdom of trade liberalisation in the first place. Even a nail, tiny and seemingly meaningless, could have cultural implications when combined with millions of other nails and millions of other goods and services bringing in foreign influences, standards, and materials. This is the essence of the trade and culture problem.

On one view, '[j]ust as quarantine laws prohibit the import of disease-bearing plants and animals, so does cultural protection seek to shield

---

[53] Ibid.
[54] See, e.g., Harry Redner, *Conserving Cultures: Technology, Globalization, and the Future of Local Cultures* (2004) 47-8, 103; George Yúdice, *The Expediency of Culture: Uses of Culture in the Global Era* (2003) 221; Guillermo de la Dehesa, *Winners and Losers in Globalization* (2006) 166-7. But see also Trebilcock and Howse, *Regulation of Trade* (3rd edn) 10-12, 451; David Hesmondhalgh, *The Cultural Industries* (2002) 174-8.
[55] David Throsby, *Economics and Culture* (2001) 28-9.
[56] Tomer Broude, 'Taking "Trade and Culture" Seriously: Geographical Indications and Cultural Protection in WTO Law' (2005) 26(4) *University of Pennsylvania Journal of International Economic Law* 623, 638-41.

the community from infection by foreign cultural influences'.[57] This description is conceptually attractive, and it helps explain the perceived contradiction between trade liberalisation and cultural policy. However, it hides another side of the relationship between trade and culture. As the many and varied international instruments on culture demonstrate, although it may be important to preserve cultures in their original form through some insulation,[58] at the same time, cultures must be encouraged to grow and flourish through exchange and interaction with other cultures.[59] Thus, unlike imported fruit, which may be unwanted if it bears foreign diseases, imports containing foreign cultural elements may be valuable precisely because of their cultural content. This adds an extra layer of complexity to the problem of trade and culture.

It is beyond the scope of this book to establish a definitive definition of culture in the abstract, or even a definition of culture for the purposes of international trade law. Culture is a slippery and amorphous concept. In the context of international law, despite the proliferation of treaties and declarations on the subject, no single agreed definition of culture exists. However, as an example of the potentially expansive meaning of culture, the preamble to the Universal Declaration on Cultural Diversity defines culture as 'the set of distinctive spiritual, material, intellectual and emotional features of society or a social group, [encompassing], in addition to art and literature, lifestyles, ways of living together, value systems, traditions and beliefs'.[60] In the context of economics, David Throsby adopts a broadly similar and equally wide-ranging definition. He identifies two particular senses in which the word 'culture' is used: 'in a broadly anthropological or sociological framework to describe a set

---

[57] Throsby, *Economics and Culture*, 132.
[58] See, e.g., Convention on Cultural Property in Armed Conflict, art. 4.3; Convention for the Protection of Cultural Heritage, art. 4; UNIDROIT Convention on Cultural Objects, art. 1; UNESCO, *Recommendation on the Safeguarding of Traditional Culture and Folklore*, 25 C/Resolutions, annex I(B), 238 (15 November 1989) [B].
[59] See, e.g., Beirut Agreement, art. III; Florence Agreement, art. I; Nairobi Protocol, [1]; UNESCO, *Declaration of the Principles of International Cultural Co-operation*, 14 C/Resolution 8 (4 November 1966) arts. IV:1, IV:4, VI, VII:1; UNESCO, *Recommendation Concerning the International Exchange of Cultural Property*, 19 C/Resolutions, annex I, 16 (26 November 1976) [2]; Universal Declaration on Cultural Diversity, art. 7.
[60] Footnote 2 to the Declaration points out: 'This definition is in line with the conclusions of the World Conference on Cultural Policies (MONDIACULT, Mexico City, 1982), of the World Commission on Culture and Development (*Our Creative Diversity*, 1995), and of the Intergovernmental Conference on Cultural Policies for Development (Stockholm, 1998).'

of attitudes, beliefs, mores, customs, values and practices which are common to or shared by any group'; and, in a more functional sense, 'denoting certain activities that are undertaken by people, and the products of those activities, which have to do with the intellectual, moral and artistic aspects of human life'.[61] According to these definitions, culture may refer both to concrete products of artistic endeavour (whether traditional or popular, commercial or non-profit) and to less tangible notions or 'ways of life'. Within these broad definitions of culture, almost any form of international trade or trade policy could reasonably be interpreted as having a cultural aspect or influence.

Three examples from WTO disputes demonstrate the kinds of trade measures that might be described as cultural. The case of *Japan – Leather II (US)*, heard by a Panel under GATT 1947, concerned a Japanese law requiring importers of certain types of leather to obtain import licences and to comply with import quotas.[62] The US complained that this violated Article XI of GATT 1947. Japan argued that the system was justified by its desire to protect the jobs of a certain minority population.[63] Japan explained that a minority group of Japanese people centred in particular districts (the Dowa people) were in an inferior position economically, socially, and culturally because of discrimination based on a class system. The Dowa people tended to work in traditional Dowa industries such as the tanning industry, which had a low level of technology and international competitiveness, and which supported several hundred thousand people and a regional economy. If the import restrictions were eliminated, Japan maintained, 'the industry would collapse with [immeasurable] social, regional economic and political problems'.[64] In this dispute the Panel decided that it could not consider 'the special historical, cultural and socio-economic circumstances referred to by Japan' under Article XI.[65] However, it is worth noting that the import quotas at issue could be framed more specifically as measures designed to preserve a threatened culture or way of life.

More recently, in *Japan – Alcoholic Beverages II*, Japan supported its differential tax rates for shochu and 'spirits' such as vodka[66] by arguing that Japanese consumers regard shochu as different from spirits and drink it in different ways and settings. For example, Japan reported that most shochu consumers drink shochu during meals, while most spirits

---

[61] Throsby, *Economics and Culture*, 3–4.   [62] GATT Panel Report, *Japan – Leather II (US)*, [8].
[63] Ibid., [15], [17]–[18].   [64] Ibid., [21]–[22].   [65] Ibid., [44].
[66] Appellate Body Report, *Japan – Alcoholic Beverages II*, [2.2]–[2.3].

consumers drink spirits after meals. Similarly, a large proportion of shochu consumers drink shochu with hot water, but few spirits consumers drink vodka with hot water. Conversely, many drink vodka with tonic water, but no shochu consumers drink shochu with tonic water.[67] Although Japan did not specifically refer to 'cultural' concerns, the differential tax scheme could be described as simply a reflection of cultural values and practices with respect to alcohol.

Similar arguments could apply to the EC directive prohibiting the sale or importation of bovine meat from animals to which certain hormones have been administered for growth promotion purposes.[68] That measure, which was considered in *EC – Hormones*, could represent an accommodation of the cultural sensitivities of the people of Europe in relation to food. Indeed, Marsha Echols maintains that, whereas Europeans typically favour traditional foods and are suspicious of new technologies (such as genetic engineering), Americans are typically willing to adopt new technologies, while being suspicious of traditional production processes (such as those used to create raw milk cheese and cured meats).[69] This suggestion about European attitudes to food, despite being a generalisation, is borne out by the evidence presented in *EC – Hormones*. The Panel and the Appellate Body both recognised the existence of consumer concerns within the EC about the use of hormones for growth promotion in animals used for food.[70] At a more general level, the EC measure could reflect a certain European cultural attitude towards risk, entailing a preference for precaution and qualitative appraisals of risk in contrast to the typical US faith in science and

---

[67] Panel Report, *Japan – Alcoholic Beverages II*, [4.54].
[68] Panel Report, *EC – Hormones (US)*, [II.2]–[II.5].
[69] Marsha Echols, 'Food Safety Regulation in the European Union and the United States: Different Cultures, Different Laws' (1998) 4 *Columbia Journal of European Law* 525, 526. See also Marsha Echols, *Food Safety and the WTO: The Interplay of Culture, Science and Technology* (2001); Bruce Silverglade, 'International Harmonization under the SPS Agreement' in National Research Council (ed.), *Incorporating Science, Economics, and Sociology in Developing Sanitary and Phytosanitary Standards in International Trade: Proceedings of a Conference* (2000) 210, 213; David Winickoff et al., 'Adjudicating the GM Food Wars: Science, Risk, and Democracy in World Trade Law' (2005) 30(1) *Yale Journal of International Law* 81, 97–9; George York, 'Global Foods, Local Tastes and Biotechnology: The New Legal Architecture of International Agriculture Trade' (2001) 7 *Columbia Journal of European Law* 423.
[70] Appellate Body Report, *EC – Hormones*, [245]; Panel Report, *EC – Hormones (Canada)*, [II.26], [IV.15]; Panel Report, *EC – Hormones (US)*, [II.26], [IV.14].

quantitative methods of risk assessment.[71] This cultural difference could have implications for the application of the SPS Agreement, in that a Member will face greater difficulties in complying with this agreement where its consumers are concerned about a matter that international standards bodies consider to be safe (as happened in this case). The relevance of 'social and cultural factors'[72] under the SPS Agreement also arose in the recent dispute on EC measures concerning genetically modified food.[73]

The cultural implications of the WTO extend beyond the SPS Agreement and GATT 1994 to many other WTO agreements. For example, several of the intellectual property rights addressed in the TRIPS Agreement relate to culture. Cultural preservation provides one possible justification for protecting 'geographical indications'[74] such as 'Champagne' in the TRIPS Agreement, with culture here encompassing such things as traditional production methods for food and wine and the historical and physical connection between particular locations and particular products.[75] The TRIPS Agreement already protects geographical indications, most extensively in connection with wines and spirits,[76] although several aspects of the relevant provisions remain contested,[77] and Members are continuing negotiations on this issue.[78] One question is whether geographical indications create a valid and effective form of cultural preservation and promotion or whether, as

---

[71] Sheila Jasanoff, 'Technological Risk and Cultures of Rationality' in National Research Council, *Incorporating Science, Economics, and Sociology*, 65, 71–2; C. Ford Runge et al., 'Differing U.S. and European Perspectives on GMOs: Political, Economic and Cultural Issues' (2001) 2(2) *The Estey Centre Journal of International Law and Trade Policy* 221, 224–5. See also Button, *Power to Protect*, 107–8.
[72] Button, *Power to Protect*, 112.
[73] See Panel Report, *EC – Biotech*; Cara Coburn, 'Out of the Petri Dish and Back to the People: A Cultural Approach to GMO Policy' (2005) 23(2) *Wisconsin International Law Journal* 283, 294–6.
[74] 'Geographical indications are ... indications which identify a good as originating in the territory of a Member, or a region or locality in that territory, where a given quality, reputation or other characteristic of the good is essentially attributable to its geographical origin': TRIPS Agreement, art. 22.
[75] Broude, 'Geographical Indications and Cultural Protection', 650–3.
[76] TRIPS Agreement, arts. 22–24.
[77] See generally Panel Reports, *EC – Trade Marks and Geographical Indications*.
[78] Hong Kong Declaration, [29]; Doha Declaration, [18]. See also G. Evans and Michael Blakeney, 'The Protection of Geographical Indications After Doha: Quo Vadis?' (2006) 9(3) *Journal of International Economic Law* 1.

Tomer Broude contends, they are merely 'legal tools for granting commercial advantages to certain products, sectors and regions'.[79]

The WTO Ministerial Conference (the WTO's highest decision-making body, comprising representatives of all WTO Members)[80] has also instructed the Council for TRIPS (which oversees the functioning of the TRIPS Agreement)[81] to examine 'the protection of traditional knowledge and folklore',[82] concepts with no authoritative WTO definition but that evidently relate to cultural issues. Thus, Johanna Gibson defines traditional knowledge as 'the totality of Indigenous and traditional cultural production'.[83] Most of the Council's work so far has focused on traditional knowledge rather than folklore, and one reason Members have put forward in favour of international action to protect this knowledge is culture.[84] Many Members are concerned that a failure to protect traditional knowledge enables private entities to appropriate and patent commercially valuable subject matter such as genetic resources of the neem tree, as well as associated research and development into their uses,[85] without obtaining permission or adequately compensating the customary owners.[86] This may hinder not only the maintenance of traditional knowledge itself, which may be inherently cultural, but also the way of life of the communities concerned, which may also have precious cultural elements.[87] For example, the 'African Group' of WTO Members

---

[79] Broude, 'Geographical Indications and Cultural Protection', 678. See also Jim Chen, 'A Sober Second Look at Appellations of Origin: How the United States Will Crash France's Wine and Cheese Party' (1996) 5 *Minnesota Journal of Global Trade* 29.
[80] Marrakesh Agreement, art. IV:1.   [81] Ibid., art. IV:5.   [82] Doha Declaration, [19].
[83] Johanna Gibson, *Community Resources: Intellectual Property, International Trade and Protection of Traditional Knowledge* (2005) 28.
[84] WTO, Council for Trade-Related Aspects of Intellectual Property Rights, *The Protection of Traditional Knowledge and Folklore: Summary of Issues Raised and Points Made – Note by the Secretariat (Revision)*, IP/C/W/370/Rev.1 (9 March 2006) [6], [9].
[85] See, e.g., WTO, Council for Trade-Related Aspects of Intellectual Property Rights, *Minutes of Meeting Held on 21 and 22 September 2000*, IP/C/M/28 (23 November 2000) [126].
[86] See, e.g., WTO, Council for Trade-Related Aspects of Intellectual Property Rights, *Article 27.3(b), Relationship between the TRIPS Agreement and the CBD and Protection of Traditional Knowledge and Folklore: Communication from Peru*, IP/C/W/447 (8 June 2005) 2–3. See also Graham Dutfield, 'Protecting Traditional Knowledge: Pathways to the Future' (working paper, International Centre for Trade and Sustainable Development, 2006) ch. 2.
[87] For further discussion of the relationship between culture and traditional knowledge, see Rosemary Coombe, 'Protecting Cultural Industries to Promote Cultural Diversity: Dilemmas for International Policymaking Posed by the Recognition of Traditional Knowledge' in Keith Maskus and Jerome Reichman (eds.), *International Public Goods and Transfer of Technology Under a Globalized Intellectual Property Regime* (2005) 599. On the human rights implications, see UN, Commission on Human Rights, Sub-Commission

has defined 'traditional knowledge' as including 'knowledge systems, innovations and adaptations, information, and practices of local communities or indigenous communities ... relating to any type of medicine or cures, agriculture, use and conservation of biological material and diversity, and any other aspect of economic, social, cultural, aesthetic or other value'.[88] The African Group has also explained that

> [t]he protection of genetic resources and traditional knowledge, particularly those originating from developing country Members, is an important means of addressing poverty and is rightly a matter of equity and due recognition for the custodians of the genetic resources and the traditional knowledge. It is also a matter of law in the context of protecting cultural rights as well as of preserving the invaluable heritage of humankind that biological diversity and traditional knowledge constitute.[89]

From this brief discussion, it is not difficult to see how a large array of other products and trade measures could be linked to cultural norms, perhaps through the medium of legal, social, or political traditions.[90] These include measures to protect the environment, giving effect to religious beliefs, or regulating education. No single characteristic distinguishes products related to culture from other products; rather, the 'continuum' of products with cultural aspects ranges from films, to cars and shoes, to cement and petroleum products.[91] Thus, US measures to protect its steel industry could be identified as necessary to protect a traditional way of life in its industrial towns.[92] Finally, some Members currently call for recognition of the 'multifunctionality' of agriculture, in that agriculture may further social or environmental policies or preserve the rural landscape.[93] Along the same lines, it could be argued

---

on the Promotion and Protection of Human Rights, *The Impact of the Agreement on Trade-Related Aspects of Intellectual Property Rights on Human Rights: Report of the High Commissioner*, E/CN.4/Sub.2/2001/13 (27 June 2001) [26].

[88] WTO, Council for Trade-Related Aspects of Intellectual Property Rights, *Taking Forward the Review of Article 27.3(b) of the TRIPS Agreement: Joint Communication from the African Group*, IP/C/W/404 (26 June 2003) 1–2.

[89] Ibid., 9.

[90] For further discussion of GATT/WTO cases that may be relevant to culture, see Chi Carmody, 'When "Cultural Identity was Not at Issue": Thinking about Canada – Certain Measures Concerning Periodicals' (1999) 30 *Law and Policy in International Business* 231, 261–76.

[91] Allen Scott and Dominic Power, 'A Prelude to Cultural Industries and the Production of Culture' in Dominic Power and Allen Scott (eds.), *Cultural Industries and the Production of Culture* (2004) 3, 4.

[92] Cf. Philippe Legrain, *Open World: The Truth about Globalisation* (2002) 26–31.

[93] See, e.g., Elie Cohen, 'Globalization and Cultural Diversity' in UNESCO (ed.), *World Culture Report: Cultural Diversity, Conflict and Pluralism* (2000) 66, 69; Stilwell and Bohanes,

that agriculture protects cultural values and deserves special treatment on that basis.

In the cases mentioned above, the respondent did not try to justify its measure on the basis of its cultural goals. In fact, in most of the examples mentioned it is highly unlikely that a WTO Member would try to defend its measure on the basis of culture. The reason for this may be primarily that, as we shall see, the WTO agreements contain virtually no explicit recognition of culture or the legitimacy of Members' cultural interests or policies. Accordingly, respondents may view cultural arguments as unlikely to succeed. Yet this is probably not the only reason for Members' reluctance to make these arguments. A respondent would also be wary of raising cultural motivations for a particular measure because of the systemic implications of doing so. The potentially vast scope of 'culture' would likely be of concern to both parties.[94] The respondent would realise that, to avoid the risk of opening up a significant area of uncertainty, the complainant would most likely vigorously oppose any cultural arguments. For the same reason, the respondent could fear the implications for its country in the future if its own cultural arguments succeeded.

1.3 Cultural industries, cultural products, and cultural policy measures

1.3.1 Definitions

It is useful to contemplate the wide-ranging issues raised by culture in order to understand the reluctance of some WTO Members to provide any special treatment for culture in the WTO rules. At the same time, it is not possible here to cover all aspects of culture that may be affected by international trade. The rest of this book therefore explores a particular notion of culture, in the form of certain defined 'cultural products' created or provided by certain 'cultural industries', as a specific example or case study of the potential conflict between trade and culture in the WTO and how such a conflict may be resolved. This narrow group of products is currently the most contentious aspect of culture within the WTO.

'Trade and Environment', 553; WTO, TPRB, *Trade Policy Review of Switzerland and Liechtenstein: Minutes of Meeting Held on 15 and 17 December 2004*, WT/TPR/M/141 (16 February 2005) [40]; TPRB, WTO, *Trade Policy Review of the Republic of Korea: Minutes of Meeting Held on 15 and 17 September 2004*, WT/TPR/M/137 (19 November 2004) [88].
[94] See below, 185.

The term 'culture industry' may have been first used in 1947 by Theodor Adorno,[95] who described film as the 'central sector' of that industry in his critique of mass culture.[96] UNESCO suggests that cultural industries 'generally [include] printing, publishing and multimedia, audio-visual, phonographic and cinematographic productions, as well as crafts and design', and that a broader definition might also encompass 'architecture, visual and performing arts, sports, manufacturing of musical instruments, advertising and cultural tourism'.[97] In this book, I refer to the cultural industries as the audiovisual industry and the printing and publishing industries.[98] In turn, I describe the relevant products of these industries as 'cultural products' (referring predominantly to film, video, radio, television, sound recording, books, magazines, periodicals, and associated services). These terms are no more than convenient labels or shorthand references, and in using them I do not intend to prejudge whether or to what extent these industries or products embody culture or should receive special treatment under WTO law. By 'cultural policy measures',[99] I mean measures that are ostensibly designed to protect or promote cultural aspects of cultural products, to the extent that they affect trade in goods or services.

1.3.2 Common cultural policy measures

Before explaining the significance of cultural products in the WTO, it is worth setting out a few examples of the types of cultural policy measures that Members may wish to adopt, focusing on those that may conflict with WTO rules. In Chapter 3, in the course of assessing the current treatment of cultural products in WTO law, I provide additional examples of the types of cultural policy measures that Members have

---

[95] Theodor Adorno, *The Culture Industry: Selected Essays on Mass Culture* (1991), edited with an introduction by J. M. Bernstein, 85; Theodor Adorno and Max Horkheimer, *Dialectic of Enlightenment* (1972), translated by John Cumming (original publication 1944).

[96] Adorno, *Culture Industry*, 87. For further discussion see John Sinclair, 'Culture and Trade: Some Theoretical and Practical Considerations' in Emile McAnany and Kenton Wilkinson (eds.), *Mass Media and Free Trade: NAFTA and the Cultural Industries* (1996) 30, 30–40; Mary Footer and Christoph Graber, 'Trade Liberalization and Cultural Policy' (2000) 3 *Journal of International Economic Law* 115, 117–18.

[97] UNESCO, *Culture, Trade and Globalization: Questions and Answers* (2000) q. 1.

[98] See Keith Acheson and Christopher Maule, *Much Ado about Culture: North American Trade Disputes* (1999) 2, 6–7.

[99] On the use of the term 'measure' in WTO disputes, see generally Alan Yanovich and Tania Voon, 'What is the Measure at Issue?' in Andrew Mitchell (ed.), *Challenges and Prospects for the WTO* (2005) 115.

used or contemplated. More extensive descriptions and classifications of these measures appear elsewhere.[100]

WTO Members often impose minimum national content quotas in the film, television, and radio industries.[101] The Canadian broadcasting policy specifically states that 'each broadcasting undertaking shall make maximum use, and in no case less than predominant use, of Canadian creative and other resources in the creation and presentation of programming'.[102] In its most recent reviews of Canadian trade policy, the TPRB (a WTO body that monitors Members' trade regulations and compliance with WTO obligations) noted restrictions imposed by the CRTC on radio and television broadcasts. Specifically, the TPRB mentioned CRTC requirements 'that for Canadian conventional, over-the-air broadcasters, Canadian programming make up 60% of television broadcast time, and 50% during the evening hours ... [and] that 35% of "popular" musical selections broadcast on radio should qualify as "Canadian" under a government-determined points system'.[103] The 'public broadcaster must maintain the same overall level of Canadian content and 60 per cent during prime time',[104] but '[t]here is no similar national control over what appears in Canadian cinemas'.[105] In France,

---

[100] See, e.g., Footer and Graber, 'Trade Liberalization and Cultural Policy', 122–6; Christoph Graber, *Handel und Kultur im Audiovisionsrecht der WTO: Völkerrechtliche, ökonomische und kulturpolitische Grundlagen einer globalen Medienordnung* (2003) ch. 6; Paolo Guerrieri, Lelio Iapadre, and Georg Koopmann (eds.), *Cultural Diversity and International Economic Integration: The Global Governance of the Audiovisual Sector* (2005); Christoph Graber, 'Audio-Visual Policy: The Stumbling Block of Trade Liberalisation?' in Damien Geradin and David Luff (eds.), *The WTO and Global Convergence in Telecommunications and Audio-Visual Services* (2004) 165, 173–97.

[101] See, e.g., WTO, *Mexico – Schedule of Specific Commitments*, GATS/SC/56 (15 April 1994) 17 (national treatment limitation in mode 3 for private film-screening services); Australian Broadcasting Authority, *Broadcasting Services (Australian Content) Standard 1999* (July 2004); Television Without Frontiers Directive, art. 4(1), 5; European Research Institute for Comparative Cultural Policy and the Arts, *A Pilot Inventory of National Cultural Policies and Measures Supporting Cultural Diversity* (July 2001) 26–8.

[102] *Broadcasting Act 1991* (Canada), s. 3.1(f).

[103] WTO, TPRB, *Trade Policy Review, Canada: Report by the Secretariat*, WT/TPR/S/78 (15 November 2000) [I:181]; WTO, TPRB, *Trade Policy Review, Canada: Report by the Secretariat*, WT/TPR/S/112/Rev.1 (19 March 2003) [IV:88]. See also Canadian Heritage, *Canadian Content in the 21st Century: A Discussion Paper about Canadian Content in Film and Television Productions* (March 2002) 8.

[104] Keith Acheson and Christopher Maule, 'Canada – Audio-Visual Policies: Impact on Trade' in Guerrieri, Iapadre, and Koopmann, *Cultural Diversity*, 156, 161.

[105] Ibid., 163.

quotas on film screening have been in place since as early as 1928,[106] while quotas for European and French programming on television go beyond the requirements of the EC's Television Without Frontiers Directive.[107] For example, for the television channel Canal Plus, France requires not only that at least 60 per cent of movies broadcast in peak hours be European (which concerns the MFN principle), but also that 40 per cent be French[108] (which could conflict with the national treatment principle).

Assistance to the film industry often takes the form of tax incentives for investment in or production of national films, with nationality determined according to various defined criteria.[109] For example, the Canadian Audio-Visual Certification Office and the Canada Revenue Agency co-administer two programmes for the provision of tax credits for film or video production. The first is provided for Canadian film or video production and the second for services rendered by Canadians to film or video production in Canada.[110] The UK provides tax incentives for investment in UK film and television production.[111] In Egypt, a producer of Egyptian films is entitled to distribute a maximum number of foreign films relative to the number of Egyptian films produced. The maximum is currently five foreign films distributed for every Egyptian film produced. The profits from distributing foreign films help finance the production of Egyptian films.[112]

---

[106] Anne Marie Condron, 'Cinema' in Sheila Perry (ed.), *Aspects of Contemporary France* (1997) 209. See also Ivan Bernier, 'Cultural Goods and Services in International Trade Law' in Dennis Browne (ed.), *The Culture/Trade Quandary: Canada's Policy Options* (1998) 109.

[107] USTR, *2002 National Trade Estimate Report on Foreign Trade Barriers* (2002) 127. See below, 94.

[108] Emmanuel Cocq and Patrick Messerlin, 'French Audio-Visual Policy: Impact and Compatibility with Trade Negotiations' in Guerrieri, Iapadre, and Koopmann, *Cultural Diversity*, 21, 27. See also Patrick Messerlin, *Measuring the Costs of Protection in Europe: European Commercial Policy in the 2000s* (2001) 328.

[109] See, e.g., European Research Institute for Comparative Cultural Policy and the Arts, *Pilot Inventory*, 26.

[110] Department of Canadian Heritage, *A Guide to Federal Programs for the Film and Video Sector* (September 2001) 24–5; <www.pch.gc.ca/progs/ac-ca/progs/bcpac-cavco/index_e.cfm> (accessed 4 August 2006).

[111] Department for Culture, Media and Sport, *Creative Industries: UK Television Exports Inquiry (The Report of the Creative Industries Task Force Inquiry into Television Exports)* (November 1999) ch. 2, [6.3]–[6.5]; Gillian Doyle and Matthew Hibberd, 'The Case of the UK Audio-Visual System' in Guerrieri, Iapadre, and Koopmann, *Cultural Diversity*, 131, 140.

[112] Ahmed Farouk Ghoneim, 'The Audio-Visual Sector in Egypt' in Guerrieri, Iapadre, and Koopmann, *Cultural Diversity*, 192, 196.

Many WTO Members also grant 'substantial subsidies' to local audiovisual industries.[113] Before the latest EC enlargement, EC funding of the audiovisual sector was estimated at €1,120 million for 2001, with France the leader, making up 40 per cent of that amount.[114] France has 'Europe's most heavily subsidised film industry',[115] and in France a tax on every cinema ticket has traditionally been used to aid French and European film-making.[116] However, subsidies for cultural products are not restricted to Europe. The WTO Secretariat reported in 1998 that, of the '44 countries (including the individual EU Member States) which have been reviewed under WTO provisions, at least 17 have aided their audiovisual industries'.[117] For example, the Australian Government funds the Australian Broadcasting Corporation ('a major part of Australia's ... cultural life'),[118] including its 'Radio Australia' broadcasts, which deliver Australian radio content to regional areas including Timor-Leste.[119] Budgetary outlays by India in this sector amounted to US$170.8 million for the year 2001-2.[120] Keith Acheson and Christopher Maule estimate the combination of Canadian subsidies and tax incentives for the audiovisual industry at $1.1 billion per year, or 30 per cent

---

[113] WTO, Council for Trade in Services, *Audiovisual Services: Background Note by the Secretariat*, S/C/W/40 (15 June 1998) [19]. See also WTO, *World Trade Report 2006: Exploring the Links between Subsidies, Trade and the WTO* (2006) 178, 187-8; GATT, Uruguay Round Group of Negotiations on Services, Working Group on Audiovisual Services, *Matters Relating to Trade in Audiovisual Services: Note by the Secretariat*, MTN.GNS/AUD/W/1 (4 October 1990) [16]; WTO, Working Party on GATS Rules, *Communication from Argentina and Hong Kong, China: Development of Multilateral Disciplines Governing Trade Distortive Subsidies in Services*, S/WPGR/W/31 (16 March 2000) [6]; WTO, Working Party on GATS Rules, *Subsidies for Services Sectors: Information Contained in WTO Trade Policy Reviews – Background Note by the Secretariat*, S/WPGR/W/25 (26 January 1998) 4; OECD, Working Party on the Information Economy, *Digital Broadband Content: Music*, DSTI/ICCP/IE(2004)12/FINAL (8 June 2005) 96; European Research Institute for Comparative Cultural Policy and the Arts, *Pilot Inventory*, 23-5.

[114] Cocq and Messerlin, 'French Audio-Visual Policy', 28-9 (citing European Audiovisual Observatory, Statistical Yearbook, vol III, 2002, Strasbourg, 97).

[115] Condron, 'Cinema', 213. See also Messerlin, *Measuring the Costs of Protection*, 327.

[116] Condron, 'Cinema', 211. See also Messerlin, *Measuring the Costs of Protection*, 326-7.

[117] WTO, Working Party on GATS Rules, *Subsidies for Services Sectors: Information Contained in WTO Trade Policy Reviews – Background Note by the Secretariat*, S/WPGR/W/25 (26 January 1998) [6].

[118] Australian Government, *Creative Nation: Commonwealth Cultural Policy* (October 1994), 'Film, Television and Radio'.

[119] Richard Alston, 'Additional Government funding guarantees Radio Australia service', press release, Minister for Communications, Information Technology and the Arts; Deputy Leader of the Government in the Senate Doc. 41/01 (28 March 2001).

[120] Arpita Mukherjee, 'Audio-Visual Policies and International Trade: The Case of India' in Guerrieri, Iapadre, and Koopmann, *Cultural Diversity* 218, 227.

of total annual production.[121] This support is provided to audiovisual production, broadcasting, and distribution.[122] Canada's Book Publishing Industry Development Program provides funding to publishers that are at least 75 per cent Canadian owned and controlled for sales of Canadian titles.[123] The principle objective of the programme is 'to ensure choice of and access to Canadian-authored books that reflect Canada's cultural diversity and linguistic duality in Canada and abroad'.[124]

1.3.3 Significance in the WTO

The significance for the trade and culture debate of cultural products, as I have defined them, is reflected in the WTO's history and current activities. During the Uruguay Round, GATT contracting parties engaged in a heated debate concerning the treatment of culture,[125] primarily in the negotiation of the new trade in services agreement, GATS. The multilateral rules under GATT 1947 concerned only goods, and the inclusion of matters such as trade in services and trade-related aspects of intellectual property rights in the Uruguay Round represented a significant expansion of the GATT 1947 regime as it transformed into the WTO. GATS is particularly important given the high proportion of global trade that involves services,[126] but it also raises sensitive issues given that many barriers to trade in services 'relate to fundamental domestic regulatory choices'.[127] As a result, GATS disciplines are generally weaker than those under GATT 1994,[128] and the levels of protection for services are much higher than for goods.[129]

---

[121] Acheson and Maule, 'Canada – Audiovisual Policies', 174.   [122] Ibid., 173, 180–1.
[123] Canadian Heritage Publishing Policy and Programs Branch, *Book Publishing Industry Activity Report: 2000–2001* (September 2001) section I; <www.pch.gc.ca/progs/ac-ca/progs/padie-bpidp/index_e.cfm> (accessed 4 August 2006).
[124] Canadian Heritage, *Book Publishing Industry Development Program (BPIDP): Applicant's Guide 2002–2003* (2002).
[125] For a detailed and authoritative account of these negotiations, see John Croome, *Reshaping the World Trading System: A History of the Uruguay Round* (2nd rev. edn, 1999) 212–15, 243–4, 310–12, 320, 324–7.
[126] Pierre Sauvé and Robert Stern (eds.), *GATS 2000: New Directions in Services Trade Liberalization* (2000) 1. On the history and achievements of GATS, see Mary Footer, 'The International Regulation of Trade in Services Following Completion of the Uruguay Round' (1995) 29 *International Lawyer* 453.
[127] Trebilcock and Howse, *Regulation of Trade* (3rd edn) 352.
[128] See Chapter 3 below.
[129] Bernard Hoekman and Patrick Messerlin, 'Liberalizing Trade in Services: Reciprocal Negotiations and Regulatory Reform' in Sauvé and Stern, *GATS 2000*, 487, 494.

As regards culture, countries such as Austria,[130] Peru, Romania, Canada, Brazil, and the Nordic countries suggested in the Uruguay Round that the protection of national or cultural identity or values should provide the basis for a general exception under GATS.[131] Egypt and India also favoured a general cultural exception in services trade.[132] Australia and the EC expressed doubts about this approach.[133] Instead, the EC was one of several countries that viewed audiovisual services as being in particular need of exemption or specific treatment, given their nature and cultural content.[134] The EC introduced a draft sectoral annex 'to ensure that the liberalization of audiovisual services ... be achieved while respecting the cultural specificities of these services'.[135] Australia supported the objectives of the draft annex, while Canada, Chile, Cuba, India, and Sweden supported the approach to varying degrees.[136] Brazil, Egypt, and Finland agreed that 'flexibility' was required 'in dealing with the specificities of the audiovisual services sector'.[137] In contrast, Japan opposed this approach,[138] and New Zealand regarded the draft annex as 'too broad and sweeping'.[139] Furthermore, the USA vigorously opposed both a general exception for culture and a cultural exception for audiovisual services.[140]

[130] Trade Negotiations Committee, GATT, *Mid-Term Meeting*, MTN.TNC/11 (21 April 1989) [II(e)(i)].
[131] Ibid., [II(g)(i)].
[132] GATT, Uruguay Round Group of Negotiations on Services, Working Group on Audiovisual Services, *Note on the Meeting of 5 and 18 October 1990*, MTN.GNS/AUD/2 (20 December 1990) [3]; GATT, Uruguay Round Group of Negotiations on Services, Working Group on Audiovisual Services, *Note on the Meeting of 27–28 August 1990*, MTN.GNS/AUD/1 (27 September 1990) [3], [6], [27], [29], [33].
[133] GATT, Uruguay Round Group of Negotiations on Services, Working Group on Audiovisual Services, *Note on the Meeting of 27–28 August 1990*, MTN.GNS/AUD/1 (27 September 1990) [7], [27], [35].
[134] GATT, Uruguay Round Group of Negotiations on Services, Working Group on Audiovisual Services, *Matters Relating to Trade in Audiovisual Services: Note by the Secretariat*, MTN.GNS/AUD/W/1 (4 October 1990) [15].
[135] GATT, Uruguay Round Group of Negotiations on Services, Working Group on Audiovisual Services, *Note on the Meeting of 5 and 18 October 1990*, MTN.GNS/AUD/2 (20 December 1990) [2] (see also [9]). In December 1993, the EC put forward a proposal to acknowledge the cultural specificity of the sector in several GATS articles: GATT, Group of Negotiations on Services, *Informal GNS Meeting – Chairman's Statement*, MTN.GNS/49 (11 December 1993) [3].
[136] GATT, Uruguay Round Group of Negotiations on Services, Working Group on Audiovisual Services, *Note on the Meeting of 5 and 18 October 1990*, MTN.GNS/AUD/2 (20 December 1990) [3], [5].
[137] Ibid., [7]. [138] Ibid., [4], [6]. [139] Ibid., [8].
[140] GATT, Uruguay Round Group of Negotiations on Services, Working Group on Audiovisual Services, *Note on the Meeting of 27–28 August 1990*, MTN.GNS/AUD/1 (27 September 1990) [2], [26].

In the final stages of the Uruguay Round, as with many other matters being negotiated, this issue depended largely on the USA and the EC reaching agreement.[141] In the last days, Mickey Kantor (for the USA) and Sir Leon Brittan (for the EC) settled this issue. The USA refused to recognise the special cultural character of audiovisual services, and the EC responded 'at the urging of various national ministries of culture'[142] by making no offers in relation to audiovisual services.[143] Thus, ultimately, GATT contracting parties 'agreed to disagree' on how to treat audiovisual services.[144] As explained further in Chapter 3, several Members exempted audiovisual services from MFN treatment (typically based on cultural objectives),[145] and relatively few Members scheduled commitments to provide national treatment or market access in the audiovisual sector[146] (although a greater proportion of Members

---

[141] Croome, *History of the Uruguay Round*, 328; GATT, Trade Negotiations Committee, *Uruguay Round – Trade Negotiations Committee Meeting*, NUR 077 (26 November 1993).

[142] William Drake and Kalypso Nicolaïdis, 'Global Electronic Commerce and GATS: The Millennium Round and Beyond' in Sauvé and Stern, *GATS 2000*, 399, 408.

[143] Croome, *History of the Uruguay Round*, 328.

[144] WTO, Council for Trade in Services, *Audiovisual Services: Background Note by the Secretariat*, S/C/W/40 (15 June 1998) [24], [30]; GATT, *Peter Sutherland Responds to Debate on Audiovisual Sector*, NUR 069 (14 October 1993).

[145] At the time of writing, forty-four Members (including the EC) have listed MFN exemptions specifically for the audiovisual sector: WTO, *Services Database: Predefined Report – All Countries' MFN Exemptions* (21 March 2005) at <http://tsdb.wto.org/wto/WTOHomepublic.htm> (accessed 4 August 2006). Saudi Arabia has acceded to the WTO since the date of this report but did not list such an exemption. In December 2005, the Ministerial Conference approved Tonga's terms of accession, which include MFN exemptions in the audiovisual sector: WTO, Ministerial Conference, *Report of the Working Party on the Accession of Tonga, Addendum: Part II – Schedule of Specific Commitments in Services, List of Article II MFN Exemptions*, WT/ACC/TON/17/Add.2, WT/MIN(05)/4/Add.2 (2 December 2005) 21. In November 2006, the General Council approved Viet Nam's membership, and it has now become the 150th Member of the WTO. Its terms of accession also include MFN exemptions: WTO, *Report of the Working Party on the Accession of Viet Nam, Schedule CLX – Viet Nam, Part II – Schedule of Specific Commitments in Services, List of Article II MFN Exemptions, Addendum*, WT/ACC/VNM/48/Add.2 (27 October 2006) 56. See also WTO, Council for Trade in Services, *Audiovisual Services: Background Note by the Secretariat*, S/C/W/40 (15 June 1998) [31]; Laura Altinger and Alice Enders, 'The Scope and Depth of GATS Commitments' (1996) 19(3) *World Economy* 307, 323–4; GATT, Uruguay Round Group of Negotiations on Services, Working Group on Audiovisual Services, *Note on the Meeting of 27–28 August 1990*, MTN.GNS/AUD/1 (27 September 1990) [12]; Martin Roy, 'Audiovisual Services in the Doha Round: "Dialogue de Sourds, The Sequel"?' (2005) 6(6) *Journal of World Investment and Trade* 923, 935–6.

[146] At the time of writing, 27 Members have made national treatment or market access commitments in relation to 'audiovisual services'. These are Armenia, Central African Republic, China, Chinese Taipei, Dominican Republic, El Salvador, Gambia, Georgia, Hong Kong, India, Israel, Japan, Jordan, Kenya, Republic of Korea, Kyrgyz Republic,

26   STALEMATE AND ITS IDEOLOGICAL ORIGINS

acceding to the WTO after the Uruguay Round were required to make these commitments).[147] In part, this failure to reach consensus was caused by negotiating mistakes (e.g., the late submission of the EC's final position, and the lack of preparation by both sides).[148] However, it can also be attributed to the intractable nature of this problem and the wide gap in the perspectives of different Members.

Of the 135 WTO Panel Reports and 80 Appellate Body Reports circulated at the time of writing, the most significant in reflecting the problem of trade and culture is the 1997 case of *Canada – Periodicals*.[149] In that case, although the Panel was at pains to point out that 'the ability of any Member to take measures to protect its cultural identity was not at issue',[150] Canada argued that magazines should 'receive unique treatment' under GATT 1994 because of their 'intellectual or cultural content'.[151] The Appellate Body took note of the Canadian Government's

---

Lesotho, Malaysia, Mexico, New Zealand, Nicaragua, Oman, Panama, Saudi Arabia, Singapore, Thailand, USA: WTO, *Services Database: Predefined Report – All Sectors in Each Country* (20 March 2005) at <http://tsdb.wto.org/wto/WTOHomepublic.htm> (accessed 4 August 2006); WTO, *The Kingdom of Saudi Arabia – Schedule of Specific Commitments*, GATS/SC/141 (29 March 2006). The terms of accession of Tonga and Viet Nam also include national treatment and market access commitments in the audiovisual sector: WTO, Ministerial Conference, *Report of the Working Party on the Accession of Tonga, Addendum: Part II – Schedule of Specific Commitments in Services, List of Article II MFN Exemptions*, WT/ACC/TON/17/Add.2, WT/MIN(05)/4/Add.2 (2 December 2005) 10; WTO, *Report of the Working Party on the Accession of Viet Nam, Schedule CLX – Viet Nam, Part II – Schedule of Specific Commitments in Services, List of Article II MFN Exemptions, Addendum*, WT/ACC/VNM/48/Add.2 (27 October 2006) 29–30. See also WTO, Council for Trade in Services, *Audiovisual Services: Background Note by the Secretariat*, S/C/W/40 (15 June 1998) [24], Table 9; Altinger and Enders, 'GATS Commitments', 315, 329; Roy, 'Audiovisual Services', 929, 934–5; Rudolf Adlung and Martin Roy, 'Turning Hills into Mountains? Current Commitments under the General Agreement on Trade in Services and Prospects for Change' (2005) 39(6) *Journal of World Trade* 1161, 1169, 1183.

[147] Roy, 'Audiovisual Services', 929.
[148] Karl Falkenberg, 'The Audiovisual Sector' in Jacques Bourgeois, Frédérique Berrod and Eric Gippini Fournier (eds.), *The Uruguay Round Results: A European Lawyers' Perspective* (1995) 429, 432.
[149] I discuss various aspects of this case in later chapters. For further background on this dispute and the Canadian regulations underlying it, see Keith Acheson and Christopher Maule, 'Canadian Magazine Policy: International Conflict and Domestic Stagnation' in Robert Stern (ed.), *Services in the International Economy* (2001) 395; Chinedu Ezetah, 'Canadian Periodicals: Canada – Certain Measures Concerning Periodicals' (1998) 9(1) *European Journal of International Law* 182; Trevor Knight, 'The Dual Nature of Cultural Products: An Analysis of the World Trade Organization's Decisions Regarding Canadian Periodicals' (1999) 57 *University of Toronto Faculty of Law Review* 165; Myra Tawfik, 'Competing Cultures: Canada and the World Trade Organization – The Lessons from *Sports Illustrated*' (1998) 36 *Canadian Yearbook of International Law* 279.
[150] Panel Report, *Canada – Periodicals*, [5.45].   [151] Ibid., [3.84].

assertion of the cultural significance of Canadian periodicals: 'The Government reaffirms its commitment to protect the economic foundations of the Canadian periodical industry, which is a vital element of Canadian cultural expression'.[152] Canada's approach to the cultural aspects of periodicals in this case was consistent with its position during the Uruguay Round, where it described the 'cultural industries' as comprising the audiovisual sector as well as broadcasting, print, and sound recording.[153]

Also in 1997, the USA challenged under Article III of GATT 1994 the imposition by Turkey of a 25 per cent municipality tax on box-office receipts generated from showing foreign-origin films (compared to zero tax on receipts from showing domestic-origin films).[154] The parties eventually resolved the dispute by agreement, with the USA withdrawing its complaint and Turkey agreeing to equalise these taxes as soon as reasonably possible.[155]

In 1998, the EC requested consultations with Canada about certain 'measures affecting film distribution services'.[156] This request stemmed from the application of Canadian foreign investment guidelines to Polygram, a European company. The guidelines restricted foreign investors in film distribution such as Polygram to distribution of proprietary products.[157] These consultations did not lead to the establishment of a Panel because Polygram was eventually sold to a Canadian company, Seagram.[158]

Divergent views remain among WTO Members about the relationship between trade and cultural products, as reflected in the latest

---

[152] Appellate Body Report, *Canada – Periodicals*, 31.
[153] GATT, Uruguay Round Group of Negotiations on Services, Working Group on Audiovisual Services, *Note on the Meeting of 27–28 August 1990*, MTN.GNS/AUD/1 (27 September 1990) [6].
[154] WTO, DSB, *Turkey – Taxation of Foreign Film Revenues: Request for Consultations by the United States*, WT/DS43/1, G/L/85 (17 June 1996); WTO, DSB, *Turkey – Taxation of Foreign Film Revenues: Request for the Establishment of a Panel by the United States*, WT/DS43/2 (10 January 1997).
[155] WTO, DSB, *Turkey – Taxation of Foreign Film Revenues: Notification of Mutually Agreed Solution*, WT/DS43/3, G/L/177 (24 July 1997).
[156] WTO, DSB, *Canada – Measures Affecting Film Distribution Services: Request for Consultations by the European Communities*, WT/DS117/1, S/L/53 (22 January 1998).
[157] WTO, TPRB, *Trade Policy Review, Canada: Report by the Secretariat*, WT/TPR/S/78 (15 November 2000) [I:187].
[158] Canadian Department of Foreign Affairs and International Trade, Cultural Industries SAGIT, *Canadian Culture in a Global World: New Strategies for Culture and Trade* (February 1999).

services negotiations. Article XIX:1 of GATS provides for Members to enter into successive rounds of negotiations, beginning by 2000 and continuing periodically thereafter, with a view to achieving a progressively higher level of liberalisation. The new services negotiations began on 25 February 2000.[159] In 2001, the Special Session of the Council for Trade in Services (which, in regular sessions, oversees the functioning of GATS)[160] adopted guidelines and procedures for the negotiations, including an agreement that '[t]here shall be no a priori exclusion of any service sector'.[161] Thus, the audiovisual sector is open to negotiation like any other. These negotiations have now been incorporated into the Doha Development Agenda, a new round of negotiations that was to conclude by 1 January 2005[162] but that continues following its suspension in July 2006[163] and the Sixth Session of the Ministerial Conference held in Hong Kong in December 2005.[164] Clearly, the cultural aspects of audiovisual services remain a contentious issue in these negotiations. Countries such as Australia, Brazil, and Switzerland have emphasised in formal communications the need for special treatment of these services on cultural grounds,[165] whereas Japan and the USA have indicated a desire to enforce and enhance GATS disciplines in this sector.[166] In June 2005, Chinese Taipei, Hong Kong, Japan, Mexico, and the USA issued a communication 'express[ing]

---

[159] WTO, Council for Trade in Services, *Report of the Meeting Held on 25 February 2000: Note by the Secretariat*, S/C/M/41 (3 April 2000).

[160] Marrakesh Agreement, art. IV:5.

[161] WTO, Council for Trade in Services, *Guidelines and Procedures for the Negotiations on Trade in Services*, S/L/93 (29 March 2001) [5]; WTO, Council for Trade in Services, *Special Session – Report of the Meeting Held on 28, 29 and 30 March 2001: Note by the Secretariat*, S/CSS/M/8 (14 May 2001) [6].

[162] Doha Declaration, [15], [45].

[163] WTO, 'Talks suspended. "Today there are only losers"', news item (24 July 2006); WTO, General Council, *Minutes of Meeting Held on 27–28 July 2006*, WT/GC/M/103, 10 October 2006, [1]–[53]; WTO, 'Lamy: "We have resumed negotiations fully across the board"', news item (7 February 2007).

[164] Hong Kong Declaration, [25]–[27].

[165] Australian Department of Foreign Affairs and Trade, *Australian Intervention on Negotiating Proposal on Audiovisual Services: Council for Trade in Services Special Session* (July 2001); WTO, Council for Trade in Services, *Communication from Brazil – Audiovisual Services*, S/CSS/W/99 (9 July 2001) [9]–[12]; WTO, Council for Trade in Services, *Communication from Switzerland – GATS 2000: Audiovisual Services*, S/CSS/W/74 (4 May 2001) [11]–[12].

[166] WTO, Council for Trade in Services, *Communication from Japan: The Negotiations on Trade in Services*, S/CSS/W/42 (22 December 2000) [36]–[37]; WTO, Council for Trade in Services, *Communication from the United States – Audiovisual and Related Services*, S/CSS/W/21 (18 December 2000) [7], [10(ii)].

great concern over efforts by some key participants in the negotiations to create an a priori exclusion for such an important sector'.[167]

1.3.4 Significance in other international contexts

Canada's initial negotiating proposal for trade in services in the WTO raises another aspect of the trade and culture problem. Canada has indicated that it will 'not make any commitment that restricts our ability to achieve our cultural policy objectives until a new international instrument, designed specifically to safeguard the right of countries to promote and preserve their cultural diversity, can be established'.[168] As discussed in Chapter 5, several organisations have been developing new instruments to promote cultural diversity in the face of international trade. In particular, UNESCO recently concluded the UNESCO Convention, which purports to deal with the problem of trade and culture.[169] These steps demonstrate that the awkward relationship between trade and culture is not exclusively the concern of the WTO. They also highlight the importance of this issue for many WTO Members and raise the possibility that the solution could be taken out of the hands of the WTO.

Certain other international agreements confirm the importance for many countries of the cultural qualities of the audiovisual, printing, and publishing industries, as well as the surrounding controversy. For example, in the EC, as part of its role in contributing to 'the flowering of the cultures of the Member States',[170] the Community is to support action by and encourage co-operation between Members in areas such as artistic and literary creation, including in the audiovisual sector;[171] the European Constitution, not in force at the time of writing, contains

---

[167] WTO, Council for Trade in Services, *Communication from Hong Kong China, Japan, Mexico, the Separate Customs Territory of Taiwan, Penghu, Kinmen and Matsu, and United States: Joint Statement on the Negotiations on Audiovisual Services*, TN/S/W/49 (30 June 2005) [4]. See also WTO, Council for Trade in Services, *Report of the Meeting Held on 27 and 30 June and 1 July 2005: Note by the Secretariat*, TN/S/M/15 (15 September 2005) [206] (Hong Kong), [231], [309] (Chinese Taipei), [260]–[261] (Japan), [284] (US).
[168] WTO, Council for Trade in Services, *Communication from Canada: Initial Canadian Negotiating Proposal*, S/CSS/W/46 and Corr.1 (14 March 2001) [9].
[169] UNESCO, 'General Conference adopts Convention on the protection and promotion of the diversity of cultural expressions', press release 2005-128 (20 October 2005).
[170] EC Treaty, art. 151(1) (see also art. 3(1)(q)).
[171] Ibid., art. 151(2). See also EC Treaty, art. 151(4), and Collette Cunningham, 'In Defense of Member State Culture: The Unrealized Potential of Article 151(4) of the EC Treaty and the Consequences for EC Cultural Policy' (2001) 34 *Cornell International Law Journal* 119.

a similar provision.[172] The Council of the European Union has, for instance, established the Media Plus programme 'to encourage the development, distribution and promotion of European audiovisual works within and outside the Community', with the objective (among others) of promoting 'linguistic and cultural diversity in Europe'.[173]

Under Article 87(1) of the EC Treaty, the granting of aid by Member States in a form that distorts competition by favouring certain undertakings or the production of certain goods (e.g. the provision of subsidies) is deemed incompatible with the common market.[174] However, this general prohibition is subject to some exceptions, including (under Article 87(3)(d) of the EC Treaty) 'aid to promote culture and heritage conservation where such aid does not affect trading conditions and competition in the Community to an extent that is contrary to the common interest'.[175] EC Member States have used this provision to justify aid on cultural grounds for cultural products such as periodicals.[176] In late 2005, in making certain recommendations to EC Member States in connection with the development of the European film industry, the European Parliament and the Council of the European Union emphasised that '[c]inematographic works are an essential component of our cultural heritage' and 'a comprehensive witness to the history of the richness of Europe's cultural identities and the diversity of its people'.[177]

NAFTA also provides a limited exemption for 'cultural industries' (basically defined as persons engaged in audiovisual, publishing or

---

[172] *Treaty establishing a Constitution for Europe*, OJ C310, 1 (signed 29 October 2004) art. III-280.

[173] Council of the European Union, EC, *Council Decision of 20 December 2000 on the Implementation of a Programme to Encourage the Development, Distribution and Promotion of European Audiovisual Works (MEDIA Plus – Development, Distribution and Promotion) (2001-2005)*, OJ L13 (2001) 34, arts. (1)(1), (1)(2)(c). See also European Commission, EC, *Proposal for a Decision of the European Parliament and the Council Concerning the Implementation of a Programme of Support for the European Audiovisual Sector (MEDIA 2007)*, COM(2004) 470 final (14 July 2004).

[174] EC Treaty, art. 87(1).

[175] For further discussion of this provision see Evangelia Psychogiopoulou, 'EC State Aid Control and Cultural Justifications' (2006) 33(1) *Legal Issues of Economic Integration* 3.

[176] See, e.g., EC, European Commission, *Authorisation for State Aid Pursuant to Articles 87 and 88 of the EC Treaty: Cases where the Commission Raises No Objections*, OJ C79 (2006) 23, 26–27 (N 542/05).

[177] EC, European Parliament and Council of the European Union, *Recommendation 2005/ 865/CE of the European Parliament and of the Council of 16 November 2005 on Film Heritage and the Competitiveness of Related Industrial Activities*, OJ L323 (2005) 57, preamble [2]–[3].

printing activities).[178] Under NAFTA Annex 2106, as between Canada and the USA, most measures adopted or maintained with respect to cultural industries, and measures of equivalent commercial effect taken in response, are governed in accordance with the earlier CUSFTA. Broadly, the relevant provisions of the CUSFTA incorporated into NAFTA are as follows. The CUSFTA exempts cultural industries from the agreement.[179] However, 'a Party may take measures of equivalent commercial effect in response to actions that would have been inconsistent' with the CUSFTA but for that exemption.[180] This means that, for example, if the USA considered that a measure imposed by Canada to protect its culture would violate the principle of national treatment but for the exemption for cultural industries, the USA could take retaliatory measures, subject to certain conditions.[181] Ivan Bernier has elaborated on the limits of the cultural exception under NAFTA,[182] while others have suggested that these two countries are more likely to resolve cultural disputes through the WTO.[183] This may depend, of course, on how the WTO jurisprudence develops.[184] In any case, NAFTA provides an important example of how the trade and culture problem has played out outside the WTO, particularly with respect to cultural products.

Another striking reminder of the controversial nature of cultural products appears in the OECD Invisibles Code,[185] which 'acknowledges the cultural character of the audiovisual industry and permits screen quotas and subsidies provided the latter do not significantly distort international competition in export markets'.[186] Certain delegations proposed a cultural exemption during OECD negotiations for an MAI,[187] which OECD members unsuccessfully attempted to negotiate

---

[178] NAFTA, art. 2107.   [179] CUSFTA, art. 2005(1).   [180] Ibid., art. 2005(2).
[181] Christine James, 'Trade, Culture and Technology: A Test of Canada's Cultural Mettle' (1997) 8(7) *Entertainment Law Review* 253, 255.
[182] Ivan Bernier, 'La dimension culturelle dans le commerce international: quelques réflexions en marge de l'accord de libre-échange Canada/Etats-Unis du 2 janvier 1988' (1987) 25 *Canadian Yearbook of International Law* 243, 251–61.
[183] Ronald Atkey, 'Canadian Cultural Industries Exemption from NAFTA – Its Parameters' (1997) 23 *Canada – United States Law Journal* 177, 197. See also John Ragosta, 'The Cultural Industries Exemption from NAFTA – Its Parameters' (1997) 23 *Canada – United States Law Journal* 165, 174.
[184] I discuss this issue further in Chapter 4.
[185] OECD Council, *Decision Updating the Invisibles Code*, C(88)110 (Final) (21 July 1988).
[186] GATT, Uruguay Round Group of Negotiations on Services, Working Group on Audiovisual Services, *Matters Relating to Trade in Audiovisual Services: Note by the Secretariat*, MTN.GNS/AUD/W/1 (4 October 1990) [18].
[187] UNCTAD, *Lessons from the MAI*, UNCTAD/ITE/IIT, UN Sales No. E.99.II (1999) 15.

from 1995 until 1998.[188] Of particular concern were cultural industries, namely the printing, press, and audiovisual sectors, and a desire not to 'undermine the results of the Uruguay Round for the audio-visual sector'.[189] This was a 'leading issue for Canada and France'.[190] In particular, one delegation proposed a general exception to all MAI obligations allowing parties to regulate investment and activities of foreign corporations 'in the framework of policies designed to preserve and promote cultural and linguistic diversity'.[191] In February 1998, the French Government made it clear that it would not agree to an MAI without a cultural exception. Prime Minister Lionel Jospin declared, 'I attach an absolute priority to the preservation of our cultural identity as well as that of Europe.'[192] Canada also maintained the need for an exception in the MAI to enable it 'to adopt or maintain policies, programs and measures that promote and preserve Canadian culture and cultural industries'.[193] The USA was strongly opposed to a general cultural exception,[194] and this was one of the outstanding issues when negotiations ceased.[195]

Finally, more recent bilateral negotiations and free trade agreements demonstrate that cultural products continue to plague the minds of several WTO Members. Korea's longstanding screen quotas[196] have been a significant sticking point in its ongoing negotiations on a free

---

[188] See generally David Henderson, *The MAI Affair: A Story and Its Lessons* (1999); Trebilcock and Howse, *Regulation of Trade* (3rd edn) 457-60.

[189] OECD, Negotiating Group on the MAI, *The Multilateral Agreement on Investment: Draft Consolidated Text*, DAFFE/MAI(98)7/REV1 (22 April 1998) 127.

[190] Henderson, *MAI Affair*, 43.

[191] OECD, Negotiating Group on the MAI, *The Multilateral Agreement on Investment: Draft Consolidated Text*, DAFFE/MAI(98)7/REV1 (22 April 1998) 127.

[192] Original: 'J'attache une priorité absolue à la préservation de notre identité culturelle ainsi qu'à celle de l'Europe.'

[193] Canadian Department of Foreign Affairs and International Trade, 'Marchi Tables Government Response to Parliamentary Committee's Report on MAI', press release 97 (23 April 1998) Recommendation 14.

[194] 'Foreign Investment: Investment Talks to Continue at OECD; MAI Now On Course for 1999 Completion' (1998) 15 *International Trade Reporter* 525; Gary Yerkey, 'Foreign Investment: U.S. to Oppose EU Bid to Exempt "Culture" from OECD Investment Accord' (23 May 1995) *BNA International Business & Finance Daily*.

[195] UNCTAD, *Lessons from the MAI*, UNCTAD/ITE/IIT, UN Sales No. E.99.II (1999) 1.

[196] See generally Joongi Kim, 'The Viability of Screen Quotas in Korea: The Cultural Exception under the International Trade Regime' (1998) 26 *Korean Journal of International and Comparative Law* 199; Karsie Kish, 'Protectionism to Promote Culture: South Korea and Japan: A Case Study' (2001) 22 *University of Pennsylvania Journal of International Economic Law* 153; Byung-il Choi, *Culture and Trade in the APEC: Case of Film Industry in Canada, Mexico and Korea*, APEC Study Series 02-01 (2002) 36-41.

trade agreement with the USA.[197] In the free trade agreement between Australia and the USA that came into effect on 1 January 2005, Australia retains the right to impose minimum local content quotas on television at a specific level, which corresponds to the level existing when the agreement was concluded.[198] Similarly, in the free trade agreement between Chile and the USA that entered into force on 1 January 2004, the Chilean '*Consejo Nacional de Televisión* may establish, as a general requirement, that programs broadcast through public (open) television channels include up to 40 percent of Chilean production'.[199] Interestingly, the parties note in a side agreement that 'the *Consejo* monitors the percentage of national content by calculating at the end of the year the content level based on a two months sample of that year. As the level of national content has never been less than that required by law, the *Consejo* has never imposed the requirement.'[200]

1.4 Towards a solution

The above overview of controversies both within and outside the WTO demonstrates the importance of cultural products as an embodiment of the trade and culture problem. Finding an answer to the cultural products conundrum may shed light on possible solutions to other aspects of the conflict between trade and culture.

This book contains my reflections on cultural products and the WTO, having listened to and understood the interests and concerns of Members and others on both sides of the debate. Although the cultural industry is a business like any other, cultural products do have cultural, non-commercial features that distinguish them from other tradable goods and services. And sales of local cultural products in the marketplace may not adequately reflect the cultural value of those products to the wider community. This 'market failure' explains why some Members may wish to intervene in support of these products. Moreover, if Members

---

[197] Jeffrey Schott, Scott Bradford, and Thomas Moll, *Negotiating the Korea–United States Free Trade Agreement*, Institute for International Economics, Policy Briefs in International Economics No. PB06-4 (June 2006) 2; Choi, *Culture and Trade in APEC*, 43.
[198] *Australia United States Free Trade Agreement* (signed 18 May 2004) annex I (Australia) 14; Australian Department of Foreign Affairs and Trade, *Australia–United States Free Trade Agreement: Guide to the Agreement* (March 2004) ch. 10.
[199] *Chile United States Free Trade Agreement* (signed 6 June 2003) annex I (Chile) 3.
[200] Letter from María Soledad Alvear Valenzuela (Chilean Minister of Foreign Relations) to Robert Zoellick (United States Trade Representative), 'Side letter on television' (6 June 2003).

see local cultural products as a means of communication among their people, or if they do not wish to stifle creativity, free speech, or the progressive development of culture, they may need to support local cultural products in a manner that discriminates expressly against foreign cultural products. The same cannot be said of discrimination between cultural products of other WTO Members. If a Member wishes to extend benefits to cultural products from Members with cultures similar to its own, it can do so by adopting objective criteria such as language to distinguish between the relevant products. In addition, trade restrictions and distortions arising from cultural policy measures should be minimised. WTO rules constructed along these lines would effectively balance the various trade and cultural values of its Members.

At present, GATT 1994 and GATS do not achieve such a balance. The Members' failure to agree on how to treat cultural products in the Uruguay Round led to a result that is unsatisfactory for all WTO Members. The distinction between cultural products as goods and as services is unclear, as are the existing exceptions for cultural products, and the obligations on Members in relation to cultural products are consequently indeterminate. Furthermore, the failure of negotiations, combined with the current GATS framework, means that further liberalisation of service sectors incorporating cultural products looks all but impossible.

The uncertainty of WTO obligations and exceptions is not limited to cultural products, and it could be improved through dispute settlement in the WTO, which plays a role in gradually clarifying the meaning of WTO provisions generally. The provisions relevant to cultural products could also evolve through reference by Panels and the Appellate Body to other relevant international laws in the interpretative process. Of course, evolution through interpretation is necessarily limited and cannot resolve the problem as a whole. The future UNESCO Convention could provide some flexibility to Members in their approach to WTO disputes and negotiations, so that they enjoy greater policy space in connection with cultural products. Moreover, in its present form, this convention should not be of significant concern to WTO Members, as it does not purport to prevail over the WTO agreements, and becoming a party to the convention is unlikely to violate any WTO provisions or otherwise nullify or impair benefits of WTO Members. But the UNESCO Convention also falls short of resolving the disagreement among WTO Members regarding the treatment of cultural products. It may even exacerbate the situation by further discouraging Members from enforcing their WTO rights and progressively opening their markets to cultural products.

No doubt the WTO provisions will evolve somewhat through WTO dispute settlement, taking into account international laws, and the UNESCO Convention is scheduled to enter into force shortly. Yet more is needed. Through negotiation, Members could begin to take steps towards a better deal on cultural products – one that addresses more closely the reasons for treating cultural products differently and the appropriate limits to this special treatment. Putting aside Members' unwavering positions of 1994, one can conceive of new ways of thinking about cultural products under GATT 1994 and GATS, keeping in mind the objectives of trade liberalisation and the cultural sovereignty of Members. Article IV of GATT 1994 is anachronistic and could be removed or at least modified, while the existing exceptions under Article XX could be retained without addition. Under GATS, perhaps cultural products can be treated differently from other services, not as an exception, but as an example of the potential for liberalising trade in services. Instead of allowing MFN exemptions and allowing Members to negotiate the content of their service schedules, national treatment, MFN, and market access could apply more widely, subject to a correspondingly wide exception for discriminatory subsidies for cultural products. These are neither predictions nor prescriptions for negotiating Members, but they are ideas to demonstrate the possibility of finding a solution at last.

The core of this book is divided into two main parts. Part I explains how Members' conflicting views about trade and culture led to the current stalemate, with cultural products benefiting from limited exceptions to the WTO rules on international trade in goods and services. One problem in addressing cultural products in the WTO is in separating the current treatment of these products from the normative question of how they should be treated. Part I of this book deals with both these issues. Chapter 2 examines the arguments for and against cultural policy measures, taking into account the objectives of trade liberalisation and cultural preservation or promotion. From this analysis I identify certain guidelines for the treatment of cultural products in the WTO. In Chapter 3, I assess the extent to which these guidelines are satisfied, and I explain my misgivings regarding the current treatment of cultural products in the WTO – that is, the WTO provisions as negotiated at the end of the Uruguay Round and as subject to negotiation in the current Doha Round. I also highlight the aspects of these provisions that seem to be problematic regardless of one's views on the legitimacy of trade-restrictive cultural policy measures.

In Part II, the remaining substantive chapters evaluate three possible solutions to the impasse. First, in Chapter 4, I examine a possible judicial solution, namely whether the WTO dispute settlement mechanism could lead to a compromise understanding of the relevant WTO provisions. Specifically, could Panels and the Appellate Body interpret these provisions in a flexible manner, taking into account the conflicting views of different WTO Members as informed by international laws on culture and cultural products? If so, this could obviate the need for further negotiation and amendments to the WTO agreements. Next, Chapter 5 looks at the possibility of a new agreement or convention, separate from the existing WTO agreements, to deal specifically with the relationship between trade and culture. Most of this chapter focuses on developments external to the WTO that may have a substantial impact on this relationship in the near future, including discussions within UNESCO as well as various independent groups of stakeholders.

Chapters 4 and 5 both demonstrate likely outcomes to the trade–culture problem if WTO Members cannot resolve the issue through negotiation. However, in Chapter 6, I examine what could be described as a parliamentary alternative within the WTO. In particular, I consider amendments to the WTO agreements that could improve the current treatment of cultural products, recalling the guidelines articulated in Chapter 3. To some extent, this chapter rehearses debates that took place during the Uruguay Round. However, the Doha Round offers a renewed opportunity for WTO Members to reach agreement on this difficult area. Chapter 6 considers some possibilities that are being discussed in the Doha Round, as well as setting out certain other proposals that may fall outside the scope of the Doha negotiations. Here I also present and evaluate suggestions by certain other authors for solutions in this area. Chapter 7, the final chapter, draws together the conclusions from earlier chapters and reassesses the Doha negotiations in this light.

2 A case study of cultural products: protectionism vs cultural policy

2.1 Introduction

What are the underlying reasons for Members' dramatically different views on cultural products, as evidenced in the Uruguay Round and beyond? Put simply, an extreme 'pro-culture' position would be that cultural products are entirely different from other traded products and that, in order to preserve or promote local culture through them, governments should be free to regulate them and impose trade barriers against foreign cultural products in any way they choose. An extreme 'pro-trade' position would be that cultural products are identical to other traded products and that the notion of preserving or promoting local culture through them masks a purely protectionist impulse (that is, a desire to protect local industry from foreign competition). Moreover, discriminatory or trade-restrictive measures simply do not work in promoting culture.

WTO Members typically adopt less extreme positions in trade negotiations. Thus, for example, Canada seeks to negotiate a new instrument on cultural diversity to 'set out clear ground rules to enable Canada and other countries to maintain policies that promote their culture while respecting the rules of the international trading system and ensuring markets for cultural exports'.[1] The USA accepts that cultural products have cultural elements distinct from other products, but it argues that the current WTO rules provide sufficient flexibility for Members to pursue their cultural objectives in connection with cultural products.[2]

---

[1] WTO, TPRB, *Trade Policy Review, Canada: Report by the Secretariat*, WT/TPR/S/112/Rev.1 (19 March 2003) [IV:90]. Chapter 5 examines the development of a new instrument in more detail.

[2] See, e.g., WTO, Council for Trade in Services, *Communication from Hong Kong China, Japan, Mexico, the Separate Customs Territory of Taiwan, Penghu, Kinmen and Matsu, and*

Before we can begin to imagine ways of reaching a compromise that better serves the interests of all Members, it is crucial to appreciate the opposing arguments. The social, economic, and legal arguments concerning State support for cultural products provide a case study of the implications of culture more generally in the WTO.

Verhoosel describes a State's domestic regulatory autonomy as encompassing two aspects: 'its autonomy as regards the policy objectives it chooses to pursue; and ... its autonomy as regards the means by which it chooses to pursue such policy objectives'.[3] The first issue to be resolved in understanding the relationship between cultural policy and protectionism is thus whether the promotion or preservation of culture through cultural products is, of itself, a legitimate regulatory objective in the context of the WTO. This depends on the extent to which cultural products can be said to embody culture, and the limitations on policy objectives imposed by the WTO rules. Assuming that this is a legitimate regulatory objective, the second issue is whether WTO Members should be free to pursue that objective using discriminatory means (whether involving discrimination against or between foreign cultural products). In answering this question, one must evaluate the peculiarities of the market for cultural products to determine whether non-discriminatory measures could work equally well or better in promoting or preserving culture through cultural products. If the answer is yes, it becomes harder to defend any exclusion of cultural products from core WTO disciplines on cultural grounds.

Below, I examine these two issues in turn before considering how cultural policy measures could be evaluated or scrutinised within the WTO to distinguish protectionist measures from genuine cultural policy. In this regard, I consider the possible motives for cultural policy measures, the effectiveness of these measures, and how their trade-restrictiveness could be minimised. One purpose of this chapter is to identify guidelines for improving the treatment of cultural products in the WTO. These guidelines form the basis of my assessment, in

---

United States: Joint Statement on the Negotiations on Audiovisual Services, TN/S/W/49 (30 June 2005) [5]; WTO, Council for Trade in Services, *Communication from the United States – Audiovisual and Related Services*, S/CSS/W/21 (18 December 2000) [7]–[8]. See also Bonnie Richardson, 'Hollywood's Vision of a Clear, Predictable Trade Framework Consistent with Cultural Diversity' in Christoph Graber, Michael Girsburger, and Mira Nenova (eds.), *Free Trade versus Cultural Diversity: WTO Negotiations in the Field of Audiovisual Services* (2004) 111, 121–2.

[3] Gaëtan Verhoosel, *National Treatment and WTO Dispute Settlement: Adjudicating the Boundaries of Regulatory Autonomy* (2002) 51.

Chapter 3, of the current treatment of cultural products, as well as my evaluation, in Part II of this book, of three possible solutions.

2.2 Legitimacy of State support for cultural products

2.2.1 The nature of cultural products

If cultural products merely entertain or help pass the time of those who 'consume' them, it is difficult to see why governments should step in to support them in a trade-restrictive manner. But it is fairly uncontroversial to suggest that cultural products do something more than entertain. On one view, audiovisual products 'serv[e] a very important function in providing information to the public and thereby in the formation of public opinion'.[4] They also have an educational purpose.[5] From a less utilitarian perspective, Article 8 of the Universal Declaration on Cultural Diversity describes 'cultural goods and services ... as vectors of identity, values and meaning, [which] must not be treated as mere commodities or consumer goods'.[6] Within the WTO, Brazil has highlighted the role of 'audiovisual services ... in the transmission and diffusion of cultural values and ideas',[7] while Australia has suggested that these services 'develo[p] and reflec[t] a sense of national and cultural identity within Australia's multicultural society'.[8] Even the USA has admitted that 'the audiovisual sector may have special cultural characteristics'.[9]

On the other hand, the economic significance of cultural products cannot be forgotten in evaluating justifications for trade-restrictive cultural policy measures. Unlike other, less tangible aspects of culture, it is undeniable that making and selling cultural products in the

---

[4] Grischa Perino and Günther Schulze, 'Competition, Cultural Autonomy and Global Governance: The Audio-Visual Sector in Germany' in Guerrieri, Iapadre, and Koopmann, *Cultural Diversity* 52, 52 (see also 54).

[5] Anton Carniaux, 'L'audiovisuel dans les accords internationaux favorisant le libre-échange: des problèmes économiques et culturels difficiles à négocier' (1995) 26 *Revue générale de droit* 455, 471.

[6] See also Ministerial Conference, WTO, *Organisation internationale de la francophonie (OIF): Statement Circulated by HE Mr Abdou Diouf, Secretary General (As an Observer)*, WT/MIN(05)/ST/57 (15 December 2005).

[7] WTO, Council for Trade in Services, *Communication from Brazil – Audiovisual Services*, S/CSS/W/99 (9 July 2001) [6].

[8] Australian Department of Foreign Affairs and Trade, *Australian Intervention*.

[9] WTO, Council for Trade in Services, *Communication from the United States – Audiovisual and Related Services*, S/CSS/W/21 (18 December 2000) [7].

domestic market and in international trade is generally motivated by profit. For example, according to a recent OECD report, the value of global recorded music sales was US$32 billion in 2003.[10] Adorno maintains that '[c]ultural entities typical of the cultural industry are no longer *also* commodities, they are commodities through and through'.[11]

Michael Trebilcock and Robert Howse suggest that '[t]here are surely deeper measures of a society's cultural evolution than how many minutes are occupied by which country's soap operas on local commercial television networks'.[12] It is hard to argue with this, and the circumstances of the dispute in *Canada – Periodicals* demonstrate a similar point. In that case, Canada had prohibited the importation of split-run editions of periodicals,[13] which are essentially editions containing editorial content that is the same as or similar to that contained in editions distributed outside Canada, but with advertising primarily directed to a Canadian market that does not appear in the foreign editions. The prohibition diminished access by non-Canadian publishers to revenue through the sale of advertising to Canadian companies, largely reserving these revenues to Canadian publishers. However, publishers could still distribute split-run editions by transmitting the content via satellite to a printing plant in Canada where Canadian advertising and material could be added. This was exactly what the American publishers of *Sports Illustrated* eventually did, avoiding the prohibited step of importation. The Canadian Government responded by imposing an 80 per cent tax on advertisements in split-run editions of periodicals.[14] This tax rendered prohibitive the cost of producing split-run editions within Canada, preventing publishers from circumventing the prohibition on these editions.[15] Before the Panel, Canada explained its 'cultural' concern that these periodicals were extracting Canadian advertising revenues without adjusting their content to target a Canadian audience.[16] It is easy to counter that sports news and swimwear competitions of the kind featured in *Sports Illustrated* are far removed from the notion of

---

[10] OECD, Working Party on the Information Economy, *Digital Broadband Content: Music*, DSTI/ICCP/IE(2004)12/FINAL (8 June 2005) 23.
[11] Adorno, *Culture Industry*, 86 (original emphasis).
[12] Michael Trebilcock and Robert Howse, *The Regulation of International Trade* (2nd edn, 1999) 14. See also Trebilcock and Howse, *Regulation of International Trade* (3rd edn) 639.
[13] The Panel found that this prohibition was 'on its terms' inconsistent with GATT Article XI:1: Panel Report, *Canada – Periodicals*, [5.5]. Canada did not appeal this finding.
[14] Ibid., [2.6]–[2.9].   [15] Knight, 'Dual Nature of Cultural Products', 171–2.
[16] Panel Report, *Canada – Periodicals*, [3.27]–[3.31].

'culture' as a 'merit good' (i.e. deserving of State support because of its inherent worth in enriching society).[17]

The fact that there may be 'deeper measures' of culture than sports magazines and soap operas does not mean that these types of products are without cultural significance. Thus, the preamble to the UNESCO Recommendation on Participation in Cultural Life points out that 'the mass media can serve as instruments of cultural enrichment, both by opening up unprecedented possibilities of cultural development, [and] in contributing to ... the preservation and popularization of traditional forms of culture, and to the creation and dissemination of new forms'. Moreover, one should avoid the temptation to place a greater value on 'high' culture such as ballet and theatre than on 'low' or 'pop' culture such as films and contemporary music.[18] All these things are businesses. Recognising the cultural value in both sets of products is therefore more democratic and likely to foster greater diversity. As Throsby points out, it is 'undeniable that a term such as "high culture" has long been associated with the cultural consumption of the wealthy and privileged classes in society'.[19]

In sum, it appears reasonable to conclude that cultural products have both cultural and commercial aspects. This does not necessarily mean that Members should be allowed to impose trade-restrictive measures on cultural products for cultural reasons. However, the dual nature of cultural products does suggest that it is worth looking further at claims that States may wish to support cultural products to promote or preserve culture.

2.2.2 *Promoting or preserving culture through cultural products*

Having established the existence of certain cultural elements in cultural products, I now examine whether the promotion or preservation of culture through cultural products is a legitimate regulatory objective of WTO Members. To begin with, for reasons set out in Chapter 1, the promotion or preservation of culture through cultural products should not be regarded as an illegitimate regulatory objective of WTO Members

---

[17] See William Baumol, 'Applied Welfare Economics' in Ruth Towse (ed.), *A Handbook of Cultural Economics* (2003) 20, 22–3.
[18] On this distinction, see Richard Caves, *Creative Industries: Contracts between Art and Commerce* (2000) 186–8.
[19] Throsby, *Economics and Culture*, 117. See also Kevin Mulcahy, 'Cultural Policy: Definitions and Theoretical Approaches' (2006) 35(4) *Journal of Arts Management, Law, and Society* 319, 324–5.

merely by virtue of its apparent exclusion from GATT Article XX.[20] Similar reasoning would apply with respect to GATS Article XIV.

The next task is to identify any evidence that this is in fact a legitimate regulatory objective of Members. The WTO agreements might contain some evidence regarding the legitimacy of cultural policy measures within the WTO (e.g., GATT Article IV). However, identifying evidence in this way is rather circular, given that this chapter aims to provide a basis for determining how cultural products *should* be treated in the WTO. It is similarly unhelpful to point to actual cultural policy measures or statements of WTO Members as evidence of the legitimacy of these measures, particularly when Members appear to have quite different views on this question in the context of international trade. Instead, it is worthwhile identifying international or multilateral non-trade bodies, agreements, or statements that indicate the value of culture (and in particular cultural products) and the need for government intervention to preserve that value. This approach is consistent with the fact that the WTO rules are not to be read 'in clinical isolation'[21] from international standards[22] or international law,[23] as discussed further in Chapter 4.

UNESCO plays a major role in relation to culture on an international plane.[24] It was created 'for the purpose of advancing, through the ... cultural relations of the peoples of the world, the objectives of international peace and of the common welfare of mankind'.[25] As at March 2005, UNESCO had 191 Member States and 6 Associate Members,[26] including all but a handful of the 150 Members of the WTO.[27]

---

[20] See above, 9–11.
[21] Appellate Body Report, *US – Gasoline*, 17. See also Gabrielle Marceau, 'A Call for Coherence in International Law – Praise for the Prohibition against "Clinical Isolation" in WTO Dispute Settlement' (1999) 33(5) *Journal of World Trade* 87.
[22] See, e.g., TBT Agreement, art. 2.4–5; SPS Agreement, art. 3.1–2; Mattoo and Subramanian, 'Regulatory Autonomy', 321.
[23] See, e.g., Appellate Body Report, *US – Shrimp*, [130].
[24] See, e.g., UNESCO, *UNESCO and the Issue of Cultural Diversity: Review and Strategy, 1946–2004* (revised version, September 2004).
[25] UNESCO, *A Constitution of the United Nations Educational, Scientific and Cultural Organization* (16 November 1945) preamble.
[26] See <www.unesco.org/general/eng/about/members.shtml> (accessed 4 August 2006).
[27] Liechtenstein and Singapore are WTO Members but not UNESCO Member States. WTO Membership is not restricted to States: Marrakesh Agreement, arts. XI:1, XII:1. The following WTO Members are not UNESCO Member States or Associate Members: the EC, Hong Kong, and Chinese Taipei. Macau is a WTO Member and a UNESCO Associate Member.

UNESCO's *Recommendation for the Safeguarding and Preservation of Moving Images* recognises the cultural significance of moving images (which are defined to include film and television).[28] The preamble to the recommendation also recognises the 'rights of States to take appropriate measures for the safeguarding and preservation of moving images'. UNESCO's *Recommendation on the Safeguarding of Traditional Culture and Folklore* provides for States to provide moral and economic support for individuals or institutions cultivating or holding items of folklore, including literature and music.[29] Paragraph 10(a) of the UNESCO Recommendation on Participation in Cultural Life provides for Member States to 'create social, economic and financial conditions which should provide artists, writers and composers of music with the necessary basis for free creative work'.

These brief examples reveal multilateral recognition in a non-trade context of the value of culture, and the appropriateness of government measures to support culture, including cultural products. Accordingly, they tend to support my conclusion that the promotion or preservation of culture through cultural products is a legitimate regulatory objective of WTO Members. The more difficult question is whether WTO rules should allow Members to pursue this objective in a discriminatory or trade-restrictive manner.

2.3 Justification for discriminatory cultural policy measures

2.3.1 The market for cultural products

Liberalisation of domestic markets or international trade 'is a means of increasing economic efficiency in a wide range of situations'.[30] If consumers in a given country prefer foreign to local cultural products, isn't it economically efficient and therefore preferable to allow that country's cultural industries to lapse? An important pro-culture response is that various market failures arise in relation to the cultural industries, and government intervention is required to correct these failures. As

---

[28] 21 C/Resolutions, annex I, 156 (27 October 1980) [1(a)].
[29] UNESCO, *Recommendation on the Safeguarding of Traditional Culture and Folklore*, 25 C/Resolutions, annex I(B), 238 (15 November 1989) [D(d)].
[30] UNCTAD and World Bank, *Liberalizing International Transactions*, 37. On the reasons for preferring economically efficient outcomes in general, see Sykes, 'Comparative Advantage', 57–9.

UNESCO's primer on trade and culture asserts, 'it is difficult to argue that self-regulation of markets alone will at some point guarantee a fair development of international trade in cultural products. So far, markets alone do not seem to be able to ensure diversity of choice, access for everyone and fair competition'.[31] Similarly, the UN Commission on Human Rights maintains that 'market forces alone cannot guarantee the preservation and promotion of cultural diversity'.[32]

In this section, I scrutinise various arguments for recognising market failures in the context of cultural products. Assuming that these failures do exist, government intervention might be justified if it involves lower costs or distortions than those created by the initial market failures.[33] Later in this chapter, I consider the type and extent of government interventions that could be countenanced. Evidently, arguments for State support of cultural products on this basis rely on the conclusions of the previous sections of this chapter, namely that cultural products have cultural as well as commercial features, and that the promotion or preservation of culture through cultural products is a legitimate regulatory objective of WTO Members.

A. US dominance

In Edwin Baker's view, which is echoed by others,[34] the fact that cultural products can generally be copied at low cost for simultaneous use by multiple users[35] explains why the USA dominates markets in audiovisual products. Specifically, he suggests that the potential revenue of a given audiovisual product depends not on the price paid by each consumer but on the number of consumers. In larger and wealthier domestic markets, the potential revenue and therefore the production budget are greater. When products are traded, consumers around the world tend to prefer those products with greater budgets, being those

---

[31] UNESCO, *Culture, Trade and Globalization*, q. 22.
[32] UN, Commission on Human Rights, *Promotion of the Enjoyment of the Cultural Rights of Everyone and Respect for Different Cultural Identities*, E/CN.4/RES/2002/26 (22 April 2002) [13].
[33] WTO, *World Trade Report 2004: Exploring the Linkage between the Domestic Policy Environment and International Trade* (2004) 151.
[34] See, e.g., Peter Grant and Chris Wood, *Blockbusters and Trade Wars: Popular Culture in a Globalized World* (2004) 45–47; Pierre Sauvé and Karsten Steinfatt, 'Towards Multilateral Rules on Trade and Culture: Protective Regulation or Efficient Protection?' in Productivity Commission (ed.), *Achieving Better Regulation of Services* (2001) 329–31.
[35] Edwin Baker, 'An Economic Critique of Free Trade in Media Products' (2000) 78 *North Carolina Law Review* 1357, 1378–9. Cf. Acheson and Maule, *Much Ado About Culture*, 93, 95.

produced for larger and wealthier domestic markets such as the USA.[36] In turn, Baker contends that countries such as the USA with a large proportion of revenue derived from exports are more likely to develop products with greater 'universal' appeal (as opposed to 'foreign' or 'domestic' appeal).[37] As a result, market failure occurs when marginally successful export-oriented products prevent the survival of domestic-oriented products with smaller audiences.[38] In other words, the market fails when audiovisual products are rendered commercially unviable 'even though their creation and distribution would be a valuable use of social resources'.[39]

Baker's arguments in favour of government intervention presume that consumers generally prefer audiovisual products made with larger budgets. This is open to question. In some cases larger budgets may mean better products – for example, by enabling the use of better costumes, sets, actors, or special effects. Moreover, as Christoph Graber and Christophe Germann argue, greater marketing budgets may also increase the likelihood of success of a given film.[40] However, more money does not necessarily mean better products or bigger audiences, and lower-budget productions may sometimes equal or surpass the success of higher-budget productions. For example, in August 2005, the relatively low-budget US film *Nine Lives* won the top award at Switzerland's Locarno film festival.[41] Similarly, although the average budget for Indian films is relatively small,[42] India produces more films than any other country,[43] and Indian television and films are in significant demand internationally:

---

[36] Cowen also suggests that the US population is younger than the European population, further diminishing the size of the European market because '[m]oviegoing is the province of the young': Tyler Cowen, *Creative Destructions: How Globalization is Reshaping World Cultures* (2002) 77. See also John Barton, 'The Economics of TRIPS: International Trade in Information-Intensive Products' (2001) 33 *George Washington International Law Review* 473, 498; John Barton, 'The International Video Industry: Principles for Vertical Agreements and Integration' (2004) 22 *Cardozo Arts and Entertainment Law Journal* 67, 85.
[37] Baker, 'Economic Critique', 1382–4.   [38] Ibid., 1386–8.   [39] Ibid., 1385.
[40] Graber, *Handel und Kultur*, 220, 331–2; Christophe Germann, 'Culture in Times of Cholera: A Vision for a New Legal Framework Promoting Cultural Diversity' (2005) 1 *ERA – Forum* 109, 116–17. See also Hesmondhalgh, *Cultural Industries*, 157–60.
[41] 'Nine Lives takes top Swiss award', *BBC News* (14 August 2005).
[42] Cited in Mukherjee, 'Audio-Visual Policies', 222–3.
[43] Ibid., 219; Julia Nielson and Daria Taglioni, *Services Trade Liberalisation: Identifying Opportunities and Gains*, OECD Trade Policy Working Paper No. 1 (2004) [34].

Expatriate Indians maintain close cultural and linguistic ties with their motherland and there is a strong and growing demand for Indian-language programmes from non-resident Indians. Other South Asian communities with similar language and culture (such as Pakistanis, Bangladeshis, Sri Lankans, etc.) have also generated substantial demand for Indian-language programmes.[44]

In addition, cultural industries in countries other than the USA may rely heavily on exports and therefore, under Baker's theory, would be more likely to make products with universal appeal. For example, in Egypt, 'domestic revenue from films does not cover production costs, hence external distribution in the Arab world is the major source of revenue'.[45] Moreover, it is not only countries with large populations that have commercial or export success. In fact, small populations may lead to export reliance. The successful music industries in Jamaica and Sweden rely heavily on exports,[46] and Australia's cultural industries are also increasingly export-oriented.[47] The Netherlands is one of the few major European exporters of television programming to the Anglophone world; the Dutch company Endemol (since acquired by Spain's Telefónica) created the reality programme *Big Brother*, which was produced in seventeen countries by 2002.[48]

Baker recognises that any tendency towards US dominance in audiovisual products will be countered to some extent by a 'cultural premium'[49] – that is, consumers' preference for local products or products in the local language concerning local issues.[50] These preferences will not necessarily run along national boundaries, and they may change over time. For instance, a preference for local cultural products is likely to diminish with increased exposure to foreign cultural

---

[44] Mukherjee, 'Audio-Visual Policies', 241. See also Nielson and Taglioni, *Services Trade Liberalisation*, [33]; Hesmondhalgh, *Cultural Industries*, 189–93.
[45] Ghoneim, 'Audio-Visual Sector in Egypt', 205. See also Acheson and Maule, 'Canada – Audiovisual Policies', 163; Nielson and Taglioni, *Services Trade Liberalisation*, [36].
[46] Dominic Power and Daniel Hallencreutz, 'Profiting from Creativity? The Music Industry in Stockholm, Sweden and Kingston, Jamaica' in Power and Scott, *Cultural Industries*, 224, 225–33.
[47] Chris Gibson and John Connell, 'Cultural Industry Production in Remote Places: Indigenous Popular Music in Australia' in Power and Scott, *Cultural Industries*, 243, 244.
[48] Deniz Eröcal, *Case Studies of Successful Companies in the Services Sector and Lessons for Public Policy*, DSTI/DOC(2005)7, OECD Directorate for Science, Technology and Industry Working Paper 2005/7 (15 June 2005) 60.
[49] Grant and Wood, *Blockbusters and Trade Wars*, 124.
[50] Baker, 'Economic Critique', 1381–2. See also István Kónya, 'Modeling Cultural Barriers in International Trade' (2006) 14(3) *Review of International Economics* 494, 495.

products.[51] This may mean that the cultural premium diminishes in countries that are used to foreign cultural products (whether dubbed or subtitled), but not in those less frequently exposed to these products.

Some commentators argue that diversity and local culture are threatened because the size of the English-speaking market means its products will always be priced lower than those of smaller linguistic communities;[52] more specifically, in several countries it is cheaper to purchase US than local cultural products.[53] Some describe US films and television programmes as being 'dumped' on foreign markets after their production costs have been recovered in the large US domestic market.[54] Graber, for example, implies that vertical integration of Hollywood studios prevents 'fair competition' in this area for this reason.[55] But given the commonality of the English language, and the broad similarities between, for example, Canadian and US culture, it is difficult to see why Canadian films should not appeal to a US audience. On the supply side, although the chain from production to distribution and exhibition may be easier to establish intranationally[56] and

---

[51] Herman Galperin, 'Cultural Industries Policy in Regional Trade Agreements: The Cases of NAFTA, the European Union and MERCOSUR' (1999) 21(5) *Media, Culture & Society* 627, 628; Günther Schulze, 'International Trade' in Towse, *Handbook* 269, 269, 273; Günther Schulze, 'International Trade in Art' (1999) 23(1) *Journal of Cultural Economics* 109, 121, 125. See also Kónya, 'Modeling Cultural Barriers', 495.

[52] Lyndel Prott, 'International Standards for Cultural Heritage' in UNESCO (ed.), *World Culture Report: Culture, Creativity and Markets* (1998) 222, 229. See also Dehesa, *Winners and Losers*, 167-8; Barton, 'Economics of TRIPS, 482.

[53] See, e.g., Australian Broadcasting Authority, 'Trade Liberalisation in the Audiovisual Services Sector and Safeguarding Cultural Diversity' (commissioned by the Asia-Pacific Broadcasting Union, July 1999) iii, 3; Carniaux, 'L'audiovisuel', 465-6; Grant and Wood, *Blockbusters and Trade Wars*, 19, 131.

[54] See, e.g., Grant and Wood, *Blockbusters and Trade Wars*, 133; Prott, 'International Standards', 229; Redner, *Conserving Cultures*, 77; Dehesa, *Winners and Losers*, 168. But see Cowen, *Creative Destructions*, 90-1; Colin Hoskins, Adam Finn, and Stuart McFadyen, 'Television and Film in a Freer International Trade Environment: US Dominance and Canadian Responses' in McAnany and Wilkinson, *Mass Media and Free Trade* 63, 70-1; Footer and Graber, 'Trade Liberalization and Cultural Policy', 135.

[55] Christoph Graber, 'WTO: A Threat to European Films?' (paper presented at the Conference on European Culture, University of Navarra, Pamplona, 28-31 October 1991) V. Cf. Bernier, 'Cultural Goods and Services', 119-21; Hesmondhalgh, *Cultural Industries*, 135-54; Messerlin, *Measuring the Costs of Protection*, 328; Jeremy Rifkin, 'When Markets Give Way to Networks ... Everything is a Service' in John Hartley (ed.), *Creative Industries* (2005) 361, 363-65; Shalini Venturelli, 'Culture and the Creative Economy in the Information Age' in Hartley, *Creative Industries*, 391, 397; Barton, 'International Video Industry', 71-2, 79-80.

[56] Richard Caves, *International Trade, International Investment and Imperfect Markets* (November 1974) 11.

partially defined by existing networks,[57] Canadian films may use the large domestic US market (in addition to the Canadian market) to increase sales and reduce prices,[58] particularly as new technologies become available for faster and cheaper distribution.[59]

Let us assume, nevertheless, that Baker and others are correct that particular aspects of cultural products and the market for them (rather than pure skill or superior products)[60] explain US dominance in this area. This means simply that, because of factors such as chance,[61] history, or the size or age of the US market,[62] the USA may have a comparative advantage in making and selling cultural products at present.[63] As already mentioned, the theory of comparative advantage underlies the WTO, and it is not clear from Baker's arguments why this raises a particular problem for cultural products. Ronald Cass and Richard Boltuck caution against demands for the elimination of 'unfairness' in international trade because, '[i]n the extreme, equality can mean the elimination of all sources of comparative advantage, a basic source of gains from trade'.[64] Thus, if the USA is simply better at making commercially successful films, this should not be characterised as a

---

[57] Sam Cameron, 'Cinema' in Towse, *Handbook* 114, 115; Bernier, 'La dimension culturelle', 246; Germann, 'Culture in Times of Cholera', 123–4; Christophe Germann, 'Diversité culturelle à l'OMC et l'UNESCO à l'exemple du cinéma' (2004) 3 *Revue Internationale de Droit Economique* 325, 338.

[58] Neil Coe and Jennifer Johns, 'Production Clusters: Towards a Critical Political Economy of Networks in the Film and Television Industries' in Power and Scott, *Cultural Industries*, 188, 199.

[59] See, e.g., Australian Department of Communications Information Technology and the Arts, *Report on Access to Overseas Markets for Australia's Creative Digital Industry* (12 December 2003) 45–62; Shaun French et al., 'Putting E-commerce in Its Place: Reflections on the Impact of the Internet on the Cultural Industries' in Power and Scott, *Cultural Industries*, 54, 63; Richardson, 'Hollywood's Vision', 119; OECD, Working Party on the Information Economy, *Digital Broadband Content: Music*, DSTI/ICCP/IE(2004)12/FINAL (8 June 2005) 31–37, 47–54.

[60] Some would say that 'the difficulties suffered by the European audiovisual industry' are in fact caused by factors related to quality such as 'unprofessional script-writing', 'a lack of professionalism', and 'production decisions taken by bankers': Eric Morgan de Rivery, 'Unresolved Issues in the Audiovisual Sector and the US/EC Conflict' in Bourgeois, Berrod, and Fournier, *Uruguay Round Results*, 435, 441–2.

[61] Sykes, 'Comparative Advantage', 56.

[62] Hoskins, Finn, and McFadyen, 'Television and Film', 71–3.

[63] Cf. Michel Ghertman and Allègre Hadida, 'Institutional Assets and Competitive Advantage of French over U.S. Cinema: 1895–1914' (2005) 35(3) *International Studies of Management and Organization* 50.

[64] Ronald Cass and Richard Boltuck, 'Antidumping and Countervailing-Duty Law: The Mirage of Equitable International Competition' in Bhagwati and Hudec, *Fair Trade and Harmonization* 351, 359 (see also 391).

source of unfairness even though it may disadvantage other film industries. If the success of US cultural products results from protectionist measures that the US Government imposes in its domestic market, the appropriate response would be to combat those measures by subjecting audiovisual services to the discipline of national treatment rather than to shield it from this discipline. If the market for supply of cultural products is too concentrated,[65] allowing suppliers to engage in anti-competitive conduct,[66] this may need to be addressed through domestic or international competition laws.[67]

Rationalising cultural policy measures by reference to US cultural products may also be overly Eurocentric. Not all WTO Members who wish to support cultural products are concerned primarily with an invasion of US products. As Arjun Appadurai explains:

[F]or the people of Irian Jaya, Indonesianization may be more worrisome than Americanization, as Japanization may be for Koreans, Indianization for Sri Lankans, Vietnamization for the Cambodians, and Russianization for the people of Soviet Armenia and the Baltic republics ... [F]or polities of smaller scale, there is always a fear of cultural absorption by polities of larger scale, especially those that are nearby.[68]

Moreover, as Acheson and Maule point out, cultural concerns may differ within WTO Members:

What the United States is to English-speaking Canada in the world English-language market, France is to French-speaking Canada in the world French-language market. An asymmetric concern is the protection of a French-language market in films, broadcasting and recorded music from the competition of English-language films from the rest of Canada or abroad.[69]

---

[65] See, e.g., Caves, *Creative Industries*, 157–8, 314; Coe and Johns, 'Production Clusters', 191, 202; David Held *et al.*, *Global Transformations: Politics, Economics and Culture* (1999) 346–50; Ruth Towse, 'Cultural Industries' in Towse, *Handbook* 170, 172–3.
[66] Grant and Wood, *Blockbusters and Trade Wars*, 87, 357.
[67] See below, 243.
[68] Arjun Appadurai, *Modernity at Large: Cultural Dimensions of Globalization* (1996) 32. See also the reference to 'Haitian imperialism' in Cowen, *Creative Destructions*, 1. Even within the EC, smaller Member States may be equally concerned with the domination of audiovisual markets by larger Member States: Carniaux, 'L'audiovisuel', 470–1.
[69] Acheson and Maule, 'Canada – Audiovisual Policies', 156. But see, in relation to the position of Quebec, Daniel Salée, 'NAFTA, Quebec, and the Boundaries of Cultural Sovereignty: The Challenge of Identity in the Era of Globalization' in Dorinda Dallmeyer (ed), *Joining Together, Standing Apart: National Identities after NAFTA* (1997) 73, 74–5.

Finally, the dynamics of the cultural product market will change as different countries develop their cultural industries. Even if the USA is the prime concern of many countries now, this may change over time,[70] particularly as new technologies make it easier to access cultural products from around the world, rendering each country less dependent on its own domestic market for profit-making and therefore reducing the importance of the size of that market in determining success. Similarly, the USA may presently benefit from economic 'clusters' of specialised labour[71] and infrastructure, facilitating the creation of successful cultural products in particular areas (most obviously the film industry in Hollywood). However, cultural industry clusters also exist outside the USA (e.g., for sound recording in Jamaica and the UK,[72] and films in Mumbai),[73] and new clusters may develop in future. For example, 'runaway' film production in Vancouver is increasingly successful and could threaten Hollywood's dominance, due to the lower production costs in Canada.[74] In these circumstances, justifications for government intervention based on the special nature of cultural products *per se* are more likely to endure than arguments decrying the dominance of US cultural industries.

B. Positive externalities of cultural products

Other arguments in favour of State support for cultural products rely on the nature of cultural products in general, rather than the cultural products of any particular country. Thus, Chris Wood writes in his co-author's note to *Blockbusters and Trade Wars*:

> Whatever problems plague the market for popular Canadian culture, they have little to do with the products of that culture or their producers. They are not even peculiarly *Canadian*. They have everything to do with the unique economic behaviour of cultural products in general. That behaviour and its negative consequences are as evident in the United States as anywhere. The failure belongs to the market, not to the culture.[75]

---

[70] On the dynamic nature of cultural flows, see Held *et al.*, *Global Transformations*, 369.
[71] Schulze, 'International Trade', 273.
[72] French *et al.*, 'Putting E-commerce in Its Place', 59.
[73] Schulze, 'International Trade', 273.
[74] Coe and Johns, 'Production Clusters', 197. See also Ted Magder, 'Film and Video Production' in Michael Dorland (ed.), *The Cultural Industries in Canada: Problems, Policies and Prospects* (1996) 145, 174; Patrick Messerlin and Emmanuel Cocq, 'Preparing Negotiations in Services: EC Audiovisuals in the Millennium Round' (paper presented at the World Services Congress on Services: Generating Global Growth and Opportunity, Atlanta, 1–3 November 1999) 13.
[75] Grant and Wood, *Blockbusters and Trade Wars*, 9 (original emphasis).

A report by the Canadian Federal Cultural Policy Review Committee describes cultural activity as a 'merit good' and emphasises 'the manifest value of cultural activity in releasing the creative potential of a society, and in illuminating and enriching the human condition'.[76] According to the Committee, the market may fail 'to reflect the demand for cultural products in its entirety'.[77] In particular, the demand by today's consumers for cultural products reveals at most only the benefits to the present generation, when in fact cultural products (unlike most other consumer products) frequently convey lasting benefits to future generations as well.[78] The Committee goes on to suggest that the public is largely unaware of the social benefits conferred by cultural activity and that intervention is required to correct this information failure.[79]

This raises an important economic argument in favour of State support for cultural products: the existence of positive externalities, which arise where people other than the consumer benefit from the consumption of cultural products.[80] For example, cultural products that celebrate local culture may encourage social bonding or inspire consumers to contribute more to their community. They may also improve the reputation of a country internationally.[81] Society could also benefit from the mere existence of these products and their promotion of national coherence and identity, to a greater extent than with other kinds of products.[82] Some people might value 'a strong and informative public broadcasting system, even though they themselves consume mostly entertainment shows on private channels'.[83] But consumers may be unwilling to pay for these broader societal benefits of cultural products,[84] either because they do not realise that they exist (incomplete information),[85] they do not care about them at all (private value is

---

[76] Canadian Department of Communications, *Report of the Federal Cultural Policy Review Committee* (1982) 68.
[77] Ibid., 65.   [78] Ibid.   [79] Ibid., 68.
[80] WTO, *World Trade Report 2004*, 150. See also Graber, *Handel und Kultur*, 67-9; Tyler Cowen, *Good and Plenty: The Creative Successes of American Arts Funding* (2006) 12.
[81] Baumol, 'Applied Welfare Economics', 22.
[82] Marcel Canoy, Jan van Ours, and Frederick van der Ploeg, 'The Economics of Books' (Working Paper No. 1414, Center for Economic Studies and Institute for Economic Research, 2005) 11-12; Bruno Frey, 'Public Support' in Towse, *Handbook*, 389, 391; Bernier, 'La dimension culturelle', 248-9; Cowen, *Good and Plenty*, 24-5.
[83] Markus Krajewski, *National Regulation and Trade Liberalization in Services: The Legal Impact of the General Agreement on Trade in Services (GATS) on National Regulatory Autonomy* (2003) 19.
[84] Throsby, *Economics and Culture*, 32.   [85] Frey, 'Public Support', 392.

lower than social value,[86] or they realise that they can enjoy them at the expense of others (free-rider problem). As a result, cultural products embodying local culture may be at risk of under-consumption and under-production. Similar externalities may explain the need for public intervention to support certain research and development activities[87] or preservation of historic sites.[88]

Public goods might be seen as a specific case of externalities.[89] Pure public goods are non-rivalrous (their consumption by one person does not diminish the ability of others to consume them) and non-excludable (they cannot be restricted to certain consumers); as a result, public goods that generate positive (rather than negative) externalities would be produced in insufficient quantities in the absence of government supply or support. 'Impure' public goods, which may be partially rivalrous or excludable, may also suffer from under-production.[90] The benefits of public goods may flow from one person to the next, one generation to the next,[91] or even (in the case of global public goods)[92] to people across the world. Like biodiversity,[93] culture or cultural diversity could be described as a public good.[94] To the extent that cultural products contribute to cultural diversity, they may also have public-good aspects.[95] Thus, in relation to broadcasting:

once a programme has been produced and transmitted, extra viewers and listeners can be accommodated at almost zero additional resource cost. Pricing above such zero cost then excludes consumers who would have been

---

[86] Conversely, 'profit-based' production decisions may 'neglec[t] social costs of imported culture': Glenn Withers, 'Broadcasting' in Towse, *Handbook*, 102, 106.
[87] WTO, *World Trade Report 2004*, 170–4.
[88] Ismail Serageldin, 'Cultural Heritage As Public Good: Economic Analysis Applied to Historic Cities' in Inge Kaul, Isabelle Grunberg, and Marc Stern (eds.), *Global Public Goods: International Cooperation in the 21st Century* (1999) 240, 241, 244.
[89] Inge Kaul, Isabelle Grunberg, and Marc Stern, 'Defining Global Public Goods' in Kaul, Grunberg, and Stern, *Global Public Goods*, 2, 5.
[90] Krajewski, *National Regulation and Trade Liberalization in Services*, 15.
[91] Todd Sandler, 'Intergenerational Public Goods: Strategies, Efficiency and Institutions' in Kaul, Grunberg, and Stern, *Global Public Goods* 20.
[92] Kaul, Grunberg, and Stern, 'Defining Global Public Goods', 2–3; Keith Maskus and Jerome Reichman, 'The Globalization of Private Knowledge Goods and the Privatization of Global Public Goods' in Maskus and Reichman, *International Public Goods*, 3, 8.
[93] Kaul, Grunberg, and Stern, 'Defining Global Public Goods', 5.
[94] Serageldin, 'Cultural Heritage as Public Good', 240.
[95] Throsby, *Economics and Culture*, 23; Baumol, 'Applied Welfare Economics', 22; Graber, *Handel und Kultur*, 62–4.

quite willing to cover the costs (zero) of their receipt of the service. This is a fundamental allocative inefficiency.[96]

It is true that cultural products may be excludable to some extent (e.g., through intellectual property) and rivalrous (e.g., only one person at a time can comfortably read a single paper copy of a book); but they also embody culture, and the existence of varied cultural products increases cultural diversity, which is less obviously excludable and rivalrous. The global public-good characteristics of cultural diversity (that is, diversity between rather than merely within countries) may also explain the perceived need for international co-operation in promoting cultural diversity.[97]

Another way of putting this is to recognise that cultural value and economic value are not necessarily coterminous. According to Throsby, a positive correlation may well exist between cultural and economic value (or social and private value), in the sense that individuals may be willing to pay a higher price for something with a higher cultural value. However, for reasons explained above, this correlation is unlikely to be perfect.[98] In at least some circumstances, the relationship between cultural and economic value may even be negative: 'For example, if "high-culture" norms were adopted (conservative, elitist, hegemonic, absolutist), it might be suggested that atonal classical music is an example of a commodity with high cultural but low economic value, and that TV soap operas are an example of a high economic/low cultural value good.'[99] To the extent that the amount that an individual is willing to pay for a cultural product fails to reflect its cultural worth to the community as a whole, the market could be said to have failed.

In the abstract, this kind of reasoning seems convincing. It explains why governments may wish to intervene in cultural industries. However, it is important to keep in mind two things about these arguments about market failures. First, if accepted too readily they could be

---

[96] Withers, 'Broadcasting', 111.
[97] See WTO, *World Trade Report 2004*, 151. See generally Lisa Martin, 'The Political Economy of International Cooperation' in Kaul, Grunberg, and Stern, *Global Public Goods*, 51. I discuss international co-operation to promote cultural diversity in Chapter 5.
[98] David Throsby, 'Cultural Capital' (1999) 23 *Journal of Cultural Economics* 3, 8; Throsby, *Economics and Culture*, 34; David Throsby, 'Seven Questions in the Economics of Cultural Heritage' in Michael Hutter and Ilde Rizzo (eds.), *Perspectives on Cultural Heritage* (1997) 13, 16. See also Jagdish Bhagwati, *The Wind of the Hundred Days: How Washington Mismanaged Globalization* (2000) 209–14.
[99] Throsby, *Economics and Culture*, 34.

used to justify intervention in a wide range of industries, given that many products (particularly services) have positive externalities and public-good aspects. Second, the existence of market failures does not in itself justify trade-restrictive measures in response. Rather, it is necessary to examine the particular circumstances to determine whether the market failures could be addressed in a non-discriminatory manner. As noted earlier, trade-distorting cultural policy measures are justified only to the extent that their costs are lower than those imposed by the market failures identified in the first place. Government intervention may also fail, for example because 'politicians are motivated by the need for re-election rather than by any direct incentive to provide welfare-maximizing cultural policies',[100] and 'politicians and public officials are exposed to the influence of pressure groups'.[101] Accordingly, I now turn to the need for discrimination in cultural policy measures.

2.3.2 The need for discrimination

A. Against foreign cultural products

On the need for discrimination against foreign cultural products, two questions arise. First, would it be possible or desirable to pursue the legitimate goal of preserving or promoting local culture or cultural diversity through origin-neutral regulation of cultural products – that is, regulation that does not discriminate expressly against foreign-source products (meaning imported goods, services supplied through one of the four GATS modes,[102] or the suppliers of these services)? If so, cultural policy measures need not involve de jure discrimination contrary to the notion of national treatment. Second, could these measures be designed to avoid de facto discrimination?

The need for cultural policy measures to discriminate expressly against foreign cultural products depends to some extent on the nature of the culture that the government is trying to promote or preserve. Baker identifies two distinct conceptions of culture. The need to protect culture in Baker's preferred 'dialogic' sense focuses on providing an opportunity for members of a community to speak to each other as they develop their identity and values as a community. Baker explains that the 'goal of the dialogic conception is to maintain (or create) a dynamic local cultural discourse. This goal requires preserving (or creating) local

---

[100] Frey, 'Public support', 395.   [101] Ibid., 396.   [102] See below, 86.

cultural industries'.[103] More specifically, in the absence of a local cultural industry, local cultural 'speakers' may be unable to speak. Put differently, some commentators highlight the role of culture and cultural products in fostering a plurality of political views and hence an effective system of democracy.[104] This conception of culture is consistent with certain statements of WTO Members regarding the need to protect culture. For example, references to culture as an instrument of 'expression'[105] or of transmitting and diffusing 'values and ideas'[106] seem to reflect a view of culture as a means of communication between members of a community.[107]

For a cultural policy measure to promote or preserve culture according to this dialogic conception, it must favour cultural products originating in the relevant cultural 'community', regardless of their content or whether they are examples of 'high' or 'low' culture. In other words, the cultural importance of a film or a book rests not on what it says but on who is saying it. An American film about France does nothing to promote French culture in a dialogic sense, while a French version of an American reality television show may well do so. But culture does not necessarily follow national boundaries.[108] Thus, the government could designate a cultural community that is located in a particular area of the country or comprises a particular minority group within the country, or the population of the country as a whole.[109] In any case, this would involve de jure discrimination against foreign cultural products, which by definition would not originate in the relevant community.

Andreu Mas-Colell describes measures of this kind as involving 'protection of national cultural production' and queries whether this

---

[103] Baker, 'Economic Critique', 1370. See also Rowland Lorimer, 'Book Publishing' in Dorland, *Cultural Industries in Canada* 3, 27.
[104] See, e.g., Germann, 'Culture in Times of Cholera', 113; Graber, *Handel und Kultur*, 72, 339–40; Mulcahy, 'Cultural Policy', 329; Ivan Bernier, 'Trade and Culture' in Macrory, Appleton, and Plummer, *The World Trade Organization* (vol. II) 747, 780–1. See also Hesmondhalgh, *Cultural Industries*, 240–1; Michael Hahn, 'Eine kulturelle Bereichsausnahme im Recht der WTO?' (1996) 56 *Zeitschrift für ausländisches öffentliches Recht und Völkerrecht* 315, 324, 345–6; Barton, 'International Video Industry', 86–8; Productivity Commission, *Broadcasting*, Inquiry Report No. 11 (3 March 2000) 328.
[105] Appellate Body Report, *Canada – Periodicals*, 31.
[106] WTO, Council for Trade in Services, *Communication from Brazil – Audiovisual Services*, S/CSS/W/99 (9 July 2001) [6].
[107] See also Gibson and Connell, 'Cultural Industry Production in Remote Places', 256.
[108] Appadurai, *Modernity at Large*, 160–1; Galperin, 'Cultural Industries in Regional Trade', 637.
[109] I address cultural groups extending beyond national boundaries below, 59.

kind of production is substantially different 'from the case of shoes'.[110] Howse points out that a 'legal economist can always imagine a hypothetical welfare-maximizing regulatory instrument that achieves a public purpose without resort to trade restrictions; the logical conclusion is that the choice of any other instrument is due to protectionist measures'.[111] The legal economist's imagination might be applied to the regulation of cultural industries as follows. In protecting or preserving national culture, a WTO Member might decide to impose regulations based not on the nationality of the film-makers or other aspects external to the 'story' in the film, but on elements contained in the story itself. In this way, a Member might hope to avoid origin-specific regulation falling foul of the national treatment obligation in the WTO agreements.

Cultural policy measures of this kind could not promote culture in a 'dialogic' sense, as already explained. However, they could promote culture in the more concrete 'museum' sense, as labelled by Baker, which focuses on the content of a particular culture. Again, certain statements of WTO Members indicate a concern with the cultural 'content'[112] of cultural products that is consistent with this understanding of culture. The museum conception of culture might focus on distinctive elements such as musical instruments used in a sound recording or languages spoken in a film or song. In many countries, language is seen as one of the most important elements of cultural diversity.[113] Moreover, as cultural products often convey messages or stories, those stories could represent wide-ranging aspects of a particular culture. For example, the story could be set in an identifiable place within a country and the characters in the story could be of a particular nationality. The characters might engage in certain rituals or pastimes that are characteristic of a given country. They might eat food typical of that country or

---

[110] Andreu Mas-Colell, 'Should Cultural Goods be Treated Differently?' (1999) 23(1) *Journal of Cultural Economics* 87, 89.
[111] Robert Howse, 'Managing the Interface between International Trade Law and the Regulatory State: What Lessons Should (and Should Not) Be Drawn from the Jurisprudence of the United States Dormant Commerce Clause' in Cottier and Mavroidis, *Regulatory Barriers*, 139, 140.
[112] Panel Report, *Canada – Periodicals*, [3.84].
[113] See, e.g., A Mattera, '"L'Union européenne assure le respect des identités nationales, régionales et locales, en particulier par l'application et la mise en œuvre du principe de la reconnaissance mutuelle" (Un article 12 A à introduire dans le future Traité?)' (2002) 2 *Revue du Droit de l'Union Européenne* 217, 221, 225.

a region in that country, and they might wear clothes associated with that country.

These cultural 'elements' are not necessarily linked to particular countries. Thus, a film set in France or in which the characters speak French is not necessarily French, in the sense that the producers, actors, and funding, etc., may not come from France. As Baker explains, when culture is seen in a museum sense, '[a] quality American film on the French Revolution could contribute more [to French culture] as an accessible representation of French history, even for the French, than a French knock-off of an American game show.'[114] In the same way, US mimicry of British comedies in films such as the Yorkshire-based *Calendar Girls*[115] could be said to advance British culture.

It would be possible to construct a measure favouring cultural products that exhibited cultural elements in this museum sense without expressly requiring that any person involved in the product or its production come from any particular place or country. In this way, a measure protecting culture in the museum sense need not be origin-specific and therefore de jure discriminatory. However, it could well involve de facto discrimination because local cultural products would be more likely to contain the requisite elements and could therefore more easily qualify for the government support.

This type of regulation (which Mas-Colell describes as involving 'protection of the production of national culture')[116] could raise several other problems. To begin with, it would require the government to identify particular elements as forming important parts of that country's culture. The government may be reluctant or unqualified to do this, assuming it can be done at all. Tyler Cowen has pointed out that governments are notoriously bad at 'picking winners' and ill-equipped to make fine artistic distinctions;[117] the same may be said of governments' ability to define or refine culture. Identifying cultural elements in this way would also be restrictive, limiting culture to certain things and preventing its development over time and through influences from other places. This would be contrary to the dynamic nature of culture and the need to encourage free thinking and new ideas in a cultural

---

[114] Baker, 'Economic Critique', 1375.
[115] 'Disney-in-the-Dales', *The Economist* (22 May 2003).
[116] Mas-Colell, 'Should Cultural Goods be Treated Differently?', 89.
[117] Cowen, *Good and Plenty*, 22, 44–5, 102.

context.[118] It may also be inconsistent with general public goals or constitutional norms regarding creativity or the freedom of speech. Therefore, it may be more consistent with a country's understanding of its own culture to adopt regulations that use origin-specific criteria as a proxy for cultural content. In other words, a WTO Member may decide to protect its cultural industries on the assumption that those industries are more likely to enrich that Member's culture by creating stories that are about or addressed to that Member's people.

In practice, cultural policy measures tend to be origin-specific, particularly in those countries that emphasise the special nature of cultural products in trade negotiations. In Canada, it is assumed that '[o]nly Canadians will make Canadian films. Therefore, the criteria by which films are judged eligible for Canadian government assistance ... must ensure not only substantial majority participation by Canadian creative personnel but also Canadian control of production.'[119] For the purposes of Canadian domestic content quotas, '[w]hether a programme appearing on a television screen is deemed Canadian content does not depend on the national aspects of its story, images or sounds but on the nationality of those who financed, managed and made it'.[120]

Cultural policy measures operate in a similar manner in France. Thus, the film *The Fifth Element* (which Patrick Messerlin describes as 'a perfect Hollywood clone made by a French director')[121] received State support as a French film even though it was shot in English and starred the American Bruce Willis.[122] Conversely, the film *Un Long Dimanche de Fiançailles* was ineligible for French subsidies because its production company was controlled by Hollywood's Warner Brothers and run by the Head of Warner Brothers France, even though it was in French, with a French director and hundreds of French actors and technicians, and was the most nominated film in the 2005 César awards in France.[123]

---

[118] See generally Bruno Frey, 'Creativity, Government and the Arts' (2002) 150(4) *De Economist* 363. See also Tyler Cowen, *In Praise of Commercial Culture* (1998) 41.
[119] Canadian Department of Communications, *Report of the Federal Cultural Policy Review Committee* (1982) 256.
[120] Acheson and Maule, 'Canada – Audiovisual Policies', 161.
[121] Patrick Messerlin, 'Regulating Culture: Has it "Gone with the Wind"?' (paper presented at the Productivity Commission and Australian National University (Joint Conference) on Achieving Better Regulation of Services, Canberra, 26–7 June 2000) 11. See also Messerlin, *Measuring the Costs of Protection*, 329.
[122] Messerlin and Cocq, 'Preparing Negotiations in Services', 3. See also Messerlin, *Measuring the Costs of Protection*, 326.
[123] 'French Films', *The Economist* (24 February 2005) 30.

Grischa Perino and Günther Schulze describe one of the rationales for German television regulation as being

> to ensure the existence of a broadcasting system that is largely free from government intervention and that mirrors the pluralistic German society and its diversity of opinions. This motivation recognizes the role the broadcasting system plays in open societies and reflects the horrible experiences of the Nazi regime when broadcasting was monopolized and abused by the government for propaganda purposes. As such, this motivation is not intended to discriminate against foreign participation, but it could have restrictive side effects.[124]

A government could have three main reasons for adopting origin-specific cultural policy measures, whether or not it articulates or even conceptualises its logic in these terms: (i) it sees culture in a dialogic sense;[125] (ii) it sees culture in a museum sense, but it is unwilling to restrict creativity and cultural evolution for the reasons described earlier; or (iii) it is in fact more concerned with protecting domestic cultural industries than local culture.[126] Later in this chapter, I return to the question of government motives for imposing cultural policy measures. For now, it is sufficient to note that Members could have legitimate reasons for imposing cultural policy measures that involve de jure or de facto discrimination against foreign cultural products.

B. Between foreign cultural products

WTO Members sometimes support not only local cultural products but also cultural products from specified other countries. In principle, this is contrary to the obligation of MFN treatment. Hahn contends that MFN deviations may support cultural co-operation and peacekeeping.[127] I therefore continue my analysis above to ask: if a Member wished to grant more favourable treatment to audiovisual products from certain countries, could this be justified on cultural grounds?

---

[124] Perino and Schulze, 'Competition, Cultural Autonomy', 54.
[125] See, e.g., Australian Department of Communications Information Technology and the Arts, *Report on Access to Overseas Markets for Australia's Creative Digital Industry* (12 December 2003) 26.
[126] 'Regulatory powers can be used as easily to achieve anti-competitive goals of the *providers* of a service as to protect *buyers* of the service from lazy or predatory providers': UNCTAD and World Bank, *Liberalizing International Transactions*, 42 (original emphasis).
[127] Hahn, 'Eine kulturelle Bereichsausnahme', 350.

I have already explained why discrimination against foreign cultural products might be necessary and why governments might wish to support local cultural products in particular. However, this does not mean that the government should try to block foreign cultural products. Here, the objectives of cultural diversity and trade liberalisation coincide, as discussed further below.[128] Assuming, then, that a WTO Member allows imports of foreign cultural products, it is unclear why that Member must discriminate expressly between these products based on their origin to further its cultural interests. Whether the Member sees culture in a dialogic or museum sense, it could identify those foreign products that contribute to local culture using certain objective cultural criteria such as language (instead of simply identifying the countries, subregions or regions from which those products originate). This would ensure that all relevant foreign products are included, rather than only those based on historical cultural ties or extraneous considerations.

Concerns about restricting creativity or stifling cultural development would be less acute in this context, because the Member would not need to define the scope or content of local culture. Rather, it could simply identify those aspects of its culture that it had in common with other countries (if it wished to advantage cultural products reflecting cultures similar to its own) or that it considered important and beneficial for local culture (if it wished to enrich local culture by advantaging cultural products reflecting cultures different from its own). Moreover, as the criteria selected would be applied only to distinguish between foreign cultural products, they would not affect the incentives of local artists or producers to create or innovate.

In short, while a Member could genuinely consider de facto discrimination between foreign cultural products necessary as part of its cultural policy, it is much harder to justify de jure discrimination of this kind.

2.4 Evaluating cultural policy measures in the WTO

2.4.1 *Motives for cultural policy measures*

So, a WTO Member might have valid cultural grounds for de jure discrimination against foreign cultural products, or for de facto discrimination against or between foreign cultural products. This does not

---

[128] See below, 64.

necessarily mean that all such discrimination in cultural policy measures is in fact motivated by cultural concerns. If cultural policy measures of WTO Members are not truly motivated by a desire to preserve or promote culture, this is a powerful reason against accepting them or providing any special treatment for them in the WTO agreements.

Unfortunately, it may be extremely difficult to differentiate between protectionist and non-protectionist motives for cultural policy measures. For example, if a WTO Member grants tax concessions to its book-publishing industry on the grounds that this will promote its culture, it may be impossible to determine whether the Member was in fact motivated by cultural or by mercantilist interests. This is a particularly tricky problem given that a WTO Member might wish to protect its local cultural industry as a means of preserving or promoting its culture. Furthermore, identifying the 'motive' for a government measure may be problematic in any legal system. First, numerous motives may underlie a particular measure. For example, different political parties and individual legislators may have varied motives for enacting a particular law. Second, the true motives underlying a particular measure may be impossible to discern. Should these motives be gleaned from public statements to the media, from parliamentary debates, or purely from the text and architecture of the measure itself?

Given the problems with sorting legitimate from illegitimate motives for cultural policy measures, in the following sections I instead consider alternative mechanisms for distinguishing legitimate and illegitimate cultural policy measures.

2.4.2 *Effectiveness of cultural policy measures*

One response to Members who claim they must impose discriminatory cultural policy measures is that these measures cannot be effective in preserving or promoting culture, or that the measures used by various WTO Members have been ineffective and inefficient.[129] Interestingly, Broude reaches a similar conclusion in relation to the effectiveness of geographical indications in protecting local culture and cultural diversity.[130] Practical reasons may explain this ineffectiveness in respect of cultural products. For example, consumers who obtain foreign films via

---

[129] See, e.g., Acheson and Maule, 'Canada – Audiovisual Policies', 164; Ghoneim, 'Audio-Visual Sector in Egypt', 212; Bernier, 'La dimension culturelle', 249–51. See also Hahn, 'Eine kulturelle Bereichsausnahme', 349.
[130] Broude, 'Geographical Indications and Cultural Protection', 678; see above, 15.

the internet or satellite may bypass a quota limiting the proportion of foreign films that may be shown in cinemas.[131] A more principled objection to such cultural policy measures is that they do not achieve their goal of promoting or preserving local culture or, worse, that they damage culture and cultural products. This is a specific example of a more general problem with measures designed to protect any enterprise or industry, which is that quality suffers, whereas exposure to domestic or international competition may improve product quality. Thus, Trebilcock and Howse refer to the Canadian book-publishing industry as being 'characterized by economically fragile companies, which seem to have developed a permanent dependence on subsidization for their survival'.[132]

Although it may be impossible to assess the 'quality' of a cultural product in an objective, abstract sense,[133] one can try to determine the impact of cultural policy measures on the nature of cultural products in particular countries. In 1982, the Canadian Federal Cultural Policy Review Committee concluded that a particular tax incentive had been ineffective in enabling 'Canadians to create fresh and distinctive Canadian films, and ... audiences in Canada and abroad to see those films'.[134] Acheson and Maule explain the view that 'there is no evidence that there is a systematic connection between ownership and content. Canadian ownership of Cineplex-Odeon, a significant exhibitor of films in Canada, has not led to an appreciable increase in the number of Canadian films appearing on Canadian screens.'[135] Patrick Messerlin and Emmanuel Cocq argue that French quotas requiring a minimum proportion of French films to be broadcast on television have led to

---

[131] See Acheson and Maule, *Much Ado about Culture*, 204; Geza Feketekuty, 'Regulatory Reform and Trade Liberalization in Services' in Sauvé and Stern, *GATS 2000*, 225, 227; Messerlin and Cocq, 'Preparing Negotiations in Services', 4.
[132] Trebilcock and Howse, *Regulation of International Trade* (3rd edn), 639.
[133] Giacomo Pignataro, 'Imperfect Information and Cultural Goods: Producers' and Consumers' Inertia' in Alan Peacock and Ilde Rizzo (eds.), *Cultural Economics and Cultural Policies* (1994) 55, 56-7.
[134] Canadian Department of Communications, *Report of the Federal Cultural Policy Review Committee* (1982) 255.
[135] Acheson and Maule, *Much Ado about Culture*, 21 (see also 254). See also Tim Burt, 'Quotas Fail to Save European Producers from an Influx of US Television Shows', *Financial Times* (Paris, 27 May 2005); Bruce Feldthusen, 'Awakening from the National Broadcasting Dream: Rethinking Television Regulation for National Cultural Goals' in David Flaherty and Frank Manning (eds.), *The Beaver Bites Back? American Popular Culture in Canada* (1993) 42.

extensive 'reruns of old French films' because of the insufficient number of successful French films being made.[136]

Evidently, the effectiveness of any particular cultural policy measure in preserving or promoting national culture will depend on its structure and operation. For example, according to Messerlin and Cocq, the 1989 'Lang Plan', which 'still remains at the heart of French film policy',[137] changed the emphasis of State support to favour high-budget instead of low-budget films.[138] As the domestic market for films in France is small,[139] the results are as follows:

> Subsidies, being a protectionist device, lead to the creation of a protected type of movie ... As far as large-budget movies are concerned, the combination of high investment with relatively low profitability calls for films to respond to specific popular demand requirements ... [T]his trend has already taken place in many cases and ... it follows two specific templates. The first strategy is domestically-oriented, with the market having influenced production in such a way that most productions opt for historical dramas or popular comedy. The second strategy is oriented towards foreign markets, focusing on movies based on the Hollywood blockbuster model.[140]

The link between State support and cultural value is also countered by the demands of the market in the Canadian context:

> The cultural rationale for content quotas and related subsidies is that Canadian production teams and money will produce programmes with a Canadian sensitivity. The commercial incentive, however, is to produce the programmes that are most profitable. Since the market for most productions, either mass-market or niche-market, is typically international, the content is tailored to international demands.[141]

Technology also influences the effectiveness of cultural policy measures, in ways that may vary from country to country and year to year. For example, in countries with high internet use, the opportunity for consumers to purchase or view films online may reduce the effectiveness

---

[136] Messerlin and Cocq, 'Preparing Negotiations in Services', 7–8. See also Patrick Messerlin, 'France and Trade Policy: Is the "French Exception" Passé?' (1996) 72(2) *International Affairs* 293, 298.
[137] Cocq and Messerlin, 'French Audio-Visual Policy', 29. For further discussion see Jonathan Buchsbaum, 'After GATT: Has the Revival of French Cinema Ended?' (2005) 23(3) *French Politics, Culture & Society* 34.
[138] Cocq and Messerlin, 'French Audio-Visual Policy', 32–5.
[139] Ibid., 37–8.   [140] Ibid., 32–9.
[141] Acheson and Maule, 'Canada – Audiovisual Policies', 162.

of screen quotas in cinemas and on television.[142] The same may happen as DVDs become more popular. In these circumstances, subsidies may be preferable to quotas.

The fact that a cultural policy measure is ineffective in protecting or promoting culture may raise some doubt about whether it genuinely stems from those goals. However, Members may have different conceptions of culture and cultural values, and the WTO may not be the right place to pass judgement on cultural values *per se* or on the effectiveness of particular measures in promoting those values.[143] What the WTO can do, as discussed in the next section, is evaluate the relationship between particular measures and cultural policy goals by assessing the measures' trade-restrictiveness.

2.4.3 *Minimising trade restrictions*

If the WTO is to limit Members' choice of cultural policy measures according to their trade-restrictiveness, it must first be established that cultural policy measures can achieve their cultural goals without necessarily restricting trade or restricting it to any particular degree. An examination of certain international agreements and instruments relating to culture and cultural diversity suggests that the trade-restrictiveness of cultural policy measures can be limited or minimised without jeopardising the underlying cultural goals. At the same time, Chinedu Ezetah suggests that encouraging cultural diversity may increase the benefits of free trade.[144] In this regard, the values of trade liberalisation run parallel to those of cultural diversity to some extent.

The Beirut Agreement provides for contracting States to exempt from customs duties, quantitative restrictions, and the requirement of import licences the import of films and sound recordings of an 'educational, scientific or cultural character' originating in any other contracting State.[145] Similarly, States parties to the Florence Agreement undertake not to apply customs duties or other charges on the importation of, among other things, books, publications, and documents; or

---

[142] Cocq and Messerlin, 'French Audio-Visual Policy', 46–7; Roy, 'Audiovisual Services', 942–3; Productivity Commission, *Broadcasting*, Inquiry Report No. 11 (3 March 2000) 417.
[143] See below, 174.
[144] Chinedu Ezetah, 'Patterns of an Emergent World Trade Organization Legalism: What Implications for NAFTA Cultural Exemption?' (1998) 21(5) *World Competition* 93, 123. See also Germann, 'Culture in Times of Cholera', 111.
[145] Beirut Agreement, arts. I, II, III:1.

visual and auditory materials of an educational, scientific, or cultural character (including films and sound recordings).[146] Subject to certain exceptions, the parties to the Nairobi Protocol agree to extend this obligation to certain additional materials.[147] These UNESCO commitments look much like trade liberalisation commitments of the kind contained in the WTO agreements.

The problems with restricting trade in cultural products in order to promote or preserve culture are also reflected in widespread multilateral recognition through UNESCO of the need to encourage the free flow of products and ideas for culture to develop and flourish. Thus, UNESCO's 1966 *Declaration of the Principles of International Cultural Co-operation* notes that cultural co-operation, by disseminating ideas, knowledge, literature, and the arts, is essential to the enrichment of cultures and cultural life.[148] Similarly, the UNESCO Recommendation on Participation in Cultural Life states that 'the mass media can serve as instruments of cultural enrichment, both by opening up unprecedented possibilities of cultural development, [and] in contributing to ... the preservation and popularization of traditional forms of culture, and to the creation and dissemination of new forms'.[149] Finally, the Universal Declaration on Cultural Diversity, adopted in 2001, confirms that creativity 'flourishes in contact with other cultures', and therefore that 'genuine dialogue among cultures' should be encouraged.[150] And so, more anecdotally, Amartya Sen writes: '*Pather Panchali*, of course, is a quintessentially Indian film, in subject matter and in style, and yet a major inspiration came from an Italian film. The Italian influence did not make *Pather Panchali* anything other than an Indian film; it simply helped to make it a great Indian film.'[151]

---

[146] Florence Agreement, art. I:1, annexes A, C. See also GATT, *Barriers to the Import and Export of Educational, Scientific and Cultural Material*, GATT/CP/12 (8 March 1949) 3.
[147] Nairobi Protocol, [1].
[148] UNESCO, *Declaration of the Principles of International Cultural Co-operation*, 14 C/Resolution 8 (4 November 1966) arts. IV:1, IV:4, VI, VII:1.
[149] UNESCO Recommendation on Participation in Cultural Life, preamble.
[150] Universal Declaration on Cultural Diversity, art. 7. See also General Conference, UNESCO, *Preliminary Report by the Director-General Setting out the Situation to be Regulated and the Possible Scope of the Regulating Action Proposed, Accompanied by the Preliminary Draft of a Convention on the Protection and of the Diversity of Cultural Contents and Artistic Expressions*, 33 C/23 (4 August 2005) [8].
[151] Amartya Sen, 'Satyajit Ray and the Art of Universalism: Our Culture, Their Culture', *The New Republic* (Washington, DC, 1 April 1996) 32. See also Keith Acheson, 'Globalization' in Towse, *Handbook*, 248, 251; United Nations Development Programme, *Human Development Report 2004: Cultural liberty in today's diverse world* (2004) 89, 98.

These pronouncements do not prove that cultural policy measures need not restrict trade at all, or that discriminatory cultural policy measures cannot be grounded in cultural interests. Indeed, many more UNESCO declarations and recommendations confirm the importance of preserving a space for all the world's cultures,[152] and WTO Members could argue that unrestricted flows of cultural products are likely to damage cultural diversity. However, the instruments highlighted above do indicate that, although cultural policy measures may have incidental trade-restrictive effects, trade restriction itself need not and should not be their goal. Accordingly, minimising trade-restrictiveness (including as a result of discrimination) may provide an appropriate guide for Members' design of cultural policy measures and for evaluating those measures within the WTO. In Aaditya Mattoo's words, in relation to national treatment under GATS, 'surely [the WTO] can question the use of an instrument which discriminates against foreigners when other suitable instruments exist which would not have a similarly discriminatory effect'.[153]

A WTO framework for minimising the trade-restrictiveness of cultural policy measures could take two main forms.[154] First, WTO Members could agree on a broad rule that these measures are allowed provided that they are no more trade-restrictive than necessary to meet the relevant cultural goals. This might look something like the existing exceptions in Article XX of GATT 1994[155] or Article 5.6 of the SPS Agreement, which requires Members to ensure that their sanitary or phytosanitary measures are 'not more trade-restrictive than required to achieve their appropriate level of sanitary or phytosanitary protection'. If challenged, individual cultural policy measures would then be evaluated through the dispute settlement process (perhaps taking into account international law on culture, as discussed further in Chapter 4).[156] Thus, this approach leaves the matter largely in the hands of the judicial bodies of the WTO, primarily Panels and the

---

[152] See above, 12, n. 58.
[153] Aaditya Mattoo, 'National Treatment in the GATS: Corner-Stone or Pandora's Box?' (1997) 31(1) *Journal of World Trade* 107, 131.
[154] For analysis of a broader range of tests to balance trade values with other values, see Trachtman, 'Trade and . . . Problems'.
[155] See below, 101.
[156] See generally Alan Sykes, 'The Least Restrictive Means' (2003) 70 *University of Chicago Law Review* 403; WTO, Working Party on Domestic Regulation, *Necessity Tests in the WTO: Note by the Secretariat*, S/WPDR/W/27 (2 December 2003).

Appellate Body, which may increase flexibility while reducing certainty and Member control.[157]

Second, WTO Members could establish more concrete and comprehensive rules, reflecting a multilateral decision *ex ante* about the types of measures that will allow Members to pursue their cultural goals in the least trade-restrictive manner (as discussed further in Chapter 6). These rules might resemble more closely Article XI of GATT 1994, which imposes a general prohibition on quantitative restrictions (reflecting the preference for tariffs as a less trade-restrictive and more transparent measure), or Article 3 of the SCM Agreement, which imposes a general prohibition on certain types of subsidies. This approach relies more on the Members of the WTO, and it may increase certainty while reducing flexibility to adapt to different circumstances.

2.5 Conclusion

This chapter has explored the arguments on both sides of the trade–culture debate in order to determine guidelines for improving the current treatment of cultural products in WTO law. Unsurprisingly, given the long and still unresolved disagreements over this issue, it is a complex problem. Much of the complexity stems from the nature of cultural products as both commercial and cultural. However, accepting the dual nature of cultural products does not mean accepting that they are unique or exceptional. Just as in other areas falling within the scope of WTO rules, it is important to scrutinise any claims that particular products or industries require protection departing from the usual WTO disciplines. Nevertheless, the above analysis has shown that preservation or promotion of culture through cultural products is a legitimate regulatory objective for the purpose of WTO law, as well as an objective supported by other international instruments.

But are Members justified in adopting discriminatory cultural policy measures, contrary to the usual principle of non-discrimination in the WTO? Although much of the concern about trade in cultural products (at least as expressed by WTO Members such as Canada and the EC) is fuelled by the success of US cultural products, more permanent reasons for wishing to protect local culture through cultural products are found in the general nature of the market for cultural products. In particular, the value of that culture is not necessarily reflected in decisions

---

[157] See above, 9, n. 42.

regarding the production or consumption of cultural products, due to the gap between their private and their social value. In protecting local culture through cultural products, Members may have well-founded, non-mercantilist reasons for preferring measures that discriminate against foreign cultural products, whether in a de jure or a de facto manner. However, Members should be able to find ways of protecting local culture through cultural products without de jure discrimination *between* foreign cultural products. In assessing whether a given measure is a genuine measure of cultural policy rather than the product of protectionist inclinations, rather than trying to establish the motives behind the measure (directly or by assessing its effectiveness), WTO Members could impose a trade-restrictiveness test. The WTO could thus sanction those measures that are no more trade restrictive than necessary to achieve their declared cultural goals. In the following chapter I consider the extent to which the existing WTO rules on cultural products accord with the rationales just outlined.

3 What's wrong with the current treatment of cultural products?

All are in agreement that the present, post-Uruguay Round situation is quite unsatisfactory inasmuch as it has left most issues unresolved.[1]

The 'do nothing' approach does not really offer a long term solution to the trade and culture issue.[2]

3.1 Introduction

This chapter highlights why all WTO Members should be concerned about the current treatment of cultural products in WTO law, regardless of their positions on the nature of these products and the rationale for discriminatory or trade-restrictive cultural policy measures. As a whole, the existing provisions under GATT 1994 and GATS do not correspond with the conclusions in the previous chapter, namely that cultural policy measures may legitimately involve some forms of discrimination and that the WTO rules should allow for this discrimination while minimising the resulting trade restrictions. Perhaps more importantly, the difference in treatment of cultural products under these agreements and the uncertainty of their provisions lead to the conclusion that the WTO needs a new approach to cultural products.

The preamble to GATS makes clear that one objective of this agreement is

the early achievement of progressively higher levels of liberalization of trade in services through successive rounds of multilateral negotiations aimed at promoting the interests of all participants on a mutually advantageous basis and at securing an overall balance of rights and obligations, while giving due respect to national policy objectives.

---

[1] Rivery, 'Unresolved Issues', 439. [2] Bernier, 'Trade and Culture', 785.

This objective is reflected in Part IV of GATS, headed 'Progressive Liberalization'. As mentioned in Chapter 1, successive rounds of negotiation are to take place 'with a view to achieving a progressively higher level of liberalization', and 'with due respect for national policy objectives'.[3] However, at least in relation to cultural products (and particularly audiovisual services), this aim is being thwarted. The failure of GATT contracting parties to achieve a satisfactory resolution to this matter during the Uruguay Round[4] means that the structure of GATS is not at all conducive to increasing liberalisation in relation to cultural products.

Others have outlined how the numerous WTO agreements apply to cultural products,[5] and in this chapter I do not purport to replicate that work. Rather, I focus on what I see as the most problematic aspects of the current treatment of cultural products in WTO law, namely the existing framework under GATT 1994 and GATS. In Chapter 6, I canvas some proposals of other authors for correcting the current situation through other WTO agreements including the TRIPS Agreement.

Below, I first outline the difficulties arising from the nature of many cultural products as both goods and services. I then explain why the concept of 'likeness', as presently interpreted in WTO law, does not provide a means by which Members may impose discriminatory cultural policy measures consistent with their national treatment and MFN obligations. This leads to the question whether the existing exceptions under GATT 1994 and GATS are sufficient to protect these measures while minimising their trade-restrictiveness. Unfortunately, these exceptions are too unbalanced and uncertain to perform this role. I demonstrate that, as a result, cultural products under GATS are subject to insufficient commitments and excessive exemptions, jeopardising the goal of progressive liberalisation.

3.2 Cultural products as goods and services

3.2.1 Basic definitions and classifications

GATS applies to 'measures by Members affecting trade in services',[6] while GATT 1994 is one of the WTO's 'Multilateral Agreements on

---

[3] GATS, art. XIX:1, 2. [4] See above, 23.
[5] See, e.g., Bernier, 'Trade and Culture', 753–78; Footer and Graber, 'Trade Liberalization and Cultural Policy', 136–41.
[6] GATS, art. I:1.

Trade in Goods', contained in Annex 1A to the Marrakesh Agreement. It is well settled as a matter of WTO law that both GATT 1994 and GATS may apply to a particular measure and that, in principle, neither takes precedence.[7] The overlap between GATT 1994 and GATS could raise thorny interpretational questions in the case of a conflict between provisions of these two agreements. The general interpretative note to Annex 1A of the Marrakesh Agreement indicates how to resolve conflicts between GATT 1994 and the other multilateral agreements on trade in goods in that annex. However, the WTO agreements contain no such indication regarding the general relationship between GATT 1994 and GATS. This may pose a particular problem for cultural policy measures, given that the cultural industries generally involve both goods and services.[8]

Under GATT 1994, cultural products may take physical forms such as film reels,[9] CDs, DVDs, video and audio tapes,[10] and books on paper.[11] These things seem like ordinary goods (things you can drop on your foot), whether ordered online and then delivered in physical form,[12] or purchased in a shop.[13] At the same time, under GATS, cultural products as I have defined them include printing and publishing services,[14] as well as audiovisual services, typically classified within communication services as follows:

---

[7] Appellate Body Report, *Canada – Periodicals*, 19; Appellate Body Report, *EC – Bananas III*, [221]. See also Joost Pauwelyn, *Conflict of Norms in Public International Law: How WTO Law Relates to other Rules of International Law* (2003) 399–405.

[8] For further analysis of the problematic distinction between goods and services, see Fiona Smith and Lorna Woods, 'A Distinction Without a Difference: Exploring the Boundary Between Goods and Services in the World Trade Organization and the European Union' (2005) 12(1) *Columbia Journal of European Law* 1.

[9] Working Group on Audiovisual Services, Uruguay Round Group of Negotiations on Services, GATT, *Note on the Meeting of 27–28 August 1990*, MTN.GNS/AUD/1 (27 September 1990) [19] (representative of Switzerland).

[10] See Harmonized System, headings 37.06, 85.24.

[11] Harmonized System, heading 49.01.

[12] '[E]lectronic ordering with subsequent physical delivery' plays a significant role in music sales: OECD, Working Party on the Information Economy, *Digital Broadband Content: Music*, DSTI/ICCP/IE(2004)12/FINAL (8 June 2005) 19.

[13] WTO, Council for Trade in Services, *The Work Programme on Electronic Commerce: Note by the Secretariat*, S/C/W/68 (16 November 1998) [30]; Andrew Mitchell, 'Towards Compatibility: The Future of Electronic Commerce Within the Global Trading System' (2001) 4(4) *Journal of International Economic Law* 683, 703; Arvind Panagariya, 'Electronic Commerce, WTO and Developing Countries' (2000) 23(8) *World Economy* 959, 960–1.

[14] Document W/120, sector 1(F)(r). During the Uruguay Round negotiations leading to GATS, contracting parties were encouraged to follow the services classification system in Document W/120 (an informal note by the GATT Secretariat).

a. Motion picture and video tape production and distribution services
b. Motion picture projection service[s]
c. Radio and television services
d. Radio and television transmission services
e. Sound recording
f. Other[15]

The USA and others have pointed out that the traditional classification of audiovisual services under GATS no longer reflects current realities and technologies in the audiovisual sector, where, for example, films and music are provided directly to consumers online or via cable.[16]

Moreover, audiovisual services may also overlap with other service sectors, such as 'recreational, cultural and sporting services'. Although this sector is specified as excluding audiovisual services, some Members have here included 'cinema theatre operation services'.[17] Turning to telecommunications services, these include, for example, voice telephone services, electronic mail, online information and database retrieval, and online information or data.[18] The GATS Annex on Telecommunications elaborates on GATS 'with respect to measures affecting access to and use of public telecommunications transport networks and services',[19] excluding cable or broadcast distribution of radio or television programming.[20] Nevertheless, in some cases it may be difficult to distinguish between telecommunications services and audiovisual services. The WTO Secretariat has suggested that, '[a]s a general rule of thumb ... it has become accepted that commitments involving programming content are classified under audiovisual services, while those purely involving the transmission of information are classified under telecommunications'.[21] However, the USA has disagreed with this suggestion.[22] In addition, Sacha Wunsch-Vincent

---

[15] Ibid., sector 2(D).
[16] WTO, Council for Trade in Services, *Communication from the United States – Audiovisual and Related Services*, S/CSS/W/21 (18 December 2000) [3], [10(i)]; Roy, 'Audiovisual Services', 947–8; Sacha Wunsch-Vincent, *The WTO, the Internet and Trade in Digital Products: EC–US Perspectives* (2006) 73–5; David Luff, 'Telecommunications and Audio-Visual Services: Considerations for a Convergence Policy at the World Trade Organization Level' (2004) 38(6) *Journal of World Trade* 1059, 1073–4, 1082.
[17] Roy, 'Audiovisual Services', 929; Document W/120, sector 10. See also Appellate Body Report, *US – Gambling*, [162]–[163].
[18] Document W/120, 2.c.   [19] GATS, Annex on Telecommunications, [1].   [20] Ibid., [2(b)].
[21] WTO, Council for Trade in Services, *Audiovisual Services: Background Note by the Secretariat*, S/C/W/40 (15 June 1998) [5]. See also Graber, *Handel und Kultur*, 206, 238.
[22] WTO, Council for Trade in Services, *Communication from the United States – Audiovisual Services*, S/C/W/78 (8 December 1998).

explains that, arguably, GATS 'merely covers services that ultimately "produce or record" content (e.g., sound recording) or that serve to "deliver" content (e.g., radio and television transmission services) but not necessarily the content itself'.[23] The definition of telecommunications services and the distinction with audiovisual services need to be revisited in view of the convergence between these sectors.[24]

3.2.2 Digital products

In *Canada – Periodicals*, the Appellate Body stated that 'a periodical is a good comprised of two components: editorial content and advertising content. Both components can be viewed as having services attributes, but they combine to form a physical product – the periodical itself.'[25] Thus, while a tax on advertising might be governed by GATS, a tax on periodicals applies to goods and is subject to GATT 1994.[26] However, not all cultural policy measures are so easily classified or judged.

A cultural product that is delivered (rather than simply ordered) via broadcasting, satellite, or the internet has both goods elements and services elements. The question of whether to classify these 'digitised' or 'digital' products as goods or services remains unresolved within the WTO[27] and is presently the subject of a work programme on electronic commerce.[28] In the EC's view, '[e]lectronic deliveries consist of supplies of services which fall within the scope of the GATS'.[29] Its preferred approach would ensure that music, films, and similar products delivered electronically fall within the EC's effective exclusion of audiovisual services from GATS instead of being subject to GATT 1994.[30] Not

---

[23] Wunsch-Vincent, *WTO, Internet and Digital Products*, 50.
[24] Marco Bronckers and Pierre Larouche, 'Telecommunications Services' in Macrory, Appleton, and Plummer, *The World Trade Organization*, 989, 1033. See also Geradin and Luff, *WTO and Global Convergence*.
[25] Appellate Body Report, *Canada – Periodicals*, 17.
[26] Harmonized System, heading 49.02; Appellate Body Report, *Canada – Periodicals*, 17–18.
[27] WTO, Council for Trade in Goods, *Work Programme on Electronic Commerce: Background Note by the Secretariat*, G/C/W/128 (5 November 1998) [1.2]; WTO Secretariat, *Fifth Dedicated Discussion on Electronic Commerce under the Auspices of the General Council on 16 May and 11 July 2003: Summary by the Secretariat of the Issues Raised*, WT/GC/W/509 (31 July 2003).
[28] Doha Declaration, [34]; WTO Secretariat, *Fifth Dedicated Discussion on Electronic Commerce under the Auspices of the General Council on 16 May and 11 July 2003: Summary by the Secretariat of the Issues Raised*, WT/GC/W/509 (31 July 2003); WTO, *Work Programme on Electronic Commerce Adopted by the General Council on 25 September 1998*, WT/L/274 (30 September 1998) [2.1], [3.1].
[29] WTO, Council for Trade in Services, *Communication from the European Communities and Their Member States: Electronic Commerce Work Programme*, S/C/W/183 (30 November 2000) [6(a)].
[30] Drake and Nicolaïdis, 'Global Electronic Commerce', 408. See above, 25.

surprisingly, the USA has suggested that, because of 'the broader reach of WTO disciplines accorded by the GATT ... there may be an advantage to a GATT versus GATS approach to [digital] products which could provide for a more trade-liberalizing outcome for electronic commerce'.[31] The failure of WTO Members to agree on the classification of digital products is thus symptomatic of a larger difficulty, namely the starkly different treatment of cultural products under GATT 1994 and GATS.[32]

The 2001 Scheduling Guidelines (contained in a WTO Secretariat document intended to assist Members in preparing their GATS schedules)[33] confirm that 'services embodied in exported goods (i.e. services supplied in or by a physical medium, such as a computer diskette or drawings) are ... examples of cross-border supply' under GATS and that the imposition of customs duties on 'the cross-border movement of goods associated with the provision of a service [are] subject to the disciplines of the GATT'.[34] However, pending consensus as to whether digital products are goods or services, WTO Members have reached an informal agreement not to impose customs duties on electronic transmissions (including electronic transmissions of cultural products), which is still in effect.[35] This situation is problematic. For one thing, the moratorium is temporary, non-binding, and rather uncertain.[36] Moreover, its effectiveness is limited. Customs duties are rarely imposed on services anyway, and 'if a Member has not made a national treatment commitment, then it remains free to impose discriminatory

---

[31] WTO, *Work Programme on Electronic Commerce: Submission by the United States*, WT/COMTD/17; WT/GC/16; G/C/2; S/C/7; IP/C/16 (12 February 1999) [7]. See also Sacha Wunsch-Vincent, 'The Digital Trade Agenda of the U.S.: Parallel Tracks of Bilateral, Regional and Multilateral Liberalization' (2003) 58 *Aussenwirtschaft* 7, 13–15; Wunsch-Vincent, *WTO, Internet and Digital Products*, 36–7, 52, 56–7.

[32] For a summary of the differences between GATT 1994 and GATS in the context of digital products, see Wunsch-Vincent, *WTO, Internet and Digital Products*, 53–4.

[33] See Appellate Body Report, *US – Gambling*, n. 236.

[34] 2001 Scheduling Guidelines, [7], [28]. See also 1993 Scheduling Guidelines, [6].

[35] Hong Kong Declaration, [46]; July Package, [1(h)]; General Council, WTO, *Dedicated Discussions under the Auspices of the General Council on Cross-Cutting Issues Related to Electronic Commerce: Report to the 24–25 July Meeting of the General Council*, WT/GC/W/505 and Corr.1 (21 July 2003) [7]; WTO, Ministerial Conference, *Declaration on Global Electronic Commerce, Adopted on 20 May 1998*, WT/MIN(98)/DEC/2 (25 May 1998); Doha Declaration, [34]; Sacha Wunsch-Vincent, United Nations Information and Communication Technologies Task Force, *WTO, E-commerce, and Information Technologies: From the Uruguay Round through the Doha Development Agenda* (19 November 2004) [40].

[36] Wunsch-Vincent, *WTO, E-commerce, and Information Technologies*, [319]; Wunsch-Vincent, *WTO, Internet and Digital Products*, 38–42.

internal taxes, so the commitment not to impose customs duties would not preclude recourse to discriminatory measures with an identical effect'.[37]

Other commentators have analysed the various arguments for classifying digital products as goods or as services.[38] For my purposes, it is sufficient to note that the ongoing uncertainty surrounding this question taints the current treatment of cultural products under WTO law.

3.3 Presumed 'likeness' of cultural products

Having established the initial (but not insurmountable) problem of distinguishing goods aspects and services aspects of cultural products, I turn to how the Appellate Body and Panels are likely to analyse and compare cultural products in assessing 'likeness' for the purposes of national treatment and MFN treatment under GATT 1994 and GATS. Specifically, I examine the extent to which these bodies might distinguish cultural products from each other (and therefore find them not to be like) based on their cultural differences, first under GATT 1994 and then under GATS. If Panels and the Appellate Body took into account cultural goals and criteria in determining likeness of cultural products, this could provide a tool for allowing legitimate discrimination while simultaneously singling out disguised protectionism. If particular domestic and imported cultural products were not like, it would be easier for Members to justify treating domestic cultural products more favourably than imports. However, at present, cultural grounds would typically play only a small role in differentiating between two products. This means that the criterion of likeness does not currently offer a way out of the core disciplines of national treatment and MFN treatment, allowing cultural policy measures that legitimately discriminate on cultural grounds.

---

[37] WTO, Council for Trade in Services, *The Work Programme on Electronic Commerce: Note by the Secretariat*, S/C/W/68 (16 November 1998) 34–5. See also Wunsch-Vincent, *WTO, Internet and Digital Products*, 40; Stewart Baker and Maury Shenk, 'Trade and Electronic Commerce' in Macrory, Appleton, and Plummer, *The World Trade Organization* (vol. II) 469, 477.

[38] See, e.g., Wunsch-Vincent, *WTO, Internet and Digital Products*, 51–62; Baker and Shenk, 'Trade and Electronic Commerce', 472–6.

3.3.1 Likeness under GATT 1994

A. Like products

Within GATT 1994, the meaning of 'like products' may differ according to the provision at issue or even the particular part of that provision.[39] The existing jurisprudence lends itself towards a discussion of 'like products' under the national treatment provisions of GATT 1994 as a starting point. The first sentence of GATT Article III:2 states:

> The products of the territory of any Member imported into the territory of any other Member shall not be subject, directly or indirectly, to internal taxes or other internal charges of any kind in excess of those applied, directly or indirectly, to *like domestic products*.[40]

According to the Appellate Body, the meaning of 'like products' in this first sentence is fairly narrow.[41] Whether a domestic product is like a given imported product will depend on

(a) the product's properties, nature and quality;
(b) the product's end-uses;
(c) consumers' tastes and habits;[42] and
(d) the tariff classification of the product under the Harmonized System.[43]

Applying these factors to cultural products, their cultural significance may have some impact on their properties, nature and quality, or end-uses. For example, domestic fiction books and imported fiction books are likely to be fairly similar in a physical sense and are both likely to be used for reading pleasure. However, they may represent different things to consumers because of their cultural nature. A fiction book written in a foreign language might be used for a particular educational purpose (learning a foreign language). Even a fiction book that has been

---

[39] See, e.g., Appellate Body Report, *EC – Asbestos*, [99]; Appellate Body Report, *Japan – Alcoholic Beverages II*, 21; Robert Hudec, '"Like Product": The Differences in Meaning in GATT Articles I and III' in Cottier and Mavroidis, *Regulatory Barriers*, 101; Donald Regan, 'Regulatory Purpose and "Like Products" in Article III:4 of the GATT (With Additional Remarks on Article III:2)' (2002) 36(3) *Journal of World Trade* 443, 444–5.
[40] Emphasis added.   [41] Appellate Body Report, *Japan – Alcoholic Beverages II*, 20–1.
[42] Appellate Body Report, *Canada – Periodicals*, 21; Appellate Body Report, *Japan – Alcoholic Beverages II*, 20; Panel Report, *Indonesia – Autos*, [14.109]–[14.110]. See also GATT Working Party Report, *Border Tax Adjustments*, [18].
[43] Appellate Body Report, *Japan – Alcoholic Beverages II*, 22; Panel Report, *Dominican Republic – Import and Sale of Cigarettes*, [7.330]. The Harmonized System was developed by the World Customs Organization and provides a widely accepted method of classifying traded goods.

translated from a foreign language into a local language might be different in nature from a book that was originally in the same local language. But what about two fiction books written in the same language? The less concrete the cultural differences, the harder it will be to establish that the products are not like.

Bernier suggests that imported and domestic products of the cultural industries are not obviously like, since they are 'characterized by their artistic and intellectual content, and for that reason cannot easily be compared one to another'.[44] According to this reasoning, taxing imported fiction books at a higher rate than domestic fiction books might not violate the first sentence of Article III:2, on the grounds that these are not like products. This assumes that imported fiction books are foreign cultural products, whereas domestically produced fiction books are local cultural products. An alternative approach, linking the cultural policy more closely to the cultural nature of the products, would be to impose a higher tax on foreign fiction books (that is, books written or published by foreigners) than on local fiction books (that is, books written or published by nationals), regardless of whether these books are imported or domestically produced. Again, the Member could argue that, from a cultural perspective, foreign fiction books are not like local fiction books, and therefore the differential tax does not violate the national treatment obligation in Article III:2, first sentence, even though the foreign books are more likely to be imported than the local books.

The reasoning of Panels and the Appellate Body in several disputes (not related to cultural products)[45] suggests that this argument is unlikely to succeed, at least where the discrimination is so broadly framed. '[C]onsumers' tastes and habits, which change from country to country', are relevant in identifying like products.[46] However, in previous cases involving alcoholic beverages, Panels and the Appellate Body have discounted consumer surveys on the basis that they have been conducted against the background of an allegedly discriminatory tax regime.[47] Thus, the Appellate Body might consider that consumer preferences for local cultural products have been shaped by

---

[44] Bernier, 'Cultural Goods and Services', 121.
[45] The Appellate Body in *Canada – Periodicals* reversed the Panel's findings on the likeness of domestic and imported periodicals. However, it was unable to make a finding itself as to the likeness of these products: Appellate Body Report, *Canada – Periodicals*, 22–3.
[46] Appellate Body Report, *Japan – Alcoholic Beverages II*, 20; GATT Panel Report, *Japan – Alcoholic Beverages I*, [5.6], [6.28]; Panel Report, *Japan – Alcoholic Beverages II*, [6.21].
[47] Panel Report, *Japan – Alcoholic Beverages II*, [6.28], [6.31].

longstanding protectionist measures. Panels and the Appellate Body have also emphasised the 'variable' nature of consumer habits[48] and the 'inevitably uncertain' nature of consumer responses.[49] Put simply, '"like" products do not become "unlike" merely because of differences in local consumer traditions within a country'.[50]

The second key national treatment provision in GATT 1994 is Article III:4, which states:

> The products of the territory of any Member imported into the territory of any other Member shall be accorded treatment no less favourable than that accorded to *like products* of national origin in respect of all laws, regulations and requirements affecting their internal sale, offering for sale, purchase, transportation, distribution or use.[51]

The Appellate Body has ruled that 'the scope of "like" in Article III:4 is broader than the scope of "like" in Article III:2, first sentence'.[52] Therefore, domestic and imported cultural products may be characterised as 'like products' under Article III:4 more readily than under the first sentence of Article III:2. In addition, the Appellate Body has held that 'a determination of "likeness" under Article III:4 is, fundamentally, a determination about the nature and extent of a competitive relationship between and among products'.[53] Focusing on the competitive relationship between domestic and imported cultural products may also increase the chance of finding likeness under Article III:4, given that they may well be intensely competitive with each other even if they are culturally quite different.

In any case, the factors Panels have examined in determining the likeness of products under Article III:4 are similar to those examined under the first sentence of Article III:2: properties, nature and quality; end-uses; consumers' tastes and habits; and tariff classification.[54] The Appellate Body has endorsed this general approach, describing the factor of consumers' tastes and habits more specifically as relating to 'the extent to which consumers perceive and treat the products as

---

[48] GATT Panel Report, *Japan – Alcoholic Beverages I*, [5.7]; Panel Report, *Japan – Alcoholic Beverages II*, [2.7].
[49] GATT Panel Report, *Japan – Alcoholic Beverages I*, [5.13]; Panel Report, *Japan – Alcoholic Beverages II*, [2.7].
[50] GATT Panel Report, *Japan – Alcoholic Beverages I*, [5.9].   [51] Emphasis added.
[52] Appellate Body Report, *EC – Asbestos*, [99].   [53] Ibid., [99].
[54] See, e.g., Panel Report, *EC – Asbestos*, [8.112]–[8.115]; Panel Report, *EC – Bananas III (Ecuador)*, [7.62]; Panel Report, *US – Gasoline*, [6.9].

alternative means of performing particular functions in order to satisfy a particular want or demand'.[55]

In *EC – Asbestos*, the Appellate Body considered that health risks associated with asbestos could affect consumers' tastes and habits, and hence the degree of likeness between certain asbestos fibres and certain substitute fibres.[56] The Appellate Body faulted the Panel for, among other things, deciding not to consider consumer preferences because they may be varied and may not provide clear results.[57] The Appellate Body also specifically stated that consumers' tastes and habits remain relevant to an analysis of likeness even 'in markets where normal conditions of competition have been disturbed by regulatory or fiscal barriers'.[58] Without more, these statements indicate openness towards the view that even consumer preferences resulting from systemic discrimination may now form part of the local culture and therefore provide a valid basis for distinguishing between products. However, the Appellate Body went on to say that in these cases 'a Member may submit evidence of latent, or suppressed, consumer demand in that market, or it may submit evidence of substitutability from some relevant third market'.[59] This suggests that the Appellate Body will not rely on actual consumer preferences to distinguish between products where those preferences appear to have been shaped by market distortions. On the contrary, it will accept evidence of likely consumer preferences in the absence of these distortions. Therefore, evidence that consumers perceive local cultural products differently from foreign cultural products might not be accepted if accompanied by evidence of existing discriminatory cultural policy measures.

The MFN obligation under Article I of GATT 1994 provides, in the words of one Panel, that 'an advantage granted to the product of any country must be accorded to the *like product* of all WTO Members without discrimination as to origin'.[60] This obligation relates to advantages including the level of customs duties imposed in connection with importation or exportation, the method of levying these duties, and rules and formalities in connection with importation and exportation,

---

[55] Appellate Body Report, *EC – Asbestos*, [100]–[103], [109], [133].
[56] Ibid., [122]. See also Mary Footer, 'European Communities – Measures Affecting Asbestos and Asbestos-Containing Products: The World Trade Organization on Trial for Its Handling of Occupational Health and Safety Issues' (2002) 3 *Melbourne Journal of International Law* 120, 136–40.
[57] Appellate Body Report, *EC – Asbestos*, [109], [117]–[123].   [58] Ibid., [123].
[59] Ibid.   [60] Panel Report, *Canada – Autos*, [10.23] (emphasis added).

as well as internal charges and regulations affecting sale, distribution, etc.[61] Relatively little WTO jurisprudence exists on the meaning of 'like product' under GATT Article I, especially at the appellate level.[62] The meaning of this concept in Article I (MFN) is not identical to that under Article III (national treatment).[63] Nevertheless, from previous GATT 1947 and WTO Panel decisions and the text of the provisions, most commentators would agree that the relevant criteria for determining likeness are similar, although the category of 'like products' under Article I is broader than under Article III:2, first sentence.[64] Accordingly, Members would face similar difficulties explaining MFN and national treatment violations on the basis that cultural products are distinguishable on cultural grounds.

B. Directly competitive or substitutable products

The second sentence of Article III:2 of GATT 1994 provides that 'no Member shall otherwise apply internal taxes or other internal charges to imported or domestic products in a manner contrary to the principles set forth' in Article III:1, an overarching provision that states:

> The Members recognize that internal taxes and other internal charges, and laws, regulations and requirements affecting the internal sale, offering for sale, purchase, transportation, distribution or use of products, and internal quantitative regulations requiring the mixture, processing or use of products in specified amounts or proportions, should not be applied to imported or domestic products so as to afford protection to domestic production.*

Ad Article III:2 (in Annex I) explains that a tax complying with Article III:2, first sentence, would violate Article III:2, second sentence, only where the dissimilarly taxed imported and domestic products were

---

[61] GATT 1994, art. I:1 states: 'With respect to customs duties and charges of any kind imposed on or in connection with importation or exportation ... and with respect to the method of levying such duties and charges, and with respect to all rules and formalities in connection with importation and exportation, and with respect to all matters referred to in paragraphs 2 and 4 of Article III,* any advantage, favour, privilege or immunity granted by any Member to any product originating in or destined for any other country shall be accorded immediately and unconditionally to the like product originating in or destined for the territories of all other Members.'

[62] See Appellate Body Report, *EC – Bananas III*, [190]; Appellate Body Report, *Canada – Autos*, [76].

[63] See above, 76, n. 39.

[64] See Trebilcock and Howse, *Regulation of International Trade* (3rd edn) 65–72; Won-Mog Choi, *'Like Products' in International Trade Law: Towards a Consistent GATT/WTO Jurisprudence* (2003) 94–7.

'directly competitive or substitutable'. This category is broader than 'like products',[65] so that two products that are not 'like' under the first sentence of Article III:2 may nevertheless be directly competitive or substitutable under the second.

The Appellate Body decision in *Canada – Periodicals*[66] provides a useful case study of the meaning of 'directly competitive or substitutable' products pursuant to the second sentence of Article III:2. In that case, the Appellate Body examined Canada's excise tax on advertisements in split-run editions of periodicals under the second sentence of GATT Article III:2.[67] In determining whether imported split-run periodicals and domestic non-split-run periodicals[68] were directly competitive or substitutable, the Appellate Body focused on 'competition in the relevant markets' and 'substitution' or 'interchangeability' of the products.[69] Canada argued that Canadian and foreign periodicals were not directly competitive or substitutable (or like), because of their different content:

> [C]ontent developed for and aimed at the Canadian market cannot be the same as foreign content. Content for the Canadian market will include Canadian events, topics, people and perspectives. The content may not be exclusively Canadian, but the balance will be recognizably and even dramatically different than that which is found in foreign publications which merely reproduce editorial content developed for and aimed at a non-Canadian market.[70]

The Appellate Body rejected Canada's arguments. It stated that the existence of the differential tax scheme showed that these periodicals competed for advertising revenue. It also referred to a report by a Canadian government-appointed task force on the magazine industry, which noted the substitutability of USA for Canadian magazines, the price competition between domestic and imported magazines, and the competition for advertising between them.[71] According to the Appellate Body:

---

[65] Appellate Body Report, *Japan – Alcoholic Beverages II*, 25; Choi, *Like Products*, 109–10.
[66] See above, 40.   [67] Panel Report, *Canada – Periodicals*, [2.6]–[2.9].
[68] The Appellate Body went on to consider whether imported split-run periodicals were taxed in excess of domestic non-split-run periodicals. Another way of approaching this question would have been to ask whether imported periodicals (split-run and non-split-run) were taxed in excess of like domestic periodicals (split-run and non-split-run). See Appellate Body Report, *EC – Asbestos*, [100]; Lothar Ehring, '*De Facto* Discrimination in World Trade Law: National and Most-Favoured-Nation Treatment – or Equal Treatment?' (2002) 36(5) *Journal of World Trade* 921, 941–2.
[69] Appellate Body Report, *Canada – Periodicals*, 25.   [70] Ibid., 6.   [71] Ibid., 26–7.

A periodical containing mainly current news is not directly competitive or substitutable with a periodical dedicated to gardening, chess, sports, music or cuisine. But newsmagazines, like TIME, TIME Canada and Maclean's, are directly competitive or substitutable in spite of the 'Canadian' content of Maclean's.[72]

Other factors that may be relevant in determining whether products are directly competitive or substitutable include (similar to the factors used to determine whether products are like): physical characteristics, end-uses, channels of distribution, prices (including cross-price elasticity), consumer preferences, and tariff classifications.[73] However, as Trevor Knight concludes from *Canada – Periodicals*, 'efforts to distinguish cultural products based on their "cultural" as opposed to "commercial" aspects likely will not get a positive reception as long as the measures to protect the cultural content of various products do so in a way that has an effect on a competitive commercial relationship'.[74]

C. Aims-and-effects test

In the context of Article III:2 of GATT 1947, two GATT Panels applied the so-called 'aims-and-effects' test.[75] Essentially, this test scrutinises the aims and effects of a measure in determining whether the domestic and imported products in question are either like or 'directly competitive or substitutable'. For example, if the aims and effects of a measure are to protect the environment, one could argue that two similar products are distinguishable (i.e. neither like nor directly competitive or substitutable) in relation to that measure if only one is environmentally friendly. Thus, the answer to whether two products are like or directly competitive may be different if the aims and effects of the relevant measure are considered, in addition to traditional criteria such as end-uses. A similar argument might be made in respect of a measure with the aims and effects of promoting local culture.

The USA[76] and certain commentators have argued that the aims-and-effects test under Article III should be used to evaluate measures that are

---

[72] Ibid., 28.
[73] Panel Report, *Chile – Alcoholic Beverages*, [7.14], [7.16]; Panel Report, *Korea – Alcoholic Beverages*, [10.40], [10.43]–[10.44].
[74] Knight, 'Dual Nature of Cultural Products', 186.
[75] GATT Panel Report, *US – Malt Beverages*, [5.25]–[5.26]; GATT Panel Report, *US – Taxes on Automobiles*, [5.9]–[5.10]. These decisions appear to be contrary to two earlier GATT Panel decisions: GATT Panel Report, *Greece – Import Taxes*, [5]; GATT Panel Report, *US – Superfund*, [5.2.4].
[76] Panel Report, *Japan – Alcoholic Beverages II*, [4.16], [4.32].

prima facie neutral, whereas the general exceptions provisions under GATT Article XX are better suited to evaluating measures that discriminate on their face against imports.[77] In part, this reflects the view that the latter type of measure is necessarily applied 'so as to afford protection', while the former is not necessarily so applied. In the former case, using the aims-and-effects test would arguably oblige Panels and the Appellate Body to analyse openly the regulatory goals underlying the measure instead of relying on an analysis of motives or a 'smell test' hidden behind sterile criteria such as 'end-use' to evaluate the measure under Article III[78] (before reaching Article XX). In these circumstances, the aims-and-effects test could protect the fiscal sovereignty of WTO Members[79] and confirm the possibility of legitimate regulatory goals beyond those specified in Article XX,[80] including cultural policy.

The relevance of the aims-and-effects test may depend on which sentence of Article III:2 applies. A differential tax measure challenged under Article III:2 of GATT 1994 will violate the second sentence only if it is applied 'so as to afford protection to domestic production' within the meaning of Article III:1. The textual basis for this requirement lies in the fact that the second sentence of Article III:2 refers to applying taxes or charges 'in a manner contrary to the principles set forth in' Article III:1. In contrast, the first sentence of Article III:2 contains no explicit reference to Article III:1. For this reason, the Appellate Body has held that the first sentence contains no separate requirement that the measure be applied 'so as to afford protection', even though Article III:1 informs both sentences of Article III:2.[81] Accordingly, in *Japan – Alcoholic Beverages II*, a WTO Panel rejected the aims-and-effects test under Article III:2, first sentence, because this test is based on the words 'so as to afford protection', which appear in Article III:1 but not in Article III:2, first sentence.[82] The Appellate Body affirmed the Panel's reasoning in relation to this provision (without explicitly ruling on

---

[77] Robert Hudec, 'GATT/WTO Constraints on National Regulation: Requiem for an "Aim and Effects" Test' (1998) 32 *International Lawyer* 619, 622-3, 626; Serena Wille, 'Recapturing a Lost Opportunity: Article III:2 GATT 1994, Japan – Taxes on Alcoholic Beverages 1996' (1998) 9(1) *European Journal of International Law*, 'Current Developments', <www.ejil.org> (online only, accessed 4 August 2006) 9-10. Cf. Regan, 'Regulatory Purpose and Like Products', 455-6, referring to 'regulatory purpose' rather than 'aims-and-effects'; Choi, *Like Products*, 81-4.

[78] Hudec, 'GATT/WTO Constraints', 634; Wille, 'Recapturing a Lost Opportunity', 6-7.

[79] Wille, 'Recapturing a Lost Opportunity', 6.

[80] See above, 10.   [81] Appellate Body Report, *Japan – Alcoholic Beverages II*, 18-19, 24.

[82] Panel Report, *Japan – Alcoholic Beverages II*, [6.16].

the aims-and-effects test).[83] In *EC – Bananas III*, the Appellate Body clearly rejected the aims-and-effects test under any part of Article III:2, even though the second sentence of Article III:2 refers explicitly to Article III:1.[84]

Nevertheless, the Appellate Body has indicated that 'the design, the architecture, and the revealing structure of a measure' are relevant in determining whether a measure is applied 'so as to afford protection' under the second sentence of Article III:2, suggesting that these may provide an 'objective' understanding of the 'underlying criteria' of the measure.[85] The Appellate Body has also stated that, although legislators' subjective intentions are irrelevant, the 'statutory purposes or objectives' are pertinent – 'that is, the purpose or objectives of a Member's legislature and government as a whole – to the extent that they are given objective expression in the statute itself'.[86] This reasoning is consistent with at least one version of the aims-and-effects test – that is, a version focusing on the objective aim of the measure as evidenced by the measure and the statute itself rather than on the subjective aims of the legislators.[87]

In *Canada – Periodicals*, the Appellate Body did look at the purpose of the differential tax on periodicals in determining whether it was applied 'so as to afford protection' contrary to the second sentence of Article III:2. However, rather than supporting Canada's argument that the relevant products were treated differently because they were culturally distinct, the Appellate Body considered that the purpose of the measure confirmed its protectionist nature. The Appellate Body considered not only legislative objectives as expressed in the statute but also 'statements of the Government of Canada's explicit policy objectives in introducing the measure',[88] including statements made by the Canadian Minister for Cultural Heritage and a government-appointed task force, as well as the government's response to the task-force report. The Appellate Body focused on evidence of the government's desire to 'protect' itself against split-run periodicals from the USA, to protect 'the

---

[83] Appellate Body Report, *Japan – Alcoholic Beverages II*, 23.
[84] Appellate Body Report, *EC – Bananas III*, [216], [241]. Cf. Regan, 'Regulatory Purpose and Like Products', 446–7.
[85] Appellate Body Report, *Japan – Alcoholic Beverages II*, 29.
[86] Appellate Body Report, *Chile – Alcoholic Beverages*, [62], [71].
[87] Cf. Hudec, 'GATT/WTO Constraints', 631–2; Regan, 'Regulatory Purpose and Like Products', 476–7.
[88] Appellate Body Report, *Canada – Periodicals*, 32.

economic foundations of the Canadian periodical industry', and to divert Canadian advertising revenues to Canadian magazines.[89] For example, the Canadian Minister of Canadian Heritage had suggested that consumers might prefer cultural aspects of US periodicals: 'Canadians are much more interested in American daily life, be it political or sports life or any other kind, than vice versa. Therefore, the reality of the situation is that we must protect ourselves against splitruns coming from foreign countries and, in particular, from the United States'.[90]

The Appellate Body quoted a ministerial statement referring to the Canadian periodical industry as 'a vital element of Canadian cultural expression' and expressing the government's commitment to 'ensuring that Canadians have access to Canadian ideas and information through genuinely Canadian magazines'.[91] However, it did not evaluate the cultural reasons underlying Canada's objective of protecting its periodical industry. This suggests that where the aim of a measure is to protect a particular cultural industry and the measure is applied accordingly, this will be contrary to Article III:1 and therefore will violate Article III:2, second sentence, regardless of whether the desire to protect that industry is merely a step towards the primary goal of promoting or preserving culture.

3.3.2 Like services and service suppliers under GATS

The national treatment obligation under GATS is contained in Article XVII, the first paragraph of which provides:

> In the sectors inscribed in its Schedule, and subject to any conditions and qualifications set out therein, each Member shall accord to services and service suppliers of any other Member, in respect of all measures affecting the supply of services, treatment no less favourable than that it accords to its own *like services and service suppliers*.[92]

GATT Article III relates to discrimination against 'imported products' (goods produced in another Member's territory) and in favour of 'like domestic products' or 'like products of national origin' (goods produced within the territory of the Member). Thus, the discrimination is based on the origin of the good: where it is produced. The GATS national treatment provision is a little different. GATS Article XVII relates to

---

[89] Ibid., 30–1.   [90] Ibid., 28 (quoting Panel Report, [3.118]).
[91] Appellate Body Report, *Canada – Periodicals*, 31.   [92] Emphasis added.

discrimination against 'services and service suppliers of any other Member' and in favour of 'its own like services and service suppliers'. Under GATS, services are supplied through one of four modes:

> Mode 1 – *cross-border supply*: supply from the territory of one Member into the territory of any other Member;
> Mode 2 – *consumption abroad*: supply in the territory of one Member to the service consumer of any other Member;
> Mode 3 – *commercial presence*: supply by a service supplier of one Member, through commercial presence in the territory of any other Member; and
> Mode 4 – *presence of natural persons:*[93] supply by a service supplier of one Member, through presence of natural persons of a Member in the territory of any other Member.[94]

For services supplied through mode 1 or 2, discrimination contrary to national treatment is based on the service supplier's location (in particular, the fact that the service supplier is located outside the Member's territory). For services supplied through mode 3 or 4, discrimination is based on the origin of the service supplier (e.g., the fact that the service supplier is not a national of the Member, despite the fact that it is located within the Member's territory).[95] In either case, discrimination does not occur unless the relevant services or service suppliers are 'like'. The term 'like service suppliers' presumably includes suppliers that supply 'like services',[96] although it might be possible to identify like service suppliers in other circumstances as well.[97]

Similarly, whereas the general MFN obligation in GATT 1994 (Article I) relates to the treatment provided to a 'product' and 'like product', the equivalent provision in GATS (Article II) relates to the treatment provided to 'services and service suppliers' and 'like services and service suppliers'. GATS Article II:1 provides:

---

[93] See also GATS, Annex on Movement of Natural Persons Supplying Services under the Agreement.
[94] GATS, art. I:2.
[95] GATS, art. XXVII(f), (g); Werner Zdouc, 'WTO Dispute Settlement Practice Relating to the GATS' (1999) 2(2) *Journal of International Economic Law* 295, 327-31. Cf. Panel Report, *Mexico – Telecoms*, [7.25]-[7.45].
[96] Panel Report, *Canada – Autos*, [10.248], [10.289]; Panel Report, *EC – Bananas III (Ecuador)*, [7.322].
[97] Zdouc, 'WTO Dispute Settlement Practice', 333-4. For further discussion see Mireille Cossy, WTO, *Determining 'Likeness' Under the GATS: Squaring the Circle?*, Staff Working Paper ERSD-2006-08 (September 2006) 7-12.

With respect to any measure covered by this Agreement, each Member shall accord immediately and unconditionally to services and service suppliers of any other Member treatment no less favourable than that it accords to *like services and service suppliers* of any other country.[98]

The Appellate Body has indicated that neither Article II nor Article XVII of GATS contains 'specific authority ... for the proposition that the "aims and effects" of a measure are in any way relevant in determining whether that measure is inconsistent with those provisions'.[99] Moreover, as the Appellate Body has rejected the aims-and-effects test in the context of GATT 1994,[100] it is unlikely that either Panels or the Appellate Body would agree to apply this test under GATS in future cases. However, as we have seen in the context of GATT 1994, this does not necessarily mean that the objectives of a measure, as reflected in its structure and design, are irrelevant.[101]

In *EC – Bananas III*, the Appellate Body criticised the Panel for interpreting the MFN treatment obligation under GATS Article II in the light of the national treatment obligation under GATT Article III, suggesting that GATS Article II would be more appropriately compared with the 'MFN and MFN-type obligations' in GATT 1994.[102] Although the Appellate Body made this suggestion in connection with the phrase 'treatment no less favourable', the same reasoning would presumably apply to the phrase 'like services and service suppliers'. In other words, it may be more appropriate to assess the likeness of services and service suppliers under GATS Article II (MFN) by reference to the meaning of like products under GATT Article I:1 (MFN) rather than GATT Article III:2 or III:4 (national treatment). The same goes for GATS Article XVII (national treatment). Nevertheless, the meaning of like products has more often been considered under the national treatment obligation than the MFN treatment obligation of GATT 1994, and, as mentioned earlier, Panels have previously used similar factors in assessing likeness under these two GATT obligations.[103]

Without forgetting that 'likeness' may mean different things under GATT 1994 and GATS and also under different provisions within these

---

[98] Emphasis added.
[99] Appellate Body Report, *EC – Bananas III*, [241]; Zdouc, 'WTO Dispute Settlement Practice', 340–2.
[100] Above, 84. [101] See, e.g., Panel Report, *EC – Bananas III (Article 21.5 – Ecuador)*, [6.127].
[102] Appellate Body Report, *EC – Bananas III*, [231].
[103] See, e.g., Panel Report, *Indonesia – Autos*, [14.141].

agreements,[104] it is reasonable to presume that the factors used to assess the likeness of products under GATT 1994 may also be relevant in assessing the likeness of services under GATS Article II. In relation to a service, these factors could therefore include:[105] properties, nature and quality[106] (which are likely to depend less on physical characteristics than in the GATT context); service classification;[107] end-uses; and consumer tastes and habits. In connection with consumer tastes and habits, much of the discussion above regarding attempts to distinguish between products under GATT Article III based on their cultural significance would probably apply equally to GATS. For the reasons already mentioned (including, in particular, the Appellate Body's decision in *Canada – Periodicals*), these attempts are unlikely to succeed except to the extent that cultural differences between services are reflected in the relevant services' properties and substitutability.

With these aspects of 'likeness' in mind, let us consider India's listed MFN exemption under GATS for co-produced film and television. The exemption applies to measures that 'grant national treatment to motion pictures and television programmes co-produced with foreign countries which maintain a co-production agreement with India'.[108] Assuming that these are measures affecting trade in services within the meaning of GATS Article I:1, their consistency with the MFN obligation under GATS would depend on their particular nature. For example, this exemption might cover a measure that allowed a film that has been co-produced through the presence of natural persons in India (pursuant to a co-production agreement) to apply for subsidies from the Indian Government to assist in meeting its production costs, while excluding non-Indian films from other countries from so applying. In the absence of the exemption, this would seem to entail less favourable treatment in

---

[104] Above, 76, n. 39. For further discussion of 'likeness' under GATS, see generally Cossy, *Determining 'Likeness' Under GATS*; Sacha Wunsch-Vincent, 'The Internet, Cross-Border Trade in Services, and the GATS: Lessons from US – Gambling' (2006) 5(3) *World Trade Review* 319, 329–35.
[105] Cf. Aaditya Mattoo, 'MFN and the GATS' in Cottier and Mavroidis, *Regulatory Barriers*, 51, 74; Cossy, *Determining 'Likeness' Under GATS*, 16–23.
[106] See Panel Report, *EC – Bananas III (Ecuador)*, [7.322]. Here the Panel referred to the 'nature and characteristics' of the services in question.
[107] Panel Report, *Canada – Autos*, [10.285], [10.289]; Panel Report, *EC – Bananas III (Ecuador)*, [7.322]. On Document W/120, see above, 71, n. 14; on the CPC, see below, 89, n. 109.
[108] WTO, *India – Final List of Article II (MFN) Exemptions*, GATS/EL/42 (15 April 1994).

breach of GATS Article II:1, provided that the relevant services or service suppliers were considered like within the meaning of that provision.

The relevant services in this example might fall within CPC[109] subclass 96121, which includes 'production and realization of motion pictures designed for showing in movie theatres'. These services would be supplied by mode 4. The service supplier could be the natural persons engaged in production in India or the employer of those persons. Regardless of whether the supplier was from a country with a co-production agreement with India or from a WTO Member without such an agreement, the characteristics of the production services would be very similar, and subject to the same classification. The end-use of the production services would also be the same, and would be embodied in the film produced. The only difference that might exist between the services is in connection with consumer tastes and habits. Only if the films produced were distinguishable based on concrete cultural features, such as the language used, might these services be unlike. This could be the result of requirements in co-production agreements that co-produced films be set in India or similar requirements. However, in other cases, the services would probably be regarded as like and the measure would be inconsistent with the MFN treatment obligation in the absence of a valid exemption.

In summary, Members would face difficulties similar to those under GATT 1994 in attempting to distinguish cultural products on cultural grounds in determining likeness under the GATS national treatment and MFN obligations. The aims-and-effects test does not currently provide an avenue for considering cultural policy, and the existing jurisprudence suggests that the criterion of consumer preferences would provide an insufficient basis for drawing distinctions on cultural grounds.

3.4 Unbalanced and uncertain exceptions

If Panels and the Appellate Body will not use likeness to allow discriminatory cultural policy measures and minimise trade restrictions, the next question is whether the existing exceptions or exemptions[110]

---

[109] The CPC is a UN system for classifying goods and services. The CPC at the time of the Uruguay Round negotiations on trade in services was UN, *Provisional Central Product Classification*, Statistical Papers, Series M, No. 77 (1991). The most recent revision is UN, *Central Product Classification Version 1.1*, Statistical Papers, Series M, No. 77 (2004).

[110] On the difference between exceptions, exemptions, reservations, and waivers in relation to culture, see Bernier, 'Trade and Culture', 785.

under GATT 1994 and GATS can serve this purpose. In this section, I examine the exceptions that are most relevant to cultural products, namely the exclusion of government-supplied services from GATS, the GATT exceptions regarding screen quotas and subsidies, and the general exception under GATT Article XX(f) for national treasures and under GATT Article XX(a) and GATS Article XIV(a) for public morals. These exceptions are unbalanced as between GATT 1994 and GATS, and not sufficiently certain to protect discriminatory cultural policy measures even to the extent that they are legitimate and not overly trade-restrictive. Additional exceptions do exist under the two agreements that might be used to defend these measures, as mentioned later (such as the allowance of anti-dumping[111] and safeguards[112] under GATT 1994, the public health exception,[113] the exception for measures necessary to secure compliance with WTO-consistent laws or regulations,[114] and the exception for free trade agreements).[115] However, these are not closely related to cultural concerns, nor are they enough to remedy the situation. As a result, most Members tend to rely on their inherent flexibility under GATS to protect their cultural policy.[116]

3.4.1 Government-supplied services

GATS simply defines 'services' as 'includ[ing] any service in any sector except services supplied in the exercise of governmental authority', which means services supplied neither on a commercial basis nor in competition with one or more service suppliers.[117] In some countries, governments supply services in the cultural industries, for example

---

[111] See below, 237.   [112] See below, 239.   [113] See below, 159.   [114] See below, 166.
[115] See below, 117. Another potentially relevant exception is for national security: GATT 1994, art. XXI; GATS, art. XIVbis. A Member could argue, for example, that it needs to take discriminatory or trade-restrictive measures in order to ensure that it retains a strong audiovisual industry (including active and independent television and radio broadcasting) reasons of national security. However, although this relates to the dialogic impact of cultural products, a measure of this kind is arguably not a 'cultural policy measure' – that is, it is not directed towards promoting or preserving culture.
[116] See below, 109.
[117] GATS, art. I:3. On the meaning of this provision, see Krajewski, *National Regulation and Trade Liberalization in Services*, 68–73; Eric Leroux, 'What is a "Service Supplied in the Exercise of Governmental Authority" Under Article I:3(b) and (c) of the General Agreement on Trade in Services?' (2006) 40(3) *Journal of World Trade* 345; Rudolf Adlung, 'Public Services and the GATS' (2006) 9(2) *Journal of International Economic Law* 455, 462–5; Markus Krajewski, 'Public Services and Trade Liberalization: Mapping the Legal Framework' (2003) 6(2) *Journal of International Economic Law* 341.

through public broadcasters.[118] Examples of public broadcasters are Prasar Bharati (India),[119] the Pakistan Broadcasting Corporation and Pakistan Television Corporation Limited,[120] the Union of Radio and Television (Egypt),[121] the Canadian Broadcasting Corporation/Radio-Canada,[122] and the British Broadcasting Corporation.[123] In several countries, such as Germany,[124] these broadcasters are financed in part by licence fees imposed on television and radio users or owners. Like many other public broadcasters, German public television channels are 'less dependent on advertising revenue and hence on high viewer numbers', so 'their portfolio is much more oriented toward information and cultural programs and much less to entertainment, fiction, and advertisement'.[125]

If GATS had no application to these services, public broadcasters could choose to air solely local programmes, regardless of the commitments made by the relevant WTO Member, and regardless of the justification for this choice. However, these services are probably not supplied 'in the exercise of governmental authority', because many public broadcasters compete with private broadcasters, and the former operate increasingly on a commercial basis. Accordingly, these services would often be subject to GATS. GATS imposes additional obligations on Members in connection with monopolies and exclusive service suppliers,[126] which might include some public broadcasters.

Governments may also produce their own films or operate their own cinemas. For example, although '[t]he Egyptian state ... ceased producing feature films in 1971 ... and has been selling the cinemas it used to own since the early 1970s', in 2001 it became engaged in producing feature films again through the establishment of a new independent body for production and distribution.[127] The Government of Egypt is

---

[118] The GATT Secretariat recognised the frequency of public monopolies in television broadcasting during the Uruguay Round negotiations on services trade: Working Group on Audiovisual Services, Uruguay Round Group of Negotiations on Services, GATT, *Matters Relating to Trade in Audiovisual Services: Note by the Secretariat*, MTN.GNS/AUD/W/1 (4 October 1990) [9], [11]. See also Withers, 'Broadcasting', 109–10; Hesmondhalgh, *Cultural Industries*, 121–6.
[119] Mukherjee, 'Audio-Visual Policies', 223.
[120] WTO, TPRB, *Trade Policy Review, Pakistan: Report by the Secretariat*, WT/TPR/S/95 (21 December 2001) [IV:93].
[121] Ghoneim, 'Audio-Visual Sector in Egypt', 194, 202.
[122] Acheson and Maule, 'Canada – Audio-Visual Policies', 158.
[123] Doyle and Hibberd, 'UK Audio-Visual System', 132.
[124] Perino and Schulze, 'Competition, Cultural Autonomy', 62. [125] Ibid., 71.
[126] GATS, art. VIII.   [127] Ghoneim, 'Audio-Visual Sector in Egypt', 193.

also 'a major producer of short documentary films that are not highly profit oriented'.[128] However, in many cases these services will still be covered by GATS because they are supplied either on a commercial basis or in competition with other service suppliers.

Accordingly, the exclusion of government-supplied services under GATS does not appear to provide a means by which Members may impose cultural policy measures that are legitimately discriminatory. Nor does it redress the imbalance in exceptions for these measures under GATT 1994 and GATS, as demonstrated in the following subsections.

3.4.2 Screen quotas

When the national treatment obligations under GATT 1947 were drafted, certain countries considered that tariffs were ineffective in protecting domestic film industries and that quotas were required. They 'argued that the regulation of the film industry was more related to domestic cultural policies than to economic considerations such as ... trade'.[129] For example, the UK maintained that 'countries will not allow their own film production which affects their own culture and ideas, to be swamped by imported films simply because the latter happen to be better organised commercially'.[130] Article IV of GATT 1994 reflects the compromise reached by WTO Members regarding the treatment of cultural products (at least as far as trade in goods is concerned), and it is worth setting it out in full:

Article IV

Special Provisions relating to Cinematograph Films

If any Member establishes or maintains internal quantitative regulations relating to exposed cinematograph films, such regulations shall take the form of screen quotas which shall conform to the following requirements:
  (a)   Screen quotas may require the exhibition of cinematograph films of national origin during a specified minimum proportion of the total screen time actually utilized, over a specified period of not less than

---

[128] Ibid.
[129] GATT, *Application of GATT to International Trade in Television Programmes: Report of the Working Party*, L/1741 (13 March 1962) [8]; GATT, Uruguay Round Group of Negotiations on Services, Working Group on Audiovisual Services, *Matters Relating to Trade in Audiovisual Services: Note by the Secretariat*, MTN.GNS/AUD/W/1 (4 October 1990) [3]. See also Jackson, *World Trade and GATT*, 293.
[130] UN, *Extract of the Summary Record of the Second Session of the Preparatory Committee of the United Nations Conference on Trade and Employment, Commission A*, E/PC/T/A/SR/10 (6 June 1947).

one year, in the commercial exhibition of all films of whatever origin, and shall be computed on the basis of screen time per theatre per year or the equivalent thereof;
(b) With the exception of screen time reserved for films of national origin under a screen quota, screen time including that released by administrative action from screen time reserved for films of national origin, shall not be allocated formally or in effect among sources of supply;
(c) Notwithstanding the provisions of subparagraph (b) of this Article, any Member may maintain screen quotas conforming to the requirements of subparagraph (a) of this Article which reserve a minimum proportion of screen time for films of a specified origin other than that of the Member imposing such screen quotas; *Provided* that no such minimum proportion of screen time shall be increased above the level in effect on April 10, 1947;
(d) Screen quotas shall be subject to negotiation for their limitation, liberalization or elimination.

On one hand, this provision contains an exception to the general national treatment obligation, allowing Members to impose minimum screen quotas for exhibiting cinematograph films of national origin. This exception is explicitly recognised in Article III:10, which states that the national treatment provisions 'of this Article shall not prevent any Member from establishing or maintaining internal quantitative regulations related to exposed cinematograph films and meeting the requirements of Article IV'. On the other hand, Article IV imposes certain disciplines on protecting national films, such as the requirements that quantitative regulations take the form of screen quotas rather than any other form, and that those quotas comply with the conditions in Article IV(a). Similarly, Article IV provides a limited exception to the general MFN obligation, allowing the use of minimum screen quotas for films of a certain origin subject to the conditions in Article IV(a), and provided that the minimum proportion reserved is not higher than the level in effect on 10 April 1947.

The provision for further negotiation in Article IV(d) signals that the debate was not over in 1947, or even in 1995. Several countries impose screen quotas that they would presumably justify under Article IV.[131] Article IV also extends to '[t]he renters' film quota in force in New Zealand on April 10, 1947'.[132] However, the scope of Article IV remains uncertain.

---

[131] See, e.g., Condron, 'Cinema', 209; Kim, 'Screen Quotas in Korea'.
[132] GATT 1994, annex A.

94 STALEMATE AND ITS IDEOLOGICAL ORIGINS

In 1961, a Working Party was established at the request of the USA to examine the application of GATT 1947 to television programmes.[133] The USA argued that television programmes are goods under GATT 1947, but that Article IV should not extend to these programmes because of the different nature of the industry compared to cinematograph films. Instead, it proposed that Members be required to balance any national regulations reserving transmission time to domestic producers with provisions for reasonable access to foreign programmes.[134] Other members of the Working Party suggested that Article IV should apply equally to television programmes, or that television programming is a service not covered by GATT 1947.[135] The Working Party made draft recommendations[136] but did not resolve this issue.[137] John Jackson wrote in 1969: 'The initial United States proposal recognized that a number of television restrictions then existed that were probably violations of GATT ... [P]resumably, the alleged violations continue.'[138]

On 3 October 1989, the Council of the EC adopted the Television Without Frontiers Directive.[139] Broadly, the Directive requires EC Member States, 'where practicable and by appropriate means', to ensure that broadcasters reserve a majority of their transmission time for European works,[140] as well as at least 10 per cent of their

[133] GATT, *Application of GATT to International Trade in Television Programmes*, L/1615 (16 November 1961).
[134] GATT, *Application of GATT to International Trade in Television Programmes: Statement Made by the United States Representative on 21 November 1961*, L/1646 (24 November 1961). See also GATT, *Application of GATT to International Trade in Television Programmes: Proposal by the Government of the United States*, L/2120 (18 March 1964); GATT, *Application of GATT to International Trade in Television Programmes: Revised United States Draft Recommendation*, L/1908 (10 November 1962) 2.
[135] GATT, *Application of GATT to International Trade in Television Programmes: Report of the Working Party*, L/1741 (13 March 1962) [6], [10]. See also GATT, Uruguay Round Group of Negotiations on Services, Working Group on Audiovisual Services, *Note on the Meeting of 27-28 August 1990*, MTN.GNS/AUD/1 (27 September 1990) [8], where Japan states that GATT Article IV does not apply to radio or television.
[136] GATT, *Application of GATT to International Trade in Television Programmes: Report of the Working Party*, L/1741 (13 March 1962) annex 1.
[137] Jon Filipek, '"Culture Quotas": The Trade Controversy over the European Community's Broadcasting Directive' (1992) 28(2) *Stanford Journal of International Law* 323, 342.
[138] Jackson, *World Trade and GATT*, 294.
[139] On the Directive and the subsequent dispute, see generally Filipek, 'Culture Quotas'; Clint Smith, 'International Trade in Television Programming and GATT: An Analysis of Why the European Community's Local Program Requirement Violates the General Agreement on Tariffs and Trade' (1993) 10(2) *International Tax & Business Lawyer* 97; Rolf Weber et al., *Kulturquoten im Rundfunk* (2006) 215-27.
[140] Television Without Frontiers Directive, art. 4(1).

transmission time, or 10 per cent of their programming budget, for European works created by producers who are independent of broadcasters.[141] The Directive specifically refers to the role of television in providing information, education, culture, and entertainment,[142] and it 'was largely drafted at France's insistence and is largely in line with the main aspects of French audio-visual policy'.[143] The USA requested consultations under GATT 1947 with the EC and several European countries regarding the Directive, claiming that certain of its provisions could require EC Member States to take actions that would violate GATT.[144] The United States Trade Representative also placed the EC on its 'Special 301 Priority Watch List'.[145] The EC contended that the Directive fell outside GATT 1947.[146] Eventually, this dispute was merged into the Uruguay Round negotiations on services.[147] Some commentators suggest that GATT Article IV cannot now be regarded as applicable to television programming because of the subsequent practice of Members (in particular, the discussion of television during the Uruguay Round negotiations on services).[148] Instead, television programmes are subsumed under the GATS treatment of audiovisual services.

---

[141] Ibid., art. 5.   [142] Ibid., arts. 4(1), 5, 19(a).
[143] Cocq and Messerlin, 'French Audio-Visual Policy', 22. See also Jean-Charles Paracuellos, 'Le paysage audiovisuel français' (1993) 191 *Regards sur l'actualité* 3, 20; Hans-Peter Siebenhaar, 'Européanisation ou américanisation? Option pour la promotion de la production audiovisuelle dans l'Union européenne' (1994) 379 *Revue du Marché Commun et de l'Union Européenne* 357.
[144] GATT, *Austria / Luxembourg / Netherlands / Norway / Spain / Sweden / Switzerland / United Kingdom – Measures to be Taken under the European Convention on Transfrontier Television: Request for Consultations under Article XXII:1 by the United States*, DS4/1 (11 September 1989); GATT, *EEC – Directive on Transfrontier Television: Request for Consultations under Article XXII:1 by the United States*, DS4/3 (8 November 1989); GATT, *France – Television Broadcasting of Cinematographic and Audiovisual Works: Request for Consultations under Article XXII:1 by the United States*, DS4/5 (8 May 1990); GATT, Uruguay Round Group of Negotiations on Services, Working Group on Audiovisual Services, *Matters Relating to Trade in Audiovisual Services: Note by the Secretariat*, MTN.GNS/AUD/W/1 (4 October 1990) n. 8.
[145] Filipek, 'Culture Quotas', 326 (citing USTR, 'Hills Announces Implementation of Special 301 and Title VII', press release (26 April 1991)).
[146] GATT, *EEC – Directive on Transfrontier Television: Response to Request for Consultations under Article XXII:1 by the United States*, DS4/4 (8 November 1989) 1.
[147] GATT, *Major Proposals Tabled on Safeguards while First Sectoral Discussions Take Place in Services Group*, NUR 029 (7 July 1989); Bruno de Witte, 'Trade in Culture: International Legal Regimes and EU Constitutional Values' in Gráinne de Búrca and Joanne Scott (eds.), *The EU and the WTO: Legal and Constitutional Issues* (2001) 237, 243.
[148] Andrew Carlson, 'The Country Music Television Dispute: An Illustration of the Tensions Between Canadian Cultural Protectionism and American Entertainment Exports' (1997) 6 *Minnesota Journal of Global Trade* 585, 599–600; Witte, 'Trade in Culture', 245–6.

96   STALEMATE AND ITS IDEOLOGICAL ORIGINS

Evidently, the precise parameters of GATT Article IV remain unclear. However, these kinds of uncertainties are not unusual in the context of the WTO, international treaties generally, or even domestic statutes. This is why dispute settlement may be needed to clarify WTO provisions.[149] A more important problem with GATT Article IV is that it is not balanced by a corresponding provision under GATS. Thus, for example, a quota exempted under GATT Article IV might appear to violate GATS Article XVI. In that case, it might be argued that the parties clearly intended to exclude these measures from their agreements and therefore that no GATS violation should be found. On the other hand, if a Member has made a specific commitment to provide market access in relation to audiovisual services and has not listed a limitation for the quota, one might conclude that the Member has waived any agreed exclusion implied by GATT Article IV.

3.4.3 *Subsidies*

A. GATT Articles III:8(b) and XVI and the SCM Agreement

Providing subsidies to domestic producers of cultural products might violate the national treatment principle by indirectly treating imported cultural products less favourably than like products of national origin. However, Article III:8(b) of GATT 1994 states explicitly that Article III 'shall not prevent the payment of subsidies exclusively to domestic producers'. Whether a particular payment falls within Article III:8(b) will depend on the precise circumstances of the payment, including from whom and to whom it is made, the procedure for payment, and whether anyone else benefits from the payment. If it does fall within Article III:8(b), a subsidy that operates to increase exports or to reduce imports of products is subject to certain transparency requirements.[150] In addition, a subsidy that does not violate the national treatment requirement, by virtue of the exception under Article III:8(b), must nevertheless comply with the additional disciplines in Article XVI of GATT 1994, as elaborated in the SCM Agreement.

Canada – Periodicals provides an example of a cultural policy measure for which a Member might claim exemption under Article III:8(b), and it clarifies the nature of payments falling within that exemption. In that case, among other things, the USA challenged the provision by the Canadian Government of funds to Canada Post (a Crown corporation)

---

[149] See below, 123.   [150] GATT 1994, art. XVI:1.

to support lower postal rates ('funded rates') for eligible Canadian publications including periodicals.[151] The eligibility requirements included Canadian ownership and control of the publication, and that the periodical be published, printed, and mailed in Canada for delivery in Canada. Persons ineligible for funded rates could instead apply to enter an agreement with Canada Post for lower postal rates ('commercial rates') for bulk mailing of periodicals within Canada. The commercial rates for periodicals published and printed in Canada were lower than those for periodicals published elsewhere, and additional discounts were available to the former but not the latter.[152]

The Panel found that the commercial rates violated GATT Article III:4,[153] and Canada did not appeal this finding. The Panel also found that the funded rates violated Article III:4, but Canada argued that the funded rates were nevertheless subsidies justified under Article III:8(b).[154] The USA responded that Article III:8(b) did not apply because Canada did not pay subsidies 'exclusively' to domestic periodical producers. Instead, it paid Canada Post.[155] The USA relied on the GATT case *EEC – Oilseeds I*, where the Panel stated that 'it can reasonably be assumed that a payment not made directly to producers is not made "exclusively" to them'.[156] Although the Panel did not disagree with this earlier Panel Report, it found that the subsidies were made exclusively to domestic producers because it considered that Canada Post did not retain any economic benefits from the funded rate scheme.[157]

On appeal, the Appellate Body stated that the *EEC – Oilseeds I* Panel's comment in relation to the 'direct' nature of the payments was *obiter dicta*.[158] This could suggest that an indirect payment to domestic producers might qualify as a subsidy under Article III:8(b). Nevertheless, the Appellate Body indicated that Article III:8(b) refers to payments involving the 'expenditure of revenue by a government'.[159] Tax credits or reductions for domestic products or producers are therefore excluded from the scope of Article III:8(b) and are governed by Articles III:2 and III:4.[160] The Appellate Body saw no 'reason to distinguish a reduction of tax rates on a product from a reduction in transportation or postal

---

[151] Panel Report, *Canada – Periodicals*, [2.10]–[2.19]. [152] Ibid., [2.10]–[2.19].
[153] Ibid., [5.39]. [154] Ibid., [5.40]. [155] Ibid., [5.41].
[156] GATT Panel Report, *EEC – Oilseeds I*, [137].
[157] Panel Report, *Canada – Periodicals*, [5.42]–[5.44].
[158] Appellate Body Report, *Canada – Periodicals*, 33. [159] Ibid., 34.
[160] Appellate Body Report, *Canada – Periodicals*, 34; Panel Report, *Indonesia – Autos*, [14.43].

rates'.[161] Although an internal transfer of government funds took place to allow Canada Post to offer funded rates to domestic periodical producers, and although these producers may have consequently obtained the benefit of lower postal rates, Canada did not actually make any payment to them. Therefore the funded rates were not subsidies, and the Appellate Body reversed the Panel's conclusion that they were justified as such.[162]

Nevertheless, Article III:8(b) of GATT 1994 grants significant flexibility to Members wishing to subsidise their cultural industries, as many do,[163] provided that the payment meets the relevant requirements of involving an expenditure by government etc. However, the situation under GATS is different.

B. GATS Article XV

Under GATS Article XV:1, 'Members recognize that, in certain circumstances, subsidies may have distortive effects on trade in services'. Presumably in response to this recognition, and in the absence of an agreement at the end of the Uruguay Round on how to discipline services subsidies, Article XV:1 goes on to state that 'Members shall enter into negotiations with a view to developing the necessary multilateral disciplines to avoid such trade-distortive effects'.

Given that disciplines are still to be agreed under Article XV,[164] as presently drafted, GATS imposes very few obligations in relation to the granting of subsidies for services or service suppliers. The main specific obligation that GATS imposes is that, pursuant to Article XV:2, where a Member 'considers that it is adversely affected by a subsidy of another Member' and requests consultations with the subsidising Member, the subsidising Member is to accord 'sympathetic consideration' to the request. This is a fairly limited obligation, and one that it would most likely be difficult to breach. Just as the Appellate Body and Panels have shown some reluctance to find that Members have violated their 'good faith' obligations,[165] so too are they likely to baulk at declaring that a Member has failed to accord sympathetic consideration to a request for consultations under Article XV:2. Therefore, without amendment, this provision is unlikely to be of much use to a Member who believes they are 'adversely affected' by another Member's subsidy, whether in the audiovisual sector or any other service sector. Accordingly, in 1993,

---

[161] Appellate Body Report, *Canada – Periodicals*, 34.   [162] Ibid., 35.
[163] Above, 22.   [164] See below, 228.   [165] See the discussion below, 206–9.

GATT Director-General Peter Sutherland issued a statement in response to the debate on the audiovisual sector, as the Uruguay Round drew to a close. Among other things, Sutherland stressed that nothing in GATS would 'prevent governments from funding audio-visual projects. Obviously, much indigenous film-making is dependent on government support and that can continue.'[166]

However, GATS may restrict Members from granting subsidies in one crucial way. The national treatment provision in GATS Article XVII contains no exemption for the granting of subsidies corresponding to the national treatment exemption for subsidies in GATT Article III:8(b). For this reason, the 1993 Scheduling Guidelines (contained in a GATT Secretariat document to assist GATT contracting parties in preparing their new GATS schedules) conclude:

> Article XVII applies to subsidy-type measures in the same way that it applies to all other measures ... Therefore, any subsidy which is a discriminatory measure within the meaning of Article XVII would have to be either scheduled as a limitation on national treatment or brought into conformity with that Article. Subsidy-type measures are also not excluded from the scope of Article II (M.f.n.). An exclusion of such measures would require a legal definition of subsidies which is currently not provided for under the GATS.[167]

The 2001 Scheduling Guidelines contain a similar statement. They also add, however, that 'a binding under Article XVII with respect to the granting of a subsidy does not require a Member to offer such a subsidy to a services supplier located in the territory of another Member',[168] because GATS does not oblige Members to take measures outside their territorial jurisdiction.[169]

Although the 1993 Scheduling Guidelines constitute neither 'context' for interpreting a Member's GATS schedule,[170] nor an authoritative interpretation of GATS Article XVII (as such interpretations can be adopted exclusively by the Ministerial Conference and the General Council),[171] the Appellate Body has found that they may be used as a 'supplementary means of interpretation' in determining the meaning

---

[166] GATT, *Peter Sutherland Responds to Debate on Audiovisual Sector*, NUR 069 (14 October 1993).
[167] 1993 Scheduling Guidelines, [9]. See also Mattoo, 'National Treatment in the GATS', 119; WTO Secretariat, *A Handbook on the GATS Agreement* (2005) 38.
[168] 2001 Scheduling Guidelines, [16].
[169] Ibid., [15]; 1993 Scheduling Guidelines, [10]. But see Mattoo, 'National Treatment in the GATS', 120–1.
[170] Appellate Body Report, *US – Gambling*, [178].   [171] Marrakesh Agreement, art. IX:2.

of ambiguous GATS provisions.[172] The Appellate Body has also made clear that the 2001 Scheduling Guidelines do not constitute 'subsequent practice' for the purpose of interpreting GATS provisions or GATS schedules pursuant to Article 31(3)(b) of the VCLT.[173]

Nevertheless, if the interpretation adopted in both sets of Scheduling Guidelines is correct, this means that GATS imposes a potentially powerful discipline on providing discriminatory services subsidies.[174] Moreover, some Members may refrain from making national treatment commitments in subsidised service sectors precisely to avoid this discipline. The conclusion that a discriminatory subsidy could violate a GATS national treatment commitment also highlights the need to resolve the overlap and inconsistency between GATT 1994 and GATS. As services are sometimes 'embodied' in goods, 'as for example, the case of a compact disc on which music is recorded', 'some subsidies affecting the supply of services appear, or are treated as, subsidies on goods'.[175] Would WTO law treat a discriminatory subsidy that violated a GATS national treatment commitment differently if the subsidy fell within the SCM Agreement and complied with its provisions? Conversely, is the freedom flowing from the dearth of subsidy disciplines under GATS illusory, given that subsidies for cultural products might in any case be caught by GATT 1994 and the SCM Agreement?

3.4.4 *General exceptions (GATT Article XX, GATS Article XIV)*

A. Structure and *chapeau*

The most relevant paragraphs of GATT Article XX for cultural products read:

---

[172] Appellate Body Report, US – Gambling, [196]. On the Appellate Body's interpretative approach in relation to the 1993 and 2001 Scheduling Guidelines, see Federico Ortino, 'Treaty Interpretation and the WTO Appellate Body Report in US – Gambling: A Critique' (2006) 9(1) *Journal of International Economic Law* 117, 128-30.
[173] Appellate Body Report, US – Gambling, [193]. Chapter 4 explains the rules for interpreting WTO provisions, including in accordance with Article 31 of the VCLT.
[174] WTO, Working Party on GATS Rules, *Communication from Argentina and Hong Kong, China: Development of Multilateral Disciplines Governing Trade Distortive Subsidies in Services*, S/WPGR/W/31 (16 March 2000) [10(e)]; WTO, Working Party on GATS Rules, *Subsidies and Trade in Services: Note by the Secretariat*, S/WPGR/W/9 (6 March 1996) 8. See also Pierre Sauvé, 'Completing the GATS Framework: Addressing Uruguay Round Leftovers' (2002) 57(3) *Aussenwirtschaft* 301, 326.
[175] WTO, Working Party on GATS Rules, *Subsidies and Trade in Services: Note by the Secretariat*, S/WPGR/W/9 (6 March 1996) 4.

Subject to the requirement that such measures are not applied in a manner which would constitute a means of arbitrary or unjustifiable discrimination between countries where the same conditions prevail, or a disguised restriction on international trade, nothing in this Agreement shall be construed to prevent the adoption or enforcement by any Member of measures:
> (a) necessary to protect public morals;
> ...
> (f) imposed for the protection of national treasures of artistic, historic or archaeological value;[176]
> ...

To date, no Member has relied on Article XX(a) or (f) to justify a cultural policy measure. However, existing jurisprudence sheds light on how this argument would fare. The Appellate Body has ruled that the appropriate way to assess a measure under Article XX is first to determine whether the nature of the measure brings it within one of the listed exceptions – in paragraphs (a) to (j) – and then, if it does, to determine whether the measure is applied consistently with the '*chapeau*' (the opening paragraph of Article XX, as set out above). The burden of proof at both stages falls upon the respondent.[177]

Thus, assuming that a cultural policy measure could be provisionally justified under one of the paragraphs of GATT Article XX, the measure would then be assessed under the Article XX *chapeau*. As already mentioned,[178] Article XX in general and the *chapeau* in particular provide one means of minimising trade restrictions through judicial resolution on a case-by-case basis. In *US – Shrimp*, the Appellate Body identified three elements that must be shown in establishing that a measure is applied in a manner that constitutes 'a means of arbitrary or unjustifiable discrimination between countries where the same conditions prevail':

> First, the application of the measure must result in *discrimination*. As we stated in *United States – Gasoline*, the nature and quality of this discrimination is different from the discrimination in the treatment of products which was already found to be inconsistent with one of the substantive obligations of the GATT 1994, such as Articles I, III or XI. Second, the discrimination must be *arbitrary* or *unjustifiable* in character. ... Third, this discrimination must occur *between countries where the same conditions prevail*.[179]

---
[176] Cf. EC Treaty, art. 30.
[177] Appellate Body Report, *US – Shrimp*, [118]; Appellate Body Report, *US – Gasoline*, 22–3.
[178] Above, 66.
[179] Appellate Body Report, *US – Shrimp*, [150] (original emphasis, footnote omitted).

In this case, the Appellate Body also confirmed that the *chapeau* encompasses both discrimination among exporting Members (or among imports) and discrimination between exporting Members and the importing Member imposing the measure (or between imported and domestic products).[180] It appears that applying a measure may involve discrimination that is 'arbitrary or unjustifiable' contrary to the *chapeau* if it treats different WTO Members or products[181] differently in the absence of specific, objective criteria,[182] or if it treats all Members or their products in the same way as domestic products, without inquiring into the different conditions prevailing in the territories of those Members.[183] For reasons explored in Chapter 2, Members may have difficulty applying cultural policy measures based on specific, objective criteria and in a way that takes into account the different conditions in different countries. This might make it harder for a Member to justify a discriminatory cultural policy measure under Article XX.

As for what constitutes a 'disguised restriction on international trade' within the meaning of the Article XX *chapeau*, the Appellate Body has been less clear. In its first Report, *US – Gasoline*, the Appellate Body stated:

It is clear to us that 'disguised restriction' includes disguised *discrimination* in international trade. It is equally clear that *concealed* or *unannounced* restriction or discrimination in international trade does *not* exhaust the meaning of 'disguised restriction.' We consider that 'disguised restriction', whatever else it covers, may properly be read as embracing restrictions amounting to arbitrary or unjustifiable discrimination in international trade taken under the guise of a measure formally within the terms of an exception listed in Article XX. Put in a somewhat different manner, the kinds of considerations pertinent in deciding whether the application of a particular measure amounts to 'arbitrary or unjustifiable discrimination', may also be taken into account in determining the presence of a 'disguised restriction' on international trade. The fundamental theme is to be found in the purpose and object of avoiding abuse or illegitimate use of the exceptions to substantive rules available in Article XX.[184]

This passage suggests that a 'disguised restriction on international trade' overlaps to some extent with 'arbitrary or unjustifiable discrimination'. However, it is worth noting that a non-discriminatory measure

---

[180] Ibid. See also Appellate Body Report, *US – Gasoline*, 23–4.
[181] Panel Report, *Argentina – Hides and Leather*, [11.314].
[182] Panel Report, *EC – Tariff Preferences*, [7.232].
[183] Appellate Body Report, *US – Shrimp*, [164]–[166].
[184] Appellate Body Report, *US – Gasoline*, [25] (original emphasis).

could still be a 'disguised restriction on international trade'. This reading suggests a somewhat higher threshold for establishing that a measure is justified under the Article XX *chapeau*. In *US – Gasoline*, in assessing whether a challenged measure involved arbitrary or unjustifiable discrimination or a disguised restriction on international trade, the Appellate Body considered whether the objective of the measure could have been achieved in a non-discriminatory manner.[185] This approach brings the requirements of the *chapeau* closer to those of the paragraphs of Article XX that specify that the measure must be 'necessary' for achieving the relevant policy objective, even though in *US – Gasoline* the Appellate Body was considering whether a challenged measure was justified under paragraph (g), which covers measures 'relating to the conservation of exhaustible natural resources' and does not include the word 'necessary'. In any case, it would be just as consistent with the text of the *chapeau* (in particular, the reference to a 'disguised restriction on international trade') to examine whether the objective of the challenged measure could have been achieved in a non-trade-restrictive, or less trade-restrictive manner, even if it is not discriminatory. Again, this would make it difficult to justify a cultural policy measure under Article XX.

The Panel in *EC – Asbestos* also considered the meaning of a 'disguised restriction on international trade' in the Article XX *chapeau*. It explained that a restriction that 'formally meets the requirements' of one of the paragraphs of Article XX 'will constitute an abuse if such compliance is in fact only a disguise to conceal the pursuit of trade-restrictive objectives'.[186] Noting the difficulty of determining the objective of the challenged measure, the Panel borrowed from previous Appellate Body jurisprudence in relation to GATT Article III. Specifically, it referred to the relevance of the 'design, architecture and ... structure' of the measure in revealing its objectives, as described by the Appellate Body in *Japan – Alcoholic Beverages II*.[187] The Panel also examined the effects of the measure to determine whether it favoured domestic over foreign producers.[188] The Panel found that the EC's challenged measure was justified under Article XX(b) of GATT 1994. Canada appealed the Panel's findings with respect to paragraph (b), but not with respect to the *chapeau*, which the Appellate Body accordingly did not address. The Panel's approach involves something like an aims-and-effects test,

---

[185] Ibid., [25], [29].   [186] Panel Report, *EC – Asbestos*, [8.236].
[187] Ibid., [8.236]–[8.238].   [188] Ibid., [8.239].

which might prove more lenient towards cultural policy measures. However, as discussed earlier in relation to GATT Article III, if the aim and effect of a cultural policy measure is to protect domestic cultural industries, this is likely to be seen as a disguised restriction on trade even if it is an interim step towards promoting local culture.

GATS contains general exceptions under Article XIV, which is broadly equivalent to GATT Article XX. A measure falling within GATS Article XIV will not violate GATS, even if it otherwise appears to be inconsistent with another provision. GATS Article XIV provides, to the extent most relevant to cultural products:

Subject to the requirement that such measures are not applied in a manner which would constitute a means of arbitrary or unjustifiable discrimination between countries where like conditions prevail, or a disguised restriction on trade in services, nothing in this Agreement shall be construed to prevent the adoption or enforcement by any Member of measures:
(a) necessary to protect public morals or to maintain public order;[5]

[5] The public order exception may be invoked only where a genuine and sufficiently serious threat is posed to one of the fundamental interests of society.

Evidently, the exceptions included in GATS Article XIV are not identical to those in GATT Article XX, and where a similar exception is included it is not necessarily in identical terms. Nevertheless, the existing jurisprudence on individual exceptions under GATT 1994 may be relevant to an analysis of the general exceptions under GATS,[189] and vice versa.[190] All the exceptions in GATS Article XIV are subject to the *chapeau*, which is in similar terms to the *chapeau* of GATT Article XX. The Appellate Body has held, mirroring its reasoning under GATT Article XX, that an analysis of whether an otherwise inconsistent measure is justified under GATS Article XIV involves two steps. First, does the measure fall within one of the sub-paragraphs of Article XIV? Second, does the measure comply with the requirements of the *chapeau*?[191]

B. National treasures

Article XX(f) applies to measures 'imposed for the protection of national treasures of artistic, historic or archaeological value'. This provision recognises that Members' decisions to impose trade barriers in relation to cultural products may arise from a valid desire to preserve their cultural

[189] Appellate Body Report, *US – Gambling*, [291].
[190] Appellate Body Report, *Dominican Republic – Import and Sale of Cigarettes*, [69]-[70].
[191] Appellate Body Report, *US – Gambling*, [292].

heritage. Unlike some of the other Article XX paragraphs, paragraph (f) merely requires the measure to be 'imposed for' the purpose specified, rather than 'necessary' for that purpose. This could suggest that 'the relationship between the measure at stake and the legitimate policy'[192] reflected in paragraph (f) need not be as close as that required under certain other paragraphs of Article XX (although the Appellate Body's strict reading of the *chapeau* may limit the significance of this distinction).

Despite the potential for Article XX(f) to provide needed flexibility for cultural products, it has several limitations. First, the item in question must be not only a 'treasure' but also 'national'. This could prevent restrictions designed to protect a treasure that overlaps national boundaries or that is a treasure at some level that is less then national. Second, the exception does not refer to 'cultural value', so this concept is covered only to the extent that it is coextensive with 'artistic, historic or archaeological value'. New or 'current' products of the audiovisual and printing-publishing industries are unlikely to be of historic or archaeological value, and they might not be of sufficient artistic value to be described as national treasures. On one view, Article XX(f) 'should properly be read as relating to specific, physical artifacts of national importance, directed mainly to justify export rather than import restrictions'.[193] Graber even declares that 'this provision *obviously* cannot be alleged when trade in audio-visual media is concerned'.[194] Finally, a major problem with relying on this exception to justify discriminatory cultural policy measures is that no equivalent exception exists under GATS. This exclusion also supports the suggestion that 'national treasures' do not include products of the cultural industries.

Chapter 4 explains how international laws on culture and cultural property could assist in interpreting Article XX(f) and perhaps render it more useful in protecting cultural policy measures.[195]

C. Public morals and public order

The USA has suggested that GATT Article XX(a) represents one way in which WTO trade rules 'take into account the special cultural qualities of the [audiovisual] sector'.[196] The term 'public morals' in Article XX(a) is not defined, but Steve Charnovitz notes certain dictionary definitions of

---

[192] Appellate Body Report, *US – Shrimp*, [135] (discussing Article XX(g)).
[193] Broude, 'Geographical Indications and Cultural Protection', 682.
[194] Graber, 'Audio-Visual Policy', 200 (emphasis added).   [195] Below, 143.
[196] WTO, Council for Trade in Services, *Communication from the United States – Audiovisual and Related Services*, S/CSS/W/21 (18 December 2000) [8].

'moral' from the period of drafting that refer to what is right and wrong.[197] 'Trade measures tend to have multiple purposes',[198] and a cultural policy measure may be motivated by both cultural and moral concerns. This might make it difficult to establish that such a measure is necessary to protect public morals alone. Alternatively, it might be possible to view cultural concerns themselves as reflecting standards of public morality. Thus, for example, to the extent that a measure preventing the exhibition of programmes containing racial vilification[199] or pornography could be described as a matter of cultural policy (in that religious or broader cultural values may inform the measure), Article XX(a) may provide an exception for cultural policy measures.[200] However, Panels and the Appellate Body would have to interpret this provision broadly if it were to cover cultural policy measures more generally, and they might be reluctant to do so because this could expose the exception to abuse, not only in relation to culture and cultural industries[201] but also in an unknown range of other areas. Moreover, this exception is much less closely linked to typical notions of culture than is Article XX(f) (national treasures).[202] Panels and the Appellate Body might therefore conclude that Article XX(f) represents the limits of the cultural exception that WTO Members intended to provide, leaving Article XX(a) to deal with other measures protecting public morals.[203]

The central question under Article XX(a) is whether the challenged measure itself is 'necessary' to protect public morals, and not whether the discrimination in that measure is necessary to protect public morals.[204] As with any paragraph of Article XX that uses the term 'necessary', assessing whether the measure is 'necessary' to protect public morals under Article XX(a) will likely involve 'a process of

---

[197] Steve Charnovitz, 'The Moral Exception in Trade Policy' (1998) 38 *Virginia Journal of International Law* 689, 700.
[198] Ibid., 692.
[199] See, e.g., *Cable Television Networks Rules 1994* (India) GSR 729 (E), r. 6(c).
[200] See Christoph Feddersen, 'Focusing on Substantive Law in International Economic Relations: The Public Morals of GATT's Article XX(a) and "Conventional" Rules of Interpretation' (1998) 7 *Minnesota Journal of Global Trade* 75, 115.
[201] Broude also counsels against an overbroad reading of Article XX(a) of GATT 1994 in relation to culture: Broude, 'Geographical Indications and Cultural Protection', 681-2.
[202] See above, 104.
[203] Cf. Charnovitz, 'Moral Exception', 692; Jeremy Marwell, 'Trade and Morality: The WTO Public Morals Exception After Gambling' (2006) 81 *New York University Law Review* 802, 823.
[204] Appellate Body Report, *US – Gasoline*, 16.

weighing and balancing a series of factors',[205] including 'whether a proposed alternative to the impugned measure is reasonably available', which will depend on 'factors such as the trade impact of the measure, the importance of the interests protected by the measure, or the contribution of the measure to the realization of the end pursued'.[206] According to the Appellate Body, '[t]he more vital or important [the] common interests or values' pursued, the easier it is to fulfil the element of necessity.[207] Justifying a cultural policy measure under Article XX(a) may therefore depend on the importance that the Panel or Appellate Body attaches to cultural values. One might expect these bodies to regard these values as less important than, say, 'the preservation of human life and health through the elimination, or reduction, of the well-known, and life-threatening, health risks posed by asbestos fibres', which the Appellate Body has described as 'both vital and important in the highest degree'.[208] Nevertheless, as discussed further in Chapter 4, the connection between cultural products and cultural rights might assist in demonstrating necessity.[209]

As with GATT Article XX(a), the USA has suggested that GATS Article XIV(a) might apply to the audiovisual sector in view of its 'special cultural qualities'.[210] The Appellate Body's recent decision in *US – Gambling* demonstrates the similarity of the Appellate Body's approach in applying the general exceptions under GATT 1994 and GATS. In interpreting the word 'necessary' in Article XIV(a), the Appellate Body referred to its earlier reasoning in relation to GATT Article XX(d). Essentially, the question is whether a WTO-consistent measure is reasonably available instead of the challenged inconsistent measure to achieve the objective of protecting public morals.[211] GATS Article XIV(a) goes beyond GATT Article XX(a), in that it also refers to the maintenance of public order and explains the meaning of this term in

---

[205] Appellate Body Report, *Korea – Beef*, [164] (in the context of GATT 1994, art. XX(d)).
[206] Appellate Body Report, *Dominican Republic – Import and Sale of Cigarettes*, [70] (in the context of GATT 1994, Article XX(d)). See also GATT Panel Report, *Thailand – Cigarettes*, [75], [81]. For criticism of this approach, see Steve Charnovitz, 'An Analysis of Pascal Lamy's Proposal on Collective Preferences' (2005) 8(2) *Journal of International Economic Law* 449, 467–9.
[207] Appellate Body Report, *Korea – Beef*, [162].
[208] Appellate Body Report, *EC – Asbestos*, [172]. See also Footer, 'EC – Asbestos', 140–1.
[209] See below, 149.
[210] WTO, Council for Trade in Services, *Communication from the United States – Audiovisual and Related Services*, S/CSS/W/21 (18 December 2000) [8].
[211] Appellate Body Report, *US – Gambling*, [307].

108   STALEMATE AND ITS IDEOLOGICAL ORIGINS

footnote 5. Mavroidis has proposed a broad reading of the public order exception.[212]

Unfortunately, *US – Gambling* provides little guidance on the meaning of public morals or public order. The Panel did, however, exhibit a desire not to restrict the diversity of Members' values and regulatory objectives, stating:

> We are well aware that there may be sensitivities associated with the interpretation of the terms 'public morals' and 'public order' in the context of Article XIV. In the Panel's view, the content of these concepts for Members can vary in time and space, depending upon a range of factors, including prevailing social, cultural, ethical and religious values ... Members should be given some scope to define and apply for themselves the concepts of 'public morals' and 'public order' in their respective territories, according to their own systems and scales of values.[213]

The Panel went on to provide the following general definitions of terms contained in Article XIV(a):

> 'public morals' denotes standards of right and wrong conduct maintained by or on behalf of a community or nation.[214]

> 'public order' refers to the preservation of the fundamental interests of a society, as reflected in public policy and law. These fundamental interests can relate, *inter alia*, to standards of law, security and morality.[215]

Referring to several supplementary sources for their interpretation (namely a separate opinion by a judge of the ICJ, WTO trade policy reviews of individual Members, a draft convention put forward within the Economic Committee of the League of Nations, and the legal systems in several other jurisdictions), the Panel concluded that 'measures prohibiting gambling and betting services ... could fall within the scope of Article XIV(a) if they are enforced in pursuance of policies, the object and purpose of which is to "protect public morals" or "to maintain public order"'.[216] The Appellate Body upheld the Panel's finding in this regard without much analysis, due at least in part to the limited ground on which Antigua and Barbuda appealed it.[217]

For reasons mentioned earlier in relation to GATT Article XX(a), Panels and the Appellate Body may be unlikely to apply the exception for public morals in GATS Article XIV(a) to a cultural policy measure,

---

[212] Mavroidis, 'Like Products', 130–1.   [213] Panel Report, *US – Gambling*, [6.461].
[214] Ibid., [6.465].   [215] Ibid., [6.467].   [216] Ibid., [6.470]-[6.474].
[217] Appellate Body Report, *US – Gambling*, [296]-[299].

except to the extent that it corresponds with other matters ordinarily regarded as relating to 'standards of right and wrong conduct'.[218] For example, in Egypt, 'it is difficult to find a foreign film that does not offend the religious and social traditions of Egyptian society and, hence, will be allowed by the Censorship Authority over audio-visual products'.[219] This measure might involve de facto discrimination against foreign films, but, if it were covered by a national treatment commitment, it could well be saved under Article XIV(a). Chinese measures to prevent the promotion of 'western ideology and politics'[220] might be less easily characterised as measures protecting public morals. In Chapter 4, I return to the interpretation of Article XIV(a) and, in particular, the possibility of recognising cultural values or imperatives as 'fundamental interests of society' within the meaning of footnote 5 in this provision.[221]

3.5 The GATS outcome

3.5.1 Limited national treatment and market access commitments

Although it is part of the single undertaking to which all WTO Members subscribe, GATS is a 'made to measure' agreement. Members have significant flexibility in crafting their rights and obligations under GATS. Yet, as presently drafted, GATS contains no equivalent to the GATT 1994 provisions on subsidies, nor to GATT Article IV or XX(f). Combined with the uncertainty of the exception for public morals, the absence of such 'escape routes' or 'safety valves' may be one reason for Members' reluctance to make commitments in relation to cultural products under GATS. Of course, Members could make commitments in relation to cultural products subject to limitations, but, given the political sensitivity and significance of this issue for many Members, this could be too much of a concession. These limitations could also be more vulnerable to negotiation in future rounds than provisions of the GATS framework itself. This may explain most Members' apparent preference for refraining from making any commitments in relation to audiovisual services

---

[218] Panel Report, *US – Gambling*, [6.465].
[219] Ghoneim, 'Audio-Visual Sector in Egypt', 201.
[220] Joe McDonald, 'China Shuts Door on New Foreign TV Channels', *The Guardian* (Beijing, 5 August 2005). See also Eric Jones, *Cultures Merging: A Historical and Economic Critique of Culture* (2006) 208.
[221] Below, 149.

rather than making commitments subject to limitations.[222] As noted in Chapter 1, commitments under national treatment and market access are particularly scarce in relation to audiovisual services.[223] The fact that existing Members have frequently managed to persuade acceding Members to make these commitments[224] does not relieve the difficulties with the audiovisual sector. The accessions process may increase the level or proportion of commitments in this sector, but it cannot alter the limited or non-existent commitments of the many Members with major audiovisual industries. Thus, accessions can provide only a partial and inequitable solution.

I have already outlined the national treatment obligation under GATS.[225] The market access obligation under GATS involves a commitment not to maintain or adopt measures such as limitations on the number of service suppliers, the total value of service transactions, the total number of natural persons that may be employed in a particular service sector, or the participation of foreign capital.[226] In some ways this is analogous to the general prohibition on quantitative restrictions under GATT Article XI. However, Members have flexibility in relation to both national treatment and market access under GATS because these obligations apply only to the sectors and to the extent specified in each Member's relevant schedule.[227] For service sectors in which a Member has made no national treatment commitment, national treatment is not required; the same applies to market access. Where Members have made national treatment or market access commitments in a given sector, their GATS schedules may include agreed limitations on those commitments. These limitations demonstrate the kinds and extent of cultural policy measures that Members may wish to take.

Although commitments to printing and publishing services are not as limited as those to audiovisual services (perhaps because many periodicals and books are traded in physical form and clearly subject to GATT 1994 anyway), national treatment and market access limitations may reflect a cultural concern with respect to both. An example of a national treatment limitation regarding books or periodicals would be a nationality or residency requirement on editors.[228] In 2002, India stopped

---

[222] Roy, 'Audiovisual Services', 934–5; Adlung and Roy, 'Hills into Mountains', 1176.
[223] Above, 25.   [224] See above, 25, n. 145, and 26, n. 147.
[225] See above, 85.   [226] GATS, art. XVI:2.   [227] GATS, arts. XVI:1; XVII:1.
[228] WTO, *Iceland – Schedule of Specific Commitments*, GATS/SC/41 (15 April 1994).

applying its national treatment limitation on mode 3 (commercial presence) for certain film and video distribution services,[229] which required a certification by a prescribed authority that the film or video had, for example, won an award in an international film festival.[230] A common market access limitation in relation to the audiovisual industry that is listed by Members in their GATS schedules or otherwise applied by Members involves quotas. For example, Malaysia makes a commitment in its GATS Schedule to 'Communication Services – Audiovisual Services – Broadcasting services: covering transmission from foreign broadcast station of foreign broadcast matter from foreign territory through television or radio (7524*)'. This is subject to the following market access limitation in mode 1 (cross-border supply): '20 per cent of total screening time; and Dubbing into the national language may be required'.[231] According to the 1993 Scheduling Guidelines, a restriction on broadcasting time available for foreign films involves a market access limitation 'on the total number of service operations or quantity of service output'[232] (Article XVI:2(c)).

The fact that a Member has listed a limitation on its national treatment or market access commitment in a particular sector does not necessarily mean that it applies that limitation. India lists a market access limitation in mode 3 (commercial presence) for 'Communication Services – Audiovisual Services – Motion picture or video tape distribution services (CPC 96113)': the 'import of titles' is restricted to 100 per year.[233] In fact, this limitation was not applied even when the Uruguay Round was concluded. It was abolished in 1992.[234] Moreover, the fact that a law is on the books does not necessarily mean that it is enforced. In Egypt, a non-binding import quota of 300 foreign films per year has applied since 1973.[235] However, a trade restriction that is not enforced or not fully enforced may still have trade-restrictive 'chilling' effects.

Many Members make horizontal commitments (typically applicable to all service sectors included in the schedule), including horizontal limitations, especially for mode 3 (commercial presence). Canada

---

[229] Mukherjee, 'Audio-Visual Policies', 231.
[230] WTO, *India – Schedule of Specific Commitments*, GATS/SC/42 (15 April 1994).
[231] WTO, *Malaysia – Schedule of Specific Commitments*, GATS/SC/52 (15 April 1994).
[232] 1993 Scheduling Guidelines, [6(c)].
[233] WTO, *India – Schedule of Specific Commitments*, 8.
[234] Mukherjee, 'Audio-Visual Policies', 231, 245.
[235] Ghoneim, 'Audio-Visual Sector in Egypt', 200.

includes, in its GATS Schedule, a horizontal commitment for mode 3 except for banks. Its market access limitations on this commitment include:

> The acquisition of control of a Canadian business, or establishment of a new business related to Canada's cultural heritage or national identity, by a non-Canadian is subject to approval...[236]

Businesses 'related to Canada's cultural heritage and national identity' are defined to include persons engaged in publishing, distributing, or selling books or periodicals; producing, distributing, selling, or exhibiting film, video, or sound recordings; and radio, television, and cable broadcasting.[237] The responsible Minister will grant approval for the relevant acquisitions 'if he is satisfied that the investment is likely to be of net benefit to Canada', taking into account, where relevant, factors such as 'the compatibility of the investment with national industrial, economic and cultural policies'.[238]

Some limitations listed or applied by Members for services supplied by mode 3 are specific to cultural products. For example, Mexico lists a requirement that investors obtain a permit for film screening.[239] Thailand lists a 49 per cent limit on foreign equity participation for radio–television production and film–video production and distribution services.[240] According to WTO trade policy reviews, Australia and the USA restrict foreign control of television broadcasting licences.[241] Canada restricts foreign broadcasting competition through its policy that 'where a Canadian service is licensed in a format competitive with that of an authorized non-Canadian satellite service, the authority for the cable carriage of the non-Canadian service could be terminated'.[242] This policy led to a major dispute between Canada and the USA under NAFTA, when the CRTC revoked authority to distribute the US satellite service Country Music Television upon the granting of a broadcasting licence to the twenty-four hour Canadian music video service The

---

[236] WTO, *Canada – Schedule of Specific Commitments*, GATS/SC/16 (15 April 1994) 3.
[237] Ibid., 3.   [238] Ibid., 2.
[239] WTO, *Mexico – Schedule of Specific Commitments*, GATS/SC/56 (15 April 1994) 16–17.
[240] WTO, *Thailand – Schedule of Specific Commitments*, GATS/SC/85 (15 April 1994) 21.
[241] WTO, TPRB, *Trade Policy Review, Australia: Report by the Secretariat*, WT/TPR/S/104 (26 August 2002) [104]; WTO, TPRB, *Trade Policy Review, United States: Report by the Secretariat*, WT/TPR/S/126 (17 December 2003) [IV:32]; cf. WTO, TPRB, *Trade Policy Review, United States: Report by the Secretariat (Revision)*, WT/TPR/S/160/Rev.1 (20 June 2006) [IV:95].
[242] CRTC, *Revised Lists of Eligible Satellite Services*, Public Notice CRTC 1994-61 (6 June 1994); CRTC, *Structural Public Hearing*, Public Notice CRTC 1993-74 (3 June 1993).

Country Network.²⁴³ The matter was eventually settled by a commercial agreement to form a single network called Country Music Television (Canada).²⁴⁴

The EC makes in its GATS Schedule a commitment to 'Business Services – Other Business Services – Printing and Publishing (CPC 88442)'. It includes as a mode 3 market access limitation on this commitment, for Italy: 'Foreign participation in publishing companies limited to 49 per cent of capital or of voting rights'.²⁴⁵ The EC also makes a commitment to 'Recreational, Cultural and Sporting Services (other than Audio-visual Services) – News and Press Agency Services (CPC 962)', including a mode 3 market access limitation for France as follows: 'Foreign participation in companies publishing publications in the French language may not exceed 20 per cent of the capital or of voting rights in the company'.²⁴⁶ This market access limitation is not applied on an MFN basis and is therefore subject to an MFN exemption.

The WTO Secretariat has also commented that, in the audiovisual industries, 'where temporary working abroad is so frequent, the level of limitations in market access commitments for the presence of natural persons [mode 4] may suggest significant trade barriers'.²⁴⁷ Moreover, generally speaking, market access limitations under GATS (just like quantitative restrictions under GATT 1994) are contrary to the conclusion reached in Chapter 2 that cultural policy measures may legitimately need to discriminate but that they need not prohibit or restrict the influx of foreign cultural products.²⁴⁸

3.5.2 Excessive MFN exemptions

As with national treatment, the MFN obligation under GATS grants Members considerable flexibility. Although the MFN obligation applies to all sectors (rather than only those sectors listed in a Member's schedule), Members may specify exemptions from the MFN obligation in their

---

²⁴³ CRTC, *'The Country Network' – A Country Music Video Service – Approved*, Decision CRTC 94-284 (6 June 1994); CRTC, *Revised Lists of Eligible Satellite Services*, Public Notice CRTC 1994-61 (6 June 1994).
²⁴⁴ 'USTR Announces Commercial Agreement in the U.S. – Canada Country Music Television Dispute', press release 96-22 (7 March 1996).
²⁴⁵ WTO, *European Communities and their Member States – Schedule of Specific Commitments*, GATS/SC/31 (15 April 1994) 47.
²⁴⁶ Ibid., 84.
²⁴⁷ WTO, Council for Trade in Services, *Audiovisual Services: Background Note by the Secretariat*, S/C/W/40 (15 June 1998) [27].
²⁴⁸ See above, 66.

schedules. Specifically, GATS Article II:2 allows Members to maintain measures inconsistent with the MFN obligation in Article II:1 'provided that such a measure is listed in, and meets the conditions of, the Annex on Article II Exemptions'.

Members' MFN exemptions help us to understand certain kinds of discriminatory measures that Members may wish to impose on cultural grounds. The listed exemptions are particularly enlightening because the relevant annex provides for Members to explain the 'Conditions creating the need for the exemption'. Where a Member has listed an exemption from MFN, this does not necessarily mean that they will actually apply the exemption.[249] Just as a distinction arises under GATT 1994 between 'bound' and 'applied' tariff rates,[250] so too may a Member choose to provide more MFN treatment than it is bound to do under GATS. Nevertheless, the extent to which a Member is willing to bind itself under GATS is important.[251] For traders, a binding MFN obligation for a particular service sector under GATS (without exemptions) is likely to provide security and predictability in relation to the treatment of that sector. Therefore, the existence of this obligation may have a greater liberalising effect than a unilateral decision by a government to ensure MFN treatment. Members' listed MFN exemptions also provide examples of contemplated cultural policy measures, whether or not these are actually imposed and enforced.

A common exemption from MFN, which is often specified to be applied for cultural reasons, is for co-production arrangements for film or television. For example, Canada listed an exemption in film, video and television programming for differential treatment accorded to co-productions subject to co-production agreements or arrangements with particular countries. The exemption is needed, *inter alia*, '[f]or reasons of cultural policy'.[252] Israel exempted co-production arrangements for the same reason,[253] while many other Members listed similar

---

[249] 'A Member *may* maintain a measure inconsistent with paragraph 1 provided that such a measure is listed in, and meets the conditions of, the Annex on Article II Exemptions' (emphasis added): GATS, art. II.
[250] A Member's 'bound' tariff rate is the maximum rate it commits to impose; its 'applied' tariff rate is the rate it actually imposes, which may be lower than the bound rate.
[251] Bernard Hoekman, 'Toward a More Balanced and Comprehensive Services Agreement' in Jeffrey Schott (ed.), *The WTO After Seattle* (2000) 119, 125.
[252] WTO, *Canada – Final List of Article II (MFN) Exemptions*, GATS/EL/16 (15 April 1994).
[253] WTO, *Israel – Final List of Article II (MFN) Exemptions*, GATS/EL/44 (15 April 1994).

exemptions 'for cultural reasons';[254] to promote 'cultural links',[255] 'common cultural objectives'[256] or 'cultural exchange';[257] or to 'maintain the Arab culture and identity'.[258] Co-production arrangements typically provide the benefit of national treatment to works covered by the arrangements, for example 'in respect of access to finance and tax concessions and simplified requirements for the temporary entry of skilled personnel'.[259]

Some MFN exemptions refer to arrangements specifically designed to promote regional culture, or the culture of a particular group of countries. Thus, Norway listed an MFN exemption for producing and distributing cinematographic works and television programmes in Nordic countries (i.e. Finland, Norway, Sweden, Iceland and Denmark). This exemption is aimed at the '[p]reservation and promotion of the regional identity of the countries concerned'.[260] An EC exemption from MFN refers to audiovisual works of 'European origin' and the need to 'promote cultural values both within EC Member States and with other countries in Europe, as well as achieving linguistic policy objectives'.[261] This exemption is presumably intended to cover the EC's Television Without Frontiers Directive.[262] However, co-production arrangements are not necessarily entered into by culturally similar or geographically close or related countries. Australia's listed MFN exemption for these arrangements covers 'Italy, UK, Canada and France and any other country where cultural co-operation might be desirable and which is prepared to exchange preferential treatment on the terms and conditions specified in the Australian co-production programme'.[263] In 2001, 85 per cent of requests for co-production status in Canada came from

---

[254] See, e.g., WTO, *New Zealand – Final List of Article II (MFN) Exemptions*, GATS/EL/62 (15 April 1994).
[255] See, e.g., WTO, *European Communities and their Member States – Final List of Article II (MFN) Exemptions*, GATS/EL/31 (15 April 1994); WTO, *The Hashemite Kingdom of Jordan – Final List of Article II MFN Exemptions*, GATS/EL/128 (15 December 2000).
[256] See, e.g., WTO, *Switzerland – Final List of Article II (MFN) Exemptions*, GATS/EL/83 (15 April 1994).
[257] See, e.g., WTO, *Brazil – Final List of Article II (MFN) Exemptions*, GATS/EL/13 (15 April 1994); WTO, *India – Final List of Article II (MFN) Exemptions*, GATS/EL/42 (15 April 1994).
[258] WTO, *Egypt – Final List of Article II (MFN) Exemptions*, GATS/EL/30 (15 April 1994).
[259] WTO, *Australia – Final List of Article II (MFN) Exemptions*, GATS/EL/6 (15 April 1994).
[260] WTO, *Norway – Final List of Article II (MFN) Exemptions*, GATS/EL/66 (15 April 1994).
[261] WTO, *European Communities and Their Member States – Final List of Article II (MFN) Exemptions*, GATS/EL/31 (15 April 1994).
[262] Above, 94.
[263] WTO, *Australia – Final List of Article II (MFN) Exemptions*, GATS/EL/6 (15 April 1994).

the UK, France, China, and Australia.[264] And Israel has co-production agreements with Australia, Belgium, Canada, France, Germany, Italy, and Sweden.[265] Co-production arrangements are not necessarily made between countries. Canada lists a separate MFN exemption for co-production arrangements with Québec.[266]

Another example of an MFN exemption, but one that could be said to involve a cultural policy measure in relation to printed material as opposed to audiovisual services, is found in the EC's list of MFN exemptions. The EC lists (under 'Newsagency services', rather than 'Printing, publishing') 'Foreign participation in companies in France publishing publications in the French language exceeding 20% of the capital or of voting rights in the company, subject to a condition of reciprocity'.[267] However, this exemption would allow more favourable treatment for countries providing similar treatment, which seems less about culture than opening foreign markets to French investment. This is consistent with the measure's justification, which is described as: 'Need to ensure effective market access and equivalent treatment for French service suppliers'.[268]

Most of these exemptions conflict with the suggestion in Chapter 2 that cultural policy measures may achieve their cultural goals without resorting to express discrimination between foreign cultural products[269] (meaning, under GATS, services or service suppliers). However, GATS itself recognises that these exemptions may be unnecessarily trade-distorting. The GATS Annex on Article II Exemptions (i.e. MFN exemptions) includes the following provisions:

5. The exemption of a Member from its obligations under paragraph 1 of Article II of the Agreement with respect to a particular measure terminates on the date provided for in the exemption.
6. In principle, such exemptions shall not exceed a period of 10 years. In any event, they shall be subject to negotiation in subsequent trade-liberalizing rounds.

---

[264] Acheson and Maule, 'Canada – Audiovisual Policies', 175.
[265] WTO, Council for Trade in Services, *Communication from Israel – Review of Article II Exemptions: Replies to Questions Posed on Israel's MFN Exemptions in the Area of Audiovisual Services in the Course of the Review of MFN Exemptions*, S/C/W/158 (10 July 2000).
[266] WTO, *Canada – Final List of Article II (MFN) Exemptions*, GATS/EL/16 (15 April 1994) 1.
[267] WTO, *European Communities and Their Member States – Final List of Article II (MFN) Exemptions*, GATS/EL/31 (15 April 1994) 6.
[268] Ibid., 6.   [269] See above, 60.

As the Marrakesh Agreement came into force on 1 January 1995, the ten-year period mentioned in paragraph 6 expired on 31 December 2004. These paragraphs could therefore provide a solution to ongoing MFN exemptions in connection with cultural products. However, the text does not state explicitly which paragraph prevails in the event of a conflict. For example, if a Member's MFN exemption is expressed to last indefinitely or to terminate after twenty years, does this express declaration, pursuant to paragraph 5, prevail over the suggestion in paragraph 6 that exemptions should last a maximum of ten years? The words '[i]n principle' in paragraph 6 could suggest that the ten-year period prevails. Alternatively, these words could suggest that the ten-year limitation is flexible and subject to express contrary indications in the exemptions listed by individual Members. WTO Members have been addressing these issues in the Council for Trade in Services and have not yet reached agreement on how to treat existing MFN exemptions.[270] Accordingly, these exemptions may remain in force despite the inbuilt time limit.

If these exemptions expired, Members would still have some leeway in pursuing cultural policy measures contrary to the MFN rule. Most significantly, GATS Article V:1 states that GATS does not prevent Members from entering economic integration agreements to liberalise trade in services. This is analogous to the exception for free trade areas and customs unions under Article XXIV:5 of GATT 1994. Nevertheless, the requirements under GATS Article V appear less stringent than the equivalent conditions in GATT Article XXIV,[271] such that it might be easier for a Member to justify a cultural policy measure under the former provision. This might exempt, for example, an agreement on co-producing film or television programmes made among parties to a broader agreement to liberalise trade in services, depending on the structure of the co-production agreement and the broader liberalisation agreement.[272]

3.6 Conclusion

The current GATS negotiations are to 'take place within and ... respect the existing structure and principles of GATS, including the right to specify sectors in which commitments will be undertaken and the four

---

[270] See, e.g., WTO, Council for Trade in Services, *Report of the Meeting Held on 30 November 2004: Note by the Secretariat*, S/C/M/76 (4 February 2005).
[271] Bernard Hoekman, *Tentative First Steps: An Assessment of the Uruguay Round Agreement on Services*, World Bank Policy Research Working Paper 1455 (1995) 8.
[272] Cocq and Messerlin, 'French Audio-Visual Policy', 25.

modes of supply'.[273] The GATS structure and principles appear to be designed to ensure 'an overall balance of rights and obligations, while giving due respect to national policy objectives', as stated in the preamble. But the outcome for audiovisual services has tipped too far in favour of Members' rights to regulate as they see fit, because few Members have made any commitments in this sector. This is not a problem merely for other Members (such as the USA and Chile)[274] seeking to diminish barriers to trade in audiovisual services. Even those Members who wish to promote or preserve their cultural industries for cultural reasons (such as the EC and Canada) may have complex motives and interests. The EC may be competitive in sound recordings[275] and wish to open foreign markets to these products. Australia may want to retain local content requirements on broadcasting[276] but open foreign markets to its own cultural products.[277] If the EC had included audiovisual policies in its GATS schedule, this could also have shielded it from 'unilateral trade pressures from the US'.[278] Opening markets for cultural products, with appropriate safeguards for cultural policy, is in all Members' interests.

The underlying problem is that cultural products are treated quite differently in WTO law depending on whether they are classified as goods or as services. To the extent that they are goods they are subject to exacting disciplines under GATT 1994. The only special treatment for these particular products is in Article IV, with respect to screen quotas. At the same time, GATT 1994 offers additional leeway for Members imposing cultural policy measures through generally applicable provisions such as the allowance for certain kinds of subsidies. In contrast, to the extent that cultural products are services, GATS simultaneously imposes fewer general disciplines and offers fewer general escape routes. Members may refrain from making national treatment or market access commitments in relation to cultural products under GATS, but if they do make unlimited commitments of this kind they may be

---

[273] WTO, Council for Trade in Services, *Guidelines and Procedures for the Negotiations on Trade in Services*, S/L/93 (29 March 2001) [4].
[274] See below, 193.   [275] Held *et al.*, *Global Transformations*, 353.
[276] See, e.g., Donald Rothwell, 'Quasi-Incorporation of International Law in Australia: Broadcasting Standards, Cultural Sovereignty and International Trade' (1999) 27(3) *Federal Law Review* 527.
[277] See generally Australian Department of Communications Information Technology and the Arts, *Report on Access to Overseas Markets for Australia's Creative Digital Industry* (12 December 2003).
[278] Falkenberg, 'Audiovisual Sector', 432.

more restricted in granting subsidies than under GATT 1994, and they do not have the comfort of an exemption for screen quotas. In the absence of a judicial willingness to accept that cultural products may not be 'like' for reasons of culture, the present GATS framework limits the amount of liberalisation that can be achieved for cultural products (particularly audiovisuals). In addition, the disparity of treatment under GATT 1994 and GATS aggravates uncertainties regarding matters such as classifying digital products as goods or services, applying more than one WTO agreement to a single cultural policy measure, and the scope of exceptions for public morals, national treasures, and screen quotas.

If the status quo were maintained, this would likely restrict further liberalisation in the cultural industries (especially under GATS), hampering the goal of liberalisation among WTO Members and its attendant benefits. It would also leave several areas of uncertainty and the likelihood of additional WTO disputes regarding the cultural industries in future. These factors should concern Members on both sides of the trade–culture debate.

PART II

Options for the future

4 Resolution through dispute settlement and international law

Article 31(3)(c) of the *Vienna Convention* ... mandates the consideration of *non*-WTO international legal rules in the interpretation of WTO treaties – rules that may reflect or prioritize other values and interests than those of trade liberalization ...[1]

4.1 Introduction

All laws involve some unsettled aspects, and ambiguity may even be deliberate, to accommodate the views of different individuals or groups involved in drafting. The drafters of the WTO agreements recognised that they could not anticipate every issue that might arise in future, revealing ambiguities in the text. Accordingly, one of the purposes of the WTO dispute settlement system is to clarify the meaning of the provisions and hence provide security and predictability in international trade.[2] One possible solution to the difficulties with the current treatment of cultural products under WTO law is to leave the relevant provisions as they stand, while allowing the organs of WTO dispute settlement to resolve uncertainties where appropriate and, perhaps, to develop pragmatic compromises in the absence of explicit guidance in the text. Effectively, this is the approach that WTO Members have taken to this problem since the WTO agreements came into force on 1 January 1995. Indeed, this is the way that WTO Members have dealt with most

---

[1] Robert Howse, 'Adjudicative Legitimacy and Treaty Interpretation in International Trade Law: The Early Years of WTO Jurisprudence' in Joseph Weiler (ed.), *The EU, the WTO and the NAFTA: Towards a Common Law of International Trade* (2000) 35, 55 (original emphasis).
[2] DSU, art. 3.2.

problems and ambiguities in the WTO agreements since the mid-1990s.[3] However, only one dispute on cultural products has proceeded to the stage of a Panel Report being circulated, namely *Canada – Periodicals*. The DSB adopted the Panel and Appellate Body Reports in that dispute on 30 July 1997.[4] This leaves considerable scope for speculation about how other cultural policy measures would be assessed if challenged in future.

One promising possibility for improving the treatment of cultural products through WTO dispute settlement arises from public international law regarding cultural products, cultural rights, and other aspects of culture. As explained below, international law affects the interpretation of WTO provisions in WTO disputes through Article 3.2 of the DSU and, indirectly, Article 31 of the VCLT. Panels and the Appellate Body have already made use of these provisions to consider international law in several previous disputes, but not yet in relation to cultural policy measures. If they extended their consideration of international law, could they improve the current treatment of cultural products under WTO law simply by interpreting existing provisions relevant to cultural products in a particular way? Below, I consider the likelihood, legitimacy, and desirability (from the perspective of the WTO Membership) of WTO law on cultural products evolving through dispute settlement and international law. For the moment, I focus on *interpretation* and leave to one side the questions of how international law on culture might influence the conduct of WTO Members, give rise to a WTO violation, or be *applied* in a WTO dispute as an independent defence to a WTO violation.

4.2 The role of international law in interpreting WTO law

In explaining the role of international law in interpreting WTO law, I first present the main legal provision on this interpretation, namely Article 3.2 of the DSU, which refers implicitly to Articles 31 and 32 of the VCLT. I then consider the Appellate Body's use of international law in interpreting specific WTO provisions in its decisions to date.

---

[3] See Tomer Broude, *International Governance in the WTO: Judicial Boundaries and Political Capitulation* (2004) 61–4.
[4] See above, 9, n. 42.

4.2.1 Relevant provisions
A. Article 3.2 of the DSU

Article 3.2 of the DSU explains the objectives of WTO dispute settlement, and the correct way of interpreting WTO provisions, as follows:

> The dispute settlement system of the WTO is a central element in providing security and predictability to the multilateral trading system. The Members recognize that it serves to preserve the rights and obligations of Members under the covered agreements, and to clarify the existing provisions of those agreements in accordance with customary rules of interpretation of public international law. Recommendations and rulings of the DSB cannot add to or diminish the rights and obligations provided in the covered agreements.

In connection with the use of international law in WTO disputes, Article 3.2 imposes two key requirements. First, public international law clearly plays a part, at least to the extent that it provides 'customary rules' regarding the 'interpretation' of WTO agreements. Along the same lines, Article 17.6(ii) of the Anti-Dumping Agreement provides, specifically in the anti-dumping context, that 'the panel shall interpret the relevant provisions of the Agreement in accordance with customary rules of interpretation of public international law'.[5] Second, public international law cannot be used to replace or supplement the WTO agreements if this would amount to increasing or diminishing the 'rights and obligations' provided under those agreements. In Howse's view, these two principles fit neatly together: 'when the AB is interpreting existing provisions in accordance with the customary rules (including their dynamic dimension) it is not, impermissibly, adding [to] or diminishing ... existing obligations'.[6] Similarly, the Appellate Body itself has stated that it has 'difficulty in envisaging circumstances in which a panel could add to the rights and obligations of a Member of the WTO if its conclusions reflected a correct interpretation and application of provisions of the covered agreements'.[7] As discussed in

---

[5] The Appellate Body has treated this first sentence of Article 17.6(ii) of the Anti-Dumping Agreement as simply confirming that the usual rules of treaty interpretation under the DSU apply: Appellate Body Report, *US – Hot-Rolled Steel*, [57].

[6] Robert Howse, 'The Most Dangerous Branch? WTO Appellate Body Jurisprudence on the Nature and Limits of the Judicial Power' in Thomas Cottier and Petros Mavroidis, *The Role of the Judge in International Trade Regulation: Experience and Lessons for the WTO* (2003) 11, 15.

[7] Appellate Body Report, *Chile – Alcoholic Beverages*, [79]. See also ILC, UN, *Fragmentation of International Law: Difficulties Arising from the Diversification and Expansion of International Law – Report of the Study Group – Finalized by Martti Koskenniemi*, A/CN.4/L.682 (13 April 2006) [447].

Chapter 5, others contend that the last sentence of Article 3.2 limits the application of non-WTO international law within WTO dispute settlement.

I now examine the meaning of 'customary rules of interpretation of public international law' in Article 3.2.

B. Article 31 of the VCLT

In its first appeal, in 1996, the Appellate Body identified Article 31(1) of the VCLT as expressing 'a fundamental rule of treaty interpretation' that had 'attained the status of a rule of customary or general international law' and was, therefore, a rule to be applied in interpreting the WTO agreements in accordance with Article 3.2 of the DSU.[8] Since then, the Appellate Body has confirmed the status of the interpretative rules in the VCLT on several occasions,[9] so that it is now 'well settled in WTO case law that the principles codified in Articles 31 and 32 of the *Vienna Convention* ... are ... customary rules' of interpretation within the meaning of Article 3.2 of the DSU.[10] In their statements at DSB meetings adopting Appellate Body Reports, Members (including the USA) have generally supported the Appellate Body's reading of Article 3.2 of the DSU as including a reference to at least certain interpretative principles in the VCLT.[11] Although, as Michael Lennard points out, the USA and some other WTO Members are not party to the VCLT,[12] this does not matter as these rules form part of customary international law.

Perhaps the most important provision of the VCLT in the context of WTO dispute settlement is Article 31, which provides:

---

[8] Appellate Body Report, *US – Gasoline*, 16–17.
[9] See, e.g., Appellate Body Report, *EC – Computer Equipment*, [84]; Appellate Body Report, *EC – Sardines*, [200]; Appellate Body Report, *India – Patents (US)*, [46]; Appellate Body Report, *Japan – Alcoholic Beverages II*, 10.
[10] Appellate Body Report, *US – Carbon Steel*, [61].
[11] See, e.g., WTO, DSB, *Minutes of Meeting Held in the Centre William Rappard 25 September 1997*, WT/DSB/M/37 (4 November 1997) 15 (statement by the EC); WTO, DSB, *Minutes of Meeting Held in the Centre William Rappard on 16 January 1998*, WT/DSB/M/40 (18 February 1998) 3, 8 (statement by India); WTO, DSB, *Minutes of Meeting Held in the Centre William Rappard on 23 May 1997*, WT/DSB/M/33 (25 June 1997) 10 (statement by the USA); WTO, DSB, *Minutes of Meeting Held in the Centre William Rappard on 23 October 2002*, WT/DSB/M/134 (29 January 2003) [48] (statement by Mexico).
[12] Michael Lennard, 'Navigating by the Stars: Interpreting the WTO Agreements' (2002) 5(1) *Journal of International Economic Law* 17, 18–19.

Article 31
General rule of interpretation
1. A treaty shall be interpreted in good faith in accordance with the ordinary meaning to be given to the terms of the treaty in their context and in the light of its object and purpose.
2. The context for the purpose of the interpretation of a treaty shall comprise, in addition to the text, including its preamble and annexes:
   (a) any agreement relating to the treaty which was made between all the parties in connection with the conclusion of the treaty;
   (b) any instrument which was made by one or more parties in connection with the conclusion of the treaty and accepted by the other parties as an instrument related to the treaty.
3. There shall be taken into account, together with the context:
   (a) any subsequent agreement between the parties regarding the interpretation of the treaty or the application of its provisions;
   (b) any subsequent practice in the application of the treaty which establishes the agreement of the parties regarding its interpretation;
   (c) any relevant rules of international law applicable in the relations between the parties.
4. A special meaning shall be given to a term if it is established that the parties so intended.

Based on Article 31(1) of the VCLT, the Appellate Body for many years gave overwhelming precedence to the text, while frequently supplementing its textual examination with a consideration of the context and object and purpose. Joseph Weiler once described this as a textual 'obsession'.[13] A primarily textual approach means that Members would be less able to justify their cultural policy measures by encouraging a particular interpretation of WTO provisions if this interpretation was not grounded in the text, regardless of the implications of international law and the legitimacy of their cultural objectives. However, from the beginning, the Appellate Body confirmed that GATT 1994 'is not to be read in clinical isolation from public international law'.[14] Moreover, more recently, 'the Appellate Body appears to be trying to emancipate itself from a rigorous textual approach'.[15] Although it may still have some way to go, this may

---

[13] See Joseph Weiler, 'The Rule of Lawyers and the Ethos of Diplomats: Reflections on the Internal and External Legitimacy of WTO Dispute Settlement' (2001) 35 *Journal of World Trade* 191, 206.
[14] Appellate Body Report, *US – Gasoline*, 17.
[15] Ortino, 'Treaty Interpretation', 120. See also Robert Howse and Susan Esserman, 'The Appellate Body, the WTO Dispute Settlement System, and the Politics of

improve the chances of public international law influencing the interpretation of WTO law as regards cultural products.

As demonstrated in the next section, the Appellate Body has used international law in interpreting WTO provisions primarily based on Article 31(1) of the VCLT, and in particular in determining the 'ordinary meaning' of particular words. In addition, the Appellate Body has sometimes referred to international law in reliance on Article 31(3)(c) of the VCLT. I consider these two situations in turn. Article 32 of the VCLT could also allow recourse to international law or preparatory material as a 'supplementary means of interpretation' to confirm the meaning resulting from Article 31 or to determine the meaning where the application of Article 31 leaves the meaning ambiguous or leads to a manifestly absurd or unreasonable result. However, Article 31 is more pertinent than Article 32 to the discussion below.

4.2.2 Use of international law by the Appellate Body
A. Significance of past Appellate Body Reports

In this section, I consider the use of international law by the Appellate Body in its decisions to date, as a basis for understanding the potential for WTO law regarding cultural products to evolve through interpretation in the light of international law. Before addressing the Appellate Body's substantive statements in this regard, I explain the precedential value of these statements in predicting future approaches, as well as my decision to focus on Reports of the Appellate Body (rather than Panels).

The DSU imposes no formal principle of *stare decisis* on Panels or the Appellate Body.[16] Accordingly, adopted Panel and Appellate Body Reports[17] 'are not binding, except with respect to resolving the particular dispute between the parties to that dispute'.[18] Nevertheless, the Appellate Body has held that adopted Panel and Appellate Body Reports[19] 'create legitimate expectations among WTO Members, and, therefore, should be taken into account where they are relevant to any dispute'.[20] In explaining this approach, the Appellate Body has noted

---

Multilateralism' in Giorgio Sacerdoti, Alan Yanovich, and Jan Bohanes (eds.), *The WTO at Ten: The Contributions of the Dispute Settlement System* (2006) 61, 72–4.

[16] See generally Raj Bhala, 'The Myth About Stare Decisis and International Trade Law (Part One of a Trilogy)' (1999) 14 *American University International Law Review* 845.
[17] Appellate Body Report, *US – Shrimp (Article 21.5 – Malaysia)*, [109].
[18] Appellate Body Report, *Japan – Alcoholic Beverages II*, 14.
[19] Appellate Body Report, *US – Shrimp (Article 21.5 – Malaysia)*, [109].
[20] Appellate Body Report, *Japan – Alcoholic Beverages II*, 14.

that Article 59 of the Statute of the ICJ indicates that '[t]he decision of the Court has no binding force except between the parties and in respect of that particular case', but this has not prevented the ICJ from developing 'a body of case law in which considerable reliance on the value of previous decisions is readily discernible'.[21]

The Appellate Body recently declared that 'following the Appellate Body's conclusions in earlier disputes is not only appropriate, but is what would be expected from panels, especially where the issues are the same'.[22] This concern for Members' expectations may stem in part from the emphasis in Article 3.2 of the DSU on dispute settlement 'providing security and predictability to the multilateral trading system'.[23] If Panels and the Appellate Body frequently adopted new interpretations of or contrary approaches to the covered agreements, it could be difficult for Members to plan and structure their trading systems and laws consistent with their WTO obligations. Therefore, Panels and the Appellate Body routinely take into account previous Panel and Appellate Body decisions, and Panel and Appellate Body Reports are typically consistent with previous Appellate Body Reports.[24] One can therefore expect that the Appellate Body will approach international law in future disputes in a manner that is broadly in line with previous decisions.

Panels have sometimes disagreed with or refused to follow particular Appellate Body rulings.[25] However, Panel demonstrations of this kind of independence are rare, as one might expect.[26] In addition, the Appellate Body has pointed out that a Panel ruling that is adopted by the DSB without being specifically appealed, while reflecting final resolution of the dispute at issue, cannot be taken as being approved by the Appellate Body and is open to re-examination in a subsequent appeal.[27] Therefore,

---

[21] Ibid., n. 30. See also Mohamed Shahabuddeen, *Precedent in the World Court* (1996).
[22] Appellate Body Report, *US – Oil Country Tubular Goods Sunset Reviews*, [188].
[23] See Appellate Body Report, *US – Softwood Lumber V*, [112].
[24] See generally Raj Bhala, 'The Precedent Setters: De Facto Stare Decisis in WTO Adjudication (Part Two of a Trilogy)' (1999) 9 *Journal of Transnational Law and Policy* 1. See also Raj Bhala, 'The Power of the Past: Towards De Jure Stare Decisis in WTO Adjudication (Part Three of a Trilogy)' (2001) 33 *George Washington International Law Review* 873.
[25] See, e.g., Panel Report, *Argentina – Preserved Peaches*, [7.24]; Panel Report, *US – Upland Cotton*, [7.623]; Panel Report, *US – Zeroing (Japan)*, [7.99]. See also Panel Report, *Brazil – Aircraft (Article 21.5 – Canada II)*, [5.243], [5.245].
[26] See Waincymer, *WTO Litigation*, 514.
[27] Appellate Body Report, *Canada – Periodicals*, n. 28.

it makes sense to pay particular attention to Appellate Body rulings. On occasion, the Appellate Body has also distanced itself from or distinguished the reasoning in a previous Appellate Body decision.[28] At other times, the Appellate Body has adopted different reasoning or a different emphasis in interpreting a particular provision, without expressly acknowledging any change.[29] It is therefore worth keeping in mind that, in the right circumstances, the Appellate Body might implicitly or explicitly accept a novel argument in relation to the use of international law.

B. Ordinary meaning (VCLT Article 31(1))

Two decisions demonstrate the Appellate Body's willingness to consider general international law in determining the ordinary meaning of particular words in accordance with Article 31(1) of the VCLT, pursuant to Article 3.2 of the DSU: *US – Shrimp* and *EC – Tariff Preferences*. I consider the Appellate Body's use of international instruments in these two disputes before turning to the time at which an interpreter should identify the 'ordinary meaning' of a treaty term.

(i) Relevance of international instruments

In one of the earliest and best-known WTO disputes, *US – Shrimp*, India, Malaysia, Pakistan, and Thailand challenged a US ban on certain shrimp imports, purportedly imposed to protect sea turtles from accidental capture during shrimp harvesting. The Panel found this ban inconsistent with Article XI:1 of GATT 1994 and not justified under GATT Article XX.[30] The appeal centred on Article XX(g), which concerns measures 'relating to the conservation of exhaustible natural resources'.[31]

The Appellate Body held that the words 'exhaustible natural resources' in Article XX(g) 'must be read by a treaty interpreter in the light of contemporary concerns of the community of nations about the protection and conservation of the environment'.[32] On this basis, it concluded

---

[28] See, e.g., the reference to the Appellate Body Report in *US – Section 211 Appropriations Act* in Appellate Body Report, *US – Corrosion-Resistant Steel Sunset Review*, n. 94.

[29] For example, compare the following two reports: Appellate Body Report, *EC – Bed Linen*, [55]–[60]; Appellate Body Report, *US – Softwood Lumber V*, [90]–[103]. See also Appellate Body Report, *Argentina – Footwear (EC)*, [130]–[131]; Appellate Body Report, *US – Steel Safeguards*, [345]–[361].

[30] Appellate Body Report, *US – Shrimp*, [2]–[7].

[31] On the general structure of Article XX of GATT 1994 and the interpretation of its *chapeau*, see above, 100.

[32] Appellate Body Report, *US – Shrimp*, [129].

that the words 'natural resources' include living resources,[33] drawing support from the *United Nations Convention on the Law of the Sea*,[34] the Convention on Biological Diversity, and the Resolution on Assistance to Developing Countries adopted in conjunction with the Convention on Migratory Species. Then, in holding that sea turtles were 'exhaustible' natural resources, within the meaning of Article XX(g), the Appellate Body referred to[35] the *Convention on International Trade in Endangered Species of Wild Fauna and Flora*.[36] The Appellate Body recognised that not all WTO Members, nor even the parties to this dispute, were party to all these international instruments.[37] This suggests that the Appellate Body considered that this was not a necessary requirement for it to examine these instruments, indicating that it did not intend to rely on them as 'relevant rules of international law applicable in the relations between the parties' under Article 31(3)(c) of the VCLT (although some authors suggest it did so).[38] Rather, it appears that the Appellate Body was relying on these instruments as evidence of the ordinary meaning of the words in question under Article 31(1) of the VCLT, an approach that seems justified.[39]

The Panel in the *EC – Biotech* case also seemed to read the Appellate Body's reference to international instruments in *US – Shrimp* in this way. The Panel stated:

[A]s we understand it, the Appellate Body drew on other rules of international law because it considered that they were informative and aided it in establishing the meaning and scope of the term 'exhaustible natural resources'. The European Communities correctly points out that the Appellate Body referred to conventions which were not applicable to all disputing parties. However, the mere fact that one or more disputing parties are not parties to a convention does not necessarily mean that a convention cannot shed light on the meaning and scope of a treaty term to be interpreted.[40]

The Panel Report was not appealed.

---

[33] Ibid., [130]–[131]. [34] 1833 UNTS 3; 21 ILM 1261 (adopted 10 December 1982).
[35] Appellate Body Report, *US – Shrimp*, [132].
[36] UNTS 243; 12 ILM 1085 (adopted 3 March 1973).
[37] Appellate Body Report, *US – Shrimp*, nn. 110–11, 113.
[38] See, e.g., Campbell McLachlan, 'The Principle of Systemic Integration and Article 31(3)(c) of the Vienna Convention' (2005) 54 *International & Comparative Law Quarterly* 279, 315. Cf Pauwelyn, *Conflict of Norms*, 256.
[39] Pauwelyn, *Conflict of Norms*, 260; McLachlan, 'Principle of Systemic Integration', 315.
[40] Panel Report, *EC – Biotech*, [7.94] (see also [7.92]).

In *US – Shrimp*, the Appellate Body went on to find that the challenged measures were measures 'relating to' the conservation of exhaustible natural resources within the meaning of Article XX(g) because the means used by the USA was 'reasonably related to the ends' of protecting sea turtles.[41] (Incidentally, this demonstrates how, in addition to the *chapeau* of Article XX, words like 'relating to' and 'necessary' in the different paragraphs of Article XX may impose a balancing or rationality test in connection with trade-restrictiveness.[42]) However, when it came to applying the *chapeau* itself, the Appellate Body found that the US measures did not comply and therefore were not justified under Article XX as a whole.[43] In reaching this conclusion, the Appellate Body relied on, among other things, the Convention on Biological Diversity, the Convention on Migratory Species, the *Rio Declaration on Environment and Development*,[44] and the *Inter-American Convention for the Protection and Conservation of Sea Turtles*, all of which focused on multilateral solutions to conservation.[45] In the Appellate Body's view, these instruments therefore demonstrated that the USA, in negotiating with some Members that exported shrimp to the USA but not with others (to find a consensual means of protecting sea turtles), engaged in unjustifiable discrimination contrary to the *chapeau*.[46] Here, as Joost Pauwelyn explains, the Appellate Body was perhaps relying on non-WTO international instruments, not so much to establish the ordinary meaning of particular words in WTO provisions, but more 'as a "factual reference" in examining whether there has been discrimination in the sense of the chapeau of GATT Art. XX'.[47]

Some time after *US – Shrimp*, in *EC – Tariff Preferences*, India challenged the EC's GSP scheme under GATT 1994 and the Enabling Clause (which provides an exception to MFN treatment for certain preferential tariffs to developing country Members).[48] In particular, India contested the

---

[41] Appellate Body Report, *US – Shrimp*, [141].
[42] See above, 66, 101.   [43] Appellate Body Report, *US – Shrimp*, [187(c)].
[44] UN, *Rio Declaration on Environment and Development*, A/CONF. 151/5/Rev.1; 31 ILM 874 (13 June 1992); Appellate Body Report, *US – Shrimp*, [41].
[45] Ibid., [167]–[169]; First written submission of the USA to the Panel, Exhibit AA.
[46] Appellate Body Report, *US – Shrimp*, [172]. But see Appellate Body Report, *US – Gambling*, [317], [336] (refusing to view bilateral consultations as a reasonably alternative measure in assessing whether a challenged measure was 'necessary' under GATS Article XIV(a) or (c)).
[47] Pauwelyn, *Conflict of Norms*, 269 (quoting Appellate Body Report, *US – Shrimp (Article 21.5 – Malaysia)*, [130]). See also Gabrielle Marceau, 'WTO Dispute Settlement and Human Rights' (2002) 13(4) *European Journal of International Law* 753, 791.
[48] Appellate Body Report, *EC – Tariff Preferences*, [98]–[99].

EC's granting of additional preferences to certain GSP beneficiaries to 'combat drug production and trafficking'.[49]

The EC argued that the 'drug problem' is a 'development, financial [or] trade need' under paragraph 3(c) of the Enabling Clause, as evidenced by certain WTO instruments, as well as non-WTO documents[50] such as the UN *Convention Against Illicit Traffic in Narcotic Drugs and Psychotropic Substances*[51] and the UN action plan on illicit drug crops.[52] The Appellate Body did not rule on this point. However, it suggested that an '*objective* standard' is required to establish a relevant need under paragraph 3(c), which standard could be provided by '[b]road-based recognition of a particular need, set out in the *WTO Agreement* or in multilateral instruments adopted by international organizations'.[53] The Appellate Body did not specify whether WTO Members or the parties to the dispute would need to be party to international conventions or instruments used to identify relevant development, financial or trade needs, again suggesting that it was not relying on these instruments by virtue of Article 31(3)(c) of the VCLT. This decision confirms the suggestion in *US – Shrimp* that the Appellate Body is willing to consider other multilateral conventions as well as, perhaps, non-binding international texts in determining the ordinary meaning of particular words in accordance with Article 31(1) of the VCLT.

In the result, the Appellate Body concluded that the EC's 'drug arrangements' did not fall within the Enabling Clause because they were limited *a priori* to twelve specific countries.[54] However, differentiation between GSP beneficiaries to address a particular 'development, financial [or] trade need' is not necessarily contrary to the Enabling Clause,[55] as long as 'preference-granting countries ... make available identical tariff preferences to all similarly-situated beneficiaries'[56] and select which beneficiaries are similarly situated according to clear and objective criteria.[57]

When the DSB adopted the Appellate Body Report, India pointed out 'the extremely worrisome consequence of this ruling ... that criteria and concepts were imported from other international organization[s],

---

[49] Ibid., [2]–[4]. [50] Ibid., n. 335; Panel Report, *EC – Tariff Preferences*, [4.73].
[51] E/CONF.82/15 (adopted 20 December 1988).
[52] General Assembly, UN, *Action Plan on International Cooperation on the Eradication of Illicit Drug Crops and on Alternative Development*, A/RES/S-20/4 (10 June 1998).
[53] Appellate Body Report, *EC – Tariff Preferences*, [163] (original emphasis).
[54] Ibid., [187]–[189]. [55] Ibid., [162]–[165]. [56] Ibid., [154]. [57] Ibid., [183], [187]–[188].

even those unrelated to the objectives of the WTO, into the law of the WTO without the consent of WTO Members'.[58] However, these concepts were not 'imported' into WTO law; the basis for considering other international instruments in interpreting the ordinary meaning of terms used in the WTO agreements is contained in Article 31(1) of the VCLT and, indirectly, Article 3.2 of the DSU, as explained above.

The Study Group of the ILC recently concluded four years' work on 'fragmentation' of international law, on the basis that 'the emergence of new and special types of law, "self-contained regimes" and geographically or functionally limited treaty-systems creates problems of coherence in international law'.[59] Martti Koskenniemi chaired the Study Group and finalised its report. On the use of Article 31(1) of the VCLT as an avenue for using international law in interpreting WTO law, the Study Group was dismissive, stating that 'taking "other treaties" into account as evidence of "ordinary meaning" appears a rather contrived way of preventing the "clinical isolation"' of WTO law from the rest of public international law.[60]

(ii) Contemporaneous or evolutionary interpretation

One question that arises in relation to the interpretation of WTO provisions in the light of international law is whether the 'ordinary meaning' of treaty terms, in the sense of Article 31(1) of the VCLT, is the meaning when the treaty was concluded (contemporaneous interpretation) or when the treaty is being interpreted (evolutionary interpretation).

The traditional rule in public international law was probably that the ordinary meaning to be given to the terms of a treaty was the meaning of the terms when the treaty was concluded. Thus, in Ian Sinclair's words, '[t]he ordinary meaning of a treaty provision should in principle be the meaning which would be attributed to it at the time of the conclusion of the treaty'.[61] Gerald Fitzmaurice described this as 'the principle of contemporaneity',[62] while Arnold McNair emphasised

---

[58] WTO, DSB, *Minutes of Meeting Held in the Centre William Rappard on 20 April 2004*, WT/DSB/M/167 (27 May 2004) [49].

[59] UN, ILC, *Fragmentation of International Law: Difficulties Arising from the Diversification and Expansion of International Law – Report of the Study Group – Finalized by Martti Koskenniemi*, A/CN.4/L.682 (13 April 2006) [15].

[60] Ibid., [450].

[61] Ian Sinclair, *The Vienna Convention on the Law of Treaties* (2nd edn, 1984) 124–5.

[62] Gerald Fitzmaurice, 'The Law and Procedure of the International Court of Justice 1951–4: Treaty Interpretation and Other Treaty Points' (1957) 33 *British Yearbook of International Law* 203, 212.

the importance of finding the common intention of the contracting parties[63] and explained the rule as follows:

> There is authority for the rule that when there is a doubt as to the sense in which the parties to a treaty used words, those words should receive the meaning which they bore at the time of the conclusion of the treaty; unless that intention is negatived by the use of terms indicating the contrary.[64]

According to Pauwelyn, in WTO law the usual rule has been reversed, so that the meaning of WTO terms is generally determined as at the time of interpretation rather than the time the WTO agreements entered into force.[65]

However, it is important to recall that Article 31(1) of the VCLT, adopted in 1969, refers to both 'ordinary meaning' and 'object and purpose'. As Article 31(1) imposes no hierarchy between the text, context, and object and purpose,[66] it may be seen as striking a balance between the current meaning of particular terms (included in the 'ordinary meaning') and the original intent in using them (included in the 'object and purpose', which can arguably be revealed or informed by the *travaux préparatoires*,[67] although Article 32 also refers to these materials explicitly as a supplementary means of interpretation). In any case, the drafters clearly intended to move away from the suggestion that interpretation seeks simply the intention of the parties, independent of the text: 'the starting point of interpretation is the elucidation of the meaning of the text, not an investigation *ab initio* into the intentions of the parties'.[68] Moreover, although it is possible to read certain ICJ decisions as supporting the principle of contemporaneity,[69] others are equally

---

[63] Arnold McNair, *The Law of Treaties* (1961) 366-7. [64] Ibid., 467.
[65] Pauwelyn, *Conflict of Norms*, 268.
[66] This was recognised in Panel Report, *US – Section 301 Trade Act*, [7.22]. However, Sinclair describes references to the object and purpose as 'a secondary or ancillary process' because the ordinary meaning in context is to be 'tested and either confirmed or modified' in the light of the object and purpose: Sinclair, *Vienna Convention*, 130. See also Appellate Body Report, *US – Shrimp*, [114]; Panel Report, *US – Corrosion-Resistant Steel Sunset Review*, [7.43]-[7.44].
[67] Sinclair acknowledges this view: Sinclair, *Vienna Convention*, 141.
[68] UN, ILC, *Yearbook*, II (1966) 220. See also T. Elias, 'The Doctrine of Intertemporal Law' (1980) 74(2) *American Journal of International Law* 285, 302-5; Lennard, 'Navigating by the Stars', 21-2; McLachlan, 'Principle of Systemic Integration', 289, 292, 313, 316-17.
[69] See, e.g., *Land and Maritime Boundary between Cameroon and Nigeria (Cameroon v Nigeria) (Merits)* [2002] ICJ Rep. 1, [59].

136   OPTIONS FOR THE FUTURE

consistent with evolutionary interpretation.[70] Accordingly, the use of international law in determining the 'ordinary meaning' of a WTO term should not be restricted, *a priori*, to international law as it existed when the relevant WTO agreement was drafted. This is consistent with the Appellate Body's general approach to date and the ILC Study Group's conclusion that 'it seems pointless to try to set any general and abstract preference between the past and the present'.[71]

In *US – Shrimp*, the Appellate Body specifically referred to previous decisions by the ICJ and concluded that the words 'exhaustible natural resources' in GATT Article XX(g) are, 'by definition, evolutionary'.[72] Accordingly, it relied on 'modern international conventions and declarations'[73] and 'the recent acknowledgement by the international community of the importance of concerted bilateral or multilateral action to protect living natural resources'[74] in determining the meaning of these words, rather than instruments relating to the meaning of these words when they were drafted 'more than 50 years ago',[75] in GATT 1947. However, the instruments relied on were adopted in the 1970s and 1990s, before the original Article XX(g) had been incorporated into GATT 1994. When the DSB adopted this Report, Thailand, Pakistan, and India (complainants), as well as the Philippines, expressed concern at the Appellate Body's use of an 'evolutionary' interpretative approach, suggesting that this would lead to unpredictable results not contemplated in the covered agreements.[76] However, the USA (respondent) and Switzerland welcomed the Appellate Body's reference to contemporary international concerns regarding the environment.[77]

---

[70] See, e.g., *Aegean Sea Continental Shelf Case (Greece v Turkey) (Jurisdiction)* [1978] ICJ Rep. 3, [77]–[80]; *Gabčíkovo-Nagymaros Project (Hungary v Slovakia) (Merits)* [1997] ICJ Rep. 7, [140]. See also McLachlan, 'Principle of Systemic Integration', 317.

[71] UN, ILC, *Fragmentation of International Law: Difficulties Arising from the Diversification and Expansion of International Law – Report of the Study Group – Finalized by Martti Koskenniemi*, A/CN.4/L.682 (13 April 2006) [478].

[72] Appellate Body Report, *US – Shrimp*, [130] (quoting *Legal Consequences for States of the Continued Presence of South Africa in Namibia (South West Africa) notwithstanding Security Council Resolution 276 (Advisory Opinion)* [1971] ICJ Rep. 16, [53]).

[73] Appellate Body Report, *US – Shrimp*, [130].

[74] Ibid., [131].   [75] Ibid., [129].

[76] WTO, DSB, *Minutes of Meeting Held in the Centre William Rappard on 6 November 1998*, WT/DSB/M/50 (14 December 1998) 3–5, 9, 14. See also Duncan French, 'Treaty Interpretation and the Incorporation of Extraneous Legal Rules' (2006) 55(2) *International & Comparative Law Quarterly* 281, 298.

[77] WTO, DSB, *Minutes of Meeting Held in the Centre William Rappard on 6 November 1998*, WT/DSB/M/50 (14 December 1998) 11, 14.

In *EC – Tariff Preferences*, the Appellate Body did not specify whether it was determining the 'ordinary meaning' of a 'development, financial [or] trade need' under paragraph 3(c) of the Enabling Clause using contemporaneous or evolutionary interpretation; nor did it specify whether the 'multilateral instruments adopted by international organizations'[78] that might be relevant in identifying these needs would be those applicable at the time of interpretation or the time of drafting. However, it is even easier to see why these needs would change over time and therefore be subject to an evolutionary approach than would 'exhaustible natural resources', as addressed in *US – Shrimp*. This approach would also be consistent with the Appellate Body's frequent reference to contemporary, post-1994 editions of dictionaries such as the *Shorter Oxford English Dictionary*[79] or *Black's Law Dictionary*[80] in identifying the ordinary meaning of particular WTO terms.

The recent Panel Reports in *EC – Chicken Cuts* concluded that 'the "ordinary meaning" is to be assessed at the time of *conclusion* of the treaty in question'.[81] The Appellate Body did not address this specific question in its Report.

C. International law between the parties (VCLT Article 31(3)(c))

Paragraph 3(c) contains another key element of Article 31 of the VCLT that may allow WTO Panels and the Appellate Body to take into account non-WTO rules of international law when interpreting WTO provisions. Under Article 31(3)(c), the treaty interpreter 'shall' take into account 'relevant rules of international law applicable in the relations between the parties'. From this requirement, two main questions arise. First, what are 'relevant rules of international law'? That is, what types of international law rules must be taken into account?

Article 38(1) of the Statute of the ICJ 'continues to form a de facto authoritative statement of points of reference for formally competent statements about the law'.[82] Although this provision does not purport to be an exhaustive statement in the abstract of the sources of

---

[78] Appellate Body Report, *EC – Tariff Preferences*, [163].
[79] See, e.g., Appellate Body Report, *US – Steel Safeguards*, nn. 196–7, 232.
[80] See, e.g., Appellate Body Report, *EC – Bed Linen*, n. 44.
[81] Panel Report, *EC – Chicken Cuts*, [7.99] (original emphasis).
[82] Martti Koskenniemi, 'Introduction' in Martti Koskenniemi (ed.), *Sources of International Law* (2000) xi, xi. See also Malcolm Shaw, *International Law* (5th edn, 2003) 66–7.

international law,[83] and although it must be read in conjunction with more recent international law,[84] it provides a useful basis for identifying the different types of international law that could be used in WTO disputes to assist in the interpretation of WTO provisions. Article 38(1) provides, to the extent relevant to this chapter:

The Court, whose function is to decide in accordance with international law such disputes as are submitted to it, shall apply:

a. international conventions, whether general or particular, establishing rules expressly recognized by the contesting states;
b. international custom, as evidence of a general practice accepted as law;
c. the general principles of law recognized by civilized nations ...

Gabrielle Marceau suggests that at least the items listed under paragraphs (a) to (c) of Article 38(1) of the Statute of the ICJ may be relevant in interpreting WTO law in accordance with Article 31(3)(c) of the VCLT,[85] although one might contend that a general 'principle' under Article 38(1)(c) of the Statute of the ICJ cannot be simultaneously a 'rule' of international law under Article 31(3)(c) of the VCLT.[86]

The second question arising from Article 31(3)(c) of the VCLT is: what are the rules 'applicable in relations between the parties'? In particular, in the context of the WTO, does this require Panels and the Appellate Body to take into account, in interpreting WTO provisions, international law rules applicable between all WTO Members, or international law rules applicable between the disputing parties? According to Marceau and the ILC Study Group on fragmentation, only WTO Members party to the dispute at issue need to be subject to the rules.[87] In contrast, Pauwelyn

---

[83] Gerald Fitzmaurice, 'Some Problems Regarding the Formal Sources of International Law' (1958) *Symbolae Verzijl* 153, 173.
[84] Robert Jennings, 'What is International Law and How Do We Tell It When We See It?' (1981) 37 *Schweitzerisches Jahrbuch für Internationales Recht* 59, 61.
[85] Gabrielle Marceau, 'Conflicts of Norms and Conflicts of Jurisdictions: The Relationship between the WTO Agreement and MEAs and Other Treaties' (2001) 35(6) *Journal of World Trade* 1081, 1087; Marceau, 'WTO Dispute Settlement and Human Rights', 780.
[86] See, e.g., Panel Report, *EC – Biotech*, [7.67]. Cf C. McLachlan, 'Principle of Systemic Integration', 290; French, 'Treaty Interpretation', 301. On the distinction between principles and rules, and the use of principles in WTO dispute settlement, see generally Andrew Mitchell, *Legal Principles in WTO Disputes* (Cambridge: Cambridge University Press, forthcoming).
[87] UN, ILC, *Fragmentation of International Law: Difficulties Arising from the Diversification and Expansion of International Law – Report of the Study Group – Finalized by Martti Koskenniemi*, A/CN.4/L.682 (13 April 2006) [472]; Marceau, 'Conflicts of Norms', 1087. See also French, 'Treaty Interpretation', 306–7.

suggests that non-WTO international law rules must apply to all WTO Members, at least through their implicit acceptance, if Panels or the Appellate Body are to use them pursuant to Article 31(3)(c) (as opposed to Article 31(1)) of the VCLT.[88] Lennard takes a similar view, pointing out that, otherwise, the meaning of WTO provisions would be uncertain and dependent on the identity of the parties to a particular dispute.[89]

I now address the Appellate Body's apparent views on these two questions, based on its decisions to date. In *US – Shrimp*, the Appellate Body referred to the principle of 'good faith' as being 'at once a general principle of law and a general principle of international law',[90] which is reflected in the *chapeau* of Article XX of GATT 1994. It went on to state, in the same paragraph:

> [O]ur task here is to interpret the language of the chapeau, seeking additional interpretative guidance, as appropriate, from the general principles of international law.[157]

[157] Vienna Convention, Article 31(3)(c).

The Appellate Body's reference to Article 31(3)(c) of the VCLT in connection with good faith indicates that it regards this provision as allowing it to take into account, at least, 'general principles of international law' (which could mean customary international law under Article 38(1)(b) of the Statute of the ICJ, a subset of customary international law, or a subset of general principles of law under Article 38(1)(c) of the Statute of the ICJ). The Appellate Body appears to use the terms 'general principle of international law' and 'principle of general international law' interchangeably. In *US – Hot-Rolled Steel*, the Appellate Body stated that 'the principle of good faith ... is, at once, a general principle of law and a principle of general international law, that informs the provisions of the ... covered agreements',[91] slightly reversing the order of the words it used to describe the same principle in *US – Shrimp*.

In two other appeals, the Appellate Body relied on the 'general principle of international law' contained in Article 28 of the VCLT[92] in interpreting WTO provisions. Article 28 provides:

---

[88] Pauwelyn, *Conflict of Norms*, 257–8, 260–1.
[89] Lennard, 'Navigating by the Stars', 35–8. See also McLachlan, 'Principle of Systemic Integration', 315.
[90] Appellate Body Report, *US – Shrimp*, [158]. See also Appellate Body Report, *US – FSC*, [166].
[91] Appellate Body Report, *US – Hot-Rolled Steel*, [101].
[92] Appellate Body Report, *Brazil – Desiccated Coconut*, 15; Appellate Body Report, *Canada – Patent Term*, [71]. See also Appellate Body Report, *EC – Bananas III*, [235].

Non-retroactivity of treaties

Unless a different intention appears from the treaty or is otherwise established, its provisions do not bind a party in relation to any act or fact which took place or any situation which ceased to exist before the date of the entry into force of the treaty with respect to that party.

Subsequently, in *EC – Sardines*, the Appellate Body characterised the non-retroactivity of treaties as an interpretative principle: 'As we have said in previous disputes, the interpretation principle codified in Article 28 is relevant to the interpretation of the covered agreements'.[93] Jeffrey Waincymer suggests that it is unclear whether Article 28 is a rule of interpretation as described directly in Article 3.2 of the DSU.[94] Perhaps the Appellate Body did not intend to suggest that it was, particularly since it has frequently referred to Articles 31 and 32 of the VCLT as codifying the customary rules of interpretation of public international law, and those Articles do not contain a 'non-retroactivity' principle (at least not explicitly). Indeed, although Article 28 and Articles 31–2 fall within Part III of the VCLT on 'Observance, application and interpretation of treaties', Articles 31–2 appear in Section 3 of Part III on 'Interpretation of treaties', whereas Article 28 appears in Section 2 of Part III on 'Application of treaties'. Instead, the Appellate Body may have meant that the international law rule regarding non-retroactivity of treaties is relevant in interpreting WTO law because, as customary international law, it is a 'relevant rule of international law applicable in the relations between the parties' under Article 31(3)(c) of the VCLT.

The Appellate Body's statements in two other appeals in connection with the rules on State responsibility suggest that it regards customary international law under Article 38(1)(b) of the Statute of the ICJ as falling within the 'relevant rules of international law applicable in the relations between the parties' under Article 31(3)(c) of the VCLT. These appeals also suggest that, when the Appellate Body refers to 'general principles of international law', 'principles of general international law', or 'rules of general international law', it is talking about customary international law.

In *US – Cotton Yarn*, the Appellate Body recognised the 'rules of general international law on State responsibility, which require that

---

[93] Appellate Body Report, *EC – Sardines*, [200] (footnote omitted).
[94] Waincymer, *WTO Litigation*, 410.

countermeasures in response to breaches by States of their international obligations be commensurate with the injury suffered'.[95] The Appellate Body referred to these rules to support its decision that, pursuant to the second sentence of Article 6.4 of the Textiles Agreement, 'the part of the total serious damage attributed to an exporting Member must be proportionate to the damage caused by the imports from that Member'.[96] In the Appellate Body's words, it would be 'absurd' if punitive safeguard measures could be imposed against increased imports (which, in contrast to dumping or certain types of subsidies, are not unfair or illegal trade practices) in the absence of any violation of law when, at the same time, the principle of proportionality in general international law requires a proportionate response to an actual violation.[97] The EC welcomed the Appellate Body's reference to proportionality.[98]

Shortly after its decision in US – Cotton Yarn, the Appellate Body in US – Line Pipe described the rules on State responsibility as 'customary international law rules' and 'rules of general international law', and it characterised the notion of proportionality in connection with countermeasures as 'a recognized principle of international law'.[99] The Appellate Body referred to these rules and principles to support its reading of the first sentence of Article 5.1 of the Safeguards Agreement as 'requiring that safeguard measures may be applied only to the extent that they address serious injury attributed to increased imports'.[100]

These decisions do not reveal whether the Appellate Body considers itself free to examine, as 'relevant rules of international law applicable in the relations between the parties' under Article 31(3)(c) of the VCLT, rules of international law applicable only between the parties to the dispute, rather than between all WTO Members. However, it is interesting to note that the Appellate Body has not referred to Article 31(3)(c) of the VCLT in connection with its reference to any 'international conventions' within the meaning of Article 38(1)(a) of the Statute of the ICJ. It is true that, frequently, the Appellate Body does not specify which provision of the VCLT it is applying at any particular stage of its interpretation. One way of reconciling the Appellate Body's decisions and placing

---

[95] Appellate Body Report, US – Cotton Yarn, [120].   [96] Ibid., [119].   [97] Ibid., [120].
[98] WTO, DSB, Minutes of Meeting Held in the Centre William Rappard on 5 November 2001, WT/DSB/M/112 (4 December 2001) [36].
[99] Appellate Body Report, US – Line Pipe, [259].   [100] Ibid., [260].

them within the framework of Article 3.2 of the DSU is to recognise that it is hesitant to rely on an international convention to which only some WTO Members are party pursuant to Article 31(3)(c) of the VCLT,[101] but that (as mentioned earlier) it is willing to use such a convention in determining the ordinary meaning of a term pursuant to Article 31(1) of the VCLT or as a 'factual' rather than legal 'reference'.[102]

Again, the Panel proceedings in the *EC – Biotech* case shed light on this issue. The Panel Report concluded that 'the rules of international law applicable in the relations between "the parties" are the rules of international law applicable in the relations between the States which have consented to be bound by the treaty which is being interpreted, and for which that treaty is in force'.[103] In the absence of an appeal, the Appellate Body had no opportunity to clarify the meaning of 'the parties' in Article 31(3)(c).

4.3 Using international law to interpret WTO law on cultural products

Having examined the basis for using international law in interpreting WTO law generally, I now address the use of international law in interpreting WTO law as it applies specifically to cultural products. In the following sections, I consider three WTO provisions that are of particular relevance to cultural products, as explained in Chapter 3. These are the exception for national treasures in Article XX(f) of GATT 1994, the exception for public morals and public order in GATS Article XIV(a) (which also exists in modified form in GATT Article XX(a)), and the exception for certain screen quotas in Article IV(c) of GATT 1994. Where it is relevant in interpreting these provisions, I assess the use of international law in determining the 'ordinary meaning' (under Article 31(1) of the VCLT) and the use of 'relevant rules of international law applicable in the relations between the parties' (under Article 31(3)(c) of the VCLT). Before turning to the exception for public morals, I introduce the possibility of a 'human rights approach' to the treatment of cultural products in WTO law, as many human rights instruments (especially regarding cultural rights) are relevant to this issue.

I then address two other exceptions that, taking a more creative view, might also relate to cultural products, namely the exception for

---

[101] See also Panel Report, *Argentina – Poultry Anti-Dumping Duties*, [7.40]-[7.41].
[102] See above, 000, 000.   [103] Panel Report, *EC – Biotech*, [7.68].

measures 'necessary to protect human, animal or plant life or health' in GATS Article XIV(b) (which is similar to the exception in Article XX(b) of GATT 1994), and the exception for measures 'necessary to secure compliance with laws or regulations which are not inconsistent with the provisions of this Agreement' in GATT Article XX(d) (which is somewhat analogous to GATS Article XIV(c)). Although these provisions appear less directly relevant to cultural products, it is still worth considering them given that, as mentioned above,[104] the Appellate Body could be open to arguments that stretch the imagination, even if they require development of previous case law.

4.3.1 National treasures

As indicated in Chapter 3, Article XX(f) of GATT 1994 provides an exception for measures 'imposed for the protection of national treasures of artistic, historic or archaeological value', subject to compliance with the *chapeau*.[105] This provision has not yet been subject to interpretation in WTO dispute settlement. However, several concepts in Article XX(f) could be said to invite an 'evolutionary' approach to interpretation. Identifying something as a 'treasure' and assessing its 'artistic, historic or archaeological value' will depend on people's shifting tastes and priorities. Similarly, whether a treasure is of national rather than merely local significance may also change over time. Indeed, these terms appear more obviously 'evolutionary' in nature than the words 'exhaustible natural resources' in Article XX(g), which the Appellate Body construed as having an evolutionary meaning as described above.[106] Accordingly, even if Article XX is regarded as having been drafted in 1947, international law since that date may be relevant in interpreting the ordinary meaning of 'national treasures of artistic, historic or archaeological value' pursuant to Article 31(1) of the VCLT.

A vast array of international law applies to cultural products and culture more generally outside the framework of the WTO. This ranges from declarations and recommendations[107] to international treaties.[108]

---

[104] Above, 130.   [105] See above, 101.   [106] Above, 136, n. 72.
[107] See, e.g., UNESCO, *Recommendation Concerning the International Exchange of Cultural Property*, 19 C/Resolutions, annex I, 16 (26 November 1976); UNESCO, *Recommendation for the Safeguarding and Preservation of Moving Images*, 21 C/Resolutions, annex I, 156 (27 October 1980); UNESCO, *Recommendation on the Safeguarding of Traditional Culture and Folklore*, 25 C/Resolutions, annex I(B), 238 (15 November 1989).
[108] See, e.g., Convention on Cultural Property in Armed Conflict; Convention for the Protection of Cultural Heritage; Indigenous and Tribal Peoples Convention.

In this section I consider just a few of the possible texts that might be used to interpret particular WTO provisions, starting with Article XX(f). In particular, international laws outside the WTO framework might assist in clarifying the kinds of things that qualify as national treasures, and whether the exception for national treasures would extend to measures imposed by a Member to protect national treasures of other Members. I consider these issues in turn, using a hypothetical cultural policy measure that a Member might wish to adopt to prevent illicit transfers of cultural property.

The UNESCO Convention on Cultural Property was adopted in 1970[109] and currently has 102 States parties, including many of the WTO's 150 Members.[110] Article 1 of this convention identifies 'cinematographic archives' as 'cultural property' of a kind that a State could designate 'as being of importance for archaeology ... history ... [or] art'. (I focus on this aspect of cultural property because it falls within my definition of cultural products, but similar reasoning would apply to other forms of cultural property.) In Article 2(1), States parties recognise that 'the illicit import, export and transfer of ownership of cultural property is one of the main causes of the impoverishment of the cultural heritage of the countries of origin of such property'. These transfers are 'illicit' when effected contrary to the convention.[111] Under Article 6, States parties undertake to introduce a certificate signifying that the export of a particular item of cultural property is authorised, and to prohibit the export of cultural property in the absence of a certificate. In addition, Article 13 provides for States parties to 'prevent by all appropriate means transfers of ownership of cultural property likely to promote the illicit import or export of such property'.

A State party to the UNESCO Convention on Cultural Property that is also a WTO Member might decide, in accordance with Article 13 of that convention, to prohibit the import of cinematographic archives from other States parties to the UNESCO Convention on Cultural Property (including other WTO Members) where the archives are not accompanied by a certificate, issued by the government of the country in which they originate, indicating that they have been legitimately exported from that country. In this way, the Member might hope to prevent illicit

---

[109] UNESCO, *Records of the General Conference, 16th Session*, vol. I: *Resolutions* (14 November 1970) 135.
[110] <www.unesco.org/culture/laws/1970/html_eng/page3.shtml> (accessed 4 August 2006).
[111] UNESCO Convention on Cultural Property, art. 3.

imports of cultural property, thereby helping other States parties to protect their cultural property and encouraging them to adopt similar measures in return.

Broadly speaking, a prohibition on imports such as this is likely to conflict with the general ban on quantitative restrictions contained in Article XI of GATT 1994. It could also potentially breach Article I of GATT 1994, in that it would treat certain imports from WTO Members that were also States parties to the UNESCO Convention on Cultural Property less favourably than imports of like products from other WTO Members. A Member defending the prohibition on imports of certain cinematographic archives could argue that the measure falls within the exception under Article XX(f) because 'treasures of artistic, historic or archaeological value' include 'cinematographic archives'. (The Member could also argue that the UNESCO Convention on Cultural Property provides some sort of defence to a WTO-inconsistency, an issue addressed in Chapter 5.)

Based on previous Appellate Body jurisprudence discussed above, it would not matter whether all WTO Members or the parties to the WTO dispute were also parties to the UNESCO Convention on Cultural Property. In fact, even if the responding Member was not a party to this convention it could still argue that the convention was relevant in identifying the ordinary meaning of 'treasures' in Article XX(f). Panels and the Appellate Body are likely to accept directly relevant statements in international instruments such as this in determining the ordinary meaning of these words or as factual evidence.[112]

Another potentially relevant instrument is the UNIDROIT Convention on Cultural Objects adopted in 1995 (currently with twenty-seven States parties),[113] which defines 'cultural objects' as including cinematographic archives.[114] It confirms the characterisation of cinematographic archives in the UNESCO Convention on Cultural Property as having 'artistic, historic or archaeological value'. Supported by other evidence and arguments, these international laws could demonstrate that such archives rise to the level of a national 'treasure' in a particular case. However, the word 'archives' highlights the historical aspect of these works, so the conventions are likely to be of less relevance in explaining why modern cinematographic works or other cultural

---

[112] See above, 132.
[113] <www.unidroit.org/english/implement/i-95.pdf> (accessed 4 August 2006).
[114] UNIDROIT Convention on Cultural Objects, art. 2, annex.

products should fall within the exception under Article XX(f). Indeed, although international laws on culture would undoubtedly affect the interpretation of Article XX(f) in relation to many cultural objects, Members wishing to rely on Article XX(f) in relation to cultural products as defined here may face a general difficulty in showing that the relevant products are national treasures.

Let us assume that cinematographic archives have the capacity to be national treasures of a particular State, leaving aside the question of the link required between the archives and the State to make them a treasure of that State.[115] In the example provided above, a WTO Member prohibits imports of cinematographic archives from States parties to the UNESCO Convention on Cultural Property in the absence of a certificate. Presumably, these archives are not national treasures of the WTO Member prohibiting their import, although they may be national treasures of the exporting State or some other State. Thus, in prohibiting their import without a certificate, the Member is most immediately protecting the 'national treasures' of other States parties to the UNESCO Convention on Cultural Property, rather than its own national treasures.[116] This raises the issue of whether the word 'national' in Article XX(f) refers solely to the nationality of the Member imposing the measure. In other words, can a WTO Member rely on Article XX(f) as an exception for measures that are 'imposed for the protection of national treasures' of other WTO Members, or only for measures to protect its own national treasures?

The WTO Member imposing the challenged measure regarding cinematographic archives could offer two broad answers to this question under Article XX(f). First, it could argue that Article XX(f) does not state explicitly that the 'national treasures' in question must be those of the

---

[115] Non-WTO laws shedding light on this question could include the exception in the EC Treaty from the prohibition on quantitative restrictions on imports or exports for 'prohibitions or restrictions on imports, exports or goods in transit justified on grounds of ... the protection of national treasures possessing artistic, historic or archaeological value': EC Treaty, art. 30.

[116] This is consistent with the purpose of the UNESCO Convention on Cultural Property, which is, according to one commentator, 'to restrain the flow of cultural property from source nations' (i.e. countries in which 'the supply of desirable cultural property exceeds the internal demand' – primarily developing countries) 'by limiting its importation by market nations' (i.e. countries in which demand for such property exceeds supply – primarily developed countries): John Merryman, 'Two Ways of Thinking about Cultural Property' (1986) 80(4) *American Journal of International Law* 831, 832, 843.

Member relying on the exception, and that therefore the Member may protect the national treasures of other States under Article XX. In a similar vein, Charnovitz maintains that the 'moral exception' in Article XX(a) of GATT 1994 cannot be restricted to measures that are 'inwardly-directed', that is, directed towards protecting public morals within the Member imposing the measure.[117] Trebilcock and Howse go so far as to suggest that 'the general view of Article XX(f) ... is that it permits not only restrictions on the export of a [Member's] own national treasures, but import import and export restrictions on national treasures of *other* [Members] as well'.[118]

To support this view in relation to Article XX(f), the Member could refer to international instruments demonstrating the importance for the world as a whole of the cultural heritage of every State. For example, the preamble of the Convention on Cultural Property in Armed Conflict emphasises that 'damage to cultural property belonging to any people whatsoever means damage to the cultural heritage of all mankind, since each people makes its contribution to the culture of the world'. Similarly, the General Conference of UNESCO has stated that 'all cultural property forms part of the common cultural heritage of mankind and that every State has a responsibility in this respect, not only towards its own nationals but also towards the international community as a whole'.[119] The Member could even argue that all States are under a duty to protect cultural property on a global level, in accordance with certain human rights instruments discussed further below. On this reading of Article XX(f), the word 'national' would still be effective, because it would indicate that a connection must exist between the 'treasure' and some 'nation'. The need for this connection is consistent with the recognition, in the preamble to the convention just mentioned, that cultural property belonging to a 'people' reflects the contribution of that 'people' to world culture.

Alternatively, if the Member failed to establish that GATT Article XX(f) encompasses measures for protecting other States' national treasures,[120] it could argue that the challenged measure does in fact protect

---

[117] Charnovitz, 'Moral Exception', 742.
[118] Trebilcock and Howse, *Regulation of Trade* (3rd edn) 523 (original emphasis).
[119] UNESCO, *Recommendation Concerning the International Exchange of Cultural Property*, 19 C/ Resolutions, annex I, 16 (26 November 1976) [2].
[120] See UN, Office of the United Nations High Commissioner for Human Rights, *Human Rights and World Trade Agreements: Using General Exception Clauses to Protect Human Rights*, HR/PUB/05/5 (2005) 17.

its own national treasures. By insisting on an export certificate from the country of origin, the Member is strengthening the system for protecting cultural property established under the UNESCO Convention on Cultural Property and thus, indirectly, protecting its own national treasures. The fact that the national treasures of the Member imposing the prohibition are likely to benefit from a stronger UNESCO system to prevent illicit imports and exports could provide a 'sufficient nexus'[121] between the prohibition and those national treasures.

It is difficult to predict the Appellate Body's response to these arguments. Its ultimate approach to whether Members may use the exceptions in Article XX to protect interests beyond their own borders is likely to be consistent across the different paragraphs of Article XX, so the implications of international laws on culture may have little weight in this decision. To date, the Appellate Body has not provided an answer. In *US – Shrimp*,[122] three complainants argued that the US import ban on shrimp could not fall within Article XX(g) because it protected exhaustible natural resources beyond the jurisdiction of the USA.[123] The Appellate Body considered that it did not need to decide whether Article XX(g) contains an 'implied jurisdictional limitation' because the sea turtles at stake were 'all known to occur in waters over which the United States exercises jurisdiction', providing a 'sufficient nexus between the migratory and endangered marine populations involved and the United States for purposes of Article XX(g)'.[124]

The above analysis has shown how various international laws might be used in determining the ordinary meaning of the words 'national treasures of artistic, historic or archaeological value' in GATT Article XX(f). It is quite likely that the Appellate Body would at least consider the kinds of instruments described above in the process of interpretation, and it would have a legitimate basis for doing so in Article 3.2 of the DSU and Article 31(1) of the VCLT. However, from the perspective of Members wishing to promote or preserve their cultural products, the scope of the category of 'national treasures' is likely to be fairly limited, even if international laws reveal that it covers things like 'cinematographic archives'. Further, Members cannot be certain that Panels or the Appellate Body would interpret Article XX(f) as encompassing measures to protect other countries' national treasures. Members might wish to impose these measures in contexts other than the one described, such

---

[121] Appellate Body Report, *US – Shrimp*, [133].   [122] See above, 130.
[123] Panel Report, *US – Shrimp*, [7.24].   [124] Appellate Body Report, *US – Shrimp*, [133].

as in a co-production arrangement to assist a developing country to expand its cultural industries.[125]

Article XX(f) is therefore unlikely to provide much additional flexibility to Members under GATT 1994 in pursuing discriminatory or otherwise trade-restrictive cultural policy measures. In turn, Members are unlikely to regard Article XX(f) as providing them with sufficient comfort in relation to their cultural policy measures to undertake further commitments to cultural products under GATS.

4.3.2 A human rights approach to cultural products

The UN High Commissioner for Human Rights has proposed a 'human rights approach' to trade and the WTO, whereby 'the norms and standards of human rights' can be used as 'a legal framework for the social dimensions of trade liberalization'.[126] Special Rapporteurs at the UN have similarly called for 'greater complementarity between the basic tenets of international trade law as administered by the WTO and international human rights law'.[127] Indeed, a common plea in the debate over trade and human rights is for decision-makers in WTO dispute settlement to interpret WTO law in a manner consistent with human rights law.[128] The ILC Study Group stated in this regard that, 'when elucidating the content of the relevant rights and obligations, WTO bodies must situate those rights and obligations within the overall context of general international law (including the relevant environmental and human rights treaties)'.[129]

---

[125] See below, 163.
[126] UN, Commission on Human Rights, *Globalization and Its Impact on the Full Enjoyment of Human Rights: Report of the High Commissioner for Human Rights Submitted in Accordance with Commission on Human Rights Resolution 2001/32*, E/CN.4/2002/54 (15 January 2002) [10]. See also UN, Office of the United Nations High Commissioner for Human Rights, *Human Rights and Trade: Statement to the Fifth Ministerial Conference of the WTO* (10–14 September 2003) 4.
[127] UN, Commission on Human Rights, Sub-Commission on the Promotion and Protection of Human Rights, *Globalization and Its Impact on the Full Enjoyment of Human Rights: Final Report Submitted by J. Oloka-Onyango and Deepika Udagama, in Accordance with Sub-Commission Decision 2000/105*, E/CN.4/Sub.2/2003/14 (25 June 2003) [26].
[128] Christine Breining-Kaufmann, 'The Legal Matrix of Human Rights and Trade Law: State Obligations versus Private Rights and Obligations' in Thomas Cottier, Joost Pauwelyn, and Elisabeth Bürgi (eds.), *Human Rights and International Trade* (2005) 95, 117; Marceau, 'WTO Dispute Settlement and Human Rights', 779.
[129] UN, ILC, *Fragmentation of International Law: Difficulties Arising from the Diversification and Expansion of International Law – Report of the Study Group – Finalized by Martti Koskenniemi*, A/CN.4/L.682 (13 April 2006) [170].

150   OPTIONS FOR THE FUTURE

More specifically, several commentators have proposed using human rights instruments in interpreting exceptions under Article XX of GATT 1994.[130] According to Robert Wai, 'the multilateral nature of the international human rights regime partially protects against protectionist motives'.[131] This means that, instead of being a cloak for protectionism, as some fear,[132] human rights could actually assist in minimising trade restrictions arising from non-trade purposes such as cultural policy. Taking account of international human rights law in interpreting WTO law could provide an opportunity for the WTO dispute settlement system to promote human rights, despite its necessarily limited jurisdiction and the consequential inability of individuals or groups of individuals to bring claims on human rights issues or otherwise to this forum.[133] This could also reduce concerns about fragmentation in international law, bringing WTO law and human rights law closer together.[134]

In understanding how human rights law might be used in interpreting WTO provisions in connection with cultural products, it is necessary first to examine the content of certain key instruments regarding cultural rights. We can begin with the UDHR, which is a Resolution of the General Assembly of the UN containing universally recognised human

---

[130] See, e.g., Robert Howse, 'Human Rights in the WTO: Whose Rights, What Humanity? Comment on Petersmann' (2002) 13(3) *European Journal of International Law* 651, 7; Robert Howse and Makau Mutua, *Protecting Human Rights in a Global Economy: Challenges for the World Trade Organization* (2000); Ernst-Ulrich Petersmann, 'Time for a United Nations "Global Compact" for Integrating Human Rights into the Law of Worldwide Organizations: Lessons from European Integration' (2002) 13(3) *European Journal of International Law* 621, 19, 22; Robert Wai, 'Countering, Branding, Dealing: Using Economic and Social Rights in and around the International Trade Regime' (2003) 14 *European Journal of International Law* 35, 61–2; Ernst-Ulrich Petersmann, 'Human Rights, Markets and Economic Welfare: Constitutional Functions of the Emerging UN Human Rights Constitution' in Frederick Abbott, Christine Breining-Kaufmann, and Thomas Cottier (eds.), *International Trade and Human Rights: Foundations and Conceptual Issues* (2006) 29, 54. Cf Joost Pauwelyn, 'Human Rights in WTO Dispute Settlement' in Cottier, Pauwelyn, and Bürgi (eds.), *Human Rights and Trade*, 205, 208.
[131] Wai, 'Countering, Branding, Dealing', 54.
[132] See, e.g., John Jackson, 'Reflections on the Possible Research Agenda for Exploring the Relationship between Human Rights Norms and International Trade Rules' in Abbott, Breining-Kaufmann, and Cottier (eds.), *Trade and Human Rights*, 19, 26.
[133] On this and other differences between WTO law and human rights law, see Thomas Cottier, 'Trade and Human Rights: A Relationship to Discover' (2002) 5(1) *Journal of International Economic Law* 111, 120–1.
[134] UN, Office of the United Nations High Commissioner for Human Rights, *Human Rights and World Trade Agreements: Using General Exception Clauses to Protect Human Rights*, HR/PUB/05/5 (2005) 12.

rights, including several that relate to culture. The UDHR has a special status, first because it provides for the recognition by Member States of the UN of rights that the UN itself is also pledged to promote under the UN Charter,[135] and second because today it is often seen as declaring customary international law, at least in part, even though it does not purport by its terms to be a binding instrument.[136] Article 22 of the UDHR provides:

> Everyone, as a member of society ... is entitled to realization, through national effort and international co-operation and in accordance with the organization and resources of each State, of the economic, social and cultural rights indispensable for his dignity and the free development of his personality.

Article 27(1) refers more specifically to the kinds of activities that cultural rights might entail. It states:

> Everyone has the right freely to participate in the cultural life of the community, to enjoy the arts and to share in scientific advancement and its benefits.

The UDHR is 'enforced' by the UN Commission on Human Rights, in the sense that complaints may be made to the Commission about State violations of human rights.[137] The Commission has reaffirmed that, 'in accordance with the [UDHR], the ideal of free human beings enjoying freedom from fear and want can be achieved only if conditions are created whereby everyone may enjoy his or her economic, social and cultural rights'.[138] The rights protected by Article 27 may be said to extend to an individual's participation in cultural life either as a creator

---

[135] UN, *Charter of the United Nations* (signed 26 June 1945) arts. 1(3), 55, 56.
[136] See, e.g., *Applicability of Article VI, Section 22, of the Convention on the Privileges and Immunities of the United Nations (Advisory Opinion)* [1989] ICJ Rep. 177, 211 (Separate Opinion of Judge Evensen); *Legal Consequences for States of the Continued Presence of South Africa in Namibia (South West Africa) notwithstanding Security Council Resolution 276 (Advisory Opinion)*, [1971] ICJ Rep. 16, 76 (Separate Opinion of Vice-President Ammoun); *United States Diplomatic and Consular Staff in Tehran (United States v Iran) (Merits)* [1980] ICJ Rep. 3, [91]; Asbjørn Eide and Gudmundur Alfredsson, 'Introduction' in Asbjørn Eide et al. (eds.), *The Universal Declaration of Human Rights: A Commentary* (1992) 5, 7; UN, Office of the United Nations High Commissioner for Human Rights, *The United Nations Human Rights Treaty System: An Introduction to the Core Human Rights Treaties and the Treaty Bodies (Fact Sheet No. 30)* 3.
[137] UN, Economic and Social Council, *Procedure for Dealing with Communications Concerning Human Rights*, Res. 2000/3 (16 June 2000); UN, Economic and Social Council, *Procedure for Dealing with Communications Relating to Violations of Human Rights and Fundamental Freedoms*, Res. 1503(XLVIII) (27 May 1970).
[138] UN, Commission on Human Rights, *Question of the Realization in All Countries of the Economic, Social and Cultural Rights Contained in the Universal Declaration of Human Rights and in the International Covenant on Economic, Social and Cultural Rights, and Study of Special*

or as an observer or 'consumer'.[139] The reference to 'the cultural life of the community' may also be broader than a reference to national culture.[140]

The ICESCR is one of two treaties derived from the UDHR.[141] It entered into force in 1976 and currently has 153 States parties.[142] Evidently, this is a large number of States, in comparison to the 192 Member States of the UN as a whole, and it includes many WTO Members.[143] The ICESCR applies not only to WTO Members that are States parties to it, but also to all other WTO Members to the extent that it codifies customary international law. Article 2(1) of the ICESCR provides that each State party

> undertakes to take steps, individually and through international assistance and co-operation, especially economic and technical, to the maximum of its available resources, with a view to achieving progressively the full realization of the rights recognized in the present Covenant by all appropriate means, including particularly the adoption of legislative measures.

Under Article 15(1)(a) of the ICESCR, which is analogous to Article 27(1) of the UDHR, the States parties recognise the right of everyone 'to take part in cultural life'.[144] Article 15(2) adds that the steps to be taken by the States parties 'to achieve the full realization of this right shall include those necessary for the conservation, the development and the diffusion of ... culture'. The Committee on Economic, Social and Cultural Rights was established in 1985 to monitor compliance of States

---

Problems which the Developing Countries Face in Their Efforts to Achieve these Human Rights, E/CN.4/RES/2003/18 (22 April 2003).

[139] Ragnar Adalsteinsson and Páll Thórhallson, 'Article 27' in Gudmundur Alfredsson and Asbjørn Eide (eds.), *The Universal Declaration of Human Rights: A Common Standard of Achievement* (1999) 575, 579.

[140] Göran Melander, 'Article 27' in Eide et al., *Universal Declaration of Human Rights Commentary* 429, 431.

[141] The other is the ICCPR. On the relationship between these three documents, see generally UN, Office of the United Nations High Commissioner for Human Rights, *The International Bill of Human Rights (Fact Sheet No. 2 (Rev. 1))* (June 1996). The UN General Assembly has reaffirmed its 'commitment to continue building on the inspiration of the [UDHR] through the development of international human rights standards and of mechanisms for their promotion and protection': General Assembly, UN, *Fiftieth Anniversary of the Universal Declaration of Human Rights*, A/RES/52/117 (12 December 1997) [10].

[142] UN, *Multilateral Treaties Deposited with the Secretary-General*, ST/LEG/SER/E/-, <http://untreaty.un.org> (accessed 4 August 2006).

[143] <www.un.org/Overview/unmember.html> (accessed 4 August 2006).

[144] See generally Roger O'Keefe, 'The "Right to Take Part in Cultural Life" under Article 15 of the ICESCR' (1998) 47 *International & Comparative Law Quarterly* 904.

parties with the ICESCR.[145] It has made clear that States parties should include in their reports to it quantitative and qualitative data showing progress over time towards the progressive realisation of the rights as described in Article 2(1) of the ICESCR.[146] The committee's guidelines on the form and content of reports of States parties shed some light on the cultural rights described in Article 15, confirming the relevance of these rights to cultural products. These guidelines provide for States to include, in relation to Article 15, information on matters such as: the 'institutional infrastructure established for the implementation of policies to promote popular participation in culture', including libraries and cinemas; the '[r]ole of mass media and communications media in promoting participation in cultural life'; and '[m]easures taken to support ... organizations and institutions engaged in ... creative activities'.[147]

The UNESCO Recommendation on Participation in Cultural Life confirms that cultural rights are human rights, recommending that UNESCO Member States 'guarantee as human rights those rights bearing on access to and participation in cultural life'.[148] Further recognition of the cultural rights contained in the UDHR and ICESCR appears in a range of domestic and international instruments.[149] However,

---

[145] UN, Economic and Social Council, *Review of the Composition, Organization and Administrative Arrangements of the Sessional Working Group of Governmental Experts on the Implementation of the International Covenant on Economic, Social and Cultural Rights*, 1985/17 (28 May 1985).

[146] UN, Committee on Economic, Social and Cultural Rights, *General Comment No. 1: Reporting by States Parties*, E/1989/22 (24 February 1989) [7].

[147] UN, Committee on Economic, Social and Cultural Rights, *Revised Guidelines Regarding the Form and Contents of Reports to be Submitted by States Parties under Articles 16 and 17 of the International Covenant on Economic, Social and Cultural Rights*, E/C.12/1991/1, annex, art. 15, [1(b)], [1(e)], [5(c)]. The Committee on Economic, Social and Cultural Rights has expressed concern regarding 'Government control of the choice and broadcasting of minority language radio programmes' in Iraq: Committee on Economic, Social and Cultural Rights, *Report on the Sixteenth and Seventeenth Sessions*, E/1998/22 (20 June 1998) [268]. It has also shown an interest in whether 'the people of Paraguay receive Brazilian and Argentine television programmes': Committee on Economic, Social and Cultural Rights, *Summary Record of the 4th Meeting: Paraguay*, E/C.12/1996/SR.4 (6 May 1996) [30].

[148] UNESCO Recommendation on Participation in Cultural Life, art. 4(a).

[149] See, e.g., *African Charter on Human and Peoples' Rights*, 1520 UNTS 217; 21 ILM 58 (adopted 27 June 1981) art. 17.2; *American Convention on Human Rights*, 1144 UNTS 143; OAS Treaty Series No. 36 (signed 22 November 1969) art. 14.1(a); Ninth International Conference of American States, *American Declaration of the Rights and Duties of Man* (1948) art. XIII; European Convention on Human Rights, arts. 9, 10; *Convention on the Rights of the Child*, 1577 UNTS 3 (adopted 20 November 1989) art. 31; *Cyprus v Turkey* (2001) ECHR

154   OPTIONS FOR THE FUTURE

cultural rights have been described as the 'least developed category of human rights'.[150]

My discussion of a human rights approach to cultural products has so far focused on cultural rights. Graber suggests that freedom of expression (more often regarded as a civil or political right than as a cultural right) could also be relevant to cultural products in the WTO. He conducts some interesting analysis relying on corresponding EC jurisprudence to support his view that the Appellate Body should revise its understanding of 'likeness'[151] based on freedom of expression. Graber argues that a cultural policy aimed at protecting freedom of expression is, in the words of the ECJ, one of the 'overriding reasons relating to the public interest'[152] that should justify a departure from free trade disciplines. In taking this approach, the ECJ highlights its role in ensuring observance of the European Convention on Human Rights.[153] In the context of the WTO, Graber identifies Article 19(2) of the ICCPR (which is the second treaty derived from the UDHR) as the source of the relevant human rights obligation. Graber states that most WTO Members are party to the ICCPR, and that WTO law should therefore be interpreted pursuant to Article 31(3)(c) of the VCLT taking into account the 'principle of diversity' reflected in Article 19.[154] Article 19(2) reads:

Everyone shall have the right to freedom of expression; this right shall include freedom to seek, receive and impart information and ideas of all kinds,

---

Application No. 25781/94, [250], [254]; Indigenous and Tribal Peoples Convention; UNESCO, *Declaration of the Principles of International Cultural Co-operation*, 14 C/Resolution 8 (4 November 1966) art. 2.2(b). See also Lyndel Prott, 'Cultural Rights as Peoples' Rights in International Law' in James Crawford (ed.), *The Rights of Peoples* (1988) 93; Bruno De Witte and Harry Post, 'Educational and Cultural Rights' in Antonio Cassese et al. (eds.), *Human Rights and the European Community: The Substantive Law* (1991) 123.

[150] Lyndel Prott, 'Understanding One Another on Cultural Rights' in Halina Niec (ed.), *Cultural Rights and Wrongs* (1998) 161, 164. See also Hélène Ruiz Fabri, *Analyse et commentaire critique de l'avant-projet de convention sur la protection de la diversité des contenus culturels et des expressions artistiques dans la version soumise pour commentaires et observations aux gouvernements des Etats membres de l'UNESCO: Etude réalisée à la demande de l'Agence intergouvernementale de la Francophonie* (August 2004) [18]; Melander, 'Article 27', 429.

[151] See above, 75.

[152] See, e.g., *Commission of the European Communities v Kingdom of the Netherlands* (C-353/89) [1991] ECR I-4069, [17]–[18] (see also [29]–[30]). See also *Criminal Proceedings Against Burmanjer* (C-20/03) [2005] ECR I, [32]; *Vereinigte Familiapress Zeitungsverlags- und vertriebs GmbH v Heinrich Bauer Verlag* (C-368/95) [1997] ECR I-3689, [18].

[153] *Elliniki Radiophonia Tiléorassi AE v Dimotiki Etairia Pliroforissis* (C-260/89) [1991] ECR I-2925, [41].

[154] Graber, *Handel und Kultur*, 341–2 ('principle of diversity' translates 'Vielfaltsprinzip' in original).

regardless of frontiers, either orally, in writing or in print, in the form of art, or through any other media of his choice.

Graber contends that, in assessing likeness, Panels and the Appellate Body should recognise Members' discretion to pursue cultural diversity under Article 19(2).[155] The Human Rights Committee, which is charged with monitoring and enforcing the ICCPR, has indicated that 'excessive concentration of the mass media' may interfere with the enjoyment of freedom of expression under Article 19(2).[156] Thus, a Member might aim to promote freedom of expression by imposing discriminatory or trade-restrictive cultural policy measures to reduce market concentration. However, one could equally argue that these measures impinge on the freedom of expression.[157] Moreover, given the Appellate Body's current approach to likeness and the aims-and-effects test as discussed in Chapter 3, Graber's argument would more likely succeed in the context of the public morals exceptions.

EC experience and jurisprudence may indeed provide a fruitful source of ideas for WTO dispute settlement in connection with cultural products. Lessons from the EC might not be formally relevant in the course of interpreting WTO law in accordance with Articles 31 and 32 of the VCLT. However, additional research in this area could be useful to identify possible alternative approaches, given the EC human rights framework and comparable trade liberalisation rules. For example, a line of EC cases[158] could provide one means of resolving the goods–services dilemma through dispute settlement rather than through amendment of WTO rules, whereby a product is treated as a service 'where the service is the main object of the transaction'.[159] However, even this rule may be problematic.[160]

---

[155] Ibid., 318.
[156] UN, Human Rights Committee, *Concluding Observations of the Human Rights Committee: Italy*, CCPR/C/79/Add.37 (3 August 1994). See also UN, Human Rights Committee, *General Comment No. 10: Freedom of Expression (Art. 19)*, reprinted HRI\GEN\1\Rev.1, 11 (29 June 1983) 10; UN, Human Rights Committee, *Consideration of Reports Submitted by States Parties under Article 40 of the Covenant: Concluding Observations of the Human Rights Committee*, CCPR/C/ITA/CO/5 (24 April 2006) [20].
[157] See Barton, 'International Video Industry', 95–8, 103–5.
[158] See, e.g., *Her Majesty's Customs and Excise v Schindler* (C-275/92) [1994] ECR I-1039, [21]–[29]; *Criminal Proceedings Against Burmanjer* (C-20/03) [2005] ECR I, [35].
[159] Smith and Woods, 'Distinction Without a Difference', 35.   [160] Ibid., 35–40.

4.3.3 Public morals and public order

As explained in Chapter 3, Article XIV(a) of GATS provides an exception for measures 'necessary to protect public morals or to maintain public order', subject to compliance with the *chapeau*.[161] GATS footnote 5 adds that the 'public order exception may be invoked only where a genuine and sufficiently serious threat is posed to one of the fundamental interests of society'. Public morals and public order are precisely the kinds of concepts that are evolutionary by definition,[162] as is the notion of the 'fundamental interests of society'. This seems to be the Appellate Body's own view, given that 'there is no suggestion in *US – Gambling* that public morals should be interpreted exclusively by reference to the content that might have been understood when the GATT was first negotiated'.[163] Accordingly, the ordinary meaning of these words under Article 31(1) of the VCLT (or the factual question of what they encompass at a given point in time) may be influenced by current international law on culture.

The exception for public morals in GATT Article XX(a) and GATS Article XIV(a) provides one of the most likely avenues for human rights to influence the interpretation of WTO law.[164] The UN High Commissioner for Human Rights has issued a report regarding the relationship between human rights and liberalising trade in services, stating:

> The protection of public morals, life and privacy are familiar themes to human rights law and their inclusion in GATS could be seen as a link to the promotion and protection of human rights... This link could... be relevant in determining the appropriate sources of international law relevant to the interpretation of the provisions of GATS in future rulings by the WTO Dispute Settlement Body...[165]

---

[161] See above, 104.
[162] Sinclair, *Vienna Convention*, 139; Marwell, 'Trade and Morality', 820; Marceau, 'WTO Dispute Settlement and Human Rights', 784; UN, Office of the United Nations High Commissioner for Human Rights, *Human Rights and World Trade Agreements: Using General Exception Clauses to Protect Human Rights*, HR/PUB/05/5 (2005) 7-8.
[163] Howse, Langille, and Burda, 'WTO and Labour Rights', 203. For discussion of *US – Gambling*, see above, 107.
[164] UN, Office of the United Nations High Commissioner for Human Rights, *Human Rights and World Trade Agreements: Using General Exception Clauses to Protect Human Rights*, HR/PUB/05/5 (2005) 4, 9.
[165] UN, Commission on Human Rights, Sub-Commission on the Promotion and Protection of Human Rights, *Liberalization of Trade in Services and Human Rights: Report of the High Commissioner*, E/CN.4/Sub.2/2002/9 (25 June 2002) annex [63].

However, the High Commissioner has also recognised the difficulties in identifying those human rights that might be encapsulated within 'public morals'.[166]

Suppose a Member imposed a 'local content' requirement on all radio stations, restricting the broadcast of foreign music to 50 per cent of playing time. Depending on the way it was framed, one would expect this measure to violate the national treatment obligation under Article XVII of GATS, if the Member had made a national treatment commitment to audiovisual services. The Member could argue that this measure falls within the exception under GATS Article XIV(a) when interpreted in the light of international instruments regarding culture and, in particular, cultural rights.

The characterisation of the UDHR and ICESCR as reflecting customary international law[167] is contested (at least in the context of the WTO).[168] However, a Member imposing the local content quota could make a strong case to this effect. If accepted, this would mean that the rights and obligations contained in the UDHR and ICESCR apply to all WTO Members, whether or not they are parties to these instruments.[169] Accordingly, they would be relevant in interpreting GATS Article XIV(a) as 'relevant rules of international law applicable in the relations between the parties' under Article 31(3)(c) of the VCLT. Even if they do not codify customary international law, the Member whose quota is challenged could argue that the UDHR and ICESCR are still relevant in interpreting this provision if the parties to the dispute are States parties to the ICESCR.[170] However, judging

---

[166] UN, Commission on Human Rights, *Analytical Study of the High Commissioner for Human Rights on the Fundamental Principle of Non-Discrimination in the Context of Globalization: Report of the High Commissioner*, E/CN.4/2004/40 (15 January 2004) [33]–[34], [52].

[167] As described in Article 38(1)(b) of the Statute of the ICJ.

[168] See, e.g., Philip Alston, 'Resisting the Merger and Acquisition of Human Rights by Trade Law: A Reply to Petersmann' (2002) 13(4) *European Journal of International Law* 815, 20; Jose Alvarez, 'How Not to Link: Institutional Conundrums of an Expanded Trade Regime' (2001) 7 *Widener Law Symposium Journal* 1, 9; Petersmann, 'Time for a Global Compact', 19.

[169] Thus, the UN High Commissioner for Human Rights has stated that 'those areas of human rights law recognized as customary international law take on universal application, which means that trade rules should be interpreted as consistent with those norms and standards whatever the treaty commitments of States in trade matters': UN, Commission on Human Rights, Sub-Commission on the Promotion and Protection of Human Rights, *Liberalization of Trade in Services and Human Rights: Report of the High Commissioner*, E/CN.4/Sub.2/2002/9 (25 June 2002) annex [5].

[170] As described in Article 38(1)(a) of the Statute of the ICJ.

by WTO appeals discussed earlier in this chapter, the Appellate Body is unlikely to accept this argument.

In any case, according to those same appeals, the status of the UDHR and ICESCR in international law would not matter for the purpose of establishing the ordinary meaning of 'public morals', 'public order', or the 'fundamental interests of society' in accordance with Article 31(1) of the VCLT. As indicated in Chapter 3, the limited WTO jurisprudence on this provision to date suggests that 'public morals' refers to 'standards of right and wrong conduct maintained by or on behalf of a community or nation',[171] and 'public order' refers to preserving the fundamental interests of a society, including standards of morality reflected in public policy and law.[172]

The UDHR and ICESCR could be said to set out standards of right and wrong conduct in relation to cultural products and to show that cultural rights represent a fundamental interest of society. Accordingly, the Member imposing the local content requirement could argue that it is protecting public morals or public order by taking steps towards the realisation of cultural rights, as envisaged in those instruments. This argument would be more forceful if the Member had a range of laws and policies in place to promote cultural rights (and not just trade-restrictive measures) and was a Member State of the UN and a State party to the ICESCR. It could also be buttressed by empirical data reflecting attitudes towards cultural rights among its people.[173]

The Appellate Body might well accept the relevance of the UDHR and ICESCR in determining the content of public morals and fundamental interests of society. However, the Member imposing the local content quota would also have to demonstrate that this measure was 'necessary' to protect public morals or public order under GATS Article XIV(a) and that it complied with the *chapeau* of Article XIV. The UN High Commissioner for Human Rights has contended that, although 'human rights should not be used as disguised barriers to trade', 'any judgement of the trade-restrictiveness of a measure should take into account States' obligations under human rights law'.[174] This would

---

[171] Panel Report, *US – Gambling*, [6.465].   [172] Ibid., [6.467].
[173] For data reflecting attitudes towards human rights issues more generally, see Adriaan van der Staay, 'Public Opinion and Global Ethics: A Descriptive Study of Existing Survey Data' in UNESCO (ed.), *World Culture Report* (1998) 266-7, 285-6.
[174] UN, Commission on Human Rights, Sub-Commission on the Promotion and Protection of Human Rights, *Liberalization of Trade in Services and Human Rights: Report of the High Commissioner*, E/CN.4/Sub.2/2002/9 (25 June 2002) annex [14], [58].

include the 'obligation to fulfil', which 'requires States to take appropriate legislative, administrative, budgetary, judicial and other measures towards the full realization' of cultural rights.[175] More specifically, the High Commissioner has stated that 'the application of national treatment provisions should not: reduce States' capacity to use local content requirements in the interests of promoting cultural rights'.[176] This could support the suggestion that the local content quota is necessary to protect public morals in the form of cultural rights. However, it might be difficult to show, in accordance with the word 'necessary' in Article XIV(a) and the *chapeau* of Article XIV, that the Member could not have used a less trade-restrictive measure to achieve its objectives in relation to cultural rights.

In sum, international human rights law may provide a valuable basis for understanding the notions of public morals and public order under Article XIV(a) of GATS. Over time, Members might test the limits of this provision in more disputes, and the more international law they have to sustain their claim of a moral reason for a WTO-inconsistent measure, the more likely they are to succeed. International law regarding cultural rights may also be used to establish a connection between cultural policy and cultural products on the one hand, and public morals and public order on the other. This could reduce some of the suspicion that cultural policies represent nothing more than protectionism. However, WTO Members seeking additional flexibility for their cultural policy measures under GATS are unlikely to agree to further commitments in reliance on the exception in Article XIV(a). Its terms are too vague and its future interpretation too uncertain. Therefore, dispute settlement in relation to this provision holds little hope of solving the problem of cultural products in the WTO in the near future.

4.3.4 *Screen quotas*

As explained in Chapter 3, Article IV(c) of GATT 1994 provides a limited exception to the MFN obligation, allowing minimum screen quotas for films of a specified origin other than national origin in the following terms:

---

[175] 'The Maastricht Guidelines on Violations of Economic, Social and Cultural Rights' in Theo van Boven *et al.* (eds.), *SIM Special No. 20: The Maastricht Guidelines on Violations of Economic, Social and Cultural Rights* (1998) 1, [6].

[176] UN, Commission on Human Rights, *Human Rights, Trade and Investment: Report of the High Commissioner for Human Rights*, E/CN.4/Sub.2/2003/9 (2 July 2003) 3.

(c) Notwithstanding the provisions of subparagraph (b) of this Article, any Member may maintain screen quotas conforming to the requirements of subparagraph (a) of this Article which reserve a minimum proportion of screen time for films of a specified origin other than that of the Member imposing such screen quotas; *Provided* that no such minimum proportion of screen time shall be increased above the level in effect on April 10, 1947 ...

Neither the Appellate Body nor any WTO Panel has had to interpret Article IV.

One question that arises from Article IV(c) is whether 'the level in effect on April 10, 1947' refers to the level of screen time reserved for films from a particular Member, or to the total level reserved for films from any other Members. In other words, if, on 10 April 1947, Member A reserved 10 per cent of screen time for films from Member B and 10 per cent for films from Member C, does this mean that Member A may now not increase the level of screen time for Member B above 10 per cent and for Member C above 10 per cent, or that it may not increase the total level of screen time reserved for films from any other country above 20 per cent? Evidently, the latter interpretation grants greater flexibility to Member A and would allow it, for example, to reserve 5 per cent of screen time for films from Member B and 15 per cent from Member D. Member A might wish to do so because, for example, a culturally distinct minority group in Member A originates from Member D. In these circumstances, Member C might challenge this approach in the WTO dispute settlement system.

In defending its measure, Member A might refer to a range of cultural instruments. The UN Commission on Human Rights has recognised on several occasions that 'the promotion and protection of the rights of persons belonging to national or ethnic, religious and linguistic minorities ... enrich the cultural heritage of society as a whole'.[177] Furthermore, according to the UN High Commissioner for Human Rights, '[m]aintaining flexibility in the use of ... local content requirements could be appropriate at times to promote the right to culture of particular cultural or linguistic minorities'.[178] However, the hypothetical measure at issue is not a 'local' content requirement (imposed by Member A for the screening of films of Member A or of certain groups

---

[177] See, e.g., UN, Commission on Human Rights, *Rights of Persons Belonging to National or Ethnic, Religious and Linguistic Minorities*, E/CN.4/RES/2000/52 (25 April 2000) preamble.

[178] UN, Commission on Human Rights, *Human Rights, Trade and Investment: Report of the High Commissioner for Human Rights*, E/CN.4/Sub.2/2003/9 (2 July 2003) 19.

within Member A) but a preferential content requirement (imposed by Member A for the screening of films of Members B and D). Nevertheless, Member A could argue that the measure will operate to protect the cultural rights of a certain minority as film viewers rather than film creators.

One international instrument confirming the importance of cultural rights of minorities is the UN Declaration on Minorities, which the General Assembly adopted in 1992. Article 1(1) provides that States 'shall protect the existence and the national or ethnic, cultural, religious and linguistic identity of minorities within their respective territories and shall encourage conditions for the promotion of that identity'. Article 1(2) specifies that States are to adopt 'appropriate legislative and other measures' to achieve this. In wording reminiscent of Article 27 of the UDHR and Article 15 of the ICESCR, Article 2(2) of the UN Declaration on Minorities proclaims that '[p]ersons belonging to minorities have the right to participate effectively in cultural ... life'.

Member A in the example above would have difficulty relying on these provisions. Article IV(c) of GATT 1994 does not refer to culture or minorities. Nor does it contain any other terms that the UN Declaration on Minorities could assist in interpreting by clarifying the 'ordinary meaning' in accordance with Article 31(1) of the VCLT. In addition, the provisions of the UN Declaration on Minorities are unlikely to have attained the status of customary international law, and they are not conventions establishing rules. Therefore they do not appear to be 'relevant rules of international law applicable in the relations between the parties' within the meaning of Article 31(3)(c) of the VCLT, and it is difficult to see how they could assist Member A in defending its challenged measure.

Perhaps Member A could turn to the ICCPR, Article 27 of which provides:

In those States in which ethnic, religious or linguistic minorities exist, persons belonging to such minorities shall not be denied the right, in community with the other members of their group, to enjoy their own culture, to profess and practise their own religion, or to use their own language.

The Human Rights Committee has emphasised that Article 27 'imposes specific obligations on States parties'.[179] In particular, 'a State party is

---

[179] UN, Human Rights Committee, *General Comment No. 23: The Rights of Minorities (Article 27)*, CCPR/C/21/Rev.1/Add.5 (8 April 1994) [9].

under an obligation to ensure that the existence and the exercise of this right are protected against their denial or violation. Positive measures of protection are ... required.'[180]

Although Article 27 of the ICCPR might represent customary international law and therefore might fall within Article 31(3)(c) of the VCLT as a law applicable to all WTO Members, it is still unlikely to help Member A in interpreting Article IV(c) of GATT 1994 as covering its preferential screening quota. Article 27 of the ICCPR may support Member A's claim that it wishes to impose this quota to protect minority rights, but this question is quite removed from the correct interpretation of Article IV(c). Referring to Article 27 seems to put the cart before the horse, asking for a particular interpretation to protect minority rights in this instance. This is problematic because the answer to whether Article IV(c) refers to a maximum overall level of screen time or a maximum level of screen time for each individual country cannot depend on the nature of the challenged measure. In other words, if Article IV(c) allows Members to reallocate the maximum screen time among different countries to protect minority rights, it must also allow this reallocation in all other circumstances. This makes it difficult to rely on the importance of minority rights in deciding this issue.

4.3.5 Protecting human life or health

Article XIV(b) of GATS, like GATT Article XX(b), contains an exception (subject to the *chapeau*)[181] for measures 'necessary to protect human, animal or plant life or health'. Again, the risks to life or health and the steps necessary to avert these risks are likely to change over time. Hence, an evolutionary interpretation of these terms may be appropriate, allowing reference to relevant international materials pursuant to Article 31(1) of the VCLT, including recognition of cultural rights.[182]

In *US – Gasoline*, the Panel found that 'a policy to reduce air pollution resulting from the consumption of gasoline was a policy within the range of those concerning the protection of human, animal and plant life or health' under GATT Article XX(b).[183] This issue was not appealed. In *EC – Asbestos*, the Appellate Body considered Article XX(b) in relation to an EC prohibition on the manufacture, sale, or import of asbestos

---

[180] Ibid., [6.1].   [181] See above, 100.
[182] See UN, Office of the United Nations High Commissioner for Human Rights, *Human Rights and World Trade Agreements: Using General Exception Clauses to Protect Human Rights*, HR/PUB/05/5 (2005) 7–8, 12.
[183] Panel Report, *US – Gasoline*, [6.21].

fibres and products containing these fibres.[184] The Appellate Body found that the Panel had not exceeded the bounds of its discretion as the trier of facts in concluding that these products pose a risk to human life or health, and it also upheld the Panel's finding that the prohibition was necessary, in that no less trade-restrictive measure was reasonably available to achieve the EC's desired level of health protection.[185] Both these cases involved risks to physical health.

This may seem a long way from cultural products. However, the Appellate Body has already recognised the need to read the exceptions in Article XX of GATT 1994 in the light of the objectives reflected in the preamble to the Marrakesh Agreement.[186] So too, a WTO Member might argue, should one interpret the exceptions in Article XIV to GATS in the light of those objectives, including the objectives of 'raising standards of living' and 'ensur[ing] that developing countries, and especially the least developed among them, secure a share in the growth in international trade commensurate with the needs of their economic development'. These objectives, when read together with international laws on culture, could confirm the relevance of cultural policy measures in achieving development and protecting human life or health.

First, consider the types of cultural policy measures that a Member might wish to adopt in relation to development. One example relates to indigenous culture in Australia:

> [M]usic releases, films, television programs, books, art – are themselves capable of expressing Indigenous perspectives and are thus crucial to the agenda of Aboriginal self-determination ... This mix of economic and expressive elements made cultural industries obvious targets of Aboriginal economic and social development programs.[187]

At an international level, a Member might also wish to adopt a cultural policy measure to assist developing country Members to develop successful cultural industries. For example, the UNCTAD Secretariat has indicated that Senegalese musicians have obtained knowledge, international reputations, and sales through 'co-production agreements with internationally known singers from the United States or EU countries'.[188] WTO Members themselves might wish to engage in co-productions

---

[184] Appellate Body Report, *EC – Asbestos*, [2].   [185] Ibid., [162], [172]–[175].
[186] Appellate Body Report, *US – Shrimp*, [129]–[130].
[187] Gibson and Connell, 'Cultural Industry Production in Remote Places', 245–6.
[188] UNCTAD, *Audiovisual Services: Improving Participation of Developing Countries – Note by the UNCTAD secretariat*, TD/B/COM.1/EM.20/2 (30 September 2002) [24].

of this kind to 'provid[e] access to export markets for audiovisual services providers of small countries'.[189] The EC, for instance, has supported film production in the African, Caribbean, and Pacific countries.[190]

Next, consider the link between cultural products, human health, and development. For a cultural policy measure to be justified under Article XIV(b), it would probably not be enough to show that the measure protected the cultural industries in a developing country Member and thereby improved those industries' contribution to the economic development of that Member. The link to human life or health in that case would be too tenuous – almost any measure imposed by or with respect to a developing country might otherwise be justified on this basis. Therefore, the fact that developing countries (or indigenous or other minorities within a developed or developing country) may stand to gain economically from successful cultural industries would not be relevant. The Panel in *EC – Tariff Preferences* seemed to adopt a similar view in addressing the EC's defence to its 'drug arrangements' under Article XX(b) of GATT 1994. The Panel stated:

> [T]here was no evidence presented before the Panel to suggest that providing improved market access is aimed at protecting human life or health in drug importing countries. Rather, all the relevant international conventions and resolutions suggest that alternative development, including improved market access, is aimed at helping the countries seriously affected by drug production and trafficking to move to sustainable development alternatives.[191]

The EC did not appeal the Panel's conclusion that its measure did not fall within the exception in Article XX(b).

Certain statements in other international bodies suggest that a closer link could exist between cultural products and human life or health. For example, the United Nations Development Programme maintains that 'allowing people full cultural expression is an important development end in itself'.[192] UNCTAD has suggested that audiovisual services

---

[189] GATT, Uruguay Round Group of Negotiations on Services, Working Group on Audiovisual Services, *Note on the Meeting of 27–28 August 1990*, MTN.GNS/AUD/1 (27 September 1990) [15] (Switzerland).
[190] UNCTAD, *Report of the Expert Meeting on Audiovisual Services: Improving Participation of Developing Countries, 13–15 November 2002*, TD/B/COM.1/56; TD/B/COM.1/EM.20/3 (4 December 2002) [23].
[191] Panel Report, *EC – Tariff Preferences*, [7.207].
[192] United Nations Development Programme, *Human Development Report 2004*, v. See also Ruiz Fabri, *Analyse et commentaire pour la Francophonie*, 12.

transmit 'civilizational values' and therefore 'deserv[e] a special place in the development of each country, regardless of its stage and level of economic development'.[193] In addition, certain UNESCO activities underline the importance of cultural development. The World Commission on Culture and Development was established in 1991[194] and later produced a report entitled *Our Creative Diversity*.[195] The report identifies two roles for culture in the context of development: the instrumental role of culture in pursuing development, and 'the role of culture as a desirable end in itself, as giving meaning to our existence'.[196] The preamble to the Action Plan on Cultural Policies for Development adopted by the Intergovernmental Conference on Cultural and Media Policies for Development in 1998 also recognises 'cultural creativity' as 'the source of human progress' and 'cultural diversity' as 'an essential factor of development'.[197] The various human rights instruments referred to earlier could also support this contention and therefore demonstrate the importance of cultural policy measures for protecting human life or health within the meaning of GATS Article XIV(b).

At this stage, this would seem quite an unusual approach to Article XIV(b) of GATS, and one to which many Members might object because of the rather tenuous link between cultural products and human life or health. It also suffers from the doubts mentioned earlier in relation to the possible territorial restrictions in Article XX of GATT 1994, because it may involve one WTO Member (most likely a developed country) justifying its measure on the basis that it protects human life or health in another WTO Member (a developing country).[198] If a measure granting preferential access to cultural products of developing country Members was a health measure in the sense of GATS Article XIV(b), it would be difficult to show that it was 'necessary' (a less trade-restrictive measure could probably be used to assist cultural development) and that it met the requirements of the *chapeau* (especially if it was provided

---

[193] UNCTAD, *Report of the Expert Meeting on Audiovisual Services: Improving Participation of Developing Countries, 13–15 November 2002*, TD/B/COM.1/56; TD/B/COM.1/EM.20/3 (4 December 2002) [1].
[194] UNESCO, *World Report on Culture and Development*, 26 C/Resolution 3.4 (6 November 1991) [1].
[195] UNESCO, *Our Creative Diversity* (1995).   [196] Ibid., Introduction.
[197] UNESCO, *Final Report: Intergovernmental Conference on Cultural Policies for Development*, CLT-98/Conf.210 (31 August 1998).
[198] See Panel Report, *EC – Tariff Preferences*, [7.210].

only to certain developing country Members rather than to all such Members). Article XIV(b) is therefore unlikely to play a significant role in justifying any cultural policy measures in the coming years. However, this possibility should be kept in mind. If Members fail to renegotiate the treatment of cultural products, some will try to stretch the existing exceptions such as Article XIV(b). Depending on how international law develops, this provision might one day prove more relevant to cultural products.

4.3.6 Securing compliance with other laws or regulations

GATT Article XX(d) and GATS Article XIV(c) relate to measures necessary to secure compliance with other laws or regulations. Neither of these provisions expressly covers cultural products or cultural policy measures. This means it would be more difficult to establish that a cultural policy measure fell under these exceptions than, say, a measure for the enforcement of privacy laws. Nevertheless, both provisions use the word 'including', which suggests that some laws or regulations other than those listed might qualify.

GATT Article XX(d) provides an exception, subject to the *chapeau*,[199] for measures

> necessary to secure compliance with laws or regulations which are not inconsistent with the provisions of this Agreement, including those relating to customs enforcement, the enforcement of monopolies operated under paragraph 4 of Article II and Article XVII, the protection of patents, trade marks and copyrights, and the prevention of deceptive practices ...

Similarly, GATS Article XIV(c) provides an exception, subject to the *chapeau*, for measures

> necessary to secure compliance with laws or regulations which are not inconsistent with the provisions of this Agreement including those relating to:
>
> (i) the prevention of deceptive and fraudulent practices or to deal with the effects of a default on services contracts;
> (ii) the protection of the privacy of individuals in relation to the processing and dissemination of personal data and the protection of confidentiality of individual records and accounts;
> (iii) safety;
>
> ...

---

[199] See above, 100.

I now turn specifically to Article XX(d) of GATT 1994, because Members have raised this provision as a defence in several disputes.[200] In *Korea – Beef*, the Appellate Body found that an otherwise WTO-inconsistent measure will be provisionally justified under Article XX(d) only if it meets two requirements. 'First, the measure must be one designed to "secure compliance" with laws or regulations that are not themselves inconsistent with some provision of the GATT 1994. Second, the measure must be "necessary" to secure such compliance.'[201] The Appellate Body has subsequently confirmed this two-step approach.[202]

Identifying 'laws or regulations which are not inconsistent with the provisions of this Agreement' under GATT Article XX(d) will necessarily depend on the laws and regulations in existence from time to time, opening the door to an interpretation of ordinary meaning under Article 31(1) of the VCLT that takes into account current circumstances. One recent dispute suggests how international laws on culture might be relevant to Article XX(d) (and also, potentially, to GATS Article XIV(c)).

In *Mexico – Taxes on Soft Drinks*, the USA alleged that Mexico's tax on the import and transfer of soft drinks and syrups was inconsistent with the national treatment obligation in Article III of GATT 1994.[203] Mexico responded that, even if the tax was inconsistent with Article III, it was justified under Article XX(d) as a measure 'necessary to secure compliance' of the USA with its obligations under NAFTA.[204] This seems to involve two original readings of Article XX(d). First, it suggests that the 'laws or regulations' in that paragraph may be not only domestic but also regional or international laws or regulations. Second, it suggests that the exempted measures may be 'necessary to secure compliance' with these laws by another WTO Member, rather than by individuals in the territory of the Member imposing the measure.

The Panel seized on both these points. As regards the meaning of 'laws or regulations', it suggested that these words refer to domestic measures and not to international agreements.[205] As regards securing compliance,

---

[200] Canada relied unsuccessfully on Article XX(d) before the Panel in *Canada – Periodicals*, but it did not appeal this point: Panel Report, *Canada – Periodicals*, [3.5], [5.11].
[201] Appellate Body Report, *Korea – Beef*, [157].
[202] See, e.g., Appellate Body Report, *Dominican Republic – Import and Sale of Cigarettes*, [65].
[203] Panel Report, *Mexico – Taxes on Soft Drinks*, [3.1]; US, WTO, *Second Submission to the Panel in Mexico – Tax Measures on Soft Drinks and Other Beverages* (21 January 2005) [9]–[10].
[204] Panel Report, *Mexico – Taxes on Soft Drinks*, [8.162]; USA, WTO, *Second Submission to the Panel in Mexico – Tax Measures on Soft Drinks and Other Beverages* (21 January 2005) [42], [49], [53].
[205] Panel Report, *Mexico – Taxes on Soft Drinks*, [8.194], [8.197].

168   OPTIONS FOR THE FUTURE

it found that this referred to enforcement by a State against its subjects, and one State imposing countermeasures against another (an interpretation supported by the examples of relevant laws or regulations provided in Article XX(d)).[206] In any case, in the circumstances of the case, the Panel was 'not convinced'[207] that Mexico's taxes could really 'contribute to securing compliance'[208] or be 'designed' to secure compliance,[209] given the uncertainty of their effect on the USA.[210]

On appeal, although the Appellate Body upheld the Panel's conclusion that Mexico's challenged measures were not justified under Article XX(d),[211] its reasoning differed somewhat from the Panel's. The Appellate Body stated that 'the "laws or regulations" with which the Member invoking Article XX(d) may seek to secure compliance do not include obligations of *another* WTO Member under an international agreement'.[212] Consequently, it agreed with the Panel that Article XX(d) does not cover measures that are allegedly necessary to 'secure compliance' by another Member with its non-WTO obligations.[213] However, the Appellate Body refined its analysis by making clear that the 'laws or regulations' in Article XX(d) include 'rules that form part of the domestic legal system of a WTO Member, including rules deriving from international agreements that have been incorporated into the domestic legal system of a WTO Member or have direct effect according to that WTO Member's legal system'.[214] The Appellate Body characterised this as one of the 'aspects' of its reasoning that differed from that of the Panel (also disagreeing with the Panel's view that a measure under Article XX(d) must be certain to secure compliance).[215] The Panel's own discussion of this point was rather oblique. It stated:

The Panel does not see that the issue of the possible direct effect of an international agreement in domestic law is relevant in the present context. Whether or not an agreement has that effect, it retains its *international* character, and it is that character and the international character of the obligations that arise from it which lead to the possible use of countermeasures to encourage respect for those obligations. Thus, even if some of the rules of the agreement become part

---

[206] Ibid., [8.175], [8.178]–[8.179]. See also Appellate Body Report, *Mexico – Taxes on Soft Drinks*, [70].
[207] Panel Report, *Mexico – Taxes on Soft Drinks*, [8.190].   [208] Ibid., [8.186].
[209] Ibid., [8.182] (quoting Appellate Body Report, *Korea – Beef*, [157]).
[210] Panel Report, *Mexico – Taxes on Soft Drinks*, [8.185]–[8.188].
[211] Ibid., [8.204], [9.3]; Appellate Body Report, *Mexico – Taxes on Soft Drinks*, [84], [85(d)].
[212] Appellate Body Report, *Mexico – Taxes on Soft Drinks*, [69] (original emphasis).
[213] Ibid., [79].   [214] Ibid.   [215] Ibid.

of national law as a result of a doctrine of direct effect, it remains the case that it is the international dimension of the agreement's rules that needs to be considered when interpreting the phrase 'laws or regulations'.[216]

Perhaps the Panel was merely indicating that the fact that an international agreement has been implemented in domestic law does not mean that Article XX(d) justifies a measure designed to secure compliance of another Member with that agreement – a point with which I suspect the Appellate Body itself would agree.[217] Contrary to the Appellate Body's reading, the Panel did not directly address the question whether a Member could rely on Article XX(d) to justify a measure designed to secure the compliance of its subjects with a domestic law or regulation that happened to implement an international agreement. Nevertheless, the Appellate Body's reasoning was certainly clearer in suggesting this possibility.

Domestic laws or regulations that implement international laws are precisely what a Member might wish to justify under Article XX(d) in connection with their cultural policy measures. Based on the Appellate Body's reading of the relevant 'laws or regulations' in *Mexico – Taxes on Soft Drinks*, could a Member justify an otherwise WTO-inconsistent cultural policy measure by pointing to an obligation under an international convention on culture (such as the UNESCO Convention)? If the Member relied on Article XX(d) to justify a WTO-inconsistent cultural policy measure that was necessary to secure the compliance of its subjects with WTO-consistent domestic laws or regulations implementing the UNESCO Convention, it could well succeed. However, the UNESCO Convention in this case would be all but irrelevant; it would not influence the WTO-consistency of the domestic laws or regulations or the availability of the Article XX(d) defence.

At first glance, the Appellate Body's decision in *Mexico – Taxes on Soft Drinks* might suggest that Article XX(d) could play a much more significant role, namely by justifying a Member's WTO-inconsistent cultural policy measure that was necessary to secure the Member's own compliance with its non-WTO international obligations, to the extent that these obligations formed part of its domestic laws or regulations and were not inconsistent with WTO law.[218] This would open the door to

---

[216] Panel Report, *Mexico – Taxes on Soft Drinks*, [8.196] (original emphasis).
[217] Appellate Body Report, *Mexico – Taxes on Soft Drinks*, [75].
[218] I made this suggestion myself in Tania Voon, 'UNESCO and the WTO: A Clash of Cultures?' (2006) 55(3) *International & Comparative Law Quarterly* 635, 648–9.

potentially vast use of public international law to justify WTO violations under Article XX(d). However, a closer reading suggests that the Appellate Body was not contemplating this scenario and that, properly interpreted, Article XX(d) would not allow it. In WTO parlance, international obligations such as those under the UNESCO Convention would not normally be described as being either consistent or 'inconsistent' with WTO law (although 'conflicts' between them could be contentious). Rather, the WTO agreements are concerned with the consistency of Members' own laws with WTO rules. As for 'secur[ing] compliance' under Article XX(d), the Appellate Body appears to regard this as referring to compliance with a Member's laws and regulations (whether or not those laws are derived from international law), not to compliance with international obligations.[219] This interpretation of Article XX(d) seems correct.

The Appellate Body also suggested in *Mexico – Taxes on Soft Drinks* that it is not equipped to determine whether Members are complying with their international obligations outside the WTO (e.g. whether the USA is complying with its NAFTA obligations):

> Mexico's interpretation would imply that, in order to resolve the case, WTO panels and the Appellate Body would have to assume that there is a violation of the relevant international agreement (such as the NAFTA) by the complaining party, or they would have to assess whether the relevant international agreement has been violated. WTO panels and the Appellate Body would thus become adjudicators of non-WTO disputes.... [T]his is not the function of panels and the Appellate Body as intended by the DSU.[220]

Panels and the Appellate Body would presumably be equally reluctant to determine whether a Member's cultural policy measure was necessary to secure compliance with the UNESCO Convention. This rationale for refusing to recognise international laws as 'laws or regulations' under Article XX(d) is more questionable. As the EC stated when the DSB adopted the Panel and Appellate Body Reports in this case, 'interpreting and applying non-WTO law and ruling on non-WTO obligations, where this was legally relevant for deciding a WTO dispute, did not mean "adjudicating" a non-WTO dispute'.[221] I return to this issue in Chapter 5, where I discuss the 'application' of non-WTO law such as the

---

[219] Appellate Body Report, *Mexico – Taxes on Soft Drinks*, [75].
[220] Ibid., [78] (footnotes omitted).
[221] WTO, DSB, *Minutes of Meeting Held in the Centre William Rappard on 24 March 2006*, WT/DSB/M/208 (28 April 2006) [7].

UNESCO Convention in WTO disputes, in the context of certain other arguments by Mexico in *Mexico – Taxes on Soft Drinks*.[222]

Despite the Appellate Body's reference to international laws in connection with Article XX(d) in *Mexico – Taxes on Soft Drinks*, that provision offers little hope of additional flexibility for cultural policy measures based on international laws on culture. The same reasoning would apply to the exception for measures 'necessary to secure compliance with laws or regulations which are not inconsistent with the provisions of this Agreement' under GATS Article XIV(c).

4.4 Conclusion

This chapter has demonstrated how WTO Panels and the Appellate Body might use various forms of international law on culture to interpret exceptions in GATT 1994 and GATS that are of particular relevance to cultural products. That this is a realistic possibility is reflected in previous disputes such as *US – Shrimp*, *EC – Tariff Preferences*, and *US – Cotton Yarn*. The legal basis for this approach is contained in Article 3.2 of the DSU, which the Appellate Body has read as referring (at least) to Articles 31 and 32 of the VCLT. Panels and the Appellate Body can be expected to use both non-binding declarations (or 'soft law')[223] and multilateral conventions in determining the 'ordinary meaning' of particular WTO terms, under Article 31(1) of the VCLT, regardless of whether all WTO Members or even the parties to the dispute are party to the conventions. They may also use rules that have risen to the status of customary international law, in accordance with Article 31(3)(c) of the VCLT, which provides for reference to 'relevant rules of international law applicable in the relations between the parties'. However, the Appellate Body's decisions to date suggest that it may be reluctant to use multilateral conventions that are not binding on the parties to the dispute or all WTO Members in interpreting WTO provisions pursuant to Article 31(3)(c) of the VCLT.

Within these parameters, the use of international law in interpreting WTO provisions is certainly legitimate. This could clarify the exceptions in GATT 1994 and GATS as they relate to cultural products, providing

---

[222] Below, 208.
[223] See French, 'Treaty Interpretation', 310–12. See generally Christine Chinkin, 'The Challenge of Soft Law: Development and Change in International Law' (1989) 38 *International & Comparative Law Quarterly* 850; Dinah Shelton, 'Normative Hierarchy in International Law' (2006) 1002(2) *American Journal of International Law* 291, 319–22.

greater certainty to Members as well as to suppliers of cultural products. International instruments on culture could also provide evidence of the need for discrimination in this area and of Members' motives in imposing cultural policy measures. Panels and the Appellate Body may be able to identify correlations between Members' alleged objectives in pursuing cultural policy measures and multilateral statements about the value of culture and cultural diversity.

However, the likely results of this approach on its own are too limited to solve the current stalemate regarding cultural products in the WTO. For example, it is unlikely to assist in assessing whether less trade-restrictive alternative measures are available to achieve the same objectives. In addition, WTO dispute settlement cannot rewrite the WTO agreements or eliminate the gap between the treatment of cultural products under GATT 1994 and GATS. Nor are Panels or the Appellate Body in a position to promote liberalisation under GATS by interpreting the existing provisions with respect to cultural products in any particular way. These limitations mean that dispute settlement alone cannot deal with all the problems with the current treatment of cultural products.

5 Constructing a new agreement outside the WTO

The ideal solution ... – the only one likely in the long term to provide a response to the current conflict on the attention given to cultural products in international trade agreements – would be a particular convention bearing on international trade in the cultural sector, namely, a convention that would set out clearly the justification for and limitations of a particular status for cultural products by emphasizing the need to preserve cultural diversity.[1]

5.1 Introduction

The previous chapter concluded that although WTO dispute settlement might clarify some of the exceptions under GATT 1994 and GATS as applied to cultural products, it alone cannot address the other problems with the current treatment of cultural products identified in Part I of this book and thereby provide a satisfactory, long-term solution to this issue. A second possibility would be to construct a new agreement specifically addressing the relationship between cultural policy measures and WTO obligations. The potential advantages of this approach, in comparison with resolution through dispute settlement, include increased predictability on a wide range of related issues, and an outcome that enjoys greater acceptance and democratic legitimacy among Members.[2] However, the possibility of WTO Members reaching such an agreement within the WTO is fairly remote. The difficulty of

---

[1] Ivan Bernier, 'Cultural Diversity and International Trade Regulations' in UNESCO (ed.), *World Culture Report* (2000) 70, 71. See also Bernier, 'Trade and Culture', 790–1.
[2] See Rostam Neuwirth, 'The Cultural Industries and the Legacy of Article IV GATT: Rethinking the Relation of Culture and Trade in Light of the New WTO Round' (paper presented at the Conference on Cultural Traffic: Policy, Culture, and the New Technologies in the European Union and Canada, Carleton University, 2002) 19; Sauvé and Steinfatt, 'Towards Multilateral Rules', 13.3.

174 OPTIONS FOR THE FUTURE

negotiating these issues explains why the Uruguay Round failed to resolve them in the first place.

From a 'pro-culture' perspective, the best possibility for improving the current WTO rules in relation to cultural products may be to reach an agreement on trade and culture outside the WTO.[3] In this context, the underlying interests and objectives of negotiators may be less trade-focused or trade-biased,[4] even though the countries involved may be WTO Members. In this chapter, I assess how realistic it is to expect an agreement of this kind and whether this could resolve the problem of cultural products in the WTO or, perhaps, aggravate the present situation. From the outset, it is evident that a one-sided agreement outside the WTO is unlikely to provide a satisfactory resolution from the perspective of all WTO Members.

Several groups have in fact promoted the idea of agreeing a new international instrument or treaty regarding 'cultural diversity', including in connection with cultural products as defined for the purposes of this book. In general, these groups are concerned with promoting cultural diversity and the need for special or exceptional measures (including trade restrictions) to achieve this goal. From the perspective of WTO Members and the WTO as an institution, the most relevant of these is the UNESCO Convention. From this convention, Françoise Benhamou identifies a 'strategic change from WTO to UNESCO as the central place for negotiating the legitimacy of cultural policies at an international level'.[5] This is a clear overstatement. The WTO was never the 'central place' for negotiating cultural policies; rather, it was and remains the 'central place' for negotiating international trade rules, which may touch on a range of other policy areas. Nevertheless, the UNESCO Convention has particular importance for the WTO given the legitimacy and scope of UNESCO as an international organisation,[6] the formality

---

[3] See, e.g., Bernier, 'Trade and Culture', 789, 791; Gilbert Gagné, 'Une Convention internationale sur la diversité culturelle et le dilemme culture-commerce' in Gilbert Gagné (ed.), *La diversité culturelle: Vers une convention internationale effective?* (2005) 37, 51–3; Joost Smiers, *Artistic Expression in a Corporate World: Do We Need Monopolistic Control?* (2004) 24–5, 33; UNCTAD, *Audiovisual Services: Improving Participation of Developing Countries – Note by the UNCTAD Secretariat*, TD/B/COM.1/EM.20/2 (30 September 2002) 16–17.

[4] Martti Koskenniemi and Päivi Leino, 'Fragmentation of International Law? Postmodern Anxieties' (2002) 15(3) *Leiden Journal of International Law* 553, 572, 574.

[5] Françoise Benhamou, 'Comment' (2004) 28 *Journal of Cultural Economics* 263, 264.

[6] See Ivan Bernier and Hélène Ruiz Fabri, *Evaluation de la faisabilité juridique d'un instrument international sur la diversité culturelle* (2002) 22–3.

and speed of its operations on this question,[7] and the clear possibility of a conflict with WTO rules.

In Chapter 4, I addressed the implications of international law for interpreting existing WTO provisions. A new international instrument on cultural diversity such as the UNESCO Convention could also affect the interpretation of WTO law.[8] However, in this chapter I leave aside this interpretative influence and focus instead on the direct effects of the UNESCO Convention on the conduct of WTO Members, potential complaints in relation to the UNESCO Convention, and its possible application in a WTO dispute. Before examining the implications of the UNESCO Convention for the WTO, it is worth surveying some of the other concrete initiatives for an international instrument on cultural diversity that have arisen in recent years. These provide a useful background for understanding the origins of the UNESCO Convention and identifying the kinds of interests pushing for such an instrument.

5.2 National and non-governmental initiatives

5.2.1 *Canadian Department of Foreign Affairs and International Trade*

In the 1980s, several 'sectoral advisory groups on international trade' were established to advise the Canadian Minister for International Trade.[9] One such group is the Cultural Industries SAGIT, which has included leading academics in this field, such as Bernier and Maule. In a 1999 report, this group considered two main options for Canada's cultural policy: exclude culture from international trade agreements, as has been done in several of Canada's bilateral free trade agreements;[10] or pursue a new international instrument on cultural diversity. The group concluded its report by recommending the second option, envisaging an instrument (preferably within the WTO framework)[11] that would

---

[7] Ruiz Fabri, *Analyse et commentaire pour la Francophonie*, [1].
[8] See, e.g., Bernier and Ruiz Fabri, *Un instrument sur la diversité culturelle*, 38–40.
[9] See Michael Hart, 'Canada' in Macrory, Appleton, and Plummer, *The World Trade Organization* (vol. III) 29, 43.
[10] See, e.g., *Canada Chile Free Trade Agreement* (signed 5 December 1996) art. O-06; NAFTA, annex 2106.
[11] Canadian Department of Foreign Affairs and International Trade, Cultural Industries SAGIT, *Canadian Culture*, recommendation 14.

176   OPTIONS FOR THE FUTURE

- recognize the importance of cultural diversity;
- acknowledge that cultural goods and services are significantly different from other products; ...
- set out rules on the kind of domestic regulatory and other measures that countries can and cannot use to enhance cultural and linguistic diversity; and
- establish how trade disciplines would apply or not apply to cultural measures that meet the agreed upon rules.[12]

In September 2002, the Cultural Industries SAGIT issued a new report, noting the efforts of, among others, the INCP and the INCD (as discussed below) in working towards an international instrument on cultural diversity. The report stated: 'There is now a lively international dialogue on the issues related to cultural diversity and globalization. The SAGIT takes some pride in having played a part in starting this dialogue with its [1999] report.'[13] The 2002 report also put forward, for consideration by the Minister, a 'proposed new instrument on cultural diversity ... to serve as a code of conduct for all those States that consider the preservation and promotion of distinct cultural expression and of cultural diversity itself as an essential component of globalization, as well as a document of reference that could be used by them as a common position in other international fora'.[14] The SAGIT now proposed that the instrument be developed outside the WTO,[15] although it did not state precisely the institutional framework envisaged.

This discussion draft of an 'International Agreement on Cultural Diversity' applies to 'measures Member States take with respect to the creation, production, distribution, performance, and exhibition of cultural content, and to the activities of cultural undertakings'.[16] In turn, 'cultural content' is defined to include 'the sounds, images and texts of films, video, sound recordings, books, magazines, broadcast programs, multimedia works, and other forms of media ... that are creative expressions of individuals',[17] and 'cultural undertakings' are defined as 'persons, organizations and firms that produce, publish, distribute, exhibit or provide cultural content'.[18] However, in general, the agreement does not extend to the manufacturing of physical goods such as

---

[12] Ibid.
[13] Canadian Department of Foreign Affairs and International Trade, Cultural Industries SAGIT, *An International Agreement on Cultural Diversity: A Model for Discussion* (September 2002) 2.
[14] Ibid., 9.   [15] Ibid., 7-9.   [16] Ibid., 12 (art. V:1).
[17] Ibid., 12 (art. V:2(b)).   [18] Ibid., 12 (art. V:4).

CDs or to goods or services provided to users or consumers that are not 'member[s] of the public'.[19]

The draft begins with a list of 'principles', which make plain the drafters' view that cultural products are different from other products and must therefore be accorded special treatment within trading frameworks. For example, the principles recognised in Article 1 include:

2. Governments have a legitimate role to play in supporting, preserving and promoting cultural diversity . . .
5. Market forces alone cannot guarantee the preservation and promotion of cultural diversity, which is the key to sustainable human development.

The draft specifies that Member States have a 'right' (but not an obligation) to take measures such as domestic content requirements in broadcasting, screen quotas in accordance with Article IV of GATT 1994, and '[m]easures to support the creation, production, distribution, exhibition, performance and sale of cultural content of national origin through subsidies, fiscal measures or other incentives to the creators of the content or to the cultural undertakings that provide them'.[20] However, certain measures are not permitted, including measures that 'abridge legal guarantees of freedom of expression as adjudged by the courts in the Member State'.[21]

The draft agreement does not specify how it relates to other international instruments covering the same or similar matters. However, it provides that Member States agree to consult and co-ordinate with respect to matters such as promoting the principles of the agreement in other international forums,[22] and that the Executive Council established to deal with institutional matters will consult and co-operate with other intergovernmental organisations 'that have responsibilities related to those of this Agreement'.[23] The draft contains a mechanism to resolve disputes between Member States regarding measures taken to preserve and promote diversity of cultural expression.[24] This dispute resolution mechanism seems to be partially based on the WTO dispute settlement system. Instead of the DSB, a 'Cultural Dispute Resolution Body' administers the system.[25] As in the WTO, parties must engage in consultations before proceeding to the establishment of a panel.[26] However, unlike in the WTO, panel decisions are 'advisory only', and

---

[19] Ibid., 12 (art. V:3).   [20] Ibid., 12, 16 (art. VI, annex 1).   [21] Ibid., 13 (art. VII:1).
[22] Ibid., 11 (art. III:1).   [23] Ibid., 14 (art. IX:8).   [24] Ibid., 11 (art III:1).
[25] Ibid., 14 (art X).   [26] Ibid., 14 (art XI).

178   OPTIONS FOR THE FUTURE

no appeal possibility exists.[27] The inclusion of this dispute settlement mechanism raises questions regarding the relationship between WTO dispute settlement and other forms of dispute settlement regarding similar or the same measures, as addressed further below.

5.2.2 International Network on Cultural Policy

The INCP is a Canadian-based organisation established following a meeting on cultural policy hosted by Canada's Minister of Canadian Heritage in 1998.[28] It provides an informal forum for ministers responsible for cultural matters to discuss and 'develop strategies to promote cultural diversity'.[29] In 2000, ministers from member countries (currently numbering sixty-eight)[30] began drafting an international convention to promote cultural diversity. In 2002, at the insistence of France, ministers agreed that UNESCO could best serve as the institution to house and implement the convention.[31] At the Sixth Annual Ministerial Meeting in October 2003, ministers from member countries reviewed a second draft 'International Convention on Cultural Diversity'[32] prepared by the Working Group on Cultural Diversity and Globalization and agreed that the INCP should bring its work into the UNESCO discussions on a new cultural diversity instrument.[33]

The objectives of the draft INCP convention include 'ensur[ing] that cultural diversity is promoted and preserved in the face of the opportunities and challenges introduced by ... globalization, trade liberalization and technology'.[34] It governs the 'cultural policies of the Parties',[35] meaning measures adopted 'with respect to cultural expression and cultural diversity'.[36] Cultural expression is defined as 'the creation ... production, distribution, communication, exhibition and sale of cultural contents',[37] including 'the sounds, images and texts of films,

---

[27] Ibid., 15 (art XIV).
[28] Canadian Heritage, 'Copps to Host International Meeting on Culture', press release (2 June 1998).
[29] <http://incp-ripc.org>, 'About Us' (accessed 4 August 2006).
[30] <http://incp-ripc.org>, 'Member Countries' (accessed 4 August 2006).
[31] Gagné, 'Une Convention internationale', 46; INCP, *Fifth INCP Annual Ministerial Meeting: Final Report* (Cape Town, 14–16 October 2002) 27.
[32] INCP, *Draft International Convention on Cultural Diversity* (29 July 2003).
[33] INCP, *Sixth INCP Annual Ministerial Meeting: Ministerial Statement* (Opatija, 16–18 October 2003).
[34] INCP, *Draft International Convention on Cultural Diversity* (29 July 2003) art. 2.
[35] Ibid., art. 3.   [36] Ibid., art. 1.3.   [37] Ibid., art. 1.2.

CONSTRUCTING A NEW AGREEMENT 179

video, sound recordings, books, magazines, newspapers, broadcast programs and other forms of media including multimedia'.[38]

The draft INCP convention establishes the following key principle:

> The Parties reaffirm, in accordance with the Charter of the United Nations and the principles of international law, their sovereign right to take measures to preserve and promote cultural diversity within their jurisdictions, and, in line with the provisions of this Convention, take on the shared responsibility to preserve and promote it globally.[39]

The convention does not require parties to adopt specific kinds of cultural policy measures to preserve or promote cultural diversity. In this way, it is similar to the draft instrument prepared by the Canadian Cultural Industries SAGIT, discussed above, focusing on the right of parties to adopt cultural policy measures as they see fit. However, the draft INCP convention does require each party, 'in accordance with its particular conditions and capabilities, [to] develop a cultural policy framework for the preservation and promotion of cultural diversity in line with the principles and objectives of this Convention'.[40] At the same time, any cultural policy measure 'must respect balance between the promotion of domestic cultural expression and openness to cultural content from other Parties'.[41]

Article 4 states that '[n]othing in this Convention shall derogate from existing rights and obligations that Parties may have to each other under any other international Treaty'. This formulation is described as 'one of the possible solutions'[42] for articulating the relationship between the draft convention and other international treaties, including the WTO agreements. This issue is expressed to be 'the subject of ongoing debate among experts' and therefore one that 'must remain subject to discussion'.[43] In addition, Article 12 imposes obligations on parties in relation to other international forums, requiring parties to 'seek to ensure coherence between their respective rights and obligations under this Convention and under any other Convention that may have an impact on cultural diversity', and to 'make their best endeavour to interpret and apply existing treaties in a manner that does not prejudice the principles and objectives of this convention'.[44] The problem of the relationship between WTO obligations and other international obligations regarding culture, as reflected in Articles 4 and 12,

---

[38] Ibid., art. 1.4. [39] Ibid., art. 6. [40] Ibid., art. 9. [41] Ibid., art. 7.
[42] Ibid., 14 (notes on art. 4). [43] Ibid., 14 (notes on art. 4). [44] Ibid., arts. 12.2, 12.3.

180   OPTIONS FOR THE FUTURE

has become critical in the context of the UNESCO Convention, as elaborated later in this chapter.

Like the SAGIT instrument, the draft INCP convention includes a mechanism for dispute settlement. However, the dispute settlement provisions are less comprehensive than those under either the SAGIT instrument or the DSU. Article 18 of the INCP convention simply provides for parties to engage in consultations together and, failing resolution of the dispute, allows them to submit the matter to the 'dispute settlement procedure'.[45] This procedure may include the 'setting up of a panel of cultural experts', but the detailed rules are to be established by the Assembly of Parties.[46] Dispute settlement is limited to disputes 'between Parties concerning their obligations to each other',[47] such as obligations to co-operate in collecting statistics relevant to cultural diversity[48] and to ensure that cultural policy measures are consistent with the principles outlined in the convention.[49] Nevertheless, the scope of this system is potentially wide-ranging, as the obligation to ensure that cultural policy measures comply with the convention means that these measures must 'respect the principle of balance, when the actual market situation and competitive conditions are taken into account'.[50] The requirement that a cultural policy measure balance the promotion of cultural expression with openness to other cultures, as mentioned earlier,[51] may indirectly involve a balancing of cultural policy against objectives of trade liberalisation. Accordingly, a measure challenged on the basis that it is not sufficiently open to cultural products of other parties might also be challenged on the basis that it is overly trade-restrictive, contrary to WTO rules. Assuming that the disputing countries were both parties to the INCP convention and WTO Members, the two dispute settlement mechanisms could conflict. I address this possibility further below in relation to the UNESCO Convention.

The Seventh Annual Ministerial Meeting of the INCP, held in October 2004, focused less on the development of the draft INCP convention and more on the role of the INCP in supporting the work within UNESCO towards the UNESCO Convention.[52]

---

[45] Ibid., art. 18.1, 18.2.   [46] Ibid., art. 18.3.   [47] Ibid., art. 18.1.   [48] Ibid., art. 14.1(b).
[49] Ibid., art. 13.1.   [50] Ibid., art. 13.2(c).   [51] Ibid., art. 7.
[52] See INCP, *Report for Ministerial Consideration on the 2003–2004 Workplan of the Working Group on Cultural Diversity and Globalization* (2004); INCP, *Seventh INCP Annual Ministerial Meeting: Ministerial Statement* (Shanghai, 14–16 October 2004).

5.2.3 International Network for Cultural Diversity

Another Canadian-based organisation, the INCD, describes itself as a worldwide 'network of artists and cultural groups dedicated to countering the homogenizing effects of globalization on culture'.[53] Like the INCP, the INCD began work on drafting a convention to promote cultural diversity in 2000. In February 2003, the INCD presented to UNESCO[54] for its consideration a 'Proposed Convention on Cultural Diversity'.[55]

One objective of the convention proposed by the INCD, as expressed in the preamble, is to 'maintain and strengthen the capacity of all sovereign states to preserve and enhance cultural diversity ... taking into account the potential impediments to these goals that may arise from international trade, investment and services disciplines'. The convention has an uncertain or even unlimited scope, as the 'Definitions' section states that 'nothing in this Convention shall be construed to limit the sovereign authority of a Party to define such terms ... as "culture" [and] "cultural diversity"'.[56] Moreover, several aspects of the convention relate to 'cultural goods and services', although it does not define these words. Parties may also determine how to distinguish cultural goods and services, for example based on 'country of origin of the artist' or 'character, content, language or informational characteristics of such goods or services'.[57]

In comparison to the draft INCP and SAGIT instruments, this proposed convention imposes detailed obligations on parties to adopt particular types of cultural policy measures. Several of these obligations are framed in terms that appear contrary to core WTO obligations. For example, under Article VII:1:

> Each Party undertakes to provide, in accordance with its capabilities, financial support and incentives in respect of activities which will achieve the objectives of this Convention. These measures may include, but are not limited to: the provision of subsidies and grants; and the granting of any advantage, favour, privilege or immunity, including tariff and/or tax preferences.

---

[53] <www.incd.net/about.html> (accessed 4 August 2006). The INCD attended the WTO Ministerial Conferences in 2001 and 2003: <www.wto.org/english/forums_e/ngo_e/ngo_e.htm> (accessed 4 August 2006).
[54] INCD, *Advancing Cultural Diversity Globally: The Role of Civil Society Movements – Report from the Fourth Annual Conference of the International Network for Cultural Diversity in Partnership with Culturelink Network/IMO* (Opatija, 13–15 October 2003) 17.
[55] INCD, *Proposed Convention on Cultural Diversity* (15 January 2003).
[56] Ibid., art. II:1.   [57] Ibid., art. II:2(b), (c).

The words 'any advantage, favour, privilege or immunity' call to mind Article I:1 of GATT 1994, which sets out the core MFN obligation in relation to trade in goods as mentioned in Chapter 1. Article VII:1 of the proposed INCD convention appears to encourage, or at least allow, cultural policy measures that are contrary not only to MFN treatment under GATT 1994 and GATS but also to national treatment under those agreements. A party to the INCD convention that is also a WTO Member might, nevertheless, be able to fulfil its obligation to undertake cultural policy measures that are not inconsistent with WTO obligations.

Article XI:2 of the proposed INCD convention requires parties to adopt 'measures intended to preserve and enhance cultural diversity, and foster the exchange of ideas, information and artistic expression regionally, nationally and internationally', such as

(a) limitations on the number of cultural service suppliers whether in the form of numerical quotas, monopolies, exclusive service suppliers or the requirements of an economic needs test; [and]
(b) limitations on the total value of cultural service transactions or assets in the form of numerical quotas or the requirement of an economic needs test . . .

Reading Article XI:2 as a whole, what is immediately striking is that sub-paragraphs (b) to (f) are almost identical to Article XVI:2(a) to (e) of GATS, which describes market access commitments as discussed in Chapter 3.[58] The *chapeau* of Article XI:2 of the proposed INCD convention makes clear that the measures described in the sub-paragraphs are examples of the types of measures that parties agree to adopt, whereas the *chapeau* of Article XVI:2 of GATS prohibits a Member from maintaining or adopting the measures described in the sub-paragraphs in sectors for which the Member has undertaken market access commitments, unless otherwise specified in its GATS schedule. Thus, the INCD proposal appears to have been deliberately drafted in opposition to GATS market access commitments.

In contrast to the 'non-derogation' principle in Article 4 of the draft INCP convention, the proposed INCD convention states that it does not derogate from existing obligations under certain intellectual property treaties, perhaps suggesting implicitly that it may derogate from other international obligations, including those in the WTO agreements.[59] It

---

[58] See above, 110.
[59] INCD, *Proposed Convention on Cultural Diversity* (15 January 2003) art. XIII.

also provides for dispute settlement procedures to be established and specifies that, '[a]s among or between Parties, disputes concerning the meaning or application of the Convention will be resolved in accordance with the dispute procedures of this Convention and not those provided for by international trade agreements that might also apply to the measures in question'.[60] This is analogous to Article 23.1 of the DSU, which states that, '[w]hen Members seek the redress of a violation of obligations or other nullification or impairment of benefits under the covered agreements or an impediment to the attainment of any objective of the covered agreements, they shall have recourse to, and abide by', the DSU.

Evidently, a dispute regarding a violation of a WTO provision (which would need to be addressed under the DSU) might also constitute a dispute concerning the meaning of the proposed INCD convention (which would need to be addressed under that convention's procedures for dispute settlement). Indeed, certain INCD statements suggest that this is precisely the kind of dispute that the proposed convention is intended to govern, to '[e]nsure that disputes about the trade in cultural goods and services are adjudicated by cultural experts, under its terms, rather than by trade experts, under trade agreements'.[61] I consider the implications of this kind of conflict in the next section, in connection with the UNESCO Convention.

5.3 UNESCO Convention on the Protection of the Diversity of Cultural Contents and Artistic Expressions

5.3.1 Background

In March 2003, a 'Preliminary study on the technical and legal aspects relating to the desirability of a standard-setting instrument on cultural diversity' prepared by the UNESCO Secretariat was placed on the agenda of the Executive Board '[o]n the initiative of Canada, France, Germany, Greece, Mexico, Monaco, Morocco and Senegal, supported by the French-speaking group of UNESCO'.[62] This study took note of international initiatives such as those of the INCP and INCD, as well as of existing international instruments relating to cultural rights and

---

[60] Ibid., art. XIV.   [61] <www.incd.net/about.html> (accessed 4 August 2006).
[62] UNESCO, *Preliminary Study on the Technical and Legal Aspects Relating to the Desirability of a Standard-Setting Instrument on Cultural Diversity*, 166 EX/28 (12 March 2003) summary.

cultural diversity.[63] It canvassed various options for 'a new, more ambitious and ... effective instrument ... fostering States' capacity to define their cultural policies',[64] including a new instrument on cultural rights, an instrument on the status of the artist, and a new protocol to the Florence Agreement.[65] On 17 October 2003, based on a recommendation by the Executive Board,[66] UNESCO's General Conference decided that protecting 'the diversity of cultural contents and artistic expressions shall be the subject of an international convention'.[67] The General Conference invited the Director-General of UNESCO to prepare a preliminary report regarding the proposed regulation of this subject, as well as a preliminary draft convention, and to submit these documents to the General Conference at its thirty-third session.

Three meetings of fifteen independent experts (in the fields of anthropology, international law, economics of culture, and philosophy)[68] took place between December 2003 and May 2004[69] to provide opinions and a draft text to the Director-General.[70] Subsequently, three intergovernmental meetings of experts were held between September 2004 and June 2005[71] to finalise the preliminary draft convention text. The first meeting (including almost 550 experts from UNESCO Member States as well as representatives of intergovernmental and non-governmental organisations) established a drafting committee,[72] which revised the draft convention taking into account comments from UNESCO Member States, fifteen NGOs, and

---

[63] Ibid., [3]–[10], annex.   [64] Ibid., [18]–[19].   [65] Ibid., [20]–[22].
[66] UNESCO, *Decisions Adopted by the Executive Board at its 166th Session*, 166 EX/Decisions (14 May 2003) 11.
[67] General Conference, UNESCO, *Resolution 34 Adopted at the 32nd Session* (29 September 2003 – 17 October 2003) [1].
[68] UNESCO, *Preliminary Draft Convention on the Protection of the Diversity of Cultural Contents and Artistic Expressions: Preliminary Report of the Director-General*, CLT/CPD/2004/CONF.201/1 (July 2004) [5], [7]. The experts included Ivan Bernier, Tyler Cowen, and David Throsby.
[69] The meetings were held at UNESCO Headquarters in Paris from 17 to 20 December 2003, 30 March to 3 April 2004, and 28 to 31 May 2004.
[70] UNESCO, *Report of the Third Meeting of Experts (Category VI) on the Preliminary Draft of the Convention on the Protection of the Diversity of Cultural Contents and Artistic Expressions*, CLT/CPD/2004/603/5 (23 June 2004).
[71] The meetings were held at UNESCO Headquarters in Paris from 20 to 24 September 2004, 31 January to 11 February 2005, and 25 May to 3 June 2005.
[72] UNESCO, *First Session of the Intergovernmental Meeting of Experts on the Preliminary Draft Convention on the Protection of the Diversity of Cultural Contents and Artistic Expressions: Report by the Secretariat*, CLT-2004/CONF.201/9 (November 2004) [2].

three intergovernmental organisations: UNCTAD, the World Intellectual Property Organization, and the WTO.[73]

The third intergovernmental meeting finalised and transmitted the text to the Director-General and recommended that the General Conference adopt the convention in October 2005 at its thirty-third session,[74] which it did.[75] Of the 156 countries voting on the convention, 148 voted in favour, with opposing votes by Israel and the USA, and abstentions by Australia, Honduras, Liberia, and Nigeria.[76] The convention will enter into force on 18 March 2007, three months after its ratification by thirty States.[77]

5.3.2 Key features of the UNESCO Convention

One of the express objectives of the UNESCO Convention in particular highlights its relevance for the WTO. It is 'to give recognition to the distinctive nature of cultural activities, goods and services as vehicles of identity, values and meaning'.[78] This objective is mirrored in the preamble, which records the parties' conviction that 'cultural activities, goods and services have both an economic and a cultural nature ... and must therefore not be treated as solely having commercial value'.[79] In pursuing this objective, the UNESCO Convention has a fairly broad scope of application, covering those 'policies and measures adopted by the Parties [that are] related to the protection and promotion of the diversity of cultural expressions',[80]

---

[73] UNESCO, *Preliminary Draft Convention on the Protection of the Diversity of Cultural Contents and Artistic Expressions: Text Revised by the Drafting Committee, 14–17 December 2004*, CLT/CPD/2004/CONF.607/6 (23 December 2004) [7]. See also UNESCO, *Preliminary Draft Convention on the Protection of the Diversity of Cultural Contents and Artistic Expressions: Presentation of Comments and Amendments*, CLT/CPD/2004/CONF.607/1, partie IV (December 2004).

[74] UNESCO, Third Intergovernmental Meeting of Experts, *Recommendation* (3 June 2005) [2], [5]. For commentary soon after the event, see Joost Pauwelyn, 'The UNESCO Convention on Cultural Diversity, and the WTO: Diversity in International Law-Making?' (15 November 2005) *ASIL Insight*; Tomer Broude, 'Cultural Diversity and the WTO: A Diverse Relationship' (21 November 2005) *ASIL Insight*; Robert Albro, 'Managing Culture at Diversity's Expense? Thoughts on UNESCO's Newest Cultural Policy Instrument' (2005) 35(3) *Journal of Arts Management, Law, and Society* 247. See also Jan Wouters and Bart De Meester, 'UNESCO's Convention on Cultural Diversity and WTO Law: Complementary or Contradictory?' (Working Paper No. 73, KU Leuven Faculty of Law, Institute for International Law, 2005).

[75] UNESCO, 'General Conference adopts Convention on the protection and promotion of the diversity of cultural expressions', press release 2005-128 (20 October 2005).

[76] Alan Riding, 'U.S. all but alone in opposing Unesco cultural pact', *International Herald Tribune* (20 October 2005).

[77] UNESCO Convention, art. 29.1; UNESCO, 'Convention on the Protection and Promotion of the Diversity of Cultural Expressions will enter into force on 18 March 2007', press release 2006-155 (18 December 2006).

[78] Ibid., art. 1(g). [79] Ibid., preamble [18]. [80] Ibid., art. 3.

which are expressions resulting from 'the creativity of individuals, groups and societies, and that have cultural content'.[81] In turn, 'cultural content' refers to 'the symbolic meaning, artistic dimension and cultural values that originate from or express cultural identities'.[82] Some WTO Members have expressed concern about these sweeping definitions, which could extend to an almost unlimited range of products including 'computer games, designer objects, architectural services, medical services, tourism services, automobiles, steel, textiles, copper, or even rice'.[83] The UNESCO Convention could therefore impinge on many areas covered by WTO agreements such as GATT 1994, GATS, and the TRIPS Agreement.[84]

The substance of the UNESCO Convention begins with certain 'Guiding Principles' in Article 2. These include: the '[p]rinciple of respect for human rights and fundamental freedoms';[85] the '[p]rinciple of sovereignty', which declares that 'States have, in accordance with the Charter of the United Nations and the principles of international law, the sovereign right to adopt measures and policies to protect and promote the diversity of cultural expressions within their territory';[86] and the '[p]rinciple of openness and balance', whereby States adopting 'measures to support the diversity of cultural expressions ... should seek to promote ... openness to other cultures of the world'.[87]

These general principles are followed by a series of provisions setting out both rights and obligations of parties. An example of a 'right' is found in Article 6, which states that parties 'may adopt measures aimed at protecting and promoting the diversity of cultural expressions within its territory',[88] such as 'public financial assistance'[89] and 'opportunities ... for the creation, production, dissemination, distribution and enjoyment of ... domestic cultural activities, goods and services'.[90] These measures could be inconsistent with national treatment obligations in the WTO.[91] Another right that could be exercised contrary to national

---

[81] Ibid., art. 4.3.   [82] Ibid., art. 4.2.
[83] See, e.g., UNESCO, *Preliminary Draft Convention on the Protection of the Diversity of Cultural Contents and Artistic Expressions: Presentation of Comments and Amendments*, CLT/CPD/2004/CONF.607/1, partie IV (December 2004) 24–5. See also Richardson, 'Hollywood's Vision', 115–16.
[84] See, e.g., WTO, Council for Trade in Services, *Report of the Meeting Held on 23 September 2004: Note by the Secretariat*, S/C/M/74 (10 November 2004) [72] (statement by Hong Kong, China).
[85] UNESCO Convention, art. 2.1.   [86] Ibid., art. 2.2.   [87] Ibid., art. 2.8.   [88] Ibid., art. 6.1.
[89] Ibid., art. 6.2(d).   [90] Ibid., art. 6.2(b).
[91] See the concerns raised by WTO Members in UNESCO, *Preliminary Draft Convention on the Protection of the Diversity of Cultural Contents and Artistic Expressions: Presentation of Comments and Amendments*, CLT/CPD/2004/CONF.607/1, partie IV (December 2004) 24.

treatment is in Article 8, which could be described as a cultural safeguard. It states that a party 'may determine the existence of special situations where cultural expressions on its territory are at risk of extinction, under serious threat, or otherwise in need of urgent safeguarding'.[92] In this situation, parties 'may take all appropriate measures to protect and preserve cultural expressions ... in a manner consistent with the provisions of this Convention'.[93] The 'obligations' under the UNESCO Convention could also raise national treatment concerns in a WTO context. For example, Article 7.1 provides:

Parties shall endeavour to create in their territory an environment which encourages individuals and social groups:

(a) to create, produce, disseminate, distribute and have access to their own cultural expressions, paying due attention to the special circumstances and needs of women as well as various social groups, including persons belonging to minorities and indigenous peoples;
(b) to have access to diverse cultural expressions from within their territory as well as from other countries of the world.

A possible conflict with respect to MFN obligations under the WTO agreements may also arise from provisions such as Article 12, which requires parties to 'endeavour to strengthen their bilateral, regional and international cooperation for the creation of conditions conducive to the promotion of the diversity of cultural expressions ... notably in order to ... encourage the conclusion of co-production and co-distribution agreements',[94] among other things. Similarly, Article 16 states:

Developed countries shall facilitate cultural exchanges with developing countries by granting, through the appropriate institutional and legal frameworks, preferential treatment to artists and other cultural professionals and practitioners, as well as cultural goods and services from developing countries.

The broad nature of this requirement could encourage WTO Members to impose measures that are inconsistent with the general MFN rule in the WTO and not exempted by any WTO provisions for special and differential treatment of developing countries.

The UNESCO Convention also includes a dispute settlement mechanism in Article 25. This requires parties to 'seek a solution by negotiation' in the event of a dispute 'concerning the interpretation or the

---

[92] UNESCO Convention, art. 8.1.   [93] Ibid., art. 8.2.   [94] Ibid., art. 12(e).

application of the Convention'.[95] Failing that, parties may jointly seek the good offices of or mediation by a third party.[96] The final option is non-binding conciliation conducted by a 'Conciliation Commission'.[97]

Finally, of interest is Part V of the convention, governing 'Relationship to Other Instruments'. Article 20.2 states that '[n]othing in this Convention shall be interpreted as modifying rights and obligations of the Parties under any other treaties to which they are parties'. However, this apparently clear statement could conflict with certain other provisions in this part. Article 20.1 states that parties 'shall foster mutual supportiveness between this Convention and the other treaties to which they are parties' and that, 'when interpreting and applying other treaties to which they are parties or when entering into other international obligations, Parties shall take into account the relevant provisions of this Convention'. Article 21 states, furthermore, that parties 'undertake to promote the objectives and principles of this Convention in other international forums' and to consult each other as appropriate for this purpose. Perhaps these two requirements apply only to the extent that they do not involve modifying rights or obligations under other treaties.

The provisions of the UNESCO Convention dealing with dispute settlement and the relationship to other instruments were among the most controversial in finalising the text.[98] They were modified in successive versions and ultimately watered down. For example, an earlier draft included the possibility of referring disputes to the ICJ for resolution,[99] and an option whereby the UNESCO Convention would prevail over existing international instruments (other than those relating to intellectual property) where the exercise of rights and obligations under these instruments 'would cause serious damage or threat to the diversity of cultural expressions'.[100]

The drafting of the UNESCO Convention arguably took place 'in the shadow of the WTO'.[101] The drafters were well aware of the existence of

---

[95] Ibid., art. 25.1.   [96] Ibid., art. 25.2.   [97] Ibid., art. 25.3.
[98] See Ruiz Fabri, *Analyse et commentaire pour la Francophonie*, [8]–[9].
[99] UNESCO, *Preliminary Draft Convention on the Protection of the Diversity of Cultural Contents and Artistic Expressions: Preliminary Report of the Director-General*, CLT/CPD/2004/CONF.201/1 (July 2004) art. 24.
[100] Ibid., art. 19 (option B).
[101] Sebastian Oberthür and Thomas Gehring, 'Institutional Interaction in Global Environmental Governance: The Case of the Cartagena Protocol and the World Trade Organization' (2006) 6(2) *Global Environmental Politics* 1, 14.

the WTO agreements and the potential for overlap or conflict, just as they had been in negotiating environmental accords such as the Cartagena Protocol.[102] The experience of those earlier negotiations would have provided valuable lessons for the UNESCO Convention and may explain why some language in the UNESCO Convention is apparently contradictory and evocative of various environmental texts. For example, the references to 'mutual supportiveness', non-modification and non-subordination in Article 20 of the UNESCO Convention also appear in the preamble to the Cartagena Protocol, which ends:

Recognizing that trade and environment agreements should be mutually supportive with a view to achieving sustainable development,
    Emphasizing that this Protocol shall not be interpreted as implying a change in the rights and obligations of a Party under any existing international agreements,
    Understanding that the above recital is not intended to subordinate this Protocol to other international agreements ...

Conflict clauses of this kind are undoubtedly 'open-ende[d]'[103] and therefore perhaps not helpful in the sense of providing concrete guidance. On the other hand, it may be their very ambiguity that enables agreement.

Table 5.1 summarises the key features of the UNESCO Convention in comparison to the other instruments mentioned earlier in this chapter.

5.3.3 *Implications for the WTO*

A. WTO Members' views on the UNESCO Convention

UNESCO has long recognised that certain of its spheres of competence overlap with those of the WTO.[104] As mentioned in Chapter 2, nearly all WTO Members are also Member States or Associate Members of UNESCO.[105] The UNESCO Convention is therefore of particular interest to WTO Members, and the drafters of the UNESCO Convention are

---

[102] Ibid., 17.
[103] UN, ILC, *Fragmentation of International Law: Difficulties Arising from the Diversification and Expansion of International Law – Report of the Study Group – Finalized by Martti Koskenniemi*, A/CN.4/L.682 (13 April 2006) [280] (referring to the concept of mutual supportiveness).
[104] See, e.g., GATT, *Barriers to the Import and Export of Educational, Scientific and Cultural Material*, GATT/CP/12 (8 March 1949) 1–2; Sabrina Safrin, 'Treaties in Collision? The Biosafety Protocol and the World Trade Organization Agreements' (2002) 96 *American Journal of International Law* 606, 614–18.
[105] Above, 42, n. 27.

Table 5.1 *Four proposed instruments on cultural protection*

Source of instrument	Measures covered	Key rights of parties	Key obligations of parties	Relationship to other instruments	Dispute settlement
Cultural Industries SAGIT, Canada	Measures that Member States take with respect to creating, producing, distributing, performing, and exhibiting cultural content, and to the activities of cultural undertakings.	To adopt measures to support cultural content of national origin.	To co-operate in information exchange and ensure transparency. To refrain from taking measures that abridge free speech.	Council to consult with other intergovernmental organisations. Parties to consult and co-ordinate in such areas as promoting the principles of this agreement in other international forums.	Consultations; advisory decisions by panels.
INCP	Cultural policies of the parties, i.e. the framework of measures adopted by public authorities with respect to cultural expression and cultural diversity.	To take measures to preserve and promote cultural diversity within their jurisdictions.	To develop a cultural policy framework for preserving and promoting cultural diversity.	No derogation from existing rights or obligations that parties may have to each other under other international treaties. Parties to try to interpret and apply existing treaties without prejudicing the principles and objectives of this convention.	Consultations; panels.

INCD	No specific provision regarding scope of measures covered.	To define 'culture', 'cultural diversity', and 'indigenous or national culture'. To adopt measures to achieve the objectives of this convention.	To provide financial support and incentives for activities to achieve the objectives of this convention.	No derogation from existing obligations under certain specified intellectual property agreements.	Procedures to be established.
UNESCO	Policies and measures adopted by the Parties related to protecting and promoting the diversity of cultural expressions.	To adopt measures to protect and promote the diversity of cultural expressions.	To endeavour to create in their territory an environment that encourages production and access to diverse cultural expressions.	Does not modify rights and obligations of parties under any other treaties. Parties to take the relevant provisions into account when interpreting and applying other treaties. Parties to promote the principles and objectives of the convention in other international forums.	Negotiation; mediation; non-binding conciliation.

appropriately interested in the observations of the WTO on their work. The Director-General of UNESCO sought feedback from the WTO Secretariat on the UNESCO Convention, and the WTO Director-General put this request to WTO Members through the relevant bodies.[106] WTO Members responded to UNESCO in an informal discussion with UNESCO's Director of the Division of Cultural Policies and Intercultural Dialogue on 11 November 2004.[107] This provided a unique opportunity for Members such as Singapore, who are not also UNESCO Member States or Associate Members, to put forward their positions on the UNESCO Convention.[108] It also went a small way towards co-ordinating the agendas of the two organisations at an institutional level.[109]

The vast majority of WTO Members, who are also involved in the drafting of the UNESCO Convention, would ideally present the same views on the draft within UNESCO and the WTO.[110] However, the need to seek WTO Members' views separately may stem in part from the fact that different government representatives, from different ministries, may be involved in these two contexts. Normally one would expect a representative from a ministry dealing with culture to attend UNESCO meetings and a representative from a ministry dealing with international trade to attend WTO meetings.[111] Australia has therefore emphasised the need for 'appropriate inter-agency coordination to

---

[106] UNESCO, *Preliminary Draft Convention on the Protection of the Diversity of Cultural Contents and Artistic Expressions: Preliminary Report of the Director-General*, CLT/CPD/2004/CONF.201/1 (July 2004) [13]; WTO, General Council, *Annual Report 2004*, WT/GC/86 (12 January 2005) 20; WTO, General Council, *Minutes of Meeting Held on 20 October 2004*, WT/GC/M/88 (11 November 2004) [64]–[85].

[107] UNESCO, *Preliminary Draft Convention on the Protection of the Diversity of Cultural Contents and Artistic Expressions: Presentation of Comments and Amendments*, CLT/CPD/2004/CONF.607/1, partie IV (December 2004) 23; General Conference, UNESCO, *Preliminary Report by the Director-General Setting out the Situation to be Regulated and the Possible Scope of the Regulating Action Proposed, Accompanied by the Preliminary Draft of a Convention on the Protection and of the Diversity of Cultural Contents and Artistic Expressions*, 33 C/23 (4 August 2005) [17].

[108] WTO, General Council, *Minutes of Meeting Held on 20 October 2004*, WT/GC/M/88 (11 November 2004) [69].

[109] On the importance of this kind of co-ordination, see generally Victor Mosoti, 'Institutional Cooperation and Norm Creation in International Organizations' in Cottier, Pauwelyn, and Bürgi, *Human Rights and Trade*, 165.

[110] See Ruiz Fabri, *Analyse et commentaire pour la Francophonie*, [4].

[111] See, e.g., Keith Acheson and Christopher Maule, 'Convention on Cultural Diversity' (2004) 28 *Journal of Cultural Economics* 243, 245, 251; Gagné, 'Une Convention internationale', 61.

guarantee a whole-of-government approach' in relation to the UNESCO Convention.[112]

It seems that, generally speaking, WTO Members agree that the UNESCO Convention and the WTO should be 'mutually supportive'.[113] However, as in the WTO negotiations, Members have expressed quite different opinions regarding the relationship between trade and culture, and the application of WTO disciplines to cultural products, in connection with the UNESCO Convention. In addition to the discussion with UNESCO in November 2004, Members have aired their views in various informal sessions organised at the WTO while the UNESCO Convention was being drafted. The WTO delegations of Chile, Chinese Taipei, Hong Kong, Japan, Mexico, and the USA organised an informal seminar in September 2004 on trade and culture 'to facilitate the exchange of views among WTO Members on the role of trade in enhancing cultural diversity and to explore the relationship between WTO instruments, UNESCO instruments and cultural diversity'.[114] These Members typically seek liberalisation in relation to cultural products, and particularly audiovisual services. Other Members are more closely aligned with the position of the INCD, which organised a seminar relating to the UNESCO Convention as part of the WTO's public symposium in April 2005.[115]

It is worth noting that WTO Members such as the USA, who take the view that cultural products do not require any special treatment beyond that provided by existing provisions, are unlikely to become a party to the UNESCO Convention, even though UNESCO's General Conference has adopted it. Or, if they do become a party, they may take advantage of the possibility of making reservations to it.[116] Indeed, at the June 2005 UNESCO meeting at which the text of the

---

[112] WTO, General Council, *Minutes of Meeting Held on 20 October 2004*, WT/GC/M/88 (11 November 2004) [65].

[113] UNESCO, *Preliminary Draft Convention on the Protection of the Diversity of Cultural Contents and Artistic Expressions: Presentation of Comments and Amendments*, CLT/CPD/2004/CONF.607/1, partie IV (December 2004) 23.

[114] WTO, Council for Trade in Services, *Report of the Meeting Held on 23 September 2004: Note by the Secretariat*, S/C/M/74 (10 November 2004) [74].

[115] WTO, *Information Note from the Director-General, WTO Public Symposium – 'WTO After 10 Years: Global Problems and Multilateral Solutions'*, 20 to 22 April 2005, WT/INF/87 (13 April 2005) 5.

[116] See generally Palitha Kohona, 'Reservations: Discussion of Recent Developments in the Practice of the Secretary-General of the United Nations as Depositary of Multilateral Treaties' (2005) 33(2) *Georgia Journal of International and Comparative Law* 415.

UNESCO Convention was finalised for consideration by the General Conference of UNESCO, several UNESCO Member States made partial or complete reservations to the final draft text.[117] The USA, for one, formally objected to certain aspects of the draft.[118] It has also described the UNESCO Convention as 'deeply flawed', with the potential to 'impair rights and obligations under other international agreements and adversely impact prospects for successful completion of the Doha Development Round negotiations'.[119] The legal effect of reservations of this kind would depend on their exact content and form.

In the following sections, I examine some of the key implications of the UNESCO Convention, for the WTO as a whole, keeping in mind the problems and guidelines identified in Part I of this book in order to determine whether the UNESCO Convention is likely to provide a positive solution. I first consider the potential influence of the UNESCO Convention on the conduct of WTO Members who are also parties to the UNESCO Convention in WTO negotiations and in resolving WTO-related disputes. I then assess the possibility for a WTO Member to challenge the UNESCO Convention as such through WTO dispute settlement. Finally, I consider whether a WTO Member that is also a party to the UNESCO Convention could point to that convention as a defence to a WTO violation independently of any of the express exceptions discussed in Chapter 4.

B. Conduct of UNESCO Convention parties in the WTO

A WTO Member that was also a party to the UNESCO Convention might wish to refrain from making offers in the GATS negotiations regarding audiovisual services. The Member could point to the recognition under GATS of the legitimacy of 'national policy objectives'[120] and the need to promote the principles of the UNESCO Convention, under Article 21, as a multilateral basis for this negotiating stance. This could support the Member's position that cultural policy objectives are not simply disguised protectionism. Indeed, Acheson and Maule suggest that the

---

[117] See, e.g., General Conference, UNESCO, *Preliminary Report by the Director-General Setting out the Situation to be Regulated and the Possible Scope of the Regulating Action Proposed, Accompanied by the Preliminary Draft of a Convention on the Protection and of the Diversity of Cultural Contents and Artistic Expressions*, 33 C/23 (4 August 2005) [58]–[59], [61], [63]. Mexico has ratified the UNESCO Convention subject to a reservation.
[118] See, e.g., ibid., [58], [59], [61], [70].
[119] Robert Martin, *Final Statement of the United States Delegation: Third Session of the Intergovernmental Meeting of Experts, UNESCO* (Paris, 3 June 2005).
[120] GATS, art. XIX:2.

UNESCO Convention may have been 'designed to improve the bargaining position of its members in WTO negotiations'.[121]

This conduct would be unlikely to violate any WTO obligations. As explained in Chapter 3, the design of GATS is intentionally flexible, so that no WTO Member is legally bound under the WTO agreements to make national treatment or market access commitments in any particular service sector, whether or not they have committed to do so or to refrain from doing so under another international instrument. However, the Member would likely have to 'pay' for its refusal to improve commitments in relation to cultural products as part of its overall negotiating package.[122] Any negotiating trade-off could affect other Members with interests in the sectors concerned. Moreover, for the WTO as an institution, and the WTO Membership as a whole, widespread reliance on the UNESCO Convention in WTO negotiations would be contrary to the WTO objective of pursuing progressive liberalisation under GATS and the WTO more generally.[123] Accordingly, in response to UNESCO's request for comments on the draft UNESCO Convention, several WTO Members expressed concern about this potential impact on WTO negotiations.[124]

A WTO Member that was also a party to the UNESCO Convention might wish to challenge a trade measure of another WTO Member and party to the UNESCO Convention on the basis that it violated rights and obligations contained in the UNESCO Convention. In these circumstances, the question arises whether the WTO Member could choose to bring the dispute within the dispute settlement mechanism established by the UNESCO Convention, rather than within the WTO dispute settlement system. Indeed, some Members have raised concerns about the potential for conflict between dispute settlement in these two settings.[125]

Recall that Article 23.1 of the DSU states:

---

[121] Acheson and Maule, 'Convention on Cultural Diversity', 251. See also Bernier and Ruiz Fabri, *Un instrument sur la diversité culturelle*, 42; Gagné, 'Une Convention internationale', 60; Trebilcock and Howse, *Regulation of International Trade* (3rd edn) 640; Wunsch-Vincent, *WTO, Internet and Digital Products*, 198–9.
[122] See Lelio Iapadre, 'Comment' (2004) 28 *Journal of Cultural Economics* 267, 269.
[123] GATS, art. XIX:1; Marrakesh Agreement, preamble.
[124] UNESCO, *Preliminary Draft Convention on the Protection of the Diversity of Cultural Contents and Artistic Expressions: Presentation of Comments and Amendments*, CLT/CPD/2004/CONF.607/1, partie IV (December 2004) 25.
[125] Ibid., 26.

When Members seek the redress of a violation of obligations or other nullification or impairment of benefits under the covered agreements or an impediment to the attainment of any objective of the covered agreements, they shall have recourse to, and abide by, the rules and procedures of this Understanding.

This suggests that a Member that chooses to 'seek the redress' of a violation of a WTO agreement cannot do so through any means other than the WTO dispute settlement system. This is confirmed by Article 23.2(a), which states that, '[i]n such cases', Members shall 'not make a determination to the effect that a violation has occurred, that benefits have been nullified or impaired or that the attainment of any objective of the covered agreements has been impeded, except through recourse to dispute settlement in accordance with' the DSU. One WTO Panel has described Article 23 as incorporating the 'fundamental principle' that the WTO dispute settlement system provides 'the exclusive means to redress any violations of any provisions of the WTO Agreement'.[126]

To date, these provisions have been raised in WTO disputes in response to unilateral actions by Members. For example, in *US – Certain EC Products*, the EC challenged retaliatory duties that the USA imposed on its imports in response to the EC's alleged failure to bring into conformity with the WTO agreements measures that were found to be WTO-inconsistent in *EC – Bananas III*.[127] The Panel found that the USA had acted inconsistently with Article 23.1 of the DSU,[128] essentially by taking matters into its own hands instead of pursuing its concerns with the EC's conduct through the WTO dispute settlement procedure. However, the 'exclusive' nature of Article 23 could also restrict a WTO Member from pursuing a dispute in another forum, such as under the UNESCO Convention. Marceau, for example, considers that Article 23 precludes Members from taking 'their WTO-related disputes ... to another forum'.[129]

In my view, this would depend on the nature of the dispute and the steps taken by the complaining Member towards its resolution. As Yuval Shany points out, Article 23 of the DSU does not impose 'watertight' exclusivity.[130] If the Member was challenging a measure on the basis

---

[126] Panel Report, *US – Certain EC Products*, [6.13].
[127] Ibid., [2.21]–[2.25].   [128] Ibid., [7.1(a)].
[129] Marceau, 'Conflicts of Norms', 1101. On overlaps between WTO disputes and international disputes in other forums, see Joost Pauwelyn, 'Adding Sweeteners to Softwood Lumber: The WTO–NAFTA "Spaghetti Bowl" is Cooking' (2006) 9(1) *Journal of International Economic Law* 197.
[130] Yuval Shany, *The Competing Jurisdictions of International Courts and Tribunals* (2003) 185.

that it violated the UNESCO Convention, it would arguably not be seeking the redress of a 'violation of obligations or other nullification or impairment of benefits under the covered agreements or an impediment to the attainment of any objective of the covered agreements' within the meaning of Article 23.1 of the DSU. It could therefore pursue the dispute under the UNESCO Convention without violating any WTO obligations.

What if a WTO Member decided, in view of its commitments under the UNESCO Convention, to refrain from pursuing a WTO dispute in relation to a cultural policy measure imposed by another WTO Member and party to the UNESCO Convention because the measure pursued the objectives of the UNESCO Convention, even though it appeared to be inconsistent with the WTO agreements? Instead, the first Member might simply consult with the other Member, as envisaged under Article 21 of the UNESCO Convention. If the purpose of the consultations was to raise concerns about WTO violations, this might involve 'seek[ing] the redress' of a WTO violation other than through the WTO dispute settlement system, contrary to Article 23.1 of the DSU. On the other hand, it would seem to go too far to interpret Article 23.1 of the DSU as preventing WTO Members from resolving WTO disputes amicably, without resorting to formal consultations within the WTO dispute settlement system. This would also be unrealistic. In practice, Members frequently engage in informal consultations before commencing formal proceedings. Indeed, Article 4.2 of the DSU may implicitly recognise that Members will consult before lodging a formal request for consultations, which must be notified to the DSB. It states, in general terms, that '[e]ach Member undertakes to accord sympathetic consideration to and afford adequate opportunity for consultation regarding any representations made by another Member concerning measures affecting the operation of any covered agreement taken within the territory of the former'. To preclude this avenue of dispute resolution would be contrary to the aim of the dispute settlement system, which is to resolve disputes, preferably through a 'mutually agreed solution'.[131]

Accordingly, as long as WTO Members do not seek to resolve disputes regarding the WTO-consistency of their measures through formal dispute settlement under the UNESCO Convention, Article 23.1 of the DSU would not appear to preclude them from consulting each

---

[131] DSU, art. 3.7.

other to resolve a dispute taking into account the objectives of that convention.[132]

In this way, the UNESCO Convention could assist Members in resolving disputes about cultural policy measures without resorting to formal dispute settlement.[133] If both Members were party to the UNESCO Convention, its terms could provide a useful background for consultations, as a set of principles and objectives on which they agree. However, this limits the effectiveness of the UNESCO Convention in resolving the WTO stalemate on cultural products, because it would help only like-minded Members resolve their disputes about cultural policy measures. A Member that was a party to the UNESCO Convention might gain some comfort from the knowledge that other Members who were also parties would likely refrain from challenging its cultural policy measures in formal WTO dispute settlement. However, the greater concern would be the response of WTO Members that are not parties to the UNESCO Convention. It is these Members who would be most likely to challenge these measures, whether or not the UNESCO Convention ultimately enters into force.

In addition, from an institutional perspective, mutually agreed solutions are not always ideal. Thus, Article 3.7 of the DSU states that a 'solution mutually acceptable to the parties to a dispute *and consistent with the covered agreements* is clearly to be preferred'.[134] A mutually agreed solution to a dispute that has been formally raised in the WTO system must be consistent with the covered agreements and must be notified to the WTO Membership through the DSB.[135] However, where Members resolve their disputes amicably without taking any formal steps towards resolution within the WTO (specifically through a formal request for consultations), other Members may be unaware of the existence of the dispute and how it is resolved. This lack of transparency and of focus on WTO-consistent dispute resolution could conflict with the objective of the WTO dispute settlement system as 'a central element in providing security and predictability to the multilateral trading system'.[136] Resolving disputes through consultations and without necessarily applying WTO rules could mean retaining cultural policy measures that are more trade-restrictive than necessary to achieve their goals. It could also prevent the

---

[132] See also Pauwelyn, *Conflict of Norms*, 317–18.
[133] A comparable situation may arise under multilateral environmental agreements. See, e.g., WTO, Committee on Trade and Environment, *Report (1996) of the Committee on Trade and Environment*, WT/CTE/1 (12 November 1996) [178].
[134] Emphasis added.   [135] DSU, arts. 3.4, 3.6.   [136] Ibid., art. 3.2.

dispute settlement system from fulfilling its role of 'preserv[ing] the rights and obligations of Members under the covered agreements, and [clarifying] the existing provisions of those agreements',[137] including the uncertain exceptions that are of particular relevance to cultural products.

C. Complaints relating to the UNESCO Convention

According to the Appellate Body, '[i]n principle, any act or omission attributable to a WTO Member can be a measure of that Member for purposes of dispute settlement proceedings',[138] and a Member may challenge another Member's measures 'as such' or 'as applied' in a particular instance.[139] The UNESCO Convention itself would not be a measure 'taken by'[140] or 'attributable to' a WTO Member, so it could probably not be challenged as an inconsistent measure in the WTO.

The most obvious way in which a WTO Member might challenge another Member's conduct in relation to the UNESCO Convention is through a 'violation' complaint[141] against another Member's measure taken in accordance with the UNESCO Convention – that is, a claim that the UNESCO Convention as applied in a particular government measure violates one or more WTO provisions. Below, I discuss whether the UNESCO Convention could provide a defence to such a measure. However, a WTO Member might also wish to challenge another Member's very entry into the UNESCO Convention. In becoming parties to the UNESCO Convention, WTO Members could take steps that could be challenged as such in WTO dispute settlement – such as signing or ratifying the UNESCO Convention. If a challenge of this kind would be likely to succeed, this would provide a strong indication that the UNESCO Convention cannot provide a solution to the trade–culture problem in the WTO. It is therefore worth considering this possibility, even though it may be improbable from a political standpoint that a Member would publicly challenge another Member's sovereign right to become a party to an international treaty.

Taking steps to become a party to the UNESCO Convention would mean, for example, accepting an obligation 'to endeavour to create in their territory an environment that encourages individuals and social groups to create, produce, disseminate, distribute and have access to their own cultural expressions'.[142] However, this obligation is unlikely

---

[137] Ibid., art. 3.2.
[138] Appellate Body Report, *US – Corrosion-Resistant Steel Sunset Review*, [81]. See also DSU, art. 3.3.
[139] Appellate Body Report, *US – Corrosion-Resistant Steel Sunset Review*, [82].
[140] See DSU, art. 3.3.   [141] GATS, art. XXIII:1.   [142] UNESCO Convention, art. 7.1(a).

of itself to violate any WTO obligations. To begin with, the obligation is merely to 'endeavour' to do something, without necessarily requiring any particular result or the use of any particular means. In addition, although the notion of privileging one's 'own cultural expressions' may seem contrary to the spirit of national treatment, governments could find ways of ensuring production of and access to these expressions without necessarily restricting foreign cultural products. Indeed, the same provision of the UNESCO Convention recognises the importance of providing access 'to diverse cultural expressions from within their territory as well as from other countries of the world'.[143]

It is true that the mere fact that a measure may be implemented in a WTO-consistent or WTO-inconsistent manner (in other words, a measure's discretionary as opposed to mandatory nature) does not necessarily mean that the measure as such is WTO-consistent.[144] But it is extremely unlikely that a Panel or the Appellate Body would declare inconsistent as such a WTO Member's decision to become a party to another multilateral treaty incorporating aspirational provisions that reflect non-trade concerns. This would be contrary to the recognition in GATS of the need to give 'due respect to national policy objectives',[145] as well as the Appellate Body's typical 'institutional sensitivity',[146] 'institutional modesty',[147] and 'sensitivity to domestic policy'.[148] It might also suggest that a WTO Member had joined the UNESCO Convention in bad faith and without regard to its other international obligations, which would be an extraordinary suggestion.[149]

This leaves the possibility of a 'non-violation' complaint[150] against a WTO Member's actions in becoming a party to the UNESCO Convention.

---

[143] Ibid., art. 7.1(b).
[144] Appellate Body Report, *US – Corrosion-Resistant Steel Sunset Review*, [93]; Panel Report, *US – Section 301 Trade Act*, [7.53].
[145] GATS, preamble, art. XIX:2.
[146] Howse, 'Adjudicative Legitimacy and Treaty Interpretation', 64.
[147] Weiler, 'Rule of Lawyers', 206.   [148] Footer, 'EC – Asbestos', 141.
[149] See below, 206.
[150] Under GATT 1994, a third type of complaint would be possible: a 'situation' complaint under Article XXIII:1(c). However, this type of complaint does not exist under GATS, and in any case it has virtually never been used under either GATT 1947 or the WTO: Peter Morrison, 'WTO Dispute Settlement in Services: Procedural and Substantive Aspects' in Ernst-Ulrich Petersmann (ed.), *International Trade Law and the GATT/WTO Dispute Settlement System* (1999) 377, 380. See also Frieder Roessler, 'The Concept of Nullification and Impairment in the Legal System of the World Trade Organization' in Ernst-Ulrich Petersmann (ed.), *International Trade Law and the GATT/WTO Dispute Settlement System* (1999) 124, 139.

In non-violation complaints, a Member argues that another Member's measure is nullifying or impairing benefits that it could reasonably have expected to accrue to it under a WTO agreement, even though the measure may not conflict with that agreement.[151] Complainants will usually find it harder to make out non-violation complaints than violation complaints.[152] A complainant challenging the UNESCO Convention as such in a non-violation complaint would probably have to show that it had a legitimate expectation of market access for its cultural products in the respondent Member's territory and that this expectation has been nullified or impaired because, by becoming a party to the UNESCO Convention, the respondent has upset the competitive relationship between its own cultural products and foreign cultural products.[153]

This would be a difficult case to establish. A Member cannot have a legitimate expectation that it will have a continuing benefit under the WTO agreements if it could reasonably have anticipated, at the end of the Uruguay Round, that this benefit would be curtailed through a measure of the kind challenged. Given the heated debates during the Uruguay Round and the failure to reach agreement on how to deal with cultural products (and particularly audiovisual services under GATS), a pro-trade Member could reasonably have anticipated that a pro-culture Member would be likely to make use of all the available flexibility in the WTO provisions to impose cultural policy measures. Moreover, merely becoming a party to the UNESCO Convention (as opposed to implementing it through specific discriminatory or trade-restrictive measures) is unlikely to upset the competitive relationship between local and foreign cultural products.

The Appellate Body might be even more reluctant to uphold a non-violation complaint, given the rarity and controversy surrounding these complaints. In particular, some favour abolishing non-violation complaints and maintain that, at the least, Panels and the Appellate Body should 'use their unusual power to grant the right to retaliate against the denial of "un-negotiated benefits" only in those rare instances in which the membership of the WTO, through consensus

---

[151] GATT 1994, art. XXIII:1(b); GATS, art. XXIII:3. See also DSU, art. 26.
[152] Appellate Body Report, *EC – Asbestos*, 186.
[153] See Panel Report, *EC – Asbestos*, [8.288]; Panel Report, *Japan – Film*, [10.61], [10.82]. See also Mary Footer and Carol George, 'The General Agreement on Trade in Services' in Macrory, Appleton, and Plummer, *The World Trade Organization* (vol. I) 799, 868.

decisions or consistent practice, has provided them with normative guidance'.[154]

In summary, then, it seems unlikely that merely becoming a party to the UNESCO Convention would involve violating existing WTO obligations or otherwise nullifying or impairing benefits of other Members under the WTO agreements. Furthermore, as already mentioned, WTO Members would probably recoil from the idea of formally questioning each other's foreign policy decisions in signing or ratifying a given treaty. From this perspective, at least, the UNESCO Convention should not be a cause for concern among WTO Members generally, or in relation to the specific problem of trade and cultural products in the WTO. However, to determine whether the UNESCO Convention could nevertheless worsen or improve the current treatment of cultural products in WTO law, it is necessary to consider whether it could be used as a defence in a WTO dispute.

D. The UNESCO Convention as a defence to a WTO violation

As a complainant is unlikely to succeed in challenging in a WTO dispute a Member's entry into the UNESCO Convention *per se*, it might instead choose to challenge a cultural policy measure taken by another Member in applying or implementing the UNESCO Convention. Could the respondent rely on the UNESCO Convention as a defence to a claim that a cultural policy measure violates its WTO obligations? The short answer to this question is no, because by its own terms the UNESCO Convention is not to be 'interpreted as modifying rights and obligations of the Parties under any other treaties to which they are parties'.[155] This limits the extent to which the UNESCO Convention could improve (or worsen) the treatment of cultural products within the WTO. It is nevertheless worth considering what might happen in the absence of this explicit 'conflict' provision, because reservations to the UNESCO Convention are possible, as highlighted above. In addition, other multilateral instruments of this kind might take a different approach.

A Member arguing that the UNESCO Convention provides a defence to a WTO violation would need to overcome two hurdles. First, it would need to establish that Panels and the Appellate Body are entitled or obliged, in resolving WTO disputes, to apply international laws not

---

[154] Frieder Roessler and Petina Gappah, 'A Re-appraisal of Non-Violation Complaints under the WTO Dispute Settlement Procedures' in Macrory, Appleton, and Plummer, *The World Trade Organization* (vol. I) 1371, 1383.
[155] UNESCO Convention, art. 20.2.

specifically set out in the WTO agreements. Second, it would need to show that the relevant conflict rules mean that, to the extent of inconsistency, the provision of the UNESCO Convention requiring or permitting the challenged measure prevails over the WTO provision prohibiting that measure. I consider these issues in turn below. If the Member managed to overcome both hurdles, this would provide it with additional flexibility in pursuing cultural objectives in a WTO-consistent manner. This could improve the current situation in the eyes of some Members and might therefore encourage them to increase their GATS commitments to cultural products.

(i) Applying the UNESCO Convention in a WTO dispute
If the Appellate Body accepted a provision of the UNESCO Convention or a similar instrument as an independent defence to a WTO violation, it would be applying that instrument in a WTO dispute, rather than merely using it as an aid to interpretation in the manner discussed in Chapter 4. Applying public international law in WTO disputes is much more controversial and problematic than using it to interpret WTO provisions. The DSU makes fairly clear that Panels and the Appellate Body are restricted to hearing claims under WTO agreements.[156] However, according to Pauwelyn, 'the fact that the substantive jurisdiction of WTO panels is limited to claims under WTO covered agreements does not mean that the applicable law available to a WTO panel is necessarily limited to WTO covered agreements'.[157] The ILC Study Group on fragmentation agreed.[158]

The DSU does not clearly specify whether Panels and the Appellate Body may apply international law in resolving WTO claims. As mentioned in Chapter 4, the second sentence of Article 3.2 of the DSU states that the dispute settlement system 'serves to preserve the rights and

---

[156] See DSU, arts. 1.1, 11, 17.6, 19.1. See also Marceau, 'Conflicts of Norms', 1107; Marceau, 'WTO Dispute Settlement and Human Rights', 763, 767; Pauwelyn, *Conflict of Norms*, 444. But see Joel Trachtman, 'Review of Joost Pauwelyn, Conflict of Norms in Public International Law: How WTO Law Relates to Other Rules of International Law' (2004) 98 *American Journal of International Law* 855, 857.
[157] Joost Pauwelyn, 'The Role of Public International Law in the WTO: How Far Can We Go?' (2001) 95 *American Journal of International Law* 535, 560. See also Lorand Bartels, 'Applicable Law in WTO Dispute Settlement Proceedings' (2001) 35(3) *Journal of World Trade* 499, 499, 502, 519.
[158] UN, ILC, *Fragmentation of International Law: Difficulties Arising from the Diversification and Expansion of International Law – Report of the Study Group – Finalized by Martti Koskenniemi*, A/CN.4/L.682 (13 April 2006) [45], [166].

obligations of Members under the covered agreements, and to clarify the existing provisions of those agreements in accordance with customary rules of interpretation of public international law'. Some commentators regard this sentence as precluding resort to customary international law rules other than interpretative rules.[159] Marceau and Trachtman use similar *a contrario* reasoning in relation to Articles 7.1 and 7.2 of the DSU. Under Article 7.1, the standard terms of reference for Panels involve examining the matter 'in the light of the relevant provisions' in the relevant WTO agreements. Under Article 7.2, Panels are required to 'address the relevant provisions in any covered agreement or agreements cited by the parties to the dispute'. This could indicate that Panels may not examine the matter before them in the light of public international law or address this law in their Reports.[160] Marceau and Trachtman also point to provisions such as Article 19.2 and the third sentence of Article 3.2 of the DSU (which preclude Panels, the Appellate Body, and the DSB from making recommendations or rulings that 'add to or diminish the rights and obligations provided in the covered agreements') as indicating that these bodies may not apply international laws that are not expressly contained or referred to in WTO provisions.[161]

In contrast, Pauwelyn maintains that WTO law is merely one branch of public international law[162] and that, except to the extent that the covered agreements exclude other international law rules, Panels and the Appellate Body may apply these rules in deciding claims properly before them.[163] According to Pauwelyn, although Article 7.2 of the DSU requires Panels to address WTO provisions, it does not prohibit them from addressing other rules of international law. In fact, Pauwelyn

---

[159] See, e.g., John McGinnis, 'The Appropriate Hierarchy of Global Multilateralism and Customary International Law: The Example of the WTO' (2003) 44 *Virginia Journal of International Law* 229, 255, 266–8.

[160] Marceau, 'Conflicts of Norms', 1102; Joel Trachtman, 'The Domain of WTO Dispute Resolution' (1999) 40(2) *Harvard International Law Journal* 333, 342.

[161] Marceau, 'Conflicts of Norms', 1102–4; Marceau, 'WTO Dispute Settlement and Human Rights', 763–4; Trachtman, 'Domain of WTO Dispute Resolution', 342. See also Debra Steger, 'The Jurisdiction of the World Trade Organization' (2004) 98 *American Society of International Law Proceedings* 142, 143–4; Joel Trachtman, 'The Jurisdiction of the World Trade Organization' (2004) 98 *American Society of International Law Proceedings* 139, 140–1.

[162] Pauwelyn, *Conflict of Norms*, 25–40. See also Pieter Jan Kuijper, 'The Law of GATT as a Special Field of International Law' (1994) *Netherlands Yearbook of International Law* 227.

[163] Pauwelyn, *Conflict of Norms*, 465. See also Bartels, 'Applicable Law in WTO Disputes', 518; Panel Report, *Korea – Procurement*, [7.96].

maintains that Article 7.1 (under which Panels' standard terms of reference provide for Panels to 'make such findings as will assist the DSB in making the recommendations or in giving the rulings provided for' in the relevant WTO agreements) and Article 11 (under which Panels are to 'make such other findings as will assist the DSB in making' these recommendations or rulings) reveal that Panels may make findings regarding international law outside the WTO agreements.[164]

From this brief overview of an intense and ongoing debate, it is clear that the provisions of the DSU may be interpreted in support of or against applying international laws in WTO disputes. My own view is that Panels and the Appellate Body are bound to apply certain limited aspects of international law even though these may not be expressly incorporated in the WTO agreements. Without this possibility, these bodies would not be able to fulfil the functions that the drafters of the agreements assigned to them. However, more important for present purposes is the Appellate Body's view on applying non-WTO international law within WTO disputes. To predict the Appellate Body's likely approach to this question in relation to the UNESCO Convention, it is necessary to examine its reasoning to date on applying international law in the WTO, as well as Members' responses to this reasoning. I begin by surveying certain early appeals involving customary international law and non-WTO treaties, before addressing several disputes that raised the international law principle of good faith, and returning to the recent case of *Mexico – Taxes on Soft Drinks*.[165]

In general, although the Appellate Body has not ruled out applying international law, it has been cautious in doing so. This is exemplified by the 1998 Appellate Body decision in *EC – Hormones*, which related to the 'precautionary principle'.[166] The Appellate Body drew a distinction between 'customary international *environmental* law' and '*general* or *customary international law*',[167] suggesting that the status of the precautionary principle might be more settled in the former field than in the latter. Noting the absence of agreement in academic and legal

---

[164] Pauwelyn, *Conflict of Norms*, 466, 469. See also Joost Pauwelyn, 'The Jurisdiction of the World Trade Organization' (2004) 98 *American Society of International Law Proceedings* 135, 138.
[165] See above, 167.
[166] See generally Gabrielle Marceau, 'La jurisprudence sur le principe de précaution dans le droit de l'OMC' (paper presented at the Leçon inaugurale, Faculté de Droit de l'Université de Genève, 19 May 2005).
[167] Appellate Body Report, *EC – Hormones*, [123] (original emphasis).

communities regarding the status of this principle, the Appellate Body declined to take a position on this question (the Panel in *EC – Biotech* reached a similar conclusion).[168] Nevertheless, the Appellate Body in *EC – Hormones* stated that the precautionary principle is reflected in Article 5.7 of the SPS Agreement.[169]

A few months later, in *Argentina – Textiles and Apparel*, the Appellate Body had to address a 'Memorandum of Understanding' between Argentina and the International Monetary Fund in a complaint by the USA against Argentina. Argentina argued that this memorandum required Argentina to impose the tax challenged by the USA, and that the USA had acquiesced in the creation of this requirement.[170] The Appellate Body found that Argentina had established neither a 'legally binding' obligation under the memorandum to impose the challenged tax, nor an 'irreconcilable conflict' between the memorandum and the relevant WTO provisions.[171] Accordingly, the Appellate Body did not need to determine which instrument would prevail in the event of a conflict.

Shortly thereafter, in *EC – Poultry*, the Appellate Body faced a bilateral agreement concluded between the disputing parties (EC and Brazil) before the WTO agreements entered into force.[172] The Appellate Body declined to examine whether the EC's GATT schedule terminated this 'Oilseeds Agreement', as argued by the EC,[173] because it considered that the Oilseeds Agreement was 'not a "covered agreement" within the meaning of Articles 1 and 2 of the DSU'[174] and therefore did not 'for[m] the legal basis for this dispute'.[175]

I turn now to the principle of good faith. Article 3.10 of the DSU provides that, 'if a dispute arises, all Members will engage in these procedures in good faith in an effort to resolve the dispute'. In *EC – Sardines*, the Appellate Body stated that '[w]e must assume that Members of the WTO will abide by their treaty obligations in good faith, as required by the principle of *pacta sunt servanda* articulated in Article 26' of the VCLT.[176] On its own, this does not necessarily mean that the

---

[168] Panel Report, *EC – Biotech*, [7.88]–[7.89].
[169] Appellate Body Report, *EC – Hormones*, [124].
[170] Appellate Body Report, *Argentina – Textiles and Apparel*, [13].
[171] Ibid., [69]. See also Deborah Siegel, 'Legal Aspects of the IMF/WTO Relationship: The Fund's Articles of Agreement and the WTO Agreements' (2002) 96 *American Journal of International Law* 561, 572-6.
[172] Appellate Body Report, *EC – Poultry*, [2].   [173] Ibid., [78]–[79].   [174] Ibid., [79].
[175] Ibid., [81].   [176] See, e.g., Appellate Body Report, *EC – Sardines*, [278].

Appellate Body regards WTO Members as bound to carry out their WTO obligations in good faith – rather, this could simply be an example of the Appellate Body showing deference to WTO Members.

In *US – Offset Act (Byrd Amendment)*, the Appellate Body addressed this question more directly, stating with reference to Article 26 of the VCLT and not to Article 3.10 of the DSU: 'Clearly, therefore, there is a basis for a dispute settlement panel to determine, in an appropriate case, whether a Member has not acted in good faith.'[177] This suggests that the Appellate Body might be willing to apply the principle of good faith beyond that articulated in the DSU. In *US – Offset Act (Byrd Amendment)*, however, the Appellate Body rejected the Panel's conclusion that the USA had not acted in good faith.[178]

During the meeting at which the DSB adopted the Panel and Appellate Body Reports in this case, the USA agreed that Members must implement their obligations in good faith under international law. However, it indicated that it was 'troubled' by the Appellate Body's suggestion that a Panel could find that a Member had not acted in good faith because the mandate of the dispute settlement system 'was to determine conformity with the "covered agreements", and not international law more generally. Nowhere in Appendix 1 to the DSU, which defined the covered agreements for purposes of the DSU, was there listed an international law principle of good faith'.[179] In relation to a subsequent Panel statement on good faith,[180] the USA made a similar criticism, pointing out that citing Appellate Body Reports on good faith is not sufficient authority for applying this principle because adopted Panel and Appellate Body Reports are not part of the covered agreements and cannot add to or diminish the rights or obligations under those agreements.[181]

Other Members have also criticised, at DSB meetings, the use by Panels of the substantive international law principle of good faith under Article 26 of the VCLT. For example, in *Korea – Procurement*, the Panel referred to Article 26 and the negotiating history of the VCLT in

---

[177] Appellate Body Report, *US – Offset Act (Byrd Amendment)*, [297].
[178] Ibid., [298]–[299]. See also Appellate Body Report, *EC – Export Subsidies on Sugar*, [319]–[320].
[179] WTO, DSB, *Minutes of Meeting – Held in the Centre William Rappard on 27 January 2003*, WT/DSB/M/142 (6 March 2003) [57].
[180] Panel Report, *Argentina – Poultry Anti-Dumping Duties*, [7.35]–[7.36].
[181] WTO, DSB, *Minutes of Meeting Held in the Centre William Rappard on 19 May 2003*, WT/DSB/M/150 (22 July 2003) [44]–[45].

concluding that WTO Members are obliged to negotiate treaties in good faith and that a failure to do so could invalidate the treaty.[182] Korea[183] and the Philippines criticised the Panel's use of international law in this regard. The Philippines, in particular, was

> concerned about this statement because panels should interpret the rights and obligations of Members in a manner consistent with the covered agreements and in accordance with the general rules of interpretation of customary international law. There was a distinction between the rules of interpretation and the rights and obligations under customary international law. Members agreed to be subject to dispute settlement proceedings to deal with disputes which involved their rights and obligations under the covered agreements. Members did not intend the WTO to be the arbiter of their rights and obligations under customary international law.[184]

More recently, in *EC - Export Subsidies on Sugar*, the EC argued that 'estoppel is a general principle of international law, which follows from the broader principle of good faith'.[185] In the circumstances, the Appellate Body did not need to determine whether estoppel is a general principle of international law.[186] However, it expressed some doubt about applying this principle in WTO dispute settlement:

> [I]it is far from clear that the estoppel principle applies in the context of WTO dispute settlement.[187]

> [E]ven assuming *arguendo* that the principle of estoppel could apply in the WTO, its application would fall within th[e] narrow parameters set out in [Articles 3.7 and 3.10 of] the DSU.[188]

In *Mexico - Taxes on Soft Drinks*, the Appellate Body explained in more detail its view of its jurisdiction and the applicable law in WTO disputes. Mexico requested the Panel to make a preliminary ruling declining to exercise jurisdiction and recommending that Mexico and the USA resolve their differences through the NAFTA dispute settlement system, which the USA had so far refused to do.[189] The Panel refused to make this ruling, on the basis that it had no discretion to decline jurisdiction and that to do so would breach its obligation to make an

---

[182] Panel Report, *Korea - Procurement*, [7.93]-[7.101].
[183] WTO, DSB, *Minutes of Meeting Held in the Centre William Rappard on 19 June 2000*, WT/DSB/M/84 (24 July 2000) [58].
[184] Ibid., [64].   [185] Appellate Body Report, *EC - Export Subsidies on Sugar*, [311].
[186] Ibid., [313].   [187] Ibid., [310].   [188] Ibid., [312].
[189] Panel Report, *Mexico - Taxes on Soft Drinks*, [4.2], [4.71]-[4.75].

objective assessment of the matter under Article 11 of the DSU, violate the rights of Members to bring complaints under Article 23 of the DSU, and diminish the rights of complaining Members contrary to Articles 3.2 and 19.2 of the DSU.[190] The Appellate Body upheld the Panel's decision, echoing the Panel's reliance on Articles 3.2, 11, 19.2, and 23 of the DSU, and maintaining that the provisions on a Panel's terms of reference in Article 7 of the DSU also require a Panel to make findings on challenged measures[191] (although the Appellate Body has ruled that Panels may exercise judicial economy in some circumstances).[192] The Appellate Body also reiterated that it saw 'no basis in the DSU for panels and the Appellate Body to adjudicate non-WTO disputes'.[193] Relying on Article 3.2 of the DSU, it implied that the WTO dispute settlement system cannot 'be used to determine rights and obligations outside the covered agreements'.[194]

The Appellate Body's generally cautious approach to applying international law in these cases is consistent with the weight it typically accords to the text in interpreting WTO provisions,[195] from which one might infer a desire to accord considerable deference to the will of the Members as reflected in the agreements they negotiated.[196] This is confirmed by the Appellate Body's own description of the WTO agreements as containing 'carefully negotiated language'[197] reflecting, variously, a 'carefully drawn balance of rights and obligations of Members',[198] a 'delicate and carefully negotiated balance',[199] a 'carefully negotiated compromise',[200] and a 'carefully negotiated balance of rights and obligations'.[201] This caution suggests that the Appellate Body would be unlikely to apply the UNESCO Convention as an independent

---

[190] Ibid., [7.8]–[7.9], [7.18].
[191] Appellate Body Report, *Mexico – Taxes on Soft Drinks*, [48]–[53].
[192] See, e.g., Appellate Body Report, *Canada – Wheat Exports and Grain Imports*, [133].
[193] Appellate Body Report, *Mexico – Taxes on Soft Drinks*, [56].
[194] Ibid.   [195] See above, 127.
[196] '[T]he method of literal interpretation is relatively safe, and ... its results are more easily accepted than results reached by other interpretative tools': Claus-Dieter Ehlermann, 'Six Years on the Bench of the "World Trade Court": Some Personal Experiences as Member of the Appellate Body of the World Trade Organization' (2002) 36(4) *Journal of World Trade* 605, 617.
[197] Appellate Body Report, *US – Underwear*, 15.
[198] Ibid. See also Appellate Body Report, *US – Wool Shirts and Blouses*, 16.
[199] Appellate Body Report, *EC – Hormones*, [177].
[200] Appellate Body Report, *US – Carbon Steel*, [90].
[201] Appellate Body Report, *Brazil – Aircraft*, [139]. See also Appellate Body Report, *EC – Bananas III*, [136], quoting the Panel with approval.

defence in a WTO dispute with no textual anchor. The likely criticism by WTO Members of such a move would be increased by the controversy surrounding cultural products in the WTO.

In some instances the Appellate Body has shown a strong reluctance to rule on particularly controversial matters, especially (but not only) where no party has specifically requested the ruling. Rudolf Adlung suggests that, '[i]n view of their status, Panels and the Appellate Body have apparently sought to exercise restraint and limit the legal coverage of rulings to what is absolutely necessary to solve a case'.[202] For instance, the Appellate Body has sometimes exercised judicial economy in relation to issues on which the parties could have benefited from additional guidance. For example, in *US – Steel Safeguards*, the Appellate Body reversed the Panel's finding that increased imports of certain steel products caused serious injury to the relevant US domestic industry in accordance with the Safeguards Agreement. However, the Appellate Body itself 'ma[d]e no finding on whether or not a causal link has been established for these products'.[203] In implementing the recommendations and rulings of the DSB arising from the Panel and Appellate Body Reports in that dispute, and in applying these recommendations to future safeguards investigations, the USA would not know whether its authorities had acted consistently with the relevant WTO provisions in establishing causation. All they would know is that several other Members had challenged the determination of causation and might do so again.[204]

Consider also the Appellate Body's approach to Article XXIV:5 of GATT 1994, which provides an exception from certain WTO obligations for certain regional trade agreements – that is, customs unions and free trade areas meeting certain requirements. The Appellate Body has found various reasons for consistently refusing to determine whether this exception allows a WTO Member to exclude from a safeguard measure partners in a regional trade agreement,[205] even though Article 2.2 of the Safeguards Agreement requires these measures to 'be applied to a product being imported irrespective of its source'. Most

---

[202] Rudolf Adlung, 'GATS and Democratic Legitimacy' (2004) 59(2) *Aussenwirtschaft* 127, 137.
[203] Appellate Body Report, *US – Steel Safeguards*, [493].
[204] See also Appellate Body Report, *EC – Export Subsidies on Sugar*, [339].
[205] See, e.g., Appellate Body Report, *Argentina – Footwear (EC)*, [109]; Appellate Body Report, *US – Line Pipe*, [198].

notably, as Pauwelyn points out,[206] the Appellate Body appears to have constructed the notion of 'parallelism' between the imports considered in a safeguard investigation and those to which the safeguard is subsequently applied in order to avoid addressing this question.[207] The suggestion that the Appellate Body is reluctant to rule on this matter is supported by former Appellate Body Member Claus-Dieter Ehlermann: 'I share the view that the political organs of the WTO might be better suited than a panel and the Appellate Body to determine ... whether a regional trade agreement is compatible with Article XXIV.'[208]

Of course, many if not all disputes that come before the Appellate Body are controversial,[209] and it does not shy away from resolving them. With time, the Appellate Body may also be growing more confident about its perceived authority and legitimacy, allowing its first separate (read 'dissenting') opinion on a particularly sensitive issue in 2005.[210] Nevertheless, in the near future the UNESCO Convention seems an unlikely candidate to be applied as a defence in a WTO dispute. The text of the WTO agreements in relation to cultural products reflects Members' failure to agree on how to treat these products in WTO law. This disagreement is continuing in the current round of negotiations. Were the Appellate Body to rule that the UNESCO Convention provides a defence to WTO violations, it would be stepping into these negotiations in an unprecedented and inappropriate manner. It would mean not only applying a non-WTO treaty directly to a WTO dispute for the first time, but also giving a significant boost to the group of WTO Members calling for special treatment of cultural products, to the despair of many others.

(ii) Resolving conflicts between the UNESCO Convention and WTO law
In the previous section I concluded that the Appellate Body (and hence a Panel) would be unlikely to apply the UNESCO Convention directly in a WTO dispute. However, if this conclusion proved incorrect, the next question would be whether the UNESCO Convention could prevail over

---

[206] Joost Pauwelyn, 'The Puzzle of WTO Safeguards and Regional Trade Agreements' (2004) 7(1) *Journal of International Economic Law* 109, 121-2.
[207] See, e.g., Appellate Body Report, *US – Steel Safeguards*, [441]; Appellate Body Report, *US – Wheat Gluten*, [98].
[208] Ehlermann, 'Six Years on the Bench', 634.
[209] See Award of the Arbitrator, *EC – Tariff Preferences*, [56].
[210] Appellate Body Report, *US – Upland Cotton*, [631]-[641]. In *EC – Asbestos*, one Appellate Body Member provided a 'concurring statement': Appellate Body Report, *EC – Asbestos*, [149]-[154].

WTO rules by providing a defence to a WTO-inconsistent measure in the absence of a specific defence in the text of the WTO agreements. On a narrow view, no conflict arises between two international agreements unless they impose mutually exclusive obligations; in other words, it is not possible to comply with both agreements at once.[211] If, for example, one agreement prohibits behaviour that another permits, the two agreements do not conflict because a country may comply with both agreements simply by refraining from engaging in the behaviour in question. A WTO Member could presumably comply with its WTO obligations and its obligations under the UNESCO Convention by taking measures to protect cultural diversity but doing so in a manner that involves no WTO-inconsistency. Thus, the respondent would not need to use the UNESCO Convention as a defence.

This interpretation would likely prevent the Member from taking certain measures that are envisaged in the UNESCO Convention. For instance, a minimum domestic content requirement could fall within the rights recognised in Article 6.2(b) of the UNESCO Convention while conflicting with the national treatment obligation under GATT 1994 or GATS. A co-production agreement granting special advantages to some countries but not to all WTO Members could fall within the obligation to 'endeavour to strengthen ... bilateral ... cooperation' under Article 12 of the UNESCO Convention while conflicting with the MFN obligation under GATT 1994 or GATS.

Taking a broader view, a conflict does arise in these circumstances because it is not possible to exercise the right granted in the second agreement without violating the first: 'If not, one would consistently elevate obligations in international law over and above rights in international law.'[212] Put differently, a conflict may be identified 'where two rules or principles suggest different ways of dealing with a problem'.[213] According to this view, a conflict arises between the UNESCO Convention and the WTO agreements if the WTO agreements prohibit a measure that is permitted or encouraged by the UNESCO Convention. As a result, a

---

[211] See, e.g., Panel Report, *Indonesia – Autos*, n. 649; Marceau, 'Conflicts of Norms', 1084; Marceau, 'WTO Dispute Settlement and Human Rights', 792–4.
[212] Pauwelyn, 'Public International Law in the WTO', 551. See also Pauwelyn, *Conflict of Norms*, 329. Cf. Erich Vranes, 'The Definition of "Norm Conflict" in International Law and Legal Theory' (2006) 17(2) *European Journal of International Law* 395, 405, 415.
[213] UN, ILC, *Fragmentation of International Law: Difficulties Arising from the Diversification and Expansion of International Law – Report of the Study Group – Finalized by Martti Koskenniemi*, A/CN.4/L.682 (13 April 2006) [25].

respondent relying on the UNESCO Convention would need to show that the conflict should be resolved in favour of the UNESCO Convention.

Conflicts are easiest to resolve where one of the two apparently conflicting provisions is contained in an instrument that specifies that it is subordinate to another instrument. In that case, pursuant to Article 30(2) of the VCLT, the other instrument prevails. Article 20.2 of the UNESCO Convention specifies that it does not modify rights and obligations of the parties under any other treaties to which they are parties. As mentioned earlier, this indicates that the UNESCO Convention as currently drafted could not provide a defence to a WTO violation, even though Article 20.1 of the UNESCO Convention states that it is not subordinate to any other treaty.

Some doubt could arise about whether Article 20.2 means that the UNESCO Convention does not modify the rights or obligations of the parties under only existing WTO agreements as they stand upon the entry into force of the UNESCO Convention, or also under WTO agreements as amended or concluded in future. However, the absence of any reference in Article 20.2 to the time when the other treaties are concluded suggests that this provision is not limited to existing treaties. The drafters of the UNESCO Convention appear to have deliberately removed this limitation: a precursor to Article 20.2 stated that '[n]othing in this Convention shall affect the rights and obligations of the States Parties under any other *existing* international instruments',[214] whereas the current Article 20.2 states that the UNESCO Convention does not modify 'rights and obligations of the Parties under *any* other treaties to which they are parties'.[215] At most, one might read Article 20.2 as leaving open the relationship between the UNESCO Convention and future WTO agreements. In that case, as will be seen further below, the general international law rules on successive treaties would likely mean that the UNESCO Convention could not modify rights or obligations of WTO Members under future WTO agreements.

I turn now to what the WTO agreements say about their relationship with other treaties, which is very little. Martti Koskenniemi and Päivi Leino contend that, '[i]n the case of conflict between, say, an

---

[214] See, e.g., UNESCO, *Preliminary Report of the Director-General Containing Two Preliminary Drafts of a Convention on the Protection of the Diversity of Cultural Contents and Artistic Expressions*, CLT/CPD/2005/CONF.203/6 (3 March 2005) appendix 1 (composite text), art. 19 (option B) (emphasis added).
[215] Emphasis added.

unincorporated human rights or environmental treaty and a WTO agreement, WTO bodies are constitutionally prevented from concluding that the WTO standard has to be set aside'.[216] But the DSU is not so categorical. Lorand Bartels suggests that the prohibition in Articles 3.2 and 19.2 of the DSU on adding to or diminishing the rights and obligations in the WTO agreements amounts to a 'conflicts rule', which 'ensure[s] that in the event of a conflict between the provisions of the covered agreements and any other applicable law, the covered agreements shall prevail'.[217] However, these provisions are far from explicit in imposing any such rule, and in any case they could probably be overridden by a treaty concluded after the WTO agreements.[218]

Assuming that neither the UNESCO Convention nor the relevant WTO agreement contained an explicit conflict provision, various conflict rules in public international law might apply.[219] The outcome would depend on the status of the disputing WTO Members under the UNESCO Convention. Article 41 of the VCLT governs '[a]greements to modify multilateral treaties between certain of the parties only'. Assuming that only some WTO Members would become parties to the UNESCO Convention, the UNESCO Convention would have to comply with Article 41. Article 41(1) allows agreements modifying multilateral treaties between certain parties if:

(a) the possibility of such a modification is provided for by the treaty; or
(b) the modification in question is not prohibited by the treaty and:
  (i) does not affect the enjoyment by the other parties of their rights under the treaty or the performance of their obligations;
  (ii) does not relate to a provision, derogation from which is incompatible with the effective execution of the object and purpose of the treaty as a whole.

Marceau suggests that these agreements may not be possible in the WTO context because they are likely to affect the rights of other Members.[220] Trachtman reaches a similar conclusion, on the basis that the explicit WTO provisions on amendment and waiver

---

[216] Koskenniemi and Leino, 'Fragmentation of International Law?', 572.
[217] Bartels, 'Applicable Law in WTO Disputes', 507.
[218] See Pauwelyn, *Conflict of Norms*, 329, 335–6, 344, 352–5.
[219] See, e.g., UN, ILC, *Fragmentation of International Law: Difficulties Arising from the Diversification and Expansion of International Law – Report of the Study Group – Finalized by Martti Koskenniemi*, A/CN.4/L.682 (13 April 2006) [56] (*lex specialis*), [225] (*lex posterior*), [361] (*jus cogens*).
[220] Marceau, 'Conflicts of Norms', 1105.

(discussed further in Chapter 6) prohibit *inter se* modifications.[221] The Panel Report in *Turkey – Textiles* appears to support these positions,[222] as does Carmody's conclusion that WTO obligations are collective rather than bilateral in nature.[223] Pauwelyn takes a different view. He maintains that '[t]he WTO treaty did not contract out of th[e] general international law rules on the interplay of norms', so *inter se* modifications are possible.[224] Again, the ILC Study Group agreed.[225]

If this is correct, and the UNESCO Convention complied with Article 41 of the VCLT, Article 30 would apply.[226] Article 30 of the VCLT governs the application of 'successive treaties relating to the same subject-matter', a description which could apply to the UNESCO Convention and certain WTO agreements.[227] Under Article 30(4)(a) of the VCLT, if the disputing Members were also parties to the UNESCO Convention, the (earlier) WTO agreements would continue to apply only to the extent that its provisions were compatible with the (later) UNESCO Convention. In other words, the UNESCO Convention would prevail to the extent of inconsistency with the WTO agreements. If, however, only the respondent was a party to the UNESCO Convention, Article 30(4)(b) provides that the WTO agreements would prevail. The outcome would be similar to that discussed earlier in relation to UNESCO Convention parties refraining from challenging WTO-inconsistent cultural policy measures in WTO disputes.[228] These parties might have a defence to WTO challenges by other UNESCO Convention parties, but not to challenges by WTO Members that are not parties to the UNESCO Convention. This would provide little security to UNESCO Convention parties in pursuing trade-restrictive or discriminatory cultural policy measures.

---

[221] Trachtman, 'Review of Pauwelyn', 858–9.
[222] Panel Report, *Turkey – Textiles*, [9.181]–[9.182].
[223] Chios Carmody, 'WTO Obligations as Collective' (2006) 17(2) *European Journal of International Law* 419, 441–2.
[224] Pauwelyn, *Conflict of Norms*, 475. See also McLachlan, 'Principle of Systemic Integration', 315.
[225] UN, ILC, *Fragmentation of International Law: Difficulties Arising from the Diversification and Expansion of International Law – Report of the Study Group – Finalized by Martti Koskenniemi*, A/CN.4/L.682 (13 April 2006) [306].
[226] Pauwelyn, *Conflict of Norms*, 382.
[227] The Arbitrators relied on Article 30(3) of the VCLT in Decision by the Arbitrators, *EC – Hormones (US) (Article 22.6 – EC)*, [51].
[228] Above, 197.

5.4 Conclusion

The frequency and speed with which various groups have demanded a new international instrument on cultural diversity, including trade-related cultural policy measures, highlights the importance of this area for many countries. Although Canada and France stand at the forefront of this movement, and several initiatives are Canadian or traceable to Canada, the support of other countries can be seen in the steps being taken in UNESCO. The UNESCO Convention as it currently stands is unlikely to have a significant impact on WTO negotiations or disputes. In particular, its assertion that it does not affect rights or obligations of parties under other international treaties means that it cannot have a major impact on the trade-culture impasse in the WTO. Even if the UNESCO Convention purported to override WTO rules, it is unlikely that Panels or the Appellate Body would allow it to do so in a WTO dispute in the near future.

This limitation to the UNESCO Convention may be a positive sign for the WTO, since the UNESCO Convention addresses this problem from a purely cultural perspective and might not adequately take into account the positive effects of trade liberalisation. Moreover, all WTO Members should be thankful that becoming a State party to the UNESCO Convention would not appear to violate the WTO agreements or otherwise nullify or impair benefits of other Members under those agreements. Nevertheless, UNESCO Convention parties may rely on the principles set out in the UNESCO Convention to restrict their offers in the current GATS negotiations and to attempt to resolve disputes regarding WTO-inconsistent cultural policy measures outside the WTO. This raises concerns for other WTO Members, as well as for the WTO as an institution. It is therefore all the more urgent for WTO Members to negotiate a solution to the problem of cultural products within the WTO.

6 Improving the existing WTO agreements

Clearly a middle ground must be found whereby the legitimate cultural needs of a country can be attained with a minimum of impact on international trade and investment flows ... [I]t is unreasonable for countries to demand *carte blanche* to promote and protect their cultural industries. But it is also unreasonable to demand that cultural products be given exactly the same treatment as the products of any other commercial activity.[1]

6.1 Introduction

As WTO dispute settlement alone cannot provide a satisfactory compromise among WTO Members regarding cultural products, and as neither the UNESCO Convention nor any other international instrument appears likely to resolve this problem, WTO Members should consider a third, final option for achieving a solution: trying again to reach agreement. This approach will give Members the best chance of reconciling cultural and trade values and the greatest control over the outcome.

Members have been locked in intense negotiations to improve and build on the Uruguay Round agreements, as part of the Doha Development Agenda. However, these negotiations are limited by tight deadlines (several of which have already been missed)[2] and a restricted mandate, not to mention the temporary suspension of the negotiations.[3] For example, as mentioned in Chapter 3, the GATS negotiations are to 'take

---

[1] William Merkin, 'United States Trade Policy and Culture: Future Strategies' in UNESCO (ed.), *World Culture Report* (2000) 68, 68.
[2] See, e.g., July Package, [3]; Doha Declaration, [45].
[3] See above, 28, n. 163.

place within and ... respect the existing structure and principles of the GATS, including the right to specify sectors in which commitments will be undertaken and the four modes of supply'.[4] Similarly, although the Doha negotiations cover some cross-cutting issues such as development, they include no general mandate to review GATT 1994. The outcome of Doha will also depend on various political matters and horse-trading. In other words, Members' positions and flexibility in relation to cultural products are likely to be influenced by factors such as lobbying by the cultural industries, and gains or concessions in other areas of the negotiations such as agriculture. Accordingly, the present chapter is intended neither as a guide for negotiators nor as a prediction of what Doha will achieve in relation to cultural products. Rather, it takes a more radical, longer-term view of possible improvements to the current treatment of cultural products, to encourage creative thinking and reflection on this area and to offer one suggestion for accommodating the different views of WTO Members.

The conclusions reached in Chapters 2 and 3 play an important role in this chapter, providing a means of assessing proposed changes. These conclusions include that: the present treatment of cultural products in WTO law on trade in goods and services is problematic, due to uncertainties and conflicts between GATT 1994 and GATS; WTO Members may have genuine cultural reasons for de facto or de jure discrimination against foreign cultural products, or for de facto discrimination between these products; and the trade-restrictiveness of cultural policy measures should be minimised.

In assessing the options for improving the existing agreements, it is also important to keep in mind the objectives of GATT 1994, GATS, and the WTO as a whole. The preamble to the Marrakesh Agreement declares the desire of Members to contribute to broader objectives, such as raising standards of living and ensuring full employment, 'by entering into reciprocal and mutually advantageous arrangements directed to the substantial reduction of tariffs and other barriers to trade and to the elimination of discriminatory treatment in international relations'. The preamble to GATT 1994 contains almost identical wording.[5] The preamble to GATS similarly reflects the desire of Members for 'the early

---

[4] WTO, Council for Trade in Services, *Guidelines and Procedures for the Negotiations on Trade in Services*, S/L/93 (29 March 2001) [4].
[5] The preamble to GATT 1994 contains the phrase quoted but ends with 'international commerce' rather than 'international relations'.

achievement of progressively higher levels of liberalization of trade in services through successive rounds of multilateral negotiations aimed at promoting the interests of all participants on a mutually advantageous basis'. This objective is reflected in the built-in agenda for successive rounds of services trade liberalisation under Article XIX of GATS and the Hong Kong Ministerial Declaration of December 2005.[6] Against this background, it seems clear that the WTO agreements aim to dismantle trade barriers over time for the mutual benefit of all Members. Therefore, in principle, any changes to or clarifications of the agreements to accommodate cultural policy measures should not weaken the existing disciplines.

In the following sections, I first address possible improvements to the treatment of cultural products under GATT 1994, before turning to GATS. Of course, changes to the two agreements must be seen as a whole. A bigger change in one agreement may mean that Members will accept a smaller change in the other. Changes must also be compatible, particularly if one of the objectives of improvement is to narrow the gap in the treatment of cultural products under GATT 1994 and GATS. Having addressed the substance or content of possible changes to GATT 1994 and GATS, including a proposal for sectoral treatment of audiovisual services analogous to the existing GATS Annexes on Telecommunications, Air Transport Services, and Financial Services, I consider the form these changes might take.

6.2 Improving treatment of cultural products under GATT 1994

6.2.1 Screen quotas: remove or modify

One way of subjecting cinematograph films to the general disciplines of GATT 1994 would be to remove Article IV. As mentioned in Chapter 3, Article IV(d) makes screen quotas subject to negotiation for their limitation, liberalisation, or elimination. Removing Article IV would mean that screen quotas would be subject to the usual GATT provisions on national treatment and MFN treatment, as well as to the usual exceptions, for example allowing certain kinds of subsidies and certain measures regarding public morals or national treasures. As explained later in this chapter, if protective measures are required, subsidies are

---

[6] Hong Kong Declaration, [26].

typically regarded as preferable to quotas or tariffs from an economic perspective, involving fewer trade distortions. However, given the long history of this provision and the reliance of several Members on it, it could be practically difficult to achieve consensus on removal of Article IV.

An alternative to deleting Article IV of GATT 1994 altogether would be to amend it slightly. Presently, screen quotas contrary to the MFN obligation (that is, minimum quotas for films of particular origin other than national origin) are subject to a standstill obligation, whereas screen quotas contrary to the national treatment obligation (that is, minimum quotas for films of national origin) are not. A relatively simple and modest change to Article IV would be to impose a standstill or rollback obligation on the latter kind of quotas. This could be done by adding to the end of Article IV(a) words derived from Article IV(c), such as '*Provided* that no such minimum proportion of screen time shall be increased above the level in effect on' a particular date determined through negotiation. The use of similar clauses in 'cultural exceptions' in other free trade agreements suggests that this proposal might be acceptable to many Members.[7] Article IV(c) could also be amended to tolerate, not measures granting preferential treatment to films of a specified origin, but measures granting preferential treatment to films that fulfil certain open and objective cultural criteria. This would accord with the suggestion in Chapter 2 that de jure discrimination between foreign cultural products is not justified.

6.2.2 A new general exception?

In Chapter 3, I discussed two existing exceptions under Article XX of GATT 1994 that might apply to cultural policy measures, namely for measures necessary to protect public morals (Article XX(a)), and for measures imposed to protect national treasures of artistic, historic, or archaeological value (Article XX(f)). Given the uncertain scope of these exceptions, perhaps a new exception under Article XX for cultural products could be useful, especially if Article IV was deleted.

Certain regional and bilateral trade agreements may be instructive about the form that an exception for cultural products might take. For example, as discussed in Chapter 1, the EC Treaty, NAFTA, and various free trade agreements provide divergent examples of cultural

---

[7] See above, 33.

exemptions,[8] representing substantive compromises that were considered acceptable by some of the WTO Members with the strongest views on this issue (the USA, the EC, and Canada) in the specific contexts of those agreements. However, the Uruguay Round and the MAI are reminders of the difficult process leading to such a compromise and of the limited chance of success.[9]

Short of a broad exemption for 'cultural industries', what other form might a new exception under Article XX of GATT 1994 take? Hahn favours a 'narrowly tailored cultural exception which strikes a reasonable balance between the preservation of cultural values on one hand and, on the other hand, market access and fair conditions of competition for efficient producers of audiovisual goods'.[10] This may be easier said than done. Hahn's preferred exception would be based on quality or genre.[11] Graber proposes a 'cultural exemption restricted to the protection of art film'.[12] Bernier suggests an exception 'for the preservation of cultural and linguistic diversity, including national cultures'.[13] Messerlin advocates a 'distinction between industrial and cultural audiovisuals', with an exemption for 'cultural audiovisuals from WTO disciplines'.[14] However, these kinds of exceptions would be difficult to negotiate and hard to limit in terms of scope. The definition of an 'art film' or 'cultural' film would likely be elusive, and the value of these films as compared to other types of films is debatable, even assuming that 'cultural' aspects of films deserve special protection.

Another problem with all these proposals for a new cultural exception, at least in the context of GATT 1994, is that they are regressive. WTO Members agreed to significant liberalisation of goods trade in concluding GATT 1994. This was a major achievement, and if it were necessary to agree on GATT 1994 again today it might not be possible.

---

[8] For further discussion, see Carniaux, 'L'audiovisuel'; Mary Footer, 'The Future for a Cultural Exception in the World Trade Organisation' (paper presented at the Meeting of the International Trade Law Committee of the International Law Association, Geneva, 22–3 June 1995).
[9] See above, 23, 31.
[10] Hahn, 'Eine kulturelle Bereichsausnahme', 352 (Hahn's English summary).
[11] Ibid., 350.
[12] Graber, 'WTO: A Threat to European Films?', 18. See also Christoph Graber, 'Audiovisual Media and the Law of the WTO' in Graber, Girsburger, and Nenova, *Free Trade versus Cultural Diversity* 15, 62, 64; Graber, 'Audio-Visual Policy', 212–14.
[13] Bernier, 'Cultural Goods and Services', 147.
[14] Messerlin, 'Regulating Culture', 17.

For example, just as some Members might wish they had held out for greater flexibility regarding treatment of cultural products, others might wish they had never agreed to the principle of national treatment at all. Rather than attempting to water down commitments agreed in 1994 (assuming Members could ever agree to this), the objective of reducing trade barriers and eliminating discriminatory treatment would be better served by considering how to address Members' concerns about cultural products while moving towards greater trade liberalisation. This could be done by focusing on Article IV of GATT 1994 and leaving open the possibility that the current general exceptions in Article XX of GATT 1994 already provide some scope for protecting cultural products (as discussed in Chapters 3 and 4).

As mentioned earlier, the UN High Commissioner for Human Rights has called for an 'approach that sets the promotion and protection of human rights [including cultural rights] as objectives of trade liberalization, not as exceptions'.[15] This could suggest that cultural rights must be promoted and protected under GATT 1994 other than through Articles IV and XX. However, as the Appellate Body has explained in relation to other WTO exceptions, '[t]he status and relative importance of a given provision does not depend on whether it is characterized, for the purpose of allocating the burden of proof, as a claim to be proven by the complaining party, or as a defence to be established by the responding party'.[16] Just as 'characterizing the Enabling Clause as an exception [does not] detract from its critical role in encouraging the granting of special and differential treatment to developing-country Members of the WTO',[17] and authorising measures for environmental conservation under the exception in Article XX(g) does not diminish 'the importance and legitimacy of environmental protection as a goal of national and international policy',[18] so too protecting cultural policy measures through Articles IV and XX of GATT 1994 is consistent with recognising the fundamental nature of cultural rights.

---

[15] UN, Commission on Human Rights, Sub-Commission on the Promotion and Protection of Human Rights, *Liberalization of Trade in Services and Human Rights: Report of the High Commissioner*, E/CN.4/Sub.2/2002/9 (25 June 2002) annex [7].
[16] Appellate Body Report, *EC – Tariff Preferences*, [98].
[17] Ibid. See above, 132.
[18] Ibid., [95]; Appellate Body Report, *US – Shrimp*, [129].

6.3 Improving treatment of cultural products under GATS

6.3.1 Digital cultural products as services

As mentioned in Chapter 3, certain difficulties arise in classifying cultural products as goods or services. One relates to the treatment of digital products such as films or music delivered electronically (such as via the internet or television or radio broadcasts). At the time of writing, Members have imposed a moratorium on applying customs duties on these products when delivered electronically.[19] The future of this moratorium raises two overlapping questions: should these products be explicitly identified as goods or services, and should Members be free to impose duties on them?

Regarding the first of these questions, it would be artificial to treat digital products as goods when they are not delivered in a tangible form recognised in the Harmonized System, just as it would be artificial to deem all digitisable products to be services even when they are delivered in tangible form (e.g., on CD). It is true that, to avoid trade distortions, a given product should ideally be treated in the same way in international trade, regardless of the form it takes or the technology used to provide it (this is the principle of 'technological neutrality', which is not specifically reflected in the WTO agreements).[20] However, the WTO system already establishes a clear distinction between goods and services. Although this distinction may be somewhat arbitrary in some circumstances and in relation to some products, the treatment of goods under GATT 1994 has a long history and is easily applicable to products traded by physically crossing borders. In contrast, products transmitted electronically via the internet or similar means fall more easily within the new world of GATS, in which Members are still learning and deciding how best to formulate trade rules.

Accordingly, I propose explicitly recognising digital cultural products as services subject to GATS and not GATT 1994. This differs slightly from the proposal by Hahn to subject all audiovisual products to either GATS or GATT 1994.[21] Under my proposal, any distortion resulting from

---

[19] Above, 74, n. 35.
[20] Aaditya Mattoo and Ludger Schuknecht, *Trade Policies for Electronic Commerce*, World Bank Policy Research Paper 2380 (2000) 11; Wunsch-Vincent, *WTO, Internet and Digital Products*, 55, 58.
[21] Hahn, 'Eine kulturelle Bereichsausnahme', 349. See also Graber, *Handel und Kultur*, 237 (proposing that production, distribution, and screening of all audiovisual programmes be subject to GATS).

treating digital cultural products differently from non-digital products (such as paper books) would be minimised if the disciplines imposed on cultural products under GATT 1994 and GATS were more closely matched, as suggested later in this chapter. This matching process would also diminish the significance of the classification issue from a political perspective. The EC argues that digital products should be treated as services, primarily because the EC has broad discretion in relation to cultural products under the present GATS framework. Conversely, the USA wants to classify digital products as goods, because of the stronger GATT disciplines.[22] If GATT 1994 and GATS were more closely aligned in connection with cultural products, these countries would have less to disagree about. This approach is preferable to the compromise suggested by Catherine Mann and Sarah Knight, which is to 'sideste[p] the classification issue and requir[e] that WTO members follow the course of most liberal treatment' of digital products, under either GATT or GATS'.[23] Such a rule is likely to cause confusion and unpredictability instead of reducing it.

Bringing cultural products in digital form squarely into GATS would require Members to resolve several related issues, such as the proper classification of audiovisual services and the distinction between audiovisual and telecommunications services, as highlighted earlier.[24] In addition, as Wunsch-Vincent points out, the existing GATS rules do not clearly specify whether a service supplied electronically from one Member to another should be covered by mode 1 or by mode 2.[25] Nevertheless, some of these classification questions would become less significant or difficult if commitments were mandated as I propose below.[26]

As for whether Members should extend their agreement not to impose customs duties on digital products, it follows that if these products are services they would ordinarily not be subject to customs duties. Moreover, technological limitations may prevent Members from imposing these duties for some time.[27] Therefore, keeping in mind the underlying objectives of GATS (including promoting the economic

---

[22] Above, 73.
[23] Catherine Mann and Sarah Knight, 'Electronic Commerce in the WTO' in Schott, *WTO After Seattle* 253, 259.
[24] Above, 72.
[25] Wunsch-Vincent, *WTO, Internet and Digital Products*, 65–70.
[26] See also ibid., 79.
[27] Mattoo and Schuknecht, *Trade Policies for Electronic Commerce*, 10, 13.

growth of all trading partners and the development of developing countries) and the means envisaged for achieving these objectives (including progressively higher levels of liberalisation of trade in services), extending the moratorium on customs duties on a permanent and binding basis seems advisable, at least for digital cultural products as defined in this book. This would likely distort trade by encouraging electronic delivery over other means, but it could also reduce distribution costs and give developing country Members easier access to foreign markets for cultural products. In addition, although the unavailability of customs duties would have some revenue implications, which could be of greater concern to developing country Members, research shows that these implications would be limited.[28] However, imposing a moratorium on customs duties for digital cultural products would not be enough to minimise the trade-restrictiveness of cultural policy measures under the current GATS framework.

6.3.2 Mandated national treatment, market access, and MFN

To bring GATS disciplines on cultural products more closely into line with those under GATT 1994, and to pursue the objective of progressively increasing liberalisation under GATS, a new approach could be adopted. Currently, the GATS framework primarily involves a 'bottom-up' or 'positive list' approach, with Members choosing the service sectors in which they are willing to make national treatment or market access commitments. In contrast, obligations under GATT 1994 regarding national treatment and quantitative restrictions apply across the board, subject to specified exceptions. This is more of a 'top-down' or 'negative list' approach.

Reversing the onus under GATS, so that national treatment and market access disciplines apply unless otherwise exempted (as is already the case for the MFN obligation under GATS), could be unrealistic and undesirable as a general proposition. As Patrick Low and Aaditya Mattoo have suggested, 'members are simply not ready to make commitments in all services sectors, and ... even if they did, they would be tempted to specify heavy-handed restricting measures in their negative lists that would take the substance out of commitments in sectors that they regarded as sensitive'.[29] However, even in 2000, Geza Feketekuty

---

[28] Ibid., 10.
[29] Patrick Low and Aaditya Mattoo, 'Is There a Better Way? Alternative Approaches to Liberalization under GATS' in Sauvé and Stern, *GATS 2000*, 449, 468.

recognised 'strong arguments for integrating GATT and GATS rules on a step-by-step basis'.[30] Additya Mattoo and Ludger Schuknecht have also suggested 'deepening and widening the limited cross-border trade commitments' under GATS,[31] while Mann and Knight propose classifying digital products 'as services, but [making] all such products subject to most favored nation and national treatment provisions'.[32] Similarly, Wunsch-Vincent maintains in relation to 'digitally-delivered content products' that 'the single best and most forward-looking method is undoubtedly the adoption of a negative list approach coupled with very limited derogations'.[33]

My proposal goes further: subject all cultural products under GATS to the requirements of national treatment and market access. This includes not only digital products such as television and music delivered over the internet, but also other forms of cultural products caught by GATS, such as film production services and publishing periodicals. For reasons explained in Chapter 2,[34] trade restrictions in the form of market access limitations should not be allowed on the grounds that they are necessary to preserve or promote culture. Culture will be better preserved and promoted in the absence of quantitative restrictions, thus ensuring a broad range of foreign and domestic voices. In addition, although some discrimination against foreign cultural products may be justified,[35] the starting point should be national treatment.

Members should reach an agreement that the many MFN exemptions relating to the audiovisual sector[36] listed as at 1 January 1995 have expired. This is consistent with paragraph 6 of the GATS Annex on Article II Exemptions (limiting the duration of these exemptions to ten years in principle) and with the need for progressive liberalisation under GATS, and it goes further than the agreed objective of WTO Members to remove or substantially reduce MFN exemptions generally.[37] However, some MFN exemptions for cultural policy measures would still be protected where they relate to members of an 'agreement

---

[30] Geza Feketekuty, 'Assessing and Improving the Architecture of GATS' in Sauvé and Stern, *GATS 2000*, 85, 110.
[31] Mattoo and Schuknecht, *Trade Policies for Electronic Commerce*, summary findings.
[32] Mann and Knight, 'Electronic Commerce', 259.
[33] Wunsch-Vincent, *WTO, Internet and Digital Products*, 78–9.
[34] Above, 64.   [35] See above, 59.   [36] Above, 25, n. 145.
[37] Hong Kong Declaration, Annex C, [1(e)(i)].

liberalizing trade in services' that complies with Article V of GATS. Thus, members of a regional trade agreement meeting the requirements of Article V may be able to accord to services and services suppliers of other members of that agreement treatment more favourable than that provided to like services and service suppliers of other WTO Members.

A negative list approach under GATS to national treatment, market access, and MFN for cultural products supplied by any of the four modes could be achieved, provided that Members had sufficient 'escape routes' for their cultural policy measures (in addition to those already provided, for example for regional trade agreements and public morals), as discussed in the next section.

6.3.3 *Escape routes*

A. Discriminatory subsidies

In goods trade, subsidies are generally seen as the least trade-distorting instrument of protection, followed by tariffs and then quotas. From an economic perspective, subsidies are also preferable to quotas (and to tariffs, assuming they can be applied as a practical matter) in the context of trade in services.[38] Moreover, 'often subsidies are the most efficient instrument for pursuing noneconomic objectives',[39] such as preserving or promoting local culture through cultural products.[40] Alan Sykes thus distinguishes between 'good' subsidies (directed towards correcting a market failure or promoting human rights) and 'bad' subsidies (directed simply towards transferring resources to 'well-organized interest groups').[41] Messerlin and Cocq propose a WTO 'reference paper'[42] on audiovisual subsidies, 'to allow subsidies for cultural reasons, while banning subsidies for mere industrial reasons'.[43] Against this background, it makes sense to allow a limited exception for Members to impose discriminatory cultural policy measures in the form of subsidies in preference to any other form. When combined with general national treatment and MFN obligations under GATS, as

---

[38] UNCTAD and World Bank, *Liberalizing International Transactions*, 53-5. See also Roy, 'Audiovisual Services', 943.
[39] Hoekman, 'A More Balanced Services Agreement', 129.
[40] See Barton, 'Economics of TRIPS', 499.
[41] Alan Sykes, 'Subsidies and Countervailing Measures' in Macrory, Appleton, and Plummer, *The World Trade Organization* (vol. II) 81, 88-9.
[42] See below, 235.   [43] Cocq and Messerlin, 'French Audio-Visual Policy', 48-9.

well as conditions and disciplines on the granting of subsidies, this approach begins to resemble that under GATT 1994.

The scarcity of statistics on subsidies in connection with trade in services has posed a problem for the negotiations on subsidies under GATS, with Members understandably reluctant to disclose information about their own subsidies schemes before disciplines are agreed, despite the exhortation to do so under Article XVI:1 itself.[44] Nevertheless, as already mentioned, 'entertainment services' comprise one area in which countries frequently use subsidies, which 'are typically predicated on cultural considerations'.[45]

Subsidies are, of course, also granted in many other sectors, and the problem of how to agree on disciplines in this area is correspondingly broad. Some of the issues to be resolved in this process include: whether to provide for Members to take unilateral countervailing measures in response to other Members' subsidies or to concentrate on multilateral disciplines enforced by the dispute settlement system;[46] how to define subsidies under GATS, given that they may often take the form of regulation or tax incentives rather than financial contributions;[47] and whether the national treatment obligation requires a Member subsidising a service supplied through one mode to provide an equivalent subsidy for the same service supplied through any other mode.[48]

---

[44] One aspect of this problem is that Members may genuinely be unable to provide accurate, comparable information before Members have agreed on a definition of subsidies for GATS purposes: WTO, Working Party on GATS Rules, *Negotiations on Subsidies: Report by the Chairperson of the Working Party on GATS Rules*, S/WPGR/10 (30 June 2003) [16]. A more sceptical explanation could be that Members do not wish to reveal information that could be used against them if WTO disciplines on services subsidies do eventually enter into force.

[45] WTO, Working Party on GATS Rules, *Subsidies and Trade in Services: Note by the Secretariat*, S/WPGR/W/9 (6 March 1996) 2–3. See also above, 22, n. 113.

[46] See, e.g., WTO, Working Party on GATS Rules, *Communication from Argentina and Hong Kong, China: Development of Multilateral Disciplines Governing Trade Distortive Subsidies in Services*, S/WPGR/W/31 (16 March 2000) [10(c)]; WTO, Working Party on GATS Rules, *Communication from Chile: The Subsidies Issue*, S/WPGR/W/10 (2 April 1996) 3; WTO, Working Party on GATS Rules, *Subsidies and Trade in Services: Note by the Secretariat*, S/WPGR/W/9 (6 March 1996) 2.

[47] See, e.g., WTO, Working Party on GATS Rules, *Communication from Chile: The Subsidies Issue*, 1; WTO, Working Party on GATS Rules, *Subsidies and Trade in Services: Note by the Secretariat*, S/WPGR/W/9 (6 March 1996) 3.

[48] WTO, Working Party on GATS Rules, *Communication from Argentina and Hong Kong, China: Development of Multilateral Disciplines Governing Trade Distortive Subsidies in Services*, S/WPGR/W/31 (16 March 2000) [10(a)]; WTO, Working Party on GATS Rules, *Subsidies and Trade in Services: Note by the Secretariat*, S/WPGR/W/9 (6 March 1996) 9.

Members have not yet reached agreement,[49] although the goal is to do so before the end of the negotiations on specific commitments (including national treatment and market access commitments).[50] It is not the purpose of this book to suggest a comprehensive solution to the problem of services subsidies.[51] The following recommendations are limited to subsidies for cultural products.

In defining subsidies in the audiovisual sector, it would be preferable to take a narrow approach focusing on financial contributions (including a direct transfer of funds or the forgoing of government revenue that is otherwise due), similar to that in the SCM Agreement.[52] This would leave regulatory or other actions, which might have equivalent economic effects, to be governed by the usual MFN, national treatment, and market access obligations. Narrowing the subsidies exception in this way would have a liberalising effect and would minimise 'problems associated with identifying and measuring subsidies'.[53]

Turning to the discriminatory use of subsidies, in the case of audiovisual products, this could be allowed subject to conditions. The granting of subsidies for audiovisual products in a manner that discriminates against foreign services or service suppliers de jure or de facto should be allowed, notwithstanding the general national treatment requirement, given my conclusion that this discrimination may be justified on cultural grounds.[54] GATS treatment depends on the origin of the service or service supplier.[55] Thus, a Member could subsidise national service suppliers (such as national film producers) or national services (national film production), without subsidising suppliers of services through any of the four modes (foreign film producers, whether located in another Member's territory and supplying through mode 1 or mode 2, or located in the subsidising Member's territory and supplying through mode 3 or

---

[49] Hong Kong Declaration, Annex C, [4(c)]; WTO, Working Party on GATS Rules, *Report of the Meeting of 10 February 2006*, S/WPGR/M/54 (22 February 2006) [17].

[50] WTO, Council for Trade in Services, *Guidelines and Procedures for the Negotiations on Trade in Services*, S/L/93 (29 March 2001) [7]; WTO, Council for Trade in Services, *Special Session – Report of the Meeting Held on 28, 29 and 30 March 2001: Note by the Secretariat*, S/CSS/M/8 (14 May 2001) [6]; WTO, Working Party on GATS Rules, *Negotiations on Subsidies: Report by the Chairperson of the Working Party on GATS Rules*, S/WPGR/10 (30 June 2003) [5].

[51] For further discussion, see Sauvé, 'Completing the GATS Framework', 327–33.

[52] SCM Agreement, art. 1.1(a)(1)(i), (ii).

[53] WTO, Working Party on GATS Rules, *Subsidies and Trade in Services: Note by the Secretariat*, S/WPGR/W/9 (6 March 1996) 3.

[54] See above, 59.

[55] GATS, art. XXVIII:(f); Zdouc, 'WTO Dispute Settlement Practice', 327–31.

mode 4) or the services they supply (producing foreign films). As in GATT 1994, some difficulties may arise in determining the origin of the relevant service or service supplier for the purpose of granting the subsidy (given that goods and services from various sources may contribute to the production of, say, a film). Members could agree on more detailed rules in this regard. Based on certain of its free trade agreements, the USA might be willing to accept the discriminatory use of subsidies in this manner.[56]

The granting of subsidies for cultural products in a manner that discriminates *between* foreign services or service suppliers de facto could also be allowed, notwithstanding the general MFN requirement. Thus, a Member could choose to subsidise only certain films of other Members, based on objective and transparent cultural criteria such as language. This is similar to the standard that applies to Members who wish to differentiate between the beneficiaries of their GSP schemes, as discussed earlier.[57] However, as explained in Chapter 2, de jure discrimination between foreign cultural products is not necessary on cultural grounds.[58]

As is evident from the SCM Agreement in the goods context, subsidies may have trade-distorting or injurious effects even if they do not discriminate against foreign products or between products from different sources. In the audiovisual sector, a Member may wish to grant subsidies to protect or promote local culture by ensuring that the cultural industries remain vibrant even though they might not be able to compete, unaided, against foreign industries. However, the legitimate need to protect culture through cultural products should not require their promotion abroad or the use of domestic over imported goods in the production process.[59] In any case, these subsidies may be less prevalent than in the goods area.[60] Therefore, as in Part II of the SCM Agreement, new GATS disciplines on subsidies in the audiovisual sector should prohibit export subsidies (being those contingent on export) and import substitution subsidies (contingent on the

---

[56] See Wunsch-Vincent, *WTO, Internet and Digital Products*, 214.
[57] Above, 133.   [58] See above, 60.
[59] However, on one view, a country that subsidises the learning of its language in another country may 'benefit both nations': Kónya, 'Modeling Cultural Barriers', 504–5.
[60] WTO, Working Party on GATS Rules, *Communication from Argentina and Hong Kong, China: Development of Multilateral Disciplines Governing Trade Distortive Subsidies in Services*, S/WPGR/W/31 (16 March 2000) [6].

use of domestic rather than imported goods or services).[61] Members could challenge a breach of this prohibition, as with a breach of most WTO provisions, through dispute settlement. Dispute settlement action could also be available in response to subsidies causing injury or other adverse effects to other Members (as in Part III of the SCM Agreement), although this could be particularly difficult to establish in a services context.[62]

Part V of the SCM Agreement addresses subsidies causing injury to the domestic industries of other Members, allowing those Members to impose countervailing duties (increased tariffs) on the subsidised products as a remedy, subject to stringent conditions. However, at least in the audiovisual context, Members often appear to use subsidies in response to domination of the market by foreign products. This foreign dominance arises most frequently from factors such as economies of scale and consumer tastes, rather than from foreign subsidisation. This differs from, for example, the situation governed by the Agreement on Agriculture, where massive subsidisation by certain (typically developed country)[63] Members often leads to a flood of cheap imports into other Members.[64] The difference in these factual scenarios suggests that, at this stage, the need to provide separately for unilateral actions to be taken against audiovisual subsidies causing adverse effects to other Members may be less pressing.[65] If countervailing measures were allowed, this could unnecessarily weaken the existing broad-based MFN obligation under GATS because they would be imposed selectively on certain subsidising Members[66] (as occurs for goods under GATT 1994). It would also be difficult to agree on disciplines governing countervailing measures in the services context.[67]

---

[61] See Adlung, 'Public Services and GATS', 485.
[62] On the application of the SCM Agreement to subsidies to attract foreign audiovisual production, see Claire Wright, 'Hollywood's Disappearing Act: International Trade Remedies to Bring Hollywood Home' (2006) 39 *Akron Law Review* 739.
[63] WTO, Working Party on GATS Rules, *Communication from Argentina and Hong Kong, China: Development of Multilateral Disciplines Governing Trade Distortive Subsidies in Services*, S/WPGR/W/31 (16 March 2000) [5].
[64] See, e.g., the recent major disputes: Appellate Body Report, *EC – Export Subsidies on Sugar*; Appellate Body Report, *US – Upland Cotton*.
[65] See Barton, 'Economics of TRIPS', 499.
[66] See WTO, Working Party on GATS Rules, *Subsidies and Trade in Services: Note by the Secretariat*, S/WPGR/W/9 (6 March 1996) 2.
[67] Hoekman, 'A More Balanced Services Agreement', 129.

B. Developing country Members

It could be argued that an allowance for discriminatory subsidies would provide an escape route for developed country Members but would be of little use to developing country Members.[68] This is perhaps a little too simplistic. Cultural products such as film and television are far more resource-intensive than some other cultural products such as books or sound recordings.[69] Nevertheless, some of the leading film-making countries, such as India, are developing countries. This is not just a developed country game. Moreover, a Member's developing country status does not necessarily mean that it lacks the capacity to grant subsidies. Thus, Article 27 of the SCM Agreement provides special and differential treatment to developing country Members in connection with their granting of subsidies. In the agricultural context, developing countries have continued to argue for special and differential treatment in relation to the granting of subsidies (that is, more lenient subsidies disciplines for developing country Members), rather than for a general prohibition on subsidies.[70] Like other Members, developing country Members may fund a discriminatory subsidy through a non-discriminatory tax, for example a tax on box-office receipts.

That said, developing countries may find subsidies less effective as cultural policy measures, whether due to insufficient funds or because they lack the technology to develop their cultural industries.[71] It may therefore be necessary to provide some additional leeway for developing countries, or at least the least developed among them, in relation to subsidies for cultural products. For example, prohibitions on export subsidies and import substitution subsidies could be applied to developed countries only, either indefinitely or for some agreed period of time.

---

[68] See Germann, 'Culture in Times of Cholera', 118.
[69] See Hesmondhalgh, *Cultural Industries*, 74–5.
[70] See, e.g., Agreement on Agriculture, art. 6.2; WTO, Ministerial Conference, *Agriculture – Framework Proposal: Joint Proposal by Argentina, Bolivia, Brazil, Chile, China, Colombia, Costa Rica, Cuba, Ecuador, El Salvador, Guatemala, India, Mexico, Pakistan, Paraguay, Peru, Philippines, South Africa, Thailand and Venezuela*, WT/MIN(03)/W/6 (4 September 2003) [1.3], [1.4], [3.4]. Many of these countries are members of the G20, which describes itself as 'the group of developing countries with special interest in agriculture': <www.g-20.mre.gov.br/> (accessed 4 August 2006).
[71] See UNCTAD, *Audiovisual Services: Improving Participation of Developing Countries – Note by the UNCTAD Secretariat*, TD/B/COM.1/EM.20/2 (30 September 2002) 11; UNCTAD, *Report of the Expert Meeting on Audiovisual Services: Improving Participation of Developing Countries, 13–15 November 2002*, TD/B/COM.1/56; TD/B/COM.1/EM.20/3 (4 December 2002) [8].

The revenue and capacity-building implications of allowing developing countries to erect certain trade barriers to cultural products may also temporarily justify the resulting trade distortion. A blanket national treatment limitation could allow developing countries to fund subsidies for cultural products through taxes on foreign enterprises creating them – that is, enterprises supplying audiovisual, printing, or publishing services through mode 3 (commercial presence). Another national treatment limitation on modes 3 and 4 could allow developing countries to require these enterprises to use some local employees (rather than only natural persons supplying services through mode 4) as a form of technical assistance.

C. Screen quotas

If GATT Article IV were removed as suggested above,[72] this would mean that no specific exemption for screen quotas would apply to films or broadcasts. However, if GATT Article IV were retained in its present or a modified form, certain changes to GATS might be required. First, to remove uncertainty, Members might wish to confirm that a measure that complied with Article IV of GATT 1994 would not be regarded as violating GATS. Second, if necessary to achieve consensus, Members could be granted a similar entitlement to impose minimum local content quotas on television and radio broadcasts (although the effectiveness of these measures is diminishing, as technology allows consumers to access audiovisual materials in a range of ways).[73] A general GATS provision applicable to all Members could recognise that national treatment commitments do not prevent the imposition or maintenance of minimum local content quotas for television and radio broadcasts up to the level imposed by the relevant Member upon a certain specified date, without the need for a specific limitation in the Member's schedule. Perhaps this standstill element could be excluded for developing country Members.

Experience with recent free trade agreements[74] suggests that the USA might accept this change,[75] which would cater for the needs of Members concerned about cultural policy measures while restricting their nature and extent.

---

[72] Above, 219. [73] Above, 64, n. 142. [74] See above, 33.
[75] See Richardson, 'Hollywood's Vision', 126.

6.4 Effecting changes

As explained above, this chapter is not intended as a practical guide for resolving the trade–culture problem in WTO negotiations, either in the Doha Round or otherwise. Nevertheless, it is worth considering the different forms that the suggested changes to the WTO agreements might take, if they were to be made. These changes are obviously intended to be taken as a package – for example, subsidies for cultural products under GATS could be exempted from national treatment and simultaneously subjected to disciplines regarding their nature; GATT Article IV could be removed or modified only together with appropriate modifications to GATS.

It would be unusual, but not unheard of, to provide sector-specific disciplines and exceptions under GATS as suggested in this chapter – in particular, mandating commitments and providing exceptions for subsidies in relation to cultural products. For example, the existing GATS Annexes on Air Transport Services and on Financial Services limit and clarify the scope of GATS application to these particular service sectors. The GATS Annex on Telecommunications goes further, imposing additional substantive obligations in relation to access to and use of public telecommunications transport networks and services. All these annexes apply to all WTO Members,[76] as do the vast majority of WTO provisions. Members could create a similar GATS sectoral annex in relation to cultural products through amendment of GATS, under Article X of the Marrakesh Agreement. This is my preferred approach.

Under Article X:5, amendments to GATS of the kind envisaged in this chapter would 'take effect for the Members that have accepted them upon acceptance by two thirds of the Members and thereafter for each Member upon acceptance by it'. Similarly, an amendment to remove or modify Article IV of GATT 1994 would be 'of a nature that would alter the rights and obligations of the Members' and, therefore, under Article X:3 of the Marrakesh Agreement, would 'take effect for the Members that have accepted them upon acceptance by two thirds of the Members and thereafter for each other Member upon acceptance by it'. At the time of writing, no amendments have ever been made to the WTO agreements, although the Members have approved an amendment in connection with the TRIPS Agreement and public health.[77] In practice, Members

---

[76] GATS, art. XXIX; Panel Report, *Mexico – Telecoms*, [7.4].
[77] WTO, General Council, *Amendment of the TRIPS Agreement: Decision of 6 December 2005*, WT/L/641 (8 December 2005).

might be reluctant to pursue an amendment in the absence of consensus. Amendments effected through consensus would avoid the problem of a 'two-tier system of WTO obligations',[78] based on acceptance of the amendment. This would be the best way of resolving the trade and culture problem in connection with cultural products.

Negotiations in some service sectors after the Uruguay Round led to some Members increasing or modifying their commitments in those sectors, still within the standard GATS framework.[79] However, given Members' widely differing views on cultural products, and the extent of the amendments suggested, it is quite likely that they could not be agreed as a practical matter unless all Members accepted them. For the same reason, it would be difficult to achieve these changes merely through the replacement of certain parts of Members' GATS schedules, although GATS Article XXI explains how Members may modify their schedules, subject to any necessary compensatory adjustment.[80] A slightly more ambitious approach would be for like-minded Members to agree on a reference paper to incorporate into their schedules (similar to the model reference paper that some Members added to their GATS schedules extending the usual GATS disciplines for the telecommunications sector)[81] or to enter a plurilateral agreement (binding only on those Members that accept it)[82] setting out the additional obligations imposed on the audiovisual sector.

It might be possible to give effect to some of the suggested changes through an interpretation under Article IX:2 of the Marrakesh Agreement. That provision states:

> The Ministerial Conference and the General Council shall have the exclusive authority to adopt interpretations of this Agreement and of the Multilateral

---

[78] Advisory Centre on WTO Law, *Giving Legal Effect to the Results of the Doha Round: An Analysis of the Methods of Changing WTO Law – Background Paper for ACWL Members and LDCs* (June 2006) [19]–[21]; Hunter Nottage and Thomas Sebastian, 'Giving Legal Effect to the Results of WTO Trade Negotiations: An Analysis of the Methods of Changing WTO Law' (2006) 9(4) *Journal of International Economic Law* 989, 992–3.

[79] See, e.g., WTO, *Fourth Protocol to the General Agreement on Trade in Services*, S/L/20 (30 April 1996) [1]; Panel Report, *Mexico – Telecoms*, [7.5].

[80] For further discussion, see Advisory Centre on WTO Law, *Giving Legal Effect to the Results of the Doha Round: An Analysis of the Methods of Changing WTO Law – Background Paper for ACWL Members and LDCs* (June 2006) [48]–[51]; Nottage and Sebastian, 'Changing WTO Law', 997–9.

[81] WTO, *Agreement on Telecommunications Services (Fourth Protocol to General Agreement on Trade in Services)*, 36 ILM 254 (1997). See also GATT, *Understanding on Commitments in Financial Services*, LT/UR/U/1 (15 April 1994).

[82] The WTO agreements include four plurilateral agreements. Two have expired, and two remain: the Agreement on Trade in Civil Aircraft and the Agreement on Government Procurement.

Trade Agreements ... The decision to adopt an interpretation shall be taken by a three-fourths majority of the Members. This paragraph shall not be used in a manner that would undermine the amendment provisions in Article X.

To date, neither the Ministerial Conference nor the General Council has adopted an interpretation under this provision, so little guidance is available on its meaning.[83] Nevertheless, the last sentence of Article IX:2 suggests that it would not provide an appropriate basis for the substantial changes I have suggested in relation to the general treatment of cultural products under GATS.[84] An interpretation could, however, be adopted to agree that digital products involve 'trade in services' under GATS Article I:1 and not trade in goods under GATT 1994. An interpretation might also be appropriate regarding paragraphs 5 and 6 of the GATS Annex on Article II Exemptions, to confirm that all MFN exemptions in relation to cultural products terminate after ten years.

Other possible forms for effecting changes to the WTO agreements include temporary waivers[85] for specific cultural policy measures adopted by individual Members,[86] and declarations by the Ministerial Conference (the WTO's highest decision-making body).[87] However, for the changes suggested in this chapter, these mechanisms seem insufficiently definitive.

6.5 Other proposals

Having set out my proposal for a new approach to cultural products in GATT 1994 and GATS, I now examine several proposals of others that

---

[83] But see WTO, General Council, *Minutes of Meeting Held on 15 and 16 February 1999*, WT/GC/M/35 (30 March 1999) 13–32; WTO, General Council, *Request for an Authoritative Interpretation Pursuant to Article IX:2 of the Marrakesh Agreement Establishing the World Trade Organization: Communication from the European Communities*, WT/GC/W/143 (5 February 1999); Claus-Dieter Ehlermann and Lothar Ehring, 'The Authoritative Interpretation under Article IX:2 of the Agreement Establishing the World Trade Organization: Current Law, Practice and Possible Improvements' (2005) 8(4) *Journal of International Economic Law* 803.

[84] See WTO, General Council, *Procedures for Amendment and Interpretation of the Dispute Settlement Understanding – Response to European Communities' Request for an Authoritative Interpretation of the Dispute Settlement Understanding pursuant to Article IX:2 of the WTO Agreement: Communication from the United States*, WT/GC/W/144 (5 February 1999) 3.

[85] Marrakesh Agreement, art. IX:3, 4. See, e.g., GATT, *Waiver Decision on the Generalized System of Preferences*, L/3545, BISD 18S/24 (25 June 1971).

[86] See Bernier, 'Trade and Culture', 787.

[87] See, e.g., WTO, Ministerial Conference, *Declaration on the TRIPS Agreement and Public Health*, WT/MIN(01)/DEC/2 (20 November 2001).

relate to aspects of the WTO agreements that I have so far left largely to one side: namely anti-dumping, safeguards, competition, and intellectual property rights. Although I do not on the whole support these proposals in preference to my own, they represent valid viewpoints and deserve serious consideration. They may also offer useful direction for future research into trade and culture.

6.5.1 Anti-dumping measures against audiovisual services

Article VI of GATT 1994 allows Members, subject to certain conditions, to impose on imported goods anti-dumping measures that might otherwise be inconsistent with tariff bindings and MFN treatment. Dumping occurs where 'products of one country are introduced into the commerce of another country at less than the normal value of the products'.[88] The rules on anti-dumping are exceedingly complex.[89] However, putting it simply, Article VI:1 recognises that 'dumping ... is to be condemned' in some circumstances, and Article VI:2 allows Members to impose anti-dumping duties on dumped imports. Before imposing anti-dumping duties, the Member must conduct an investigation that complies with stringent conditions as elaborated in the Anti-Dumping Agreement. Essentially, the investigation must demonstrate that imports of the relevant product are being dumped, and that the dumped imports are causing injury to the domestic industry producing the like product.[90] Anti-dumping duties cannot exceed the dumping margin calculated for the relevant exporter or producer (or, in some cases, the relevant country).[91] However, they may exceed tariff bindings, and (since they are imposed only on exporters, producers or countries that are engaged in dumping) they need not be imposed on all WTO Members, contrary to the MFN rule.

Most WTO anti-dumping disputes that have reached the Panel stage involve industrial products.[92] A Member might impose anti-dumping measures on goods that are relevant to cultural products, such as

---

[88] GATT 1994, art. VI. See also Anti-Dumping Agreement, art. 2.1.
[89] For comprehensive coverage of the WTO rules on anti-dumping, see Judith Czako et al., *A Handbook on Anti-Dumping Investigations* (2003).
[90] Anti-Dumping Agreement, arts. 1–3; GATT 1994, art. VI:6(a).
[91] Anti-Dumping Agreement, arts. 6.10, 9.3.
[92] See, e.g., Appellate Body Report, *EC – Tube or Pipe Fittings*; Appellate Body Report, *Thailand – H-Beams*; Appellate Body Report, *US – Hot-Rolled Steel*; Appellate Body Report, *US – Corrosion-Resistant Steel Sunset Review*.

television receivers.[93] However, Members are less likely to impose anti-dumping measures on cultural products themselves, and no disputes regarding any such measures have been the subject of a WTO Panel Report.

GATS contains no explicit disciplines on or exceptions for anti-dumping measures; nor does it foreshadow their negotiation in future. Complications would arise in trying to impose anti-dumping duties on foreign services, given that most services do not cross the border in the way that goods do. Indeed, according to the WTO Secretariat, it is impossible to impose 'tariff-type measures across large segments of services trade'.[94] However, assuming that a Member wished and was able to impose these duties on services 'dumped' by certain Members (whatever that may mean, in the context of services), this would likely violate the MFN treatment obligation under GATS, unless the Member had a current, valid MFN exemption covering these duties. This may explain why the EC lists an MFN exemption for distributing audiovisual works that covers '[r]edressive duties which may be imposed in order to respond to unfair pricing practices, by certain third countries distributors of audiovisual works'.[95] The EC explains that this exemption is required because '[u]nfair pricing practices may cause serious disruption to the distribution of European works'.[96] Bonnie Richardson, speaking on behalf of the Motion Picture Association of America, has responded that this is 'simply bad trade policy'.[97]

In the post-Uruguay services negotiations, some have suggested allowing Members to impose anti-dumping measures in a services context, and particularly in response to 'dumping' of audiovisual services.[98] This will not happen in the Doha Round, given the absence of any

---

[93] See, e.g., WTO, DSB, *United States – Imposition of Anti-Dumping Duties on Imports of Colour Television Receivers from Korea: Communication from Korea*, WT/DS89/9 (18 September 1998); WTO, DSB, *United States – Imposition of Anti-Dumping Duties on Imports of Colour Television Receivers from Korea: Request for the Establishment of a Panel by Korea*, WT/DS89/7 (7 November 1997).

[94] WTO Secretariat, *Handbook on GATS*, 17. See also Mattoo, 'National Treatment in the GATS', 113.

[95] WTO, *EC MFN Exemptions*, 1.   [96] Ibid.   [97] Richardson, 'Hollywood's Vision', 123.

[98] WTO, Council for Trade in Services, *Communication from Brazil – Audiovisual Services*, S/CSS/W/99 (9 July 2001) [10]; WTO, Council for Trade in Services, *Report of the Meeting Held on 19–22 March 2002: Note by the Secretariat*, TN/S/M/1 (5 June 2002) [316].

mandate to negotiate this issue. The suggestion that audiovisual producers dump products in foreign markets after recovering costs in the domestic market (typically the USA)[99] is also contrary to the way in which business is actually conducted in this sector.

In any case, I would not endorse this approach, for two main reasons. First, the economic justification for imposing anti-dumping measures and the utility of doing so are highly questionable. Many economists point out that, when a country dumps products (in a WTO sense, meaning that they are exported at prices below their normal value in the home market),[100] consumers in the importing country benefit from the lower prices. By imposing anti-dumping duties on the imports, the importing country may appease the competing domestic industry, but at the expense of consumers and industrial users of the imports, who must then generally pay higher prices to cover the additional duties. The widespread use of anti-dumping measures, traditionally by developed countries but now also by some developing countries, is often seen as an outbreak of protectionism.[101] Therefore, it would be unwise to allow this new form of trade-distorting measure in the services context, particularly when the structure of GATS already provides Members with substantial flexibility in making commitments. Second, it is far from clear how a Member could impose anti-dumping measures in a services context. The goods model would provide little guidance, because it is largely based on imposing tariffs when imports cross the border. In addition, the value and price of services in different countries is much harder to compare, given variables such as differing labour costs and regulatory standards. Price discrimination between markets may also be justified.[102]

6.5.2 *Cultural diversity safeguards*

Article XIX of GATT 1994 is titled 'Emergency Action on Imports of Particular Products'. Emergency safeguard measures against imports of a particular product may take the form of increased tariffs (even if these exceed tariff bindings) or import quotas (contrary to the general elimination of quantitative restrictions under GATT 1994), but generally they should apply on an MFN basis – that is, to all imports of the

---

[99] Above, 47.   [100] GATT 1994, art. VI:1; Anti-Dumping Agreement, art. 2.1.
[101] See generally, e.g., Michael Finger, Francis Ng, and Sonam Wangchuk, *Antidumping as Safeguard Policy*, World Bank Policy Research Working Paper 2730 (2001).
[102] Barton, 'Economics of TRIPS', 496.

relevant product.[103] The Safeguards Agreement elaborates on the conditions subject to which Members may impose emergency safeguard measures.[104] Members may impose these measures after conducting an investigation that establishes that, 'as a result of unforeseen developments',[105] the relevant product 'is being imported into its territory in such increased quantities ... and under such conditions as to cause or threaten to cause serious injury to the domestic industry that produces like or directly competitive products'.[106] Members may apply safeguards 'only to the extent necessary to prevent or remedy serious injury and to facilitate adjustment'.[107]

Like anti-dumping duties, safeguards have typically been applied against industrial products,[108] and sometimes on food or agricultural products.[109] However, the possibility of imposing safeguards to combat an unexpected flood of imports of cultural products that are goods provides one escape route for Members. This contrasts from the position under GATS.

GATS Article XXI allows Members to modify or withdraw any commitment in their services schedule, after three years have passed since the commitment was made, and subject to negotiation. For original WTO Members, this period has expired. GATS Article X:2 provides some scope for modification in emergency circumstances. For temporary, unilateral (that is, non-negotiated) modification or withdrawal of commitments, GATS Article X:1 merely provides:

> There shall be multilateral negotiations on the question of emergency safeguard measures based on the principle of non-discrimination. The results of such negotiations shall enter into effect on a date not later than three years from the date of entry into force of the WTO Agreement.

Accordingly, negotiations on safeguards under GATS should have concluded before 1 January 1998. However, in the absence of agreement,

---

[103] Safeguards Agreement, art. 2.2. On the relationship between GATT Article XXIV and Article 2.2 of the Safeguards Agreement, see Pauwelyn, 'Puzzle of WTO Safeguards'.
[104] For in-depth analysis of the WTO rules on safeguards in relation to trade in goods, see Yong-Shik Lee, *Safeguard Measures in World Trade: The Legal Analysis* (2003).
[105] GATT 1994, art. XIX:1(a); Appellate Body Report, *US – Lamb*, [72].
[106] Safeguards Agreement, art. 2.1.   [107] Ibid., art. 5.1.
[108] See, e.g., Appellate Body Report, *US – Steel Safeguards*; Appellate Body Report, *US – Line Pipe*.
[109] See, e.g., Appellate Body Report, *Chile – Price Band System*; Appellate Body Report, *Korea – Dairy*; Appellate Body Report, *US – Wheat Gluten*; Appellate Body Report, *US – Lamb*.

the Council for Trade in Services has extended this deadline several times,[110] most recently stating: 'Subject to the outcome of the mandate ... the results of such negotiations shall enter into effect on a date not later than the date of entry into force of the results of the current round of services negotiations.'[111]

One group of Members 'feels that the availability of safeguards in the event of unforeseeable market disruptions would encourage more liberal commitments in services negotiations' more generally.[112] In the Doha Round, some Members have proposed a specific 'cultural diversity safeguard'.[113] I do not wish to attempt to resolve the entire problem of safeguards for services.[114] Indeed, despite the attention paid to this broader issue by the Working Party on GATS Rules (also addressing subsidies and government procurement under GATS) during a period of several years, little progress has been made to date, and Members have not even reached agreement on such fundamental matters as whether it is desirable or feasible to provide a safeguard mechanism under GATS.[115] However, Bernard Hoekman avows that the 'economic

---

[110] WTO, Council for Trade in Services, *Decision on Negotiations on Emergency Safeguard Measures*, S/L/43 (2 December 1997); WTO, Council for Trade in Services, *Fifth Decision on Negotiations on Emergency Safeguard Measures*, S/L/159 (17 March 2004); WTO, Council for Trade in Services, *Fourth Decision on Negotiations on Emergency Safeguard Measures*, S/L/102 (27 March 2002); WTO, Council for Trade in Services, *Second Decision on Negotiations on Emergency Safeguard Measures*, S/L/73 (5 July 1999); WTO, Council for Trade in Services, *Third Decision on Negotiations on Emergency Safeguard Measures*, S/L/90 (8 December 2000).

[111] WTO, Council for Trade in Services, *Fifth Decision on Negotiations on Emergency Safeguard Measures*, S/L/159 (17 March 2004) [2].

[112] WTO Secretariat, *Handbook on GATS*, 37.

[113] See, e.g., WTO, Council for Trade in Services, *Report of the Meeting Held on 19–22 March 2002: Note by the Secretariat*, TN/S/M/1 (5 June 2002) [315]–[317]. See also Graber, 'Audio-Visual Policy', 212.

[114] For further discussion, see Yong-Shik Lee, 'Emergency Safeguard Measures under Article X in GATS: Applicability of the Concepts in the WTO Agreement on Safeguards' (1999) 33(4) *Journal of World Trade* 47, 51–8; Sauvé, 'Completing the GATS Framework', 311–24.

[115] See, e.g., Hong Kong Declaration, Annex C, [4(a)]; WTO, Working Party on GATS Rules, *Report of the Meeting of 10 February 2006*, S/WPGR/M/54 (22 February 2006) [2]; WTO, Working Party on GATS Rules, *Annual Report of the Working Party on GATS Rules to the Council for Trade in Services (2004)*, S/WPGR/14 (25 November 2004) [2]; WTO, Working Party on GATS Rules, *Communication from the United States: Desirability of a Safeguard Mechanism for Services: Promoting Liberalization of Trade in Services*, S/WPGR/W/37 (2 October 2001); WTO, Working Party on GATS Rules, *Negotiations on Emergency Safeguard Measures: Report by the Chairperson of the Working Party on GATS Rules*, S/WPGR/9 (14 March 2003) [18, 22]. See also Hoekman, 'A More Balanced Services Agreement', 130; Lee, 'Safeguard Measures under GATS', 48–51; Sauvé, 'Completing the GATS Framework', 308–10.

case for safeguards instruments' in GATS is 'weak'.[116] Moreover, a safeguard measure to respond to a significant increase in the screening of foreign cinematograph films seems unnecessary, as long as GATT Article IV remains. Similarly, increased imports of physical books, or music or film on DVDs, CDs, or similar media, would be covered by GATT Article XIX and the Safeguards Agreement. In addition, the need for such emergency measures should be significantly reduced if Members are all able to provide discriminatory subsidies for cultural products.

Graber proposes a variation on the cultural diversity safeguard.[117] He suggests creating a reference paper to oblige Members adopting it to provide national treatment and market access commitments in the audiovisual sector. Like the telecommunications reference paper, Graber's proposed solution for audiovisual products would thus open audiovisual markets while providing a safeguard for cultural policy measures in the form of a 'universal service' clause allowing Members to maintain diversity in broadcasting and film supply.[118] The equivalent clause in the standard telecommunications reference paper states:

> Any Member has the right to define the kind of universal service obligation it wishes to maintain. Such obligations will not be regarded as anti-competitive *per se*, provided they are administered in a transparent, non-discriminatory and competitively neutral manner and are not more burdensome than necessary for the kind of universal service defined by the Member.[119]

In Graber's version, the requirement of 'non-discrimination' in the universal service clause would apply only to audiovisual programs defined as 'high-budget', being those with a marketing and production budget of say $5 million or more.[120] (Graber also calls for an interpretative note to the Annex on Article II Exemptions to the effect that high- and low-budget films are not 'like' for the purpose of the GATS MFN obligation.[121]) This is one way Graber suggests for operationalising his distinction between 'arthouse' and other films.[122] As suggested earlier, I find this distinction rather blunt and uncertain and therefore unlikely

---

[116] Hoekman, 'A More Balanced Services Agreement', 130.
[117] Graber uses the words 'cultural diversity safeguard' in Graber, 'Audio-Visual Policy', 212–14.
[118] Graber, *Handel und Kultur*, 333–4. See also Barton, 'International Video Industry', 101.
[119] WTO, *Agreement on Telecommunications Services (Fourth Protocol to General Agreement on Trade in Services)*, 36 ILM 254 (1997) 368.
[120] Graber, *Handel und Kultur*, 335–6.   [121] Ibid., 332.
[122] See above, 221; Graber, 'Audio-Visual Policy', 212–14.

to assist in progressively liberalising the audiovisual sector. Graber's focus on budgets also conflicts with my understanding of the underlying justification for discriminatory cultural policy measures, as explained in Chapter 2.

6.5.3 Intellectual property rights and anti-competitive conduct

This book has concentrated on cultural products under GATT 1994 and GATS. The TRIPS Agreement also has widespread implications for cultural products and cultural policy measures.[123] However, these differ somewhat from the implications of GATT 1994 and GATS. Whereas to some extent the trade and culture problem pits liberalisation of goods and services trade against cultural policy measures, the goals of cultural diversity are closely aligned with the TRIPS Agreement. Both cultural rights and intellectual property rights seek to 'strike a balance between promoting general public interests in accessing new knowledge as easily as possible and in protecting the interests of authors and inventors in such knowledge'.[124] The TRIPS Agreement may, through copyright, 'make idea generation more profitable and bring us a wider menu of cultural choices',[125] such that cultural rights and authors' rights go hand in hand.[126] However, Macmillan points out that the

---

[123] For discussion of the intersection between trade, culture, and intellectual property, see Americo Beviglia-Zampetti, 'WTO Rules in the Audio-Visual Sector' in Guerrieri, Iapadre, and Koopmann, *Cultural Diversity* 261, 274–9; Footer and Graber, 'Trade Liberalization and Cultural Policy', 126–30; Pamela Samuelson, 'Implications of the Agreement on Trade Related Aspects of Intellectual Property Rights for the Cultural Dimension of National Copyright Laws' (1999) 23 *Journal of Cultural Economics* 95, 99–100; Stephen Fraser, 'Berne, CFTA, NAFTA and GATT: The Implications of Copyright Droit Moral and Cultural Exemptions in International Trade Law' (1996) 18 *Hastings Communications and Entertainment Law Journal* 287; Keith Acheson and Christopher Maule, 'Copyright, Contract, the Cultural Industries, and NAFTA' in McAnany and Wilkinson, *Mass Media and Free Trade*, 351. See also WTO, DSB, *Japan – Measures Concerning Sound Recordings: Notification of a Mutually-Agreed Solution*, WT/DS42/4, IP/D/4/Add.1 (17 November 1997); WTO, DSB, *Japan – Measures Concerning Sound Recordings: Request for Consultations from the European Communities*, WT/DS42/1, IP/D/4 (4 June 1996); Rosemary Coombe, *The Cultural Life of Intellectual Properties: Authorship, Appropriation, and the Law* (1998).

[124] UN, Commission on Human Rights, Sub-Commission on the Promotion and Protection of Human Rights, *The Impact of the Agreement on Trade-Related Aspects of Intellectual Property Rights on Human Rights: Report of the High Commissioner*, E/CN.4/Sub.2/2001/13 (27 June 2001) [10].

[125] Cowen, *Good and Plenty*, 103 (see also 113).

[126] Thierry Desurmont, 'Réflexions sur les rapports entre la convention sur la protection et la promotion de la diversité des expressions culturelles et la protection du droit d'auteur' (2006) 208 *Revue internationale du droit d'auteur* 2, 5, 13.

relationship between copyright and culture is more 'instrumental' than 'fundamental':

> A fundamental approach to cultural output would entail encouraging and protecting it on the basis that it has an intrinsic and non-economic value, not only as an expression of human creativity and autonomy, but also [as] a means of communication within the larger cultural, social, and political domain. The instrumental approach that copyright has instead adopted focuses upon the realization of future economic value through the promotion of trade in the cultural output that comes within its purview.[127]

Regarding the problem of classifying digital products, Wunsch-Vincent maintains that the TRIPS Agreement does not provide a solution because it does not provide for market access in the way that GATT 1994 and GATS do.[128] Nevertheless, digitalisation changes the impact of the TRIPS Agreement on cultural products, for example by simplifying the creation and distribution of pirated films or increasing the strength of copyright in books when they take an electronic form.[129] Thus, technological changes may either reduce the value of copyright by creating new avenues for distribution or areas where copyright is unenforceable, or increase its significance if it is applied equally to electronic and traditional forms of cultural products.[130] Some contend that copyright in cultural products has become too strong and now threatens cultural diversity instead of nurturing it,[131] particularly because copyright in cultural products tends to be concentrated in a few hands.[132]

---

[127] Fiona Macmillan, 'Commodification and Cultural Ownership' in Jonathan Griffiths and Uma Suthersanen (eds.), *Copyright and Free Speech: Comparative and International Analyses* (2005) 35, 41 (footnotes omitted).

[128] Wunsch-Vincent, *WTO, Internet and Digital Products*, 61.

[129] Cowen, *Good and Plenty*, 125, 128-9. See also Jacco Hakfoort, 'Copyright in the Digital Age: The Economic Rationale Re-examined' in Ruth Towse (ed.), *Copyright in the Cultural Industries* (2002) 63, 76-7; Canadian House of Commons, *Scripts, Screens and Audiences: A New Feature Film Policy for the 21st Century – Report of the Standing Committee on Canadian Heritage* (November 2005) 137.

[130] See Macmillan, 'Commodification', 48-50; Hakfoort, 'Copyright in the Digital Age', 80-1.

[131] See, e.g., Johnlee Curtis, 'Culture and the Digital Copyright Chimera: Assessing the International Regulatory System of the Music Industry in Relation to Cultural Diversity' (2006) 13(1) *International Journal of Cultural Property* 59, 80; Graber, *Handel und Kultur*, 220-1. Cf. Barton, 'Economics of TRIPS', 498.

[132] Macmillan, 'Commodification', 45-8, 54-5.

The same has been said more broadly of the relationship between intellectual property rights (including trade marks and traditional knowledge) and culture.[133]

One proposed solution to the problem of over-broad intellectual property rights is competition laws, which are currently outside the negotiating mandate of WTO Members and left largely to domestic regulation.[134] The utility of a competition-based approach to prevent the TRIPS Agreement from infringing the right to health is under debate.[135] Graber suggests the same approach in connection with cultural products: introduce antitrust or competition principles into the TRIPS Agreement to counteract the highly concentrated audiovisual industry.[136] Germann makes a slightly different proposal, suggesting that existing provisions in the TRIPS Agreement (including Articles 7, 8 and 40)[137] are flexible enough to prevent

---

[133] Cf. Jason Bosland, 'The Culture of Trade Marks: An Alternative Cultural Theory Perspective' (2005) 10(2) *Media & Arts Law Review* 99, 101; Witte, 'Trade in Culture', 248; Gibson, *Community Resources*, 187.

[134] July Package, [1(g)].

[135] UN, Commission on Human Rights, Sub-Commission on the Promotion and Protection of Human Rights, *The Impact of the Agreement on Trade-Related Aspects of Intellectual Property Rights on Human Rights: Report of the High Commissioner*, E/CN.4/Sub.2/2001/13 (27 June 2001) [64]; Frederick Abbott, 'The "Rule of Reason" and the Right to Health: Integrating Human Rights and Competition Principles in the Context of TRIPS' in Cottier, Pauwelyn, and Bürgi, *Human Rights and Trade*, 279, 296; Sisule Musungu, 'The Right to Health, Intellectual Property, and Competition Principles' in Cottier, Pauwelyn, and Bürgi, *Human Rights and Trade*, 301, 308.

[136] Graber, *Handel und Kultur*, 327–8, 343 (referring to Eleanor Fox, 'Competition Law and the Millennium Round' (1999) *Journal of International Economic Law* 665, 672–3).

[137] These provisions read, to the extent most relevant:

> 7: The protection and enforcement of intellectual property rights should contribute to the promotion of technological innovation and to the transfer and dissemination of technology, to the mutual advantage of producers and users of technological knowledge and in a manner conducive to social and economic welfare, and to a balance of rights and obligations.
>
> 8.1: Members may, in formulating or amending their laws and regulations, adopt measures necessary to protect public health and nutrition, and to promote the public interest in sectors of vital importance to their socio-economic and technological development, provided that such measures are consistent with the provisions of this Agreement.
>
> 40.1: Members agree that some licensing practices or conditions pertaining to intellectual property rights which restrain competition may have adverse effects on trade and may impede the transfer and dissemination of technology.

anti-competitive conduct in the cultural industries,[138] as is Article IX of GATS.[139]

In Chapter 2, I explained why some Members might have a legitimate need to impose certain discriminatory cultural policy measures on cultural grounds. However, unlike those of Graber and Germann, my views in this regard do not stem from an apprehension of anti-competitive conduct in the cultural industries. Accordingly, their proposals regarding competition laws go beyond the trade-culture issues that I identified in Chapter 2 and the problems with the current treatment of cultural products that I highlighted in Chapter 3. These proposals nevertheless warrant further consideration.

6.6 Conclusion

This chapter has suggested ways of improving the existing WTO agreements on trade in goods and services as applied to cultural products, primarily by increasing liberalisation, harmonising the treatment of cultural products under GATT 1994 and GATS, and reducing uncertainty about the treatment of cultural products. To increase liberalisation under GATT 1994, Article IV should be removed or modified, and no new exception under Article XX should be introduced for cultural products. Under GATS, MFN exemptions should be confirmed to terminate after ten years, and national treatment and market access commitments should apply to cultural products across the board. This would be subject to an exception for discriminatory subsidies for cultural products under GATS. If Article IV is retained, it should be made effective by a provision in GATS confirming that a measure complying with GATT Article IV will not violate GATS. If necessary, an analogous allowance for local content quotas in television and radio broadcasting under GATS could also be introduced. This would correspond with an acknowledgement that these and other digital products delivered electronically are services under GATS and not goods under GATT 1994. The moratorium on customs duties applied to these products should be extended on a more formal and permanent basis. Certain special and differential

---

[138] Germann, 'Culture in Times of Cholera', 118–19.
[139] Germann, 'Diversité culturelle', 338–9. GATS Article IX:1 provides: 'Members recognize that certain business practices of service suppliers, other than those falling under Article VIII, may restrain competition and thereby restrict trade in services.'

treatment provisions should be included, recognising the special needs of developing country Members.

What would the 'pro-trade' and 'pro-culture' WTO Members get out of these changes? Countries like the USA, which seek increased liberalisation in relation to cultural products, would have the comfort of national treatment and market access commitments subject to certain agreed exceptions, primarily for subsidies. Members like the EC and Canada, who seek the right to impose discriminatory cultural policy measures, would benefit from the guaranteed subsidy exemption. Minimal trade-restrictiveness of cultural policy measures would be ensured by requiring the use of subsidies rather than more trade-distorting quotas or regulations.

As mentioned at the start of this chapter, the proposals outlined here are not intended to be practical suggestions to be implemented in the Doha Round of negotiations. Many of the changes proposed fall outside the scope of those negotiations, which largely accept the broad GATT 1994 and GATS frameworks. In addition, although matters such as subsidies and safeguards are being examined, these areas are controversial in themselves, meaning that any attempt to marry them with provisions specific to cultural products would likely be rebuffed. Nevertheless, this chapter has identified certain possible approaches to the problem of cultural products in the WTO that further the objectives of the WTO agreements. This shows that a solution is possible, and Members should not resign themselves to an indefinite stalemate.

7 Conclusion

The movement of goods, people, and services has played an important role in the evolution and dissemination of culture throughout the world for thousands of years. However, the new scale of international trade has made cultural homogenisation a significant public concern about globalisation. The fear that cultural identities, traditions, and rituals are under threat is part of a broader anxiety about growing interconnectedness and faster rates of change in life. In addition to unease at the level of individuals, cultural and many other industries face increasingly intense competition from global sources. Perceived conflicts between trade and culture arise at many levels (local, national, regional, and global) and in relation to many things, from agriculture and tourism to handicrafts and sacred sites.

This book has attempted to contribute to the debate on trade and culture with respect to one particular aspect: cultural products in the context of the WTO. Given the size of the WTO Membership, the scope and complexity of its framework of binding rules, and the increasing amount of international trade in goods and services, the WTO is an obvious choice for assessing the legal aspects of trade in cultural products. These products of the cultural industries – especially film, radio, television, sound recording, books, magazines, periodicals, and associated services – present some of the most difficult conceptual questions in balancing cultural values and the objectives of trade liberalisation, precisely because of their substantial economic implications. They also lie at the heart of WTO Members' concerns in relation to culture. This is reflected in the drawn-out Uruguay Round negotiations on audiovisual services and the extended Doha Round negotiations relating to GATS, the early WTO dispute in *Canada – Periodicals*, and the involvement of many WTO Members in the UNESCO Convention. Cultural products therefore provide a valuable basis for understanding different views regarding culture in the WTO, even though many other internationally traded goods and services may also have some cultural characteristics.

Part I of this book demonstrated that the existing situation in the WTO regarding cultural products is unsatisfactory and unsustainable, regardless of one's perspective on the distinctiveness of cultural products compared to other products. It showed that the agreement to disagree at the end of the Uruguay Round of negotiations is better characterised as a failure and a stalemate than as a compromise or a pragmatic solution.[1]

Chapter 2 clarified Members' views on cultural products and tested the policy arguments on each side. Members are yet to resolve their differences in relation to cultural products. For Members such as Hong Kong,[2] Mexico,[3] and the USA,[4] cultural products are much like other tradable products and deserve only limited special treatment in WTO rules. On this view, cultural policy measures frequently fail to achieve their cultural goals and more often than not represent disguised protectionism. For Members such as the EC,[5] Canada,[6] and Australia,[7] cultural policy measures fall within their legitimate spheres of regulatory competence and should not be curtailed in the name of international trade. Otherwise, their cultural industries and cultures more generally risk being stifled or overrun by foreign influences. This

---

[1] For example, Guerrieri and Iapadre state that 'the cultural exception, excluded in principle, was accepted *de facto* on a temporary basis, postponing a neater solution of the problem to the current negotiating round': Paolo Guerrieri and Lelio Iapadre, 'Introduction' in Guerrieri, Iapadre, and Koopmann, *Cultural Diversity*, 1, 8.
[2] See, e.g., WTO, Council for Trade in Services, *Report of the Meeting Held on 9 December 2002 – 13 January 2003: Note by the Secretariat*, TN/S/M/5 (21 February 2003) [90].
[3] WTO, Council for Trade in Services, *Report of the Meeting Held on 19–22 May 2003: Note by the Secretariat*, TN/S/M/7 (30 June 2003) [85].
[4] See, e.g., WTO, Council for Trade in Services, *Communication from the United States – Audiovisual and Related Services*, S/CSS/W/21 (18 December 2000) [7]–[9].
[5] See, e.g., EC, Council of the European Union, *Council Decision of 20 December 2000 on the Implementation of a Programme to Encourage the Development, Distribution and Promotion of European Audiovisual Works (MEDIA Plus – Development, Distribution and Promotion) (2001–2005)*, OJ L13 (2001) 34, preamble [15]. See also WTO, Council for Trade in Services, *Communication from Norway: The Negotiations on Trade in Services*, S/CSS/W/59 (21 March 2001) [6]; WTO, Council for Trade in Services, *Communication from Slovenia, Bulgaria, Czech Republic, Poland and Slovak Republic: Note on Assessment of Trade in Services in Certain Transition Economies*, S/CSS/W/18 (5 December 2000) [15].
[6] See, e.g., WTO, Council for Trade in Services, *Communication from Canada: Initial Canadian Negotiating Proposal*, S/CSS/W/46 and Corr.1 (14 March 2001) [3].
[7] See, e.g., Australian Department of Foreign Affairs and Trade, *Australian Intervention*.

chapter concluded that the social and cultural value of cultural products is sometimes greater than the price that individual consumers are willing to pay for them. As a result, some Members may have a genuine and legitimate desire to support local cultural products. Moreover, to achieve an optimal level of production and consumption of these products, Members may be compelled to adopt cultural policy measures involving de jure or de facto discrimination against foreign cultural products, and to adopt measures that discriminate de facto between cultural products. Although this discrimination would ordinarily violate the national treatment and MFN principles in WTO law, it may be justifiable provided that it is coupled with minimal restrictions on or distortions of international trade.

Chapter 3 explained the problems with WTO provisions that are most directly relevant to cultural products, concentrating on GATT 1994 and GATS. It revealed that cultural products are largely subject to the core obligations of national treatment and MFN treatment, just like any other products. Cultural products do benefit from some exceptional provisions under GATT 1994 (most notably Articles IV, XX(a), and XX(f)), while the inbuilt flexibility of GATS leaves WTO Members with significant policy space in imposing measures on cultural products. However, the distinction between goods and services is particularly difficult to apply to cultural products, which may take different forms and be supplied in different ways. This problematic distinction, when combined with the difference in treatment of cultural products under GATT 1994 and GATS, creates uncertainties in predicting whether particular cultural policy measures imposed by WTO Members are consistent with their WTO obligations. These add to the ambiguities in the text of individual exceptions under GATT 1994 and GATS. Perhaps the greatest challenge presented by the current treatment of cultural products in the WTO is how to encourage additional commitments under GATS with respect to cultural products when the Members have been unable to agree on how they should be treated.

It is unlikely that the current treatment of cultural products in the WTO will remain static, because the interpretation of relevant WTO provisions is sure to evolve through dispute settlement, and the UNESCO Convention, once it comes into force, will have a substantial impact on trade in cultural products. WTO negotiations on matters not specific to cultural products are also likely to affect the treatment of cultural policy measures in WTO law. But assuming for a moment that the status quo could be maintained, what would this mean for WTO Members with different views on the nature of cultural products?

First, it would mean continued ambiguity in the distinction between cultural goods and cultural services, including electronically delivered cultural products. This could in turn lead to overlapping and possibly conflicting obligations under the WTO agreements regarding cultural products. Second, it would mean continuing the limited and uncertain recognition in GATT 1994 and GATS of the special nature of these products as distinct from other goods and services. Third, and perhaps most importantly, it would mean maintaining the current situation under GATS in which Members ensure freedom in relation to cultural products by not making national treatment or market access commitments to these products. This leaves little room for 'achieving a progressively higher level of liberalization', as foreseen in GATS Article XIX:1, or for contributing to the WTO objectives of 'ensuring full employment and a large and steadily growing volume of real income and effective demand' through the 'substantial reduction of ... barriers to trade and ... the elimination of discriminatory treatment in international commerce', as proposed in the GATT preamble. Of course, Members who insist on withholding commitments and on listing MFN exemptions under GATS must 'pay' for this in negotiations, perhaps in other service sectors or in unrelated areas of the Doha negotiations. The status quo is, therefore, less than ideal for many WTO Members.

In Part II, I drew on the conclusions reached in Part I to evaluate three main options for dealing with cultural products in the WTO in future: dispute settlement, a new agreement, or improvements to the existing agreements.

Chapter 4 addressed the possibility of leaving the relevant WTO provisions as they are but allowing them to evolve through dispute settlement by Panels and the Appellate Body, using international laws on culture to interpret the provisions where appropriate. This approach would fall within the interpretative rules under the DSU and international law, and it could certainly clarify some of the exceptions that could be applied to cultural products, and perhaps the distinction between goods and services in WTO law. It could also provide a broader basis for assessing the motives behind some cultural policy measures, lending them legitimacy when supported by multilateral declarations or instruments. But it could not remove the major divergence in treatment of cultural products under GATT 1994 and GATS. Nor could it resolve the underlying dispute between Members on cultural products and thereby increase Members' willingness to make GATS commitments for audiovisual services.

In the absence of a negotiated solution, it is quite likely that Members' cultural policy measures will end up in more WTO disputes. Panels and the Appellate Body may provide answers to such questions as: is the exemption in GATT Article IV from the MFN rule limited to screen quotas at the level they stood in 1947 collectively or individually? What is the meaning of a 'national treasure' in the exception in GATT Article XX(f)? What are the implications of international recognition of cultural rights for interpreting the exception for public morals under GATS Article XIV(a)? Some of these questions may arise in any case, outside the context of cultural products; others will probably remain unasked if Members can negotiate a solution to cultural products. Whatever the outcome, many Members will wish they had resolved the problem of cultural products diplomatically rather than judicially. The conceptual victors, with judicial reports to support them, will be even less likely to negotiate the issue in future.

Like Chapter 4, Chapter 5 considered an approach that would involve WTO Members doing little to reach the agreement on cultural products that they failed to reach during the Uruguay Round. Rather than leaving Panels and the Appellate Body to sort out the details, the Members would leave another international body to negotiate a new instrument on cultural diversity, including the treatment of cultural products in connection with international trade. In fact, this is already happening and seems quite likely to be completed, whether or not WTO Members also negotiate a solution within the WTO.

The WTO's Doha Round was originally scheduled to end on 1 January 2005,[8] and then by the end of 2006;[9] it is still stumbling along.[10] Meanwhile, UNESCO has marched ahead and adopted the UNESCO Convention, reaffirming States' 'sovereign right to formulate and implement their cultural policies and to adopt measures to protect and promote the diversity of cultural expressions'.[11] In some ways, this timing could be fortunate. For WTO Members it should at least bring home the need to

---

[8] Doha Declaration, [45].
[9] Hong Kong Declaration, [1]. See also WTO, *Report by the Chairman of the Trade Negotiations Committee to the General Council*, TN/C/5 (28 July 2005) 2–3.
[10] See above, 28, n. 163.
[11] UNESCO Convention, art. 5(1).

address cultural products in these negotiations, albeit not before the UNESCO Convention enters into force.[12] The UNESCO Convention in its present form could amount to a representation by a respected multilateral body that WTO rules conflict with the values of cultural diversity and cultural rights. This need not be the case. It would be far preferable for WTO Members themselves to agree on how to reconcile trade and culture and prevent increasing conflicts in international norms.

Unfortunately, the UNESCO Convention cannot be seen as a co-production between the WTO and UNESCO, blending visions of free trade and cultural diversity. The culture-focused origins and objectives of the UNESCO Convention are liable to obscure the benefits of trade liberalisation. In particular, the UNESCO Convention may well cause those WTO Members who seek greater leeway for their cultural policy measures to dig in their heels and refuse to increase their commitments in relation to cultural products under GATS. Pursuant to the UNESCO Convention, these Members may also be inclined, among themselves, to withdraw their disputes regarding cultural products from the WTO arena. This could diminish the effectiveness of the WTO agreements, the transparency of dispute settlement, and the coherence of the WTO. Thus, the UNESCO Convention cannot solve the problem of cultural products in the WTO. More worryingly, it may aggravate the present WTO stalemate.

A better solution is set out in Chapter 6. This chapter proposed wide-ranging amendments to GATT 1994 and GATS, not as a strict guide for WTO Members in Doha or otherwise, but as an example of how the WTO agreements could better balance the cultural and trade objectives of all Members. My suggestion would involve removing the exception for screen quotas in Article IV of GATT 1994, or at least modifying it so that the national treatment exception was linked to a standstill requirement, as is the current MFN exception in Article IV. Then, rather than adding a new exception for cultural products to GATT 1994 and thereby reducing the degree of trade liberalisation that Members already accepted in 1994, changes for cultural products could be directed towards GATS. Specifically, Chapter 6 suggested that digital products (that is, cultural products delivered in electronic form) be classified as services, but that all Members accept broad MFN, national treatment, and market access obligations in relation to cultural products under

---

[12] See above, 185.

GATS. This would contribute to the objective of progressive liberalisation of trade in services, but it could be tempered by an allowance for certain measures to pursue cultural objectives without being unduly trade-restrictive. These would primarily take the form of subsidies, with some additional flexibility for developing and least developed countries.

To date, based on the GATS offers that are publicly available, the signs are not encouraging that Members are prepared to engage in real negotiation on this issue in the Doha Round. To the extent that it is possible to glean Members' positions and the state of the negotiations from public information, little progress appears to have been made in approaching a middle ground on cultural products. As in the Uruguay Round, the picture looks somewhat better for printing and publishing than for audiovisual services. In their offers, several Members have included market access and national treatment commitments for printing and publishing services, although often excluding mode 4.[13] Yet a number of these Members already make these commitments in their GATS schedules and do not propose to expand or improve them. In relation to audiovisual services, the few market access and national treatment commitments proposed are largely unchanged from (or even more restrictive than) their current form, as negotiated at the end of the Uruguay Round or upon accession.[14] Moreover, many

---

[13] WTO, Council for Trade in Services, *Communication from the European Communities and Its Member States: Conditional Revised Offer*, TN/S/O/EEC/Rev.1 (29 June 2005) 172–3; WTO, Council for Trade in Services, *Iceland: Revised Offer on Services*, TN/S/O/ISL/Rev.1 (14 June 2005) 15; WTO, Council for Trade in Services, *Japan: Revised Offer*, TN/S/O/JPN/Rev.1 (24 June 2005) 45; WTO, Council for Trade in Services, *Republic of Korea: Revised Offer on Services*, TN/S/O/KOR/Rev.1 (14 June 2005) 25; WTO, Council for Trade in Services, *Liechtenstein: Revised Offer*, TN/S/O/LIE/Rev.1 (20 July 2005) 17; WTO, Council for Trade in Services, *Norway: Revised Offer*, TN/S/O/NOR/Rev.1 (28 June 2005) 18; WTO, Council for Trade in Services, *Pakistan: Conditional Initial Offer on Services*, TN/S/O/PAK (30 May 2005) 13; WTO, Council for Trade in Services, *Communication from the United States: Initial Offer*, TN/S/O/USA (9 April 2003) 48.

[14] WTO, Council for Trade in Services, *Communication from the United States: Initial Offer*, TN/S/O/USA (9 April 2003) 56–59; WTO, Council for Trade in Services, *Japan Revised Offer*, 53–54; WTO, Council for Trade in Services, *New Zealand: Revised Conditional Offer*, TN/S/O/NZL/Rev.1 (17 June 2005) 25–26; WTO, Council for Trade in Services, *Republic of Korea: Revised Offer on Services*, TN/S/O/KOR/Rev.1 (14 June 2005) 33; WTO, Council for Trade in Services, *Malaysia: Revised Offer*, TN/S/O/MYS/Rev.1 (31 January 2006) 29; WTO, Council for Trade in Services, *Oman: Initial Offer*, TN/S/O/OMN (14 March 2006) 13. See also WTO, Council for Trade in Services, *Communication from Hong Kong China, Japan, Mexico, the Separate Customs Territory of Taiwan, Penghu, Kinmen and Matsu, and United States: Joint Statement on the Negotiations on Audiovisual Services*, TN/S/W/49 (30 June 2005) [5].

Members propose to retain their existing MFN exemptions in this area.[15]

If Members do not address cultural products in the Doha Round of negotiations, they will be left with unsatisfactory legal provisions and the likelihood that matters will be taken out of their hands through judicial interpretation and UNESCO activity. At the same time, there is no point in Members simply reiterating arguments made during the Uruguay Round. The views on each side are extremely strong and neither is going to 'win' by waiting for the other to give up altogether. Instead, the situation requires a willingness to co-operate and to devise ways of amending the existing provisions and encouraging new commitments while taking into account cultural concerns. Co-operation in this area will provide a starting point for tackling broader issues of trade and culture in the WTO.

To begin with, Members should accept the legitimacy of cultural policy objectives, and the right of WTO Members to pursue these objectives in relation to cultural products. At the same time, it goes without saying that the value of cultural industries is economic as well as cultural. As with any other industry, Members should therefore be wary of protectionism disguised as cultural policy. Cultural policy measures entailing de jure discrimination against foreign cultural products or de facto discrimination between these products may be justified, but they need not restrict imports. Preserving and promoting culture and cultural diversity does not mean isolating it from foreign influences. In this regard, economic efficiency and cultural objectives go hand in hand: protecting local cultural industries from foreign imports is likely to impair not only their competitiveness but also their contribution to local culture and its development. WTO rules should therefore focus on minimising the trade-restrictiveness of cultural policy measures, taking into account cultural objectives, but without evaluating the underlying

---

[15] WTO, Council for Trade in Services, *Australia: Revised Services Offer*, TN/S/O/AUS/Rev.1 (31 May 2005) 67; WTO, Council for Trade in Services, *Canada: Revised Conditional Offer on Services*, TN/S/O/CAN/Rev.1 (23 May 2005) 111; WTO, Council for Trade in Services, *Chile: Conditional Revised Offer*, TN/S/O/CHL/Rev.1 (5 July 2005) 50; WTO, Council for Trade in Services, *Colombia: Initial Offer*, TN/S/O/COL (18 September 2003) 36; WTO, Council for Trade in Services, *EC Revised Offer*, 415–18; WTO, Council for Trade in Services, *Iceland Revised Offer*, 38–39; WTO, Council for Trade in Services, *Liechtenstein Revised Offer*, 37; WTO, Council for Trade in Services, *NZ Revised Offer*, 53; WTO, Council for Trade in Services, *Norway Revised Offer*, 46–7.

motives of individual Members or the effectiveness of their cultural policy measures in achieving those objectives.

The story of cultural products in the WTO might be shot in a film noir style, with gloomy lighting and fatalistic characters. The Uruguay Round could be portrayed as just one in a string of failures to reconcile trade and cultural objectives in a multilateral setting. However, going forward the story can change dramatically. Although WTO dispute settlement and the UNESCO Convention cannot provide the vehicle for the necessary alterations, the Doha Round offers a new opportunity for concerted action by WTO Members to resolve this longstanding dilemma. I have proposed one solution, which involves harmonising the treatment of cultural products as goods and services and introducing mandatory commitments alongside blanket exceptions for cultural products under GATS. WTO Members can no doubt come up with others. In any case, it is clear that the treatment of cultural products in the WTO must be transformed with a more optimistic script that better accommodates cultural and economic aspirations on a global scale.

Bibliography

NON-WTO AGREEMENTS, CASES, STATUTES, AND TREATIES

Aegean Sea Continental Shelf Case (Greece v Turkey) (Jurisdiction) [1978] ICJ Rep. 3.
African Charter on Human and Peoples' Rights, 1520 UNTS 217; 21 ILM 58 (adopted 27 June 1981).
Agreement for Facilitating the International Circulation of Visual and Auditory Materials of an Educational, Scientific and Cultural Character, 197 UNTS 3 (adopted 10 December 1948).
Agreement on the Importation of Educational, Scientific and Cultural Materials, 131 UNTS 25 (adopted 17 June 1950).
American Convention on Human Rights, 1144 UNTS 143; OAS Treaty Series No. 36 (signed 22 November 1969).
Applicability of Article VI, Section 22, of the Convention on the Privileges and Immunities of the United Nations (Advisory Opinion) [1989] ICJ Rep. 177.
Australia United States Free Trade Agreement (signed 18 May 2004).
Broadcasting Act 1991 (Canada) Ch. B-9.01.
Cable Television Networks Rules 1994 (India) GSR 729 (E).
Canada Chile Free Trade Agreement (signed 5 December 1996).
Canada United States Free Trade Agreement, 27 ILM 281; 2 BDIEL 359 (signed 2 January 1988).
Cartagena Protocol on Biosafety to the Convention on Biological Diversity, 39 ILM 1027 (adopted 29 January 2000).
Chile United States Free Trade Agreement (signed 6 June 2003).
Commission of the European Communities v Kingdom of the Netherlands (C-353/89) [1991] ECR I-4069.
Convention Against Illicit Traffic in Narcotic Drugs and Psychotropic Substances, E/CONF.82/15 (adopted 20 December 1988).
Convention for the Protection of Cultural Property in the Event of Armed Conflict, 249 UNTS 240 (adopted 14 May 1954).
Convention for the Protection of Human Rights and Fundamental Freedoms, 213 UNTS 221; ETS 5 (signed 4 November 1950), as amended by Protocol No. 11 (ETS 155).

257

Convention for the Protection of the World Cultural and Natural Heritage, 1037 UNTS 151 (adopted 16 November 1972).
Convention on Biological Diversity, 1760 UNTS 79; 31 ILM 818 (adopted 5 June 1992).
Convention on the Conservation of Migratory Species of Wild Animals, 1651 UNTS 333; 19 ILM 11 (adopted 23 June 1979).
Convention on International Trade in Endangered Species of Wild Fauna and Flora, 99 UNTS 243; 12 ILM 1085 (adopted 3 March 1973).
Convention on the Means of Prohibiting and Preventing the Illicit Import, Export and Transfer of Ownership of Cultural Property, [1972] UNTS 230 (adopted 14 November 1970).
Convention on the Rights of the Child, 1577 UNTS 3 (adopted 20 November 1989).
Criminal Proceedings Against Burmanjer (C-20/03) [2005] ECR I.
Cyprus v Turkey (2001) ECHR Application No. 25781/94.
Elliniki Radiophonia Tiléorassi AE v Dimotiki Etairia Pliroforissis (C-260/89) [1991] ECR I-2925.
Gabčíkovo-Nagymaros Project (Hungary v Slovakia) (Merits) [1997] ICJ Rep. 7.
Her Majesty's Customs and Excise v Schindler (C-275/92) [1994] ECR I-1039.
Indigenous and Tribal Peoples Convention, ILO Convention 169 (adopted 27 June 1989).
International Convention on the Harmonized Commodity Description and Coding System (signed 14 June 1983).
International Covenant on Civil and Political Rights, 999 UNTS 171 (adopted 16 December 1966).
Land and Maritime Boundary between Cameroon and Nigeria (Cameroon v Nigeria) (Merits) [2002] ICJ Rep. 1.
Legal Consequences for States of the Continued Presence of South Africa in Namibia (South West Africa) notwithstanding Security Council Resolution 276 (Advisory Opinion) [1971] ICJ Rep. 16.
North American Free Trade Agreement, 32 ILM 289 and 605 (signed 17 December 1992).
Protocol to the Agreement on the Importation of Educational, Scientific and Cultural Materials, 1259 UNTS 3 (adopted 26 November 1976).
Treaty Establishing a Constitution for Europe, OJ C310, 1 (signed 29 October 2004).
Treaty Establishing the European Community, OJ C340, 173; 37 ILM 79 (signed 25 March 1957).
UNIDROIT Convention on Stolen or Illegally Exported Cultural Objects, Diplomatic Conference for the Adoption of the Draft UNIDROIT Convention on the International Return of Stolen or Illegally Exported Cultural Objects, Rome – Acts and Proceedings 1996 (adopted 24 June 1995).
United Nations Convention on the Law of the Sea, 1833 UNTS 3; 21 ILM 1261 (adopted 10 December 1982).
United States Diplomatic and Consular Staff in Tehran (United States v Iran) (Merits) [1980] ICJ Rep. 3.
Vereinigte Familiapress Zeitungsverlags- und vertriebs GmbH v Heinrich Bauer Verlag (C-368/95) [1997] ECR I-3689.
Vienna Convention on the Law of Treaties, 1155 UNTS 331 (adopted 22 May 1969).

OTHER OFFICIAL DOCUMENTS AND REPORTS

Advisory Centre on WTO Law, *Giving Legal Effect to the Results of the Doha Round: An Analysis of the Methods of Changing WTO Law – Background Paper for ACWL Members and LDCs* (June 2006).

Australian Broadcasting Authority, *Broadcasting Services (Australian Content) Standard 1999* (July 2004).

'Trade Liberalisation in the Audiovisual Services Sector and Safeguarding Cultural Diversity' (working paper, commissioned by the Asia-Pacific Broadcasting Union, July 1999).

Australian Department of Communications Information Technology and the Arts, *Report on Access to Overseas Markets for Australia's Creative Digital Industry* (12 December 2003).

Australian Department of Foreign Affairs and Trade, *Australia–United States Free Trade Agreement: Guide to the Agreement* (March 2004).

Australian Intervention on Negotiating Proposal on Audiovisual Services: Council for Trade in Services Special Session (July 2001).

Australian Government, *Creative Nation: Commonwealth Cultural Policy* (October 1994).

Canadian Department of Communications, *Report of the Federal Cultural Policy Review Committee* (1982).

Canadian Department of Foreign Affairs and International Trade, 'Marchi Tables Government Response to Parliamentary Committee's Report on MAI', press release 97 (23 April 1998).

Canadian Department of Foreign Affairs and International Trade, Cultural Industries SAGIT, *Canadian Culture in a Global World: New Strategies for Culture and Trade* (February 1999).

An International Agreement on Cultural Diversity: A Model for Discussion (September 2002).

Canadian Heritage, *Book Publishing Industry Development Program (BPIDP): Applicant's Guide 2002-2003* (2002).

Canadian Content in the 21st Century: A Discussion Paper about Canadian Content in Film and Television Productions (March 2002).

'Copps to Host International Meeting on Culture', press release (2 June 1998).

A Guide to Federal Programs for the Film and Video Sector (September 2001).

Canadian Heritage Publishing Policy and Programs Branch, *Book Publishing Industry Activity Report: 2000-2001* (September 2001).

Canadian House of Commons, *Scripts, Screens and Audiences: A New Feature Film Policy for the 21st Century – Report of the Standing Committee on Canadian Heritage* (November 2005).

CRTC, *'The Country Network' – A Country Music Video Service – Approved*, Decision CRTC 94-284 (6 June 1994).

Revised Lists of Eligible Satellite Services, Public Notice CRTC 1994-61 (6 June 1994).

Structural Public Hearing, Public Notice CRTC 1993-74 (3 June 1993).

Customs Cooperation Council, *Explanatory Notes to the Harmonized Commodity Description and Coding System* (1986).

260   BIBLIOGRAPHY

EC, Council of the European Communities, *Council Directive 89/552/EEC of 3 October 1989 on the Coordination of Certain Provisions Laid Down by Law, Regulation or Administrative Action in Member States Concerning the Pursuit of Television Broadcasting Activities*, OJ L298, 23 (17 October 1989), as amended by European Parliament and Council of the European Union, *Directive 97/36/EC of the European Parliament and of the Council of 30 June 1997 Amending Council Directive 89/552/EEC on the Coordination of Certain Provisions Laid Down by Law, Regulation or Administrative Action in Member States Concerning the Pursuit of Television Broadcasting Activities*, OJ L202, 60 (30 July 1997).

EC, Council of the European Union, *Council Decision of 20 December 2000 on the Implementation of a Programme to Encourage the Development, Distribution and Promotion of European Audiovisual Works (MEDIA Plus – Development, Distribution and Promotion) (2001–2005)*, OJ L13 (2001) 34.

EC, European Commission, *Authorisation for State Aid pursuant to Articles 87 and 88 of the EC Treaty: Cases Where the Commission Raises No Objections*, OJ C79 (2006) 23.

Proposal for a Decision of the European Parliament and the Council Concerning the Implementation of a Programme of Support for the European Audiovisual Sector (MEDIA 2007), COM(2004) 470 final (14 July 2004).

EC, European Parliament and Council of the European Union, *Recommendation 2005/865/CE of the European Parliament and of the Council of 16 November 2005 on Film Heritage and the Competitiveness of Related Industrial Activities*, OJ L323 (2005) 57.

European Research Institute for Comparative Cultural Policy and the Arts, *A Pilot Inventory of National Cultural Policies and Measures Supporting Cultural Diversity* (July 2001).

GATT, *Application of GATT to International Trade in Television Programmes*, L/1615 (16 November 1961).

Application of GATT to International Trade in Television Programmes: Proposal by the Government of the United States, L/2120 (18 March 1964).

Application of GATT to International Trade in Television Programmes: Report of the Working Party, L/1741 (13 March 1962).

Application of GATT to International Trade in Television Programmes: Revised United States Draft Recommendation, L/1908 (10 November 1962).

Application of GATT to International Trade in Television Programmes: Statement made by the United States Representative on 21 November 1961, L/1646 (24 November 1961).

Austria / Luxembourg / Netherlands / Norway / Spain / Sweden / Switzerland / United Kingdom – Measures to be Taken under the European Convention on Transfrontier Television: Request for Consultations under Article XXII:1 by the United States, DS4/1 (11 September 1989).

Barriers to the Import and Export of Educational, Scientific and Cultural Material, GATT/CP/12 (8 March 1949).

Countdown for the Uruguay Round: Address by Peter Sutherland to the Forum de l'Expansion, Paris, 19 October 1993, NUR 070 (20 October 1993).

EEC – Directive on Transfrontier Television: Request for Consultations under Article XXII:1 by the United States, DS4/3 (8 November 1989).

EEC – Directive on Transfrontier Television: Response to Request for Consultations under Article XXII:1 by the United States, DS4/4 (8 November 1989).
France – Television Broadcasting of Cinematographic and Audiovisual Works: Request for Consultations under Article XXII:1 by the United States, DS4/5 (8 May 1990).
Major Proposals Tabled on Safeguards while First Sectoral Discussions Take Place in Services Group, NUR 029 (7 July 1989).
Ministerial Declaration to Launch the Uruguay Round of Multilateral Trade Negotiations MIN.DEC (20 September 1986).
Peter Sutherland Responds to Debate on Audiovisual Sector, NUR 069 (14 October 1993).
Understanding on Commitments in Financial Services, LT/UR/U/1 (15 April 1994).
Waiver Decision on the Generalized System of Preferences, L/3545, BISD 18S/24 (25 June 1971).
GATT, Group of Negotiations on Services, *Informal GNS Meeting – Chairman's Statement*, MTN.GNS/49 (11 December 1993).
GATT, Trade Negotiations Committee, *Mid-Term Meeting*, MTN.TNC/11 (21 April 1989).
Uruguay Round – Trade Negotiations Committee Meeting, NUR 077 (26 November 1993).
GATT, Uruguay Round Group of Negotiations on Services, *Scheduling of Initial Commitments in Trade in Services: Explanatory Note*, MTN.GNS/W/164 (3 September 1993).
Services Sectoral Classification List – Note by the Secretariat, MTN.GNS/W/120 (10 July 1991).
GATT, Uruguay Round Group of Negotiations on Services, Working Group on Audiovisual Services, *Matters Relating to Trade in Audiovisual Services: Note by the Secretariat*, MTN.GNS/AUD/W/1 (4 October 1990).
Note on the Meeting of 5 and 18 October 1990, MTN.GNS/AUD/2 (20 December 1990).
Note on the Meeting of 27–28 August 1990, MTN.GNS/AUD/1 (27 September 1990).
INCD, *Advancing Cultural Diversity Globally: The Role of Civil Society Movements – Report from the Fourth Annual Conference of the International Network for Cultural Diversity in Partnership with Culturelink Network/IMO* (Opatija, 13–15 October 2003).
Proposed Convention on Cultural Diversity (15 January 2003).
INCP, *Draft International Convention on Cultural Diversity* (29 July 2003).
Fifth INCP Annual Ministerial Meeting: Final Report (Cape Town, 14–16 October 2002).
Report for Ministerial Consideration on the 2003–2004 Workplan of the Working Group on Cultural Diversity and Globalization (2004).
Seventh INCP Annual Ministerial Meeting: Ministerial Statement (Shanghai, 14–16 October 2004).
Sixth INCP Annual Ministerial Meeting: Ministerial Statement (Opatija, 16–18 October 2003).
Ninth International Conference of American States, *American Declaration of the Rights and Duties of Man* (1948).

OECD Council, *Decision Updating the Invisibles Code*, C(88)110 (Final) (21 July 1988).
OECD, Negotiating Group on the MAI, *The Multilateral Agreement on Investment: Draft Consolidated Text*, DAFFE/MAI(98)7/REV1 (22 April 1998).
OECD, Working Party on the Information Economy, *Digital Broadband Content: Music*, DSTI/ICCP/IE(2004)12/FINAL (8 June 2005).
UK, Department for Culture, Media and Sport, *Creative Industries: UK Television Exports Inquiry (The Report of the Creative Industries Task Force Inquiry into Television Exports)* (November 1999).
UN, *Central Product Classification Version 1.1*, Statistical Papers, Series M, No. 77 (2004).
Charter of the United Nations (signed 26 June 1945).
Extract of the Summary Record of the Second Session of the Preparatory Committee of the United Nations Conference on Trade and Employment, Commission A, E/PC/T/A/SR/10 (6 June 1947).
Multilateral Treaties Deposited with the Secretary-General, ST/LEG/SER/E/-, <http://untreaty.un.org> (accessed 4 August 2006).
Provisional Central Product Classification, Statistical Papers, Series M, No. 77 (1991).
Rio Declaration on Environment and Development, A/CONF. 151/5/Rev.1; 31 ILM 874 (13 June 1992).
Universal Declaration of Human Rights, GA Res. 217A(III) (10 December 1948).
UN, Commission on Human Rights, *Analytical Study of the High Commissioner for Human Rights on the Fundamental Principle of Non-Discrimination in the Context of Globalization: Report of the High Commissioner*, E/CN.4/2004/40 (15 January 2004).
Globalization and Its Impact on the Full Enjoyment of Human Rights: Report of the High Commissioner for Human Rights Submitted in Accordance with Commission on Human Rights Resolution 2001/32, E/CN.4/2002/54 (15 January 2002).
Promotion of the Enjoyment of the Cultural Rights of Everyone and Respect for Different Cultural Identities, E/CN.4/RES/2002/26 (22 April 2002).
Question of the Realization in All Countries of the Economic, Social and Cultural Rights Contained in the Universal Declaration of Human Rights and in the International Covenant on Economic, Social and Cultural Rights, and Study of Special Problems which the Developing Countries Face in Their Efforts to Achieve These Human Rights, E/CN.4/RES/2003/18 (22 April 2003).
Rights of Persons Belonging to National or Ethnic, Religious and Linguistic Minorities, E/CN.4/RES/2000/52 (25 April 2000).
UN, Commission on Human Rights, Sub-Commission on the Promotion and Protection of Human Rights, *Globalization and Its Impact on the Full Enjoyment of Human Rights: Final Report Submitted by J. Oloka-Onyango and Deepika Udagama, in Accordance with Sub-Commission Decision 2000/105*, E/CN.4/Sub.2/2003/14 (25 June 2003).
Human Rights, Trade and Investment: Report of the High Commissioner for Human Rights, E/CN.4/Sub.2/2003/9 (2 July 2003).
The Impact of the Agreement on Trade-Related Aspects of Intellectual Property Rights on Human Rights: Report of the High Commissioner, E/CN.4/Sub.2/2001/13 (27 June 2001).

Liberalization of Trade in Services and Human Rights: Report of the High Commissioner, E/CN.4/Sub.2/2002/9 (25 June 2002).
UN, Committee on Economic, Social and Cultural Rights, *General Comment No. 1: Reporting by States Parties*, E/1989/22 (24 February 1989).
Report on the Sixteenth and Seventeenth Sessions, E/1998/22 (20 June 1998).
Revised Guidelines Regarding the Form and Contents of Reports to be Submitted by States Parties under Articles 16 and 17 of the International Covenant on Economic, Social and Cultural Rights, E/C.12/1991/1, annex.
Summary Record of the 4th Meeting: Paraguay, E/C.12/1996/SR.4 (6 May 1996).
UN, Economic and Social Council, *Procedure for Dealing with Communications Concerning Human Rights*, Res. 2000/3 (16 June 2000).
Procedure for Dealing with Communications Relating to Violations of Human Rights and Fundamental Freedoms, Res. 1503(XLVIII) (27 May 1970).
Review of the Composition, Organization and Administrative Arrangements of the Sessional Working Group of Governmental Experts on the Implementation of the International Covenant on Economic, Social and Cultural Rights, 1985/17 (28 May 1985).
UN, General Assembly, *Action Plan on International Cooperation on the Eradication of Illicit Drug Crops and on Alternative Development*, A/RES/S-20/4 (10 June 1998).
Declaration on the Rights of Persons Belonging to National or Ethnic, Religious and Linguistic Minorities, A/RES/47/135 (18 December 1992).
Fiftieth Anniversary of the Universal Declaration of Human Rights, A/RES/52/117 (12 December 1997).
UN, Human Rights Committee, *Concluding Observations of the Human Rights Committee: Italy*, CCPR/C/79/Add.37 (3 August 1994).
Consideration of Reports Submitted by States Parties under Article 40 of the Covenant: Concluding Observations of the Human Rights Committee, CCPR/C/ITA/CO/5 (24 April 2006).
General Comment No. 10: Freedom of Expression (Art. 19), reprinted HRI\GEN\1\Rev.1, 11 (29 June 1983).
General Comment No. 23: The Rights of Minorities (Article 27), CCPR/C/21/Rev.1/Add.5 (8 April 1994).
UN, ILC, *Fragmentation of International Law: Difficulties Arising from the Diversification and Expansion of International Law – Report of the Study Group – Finalized by Martti Koskenniemi*, A/CN.4/L.682 (13 April 2006).
Fragmentation of International Law: Difficulties Arising from the Diversification and Expansion of International Law – Report of the Study Group, A/CN.4/L.702 (18 July 2006).
Yearbook, II (1966).
UN, Office of the United Nations High Commissioner for Human Rights, *Human Rights and Trade: Statement to the Fifth Ministerial Conference of the WTO* (10–14 September 2003).
Human Rights and World Trade Agreements: Using General Exception Clauses to Protect Human Rights, HR/PUB/05/5 (2005).
The International Bill of Human Rights (Fact Sheet No. 2 (Rev. 1)) (June 1996).

The United Nations Human Rights Treaty System: An Introduction to the Core Human Rights Treaties and the Treaty Bodies (Fact Sheet No. 30).

UNCTAD, *Audiovisual Services: Improving Participation of Developing Countries – Note by the UNCTAD Secretariat*, TD/B/COM.1/EM.20/2 (30 September 2002).

Lessons from the MAI, UNCTAD/ITE/IIT, UN Sales No. E.99.II (1999).

Report of the Expert Meeting on Audiovisual Services: Improving Participation of Developing Countries, 13–15 November 2002, TD/B/COM.1/56; TD/B/COM.1/EM.20/3 (4 December 2002).

UNCTAD and World Bank, *Liberalizing International Transactions in Services: A Handbook* (New York, Geneva: UN, 1994).

UNESCO, *A Constitution of the United Nations Educational, Scientific and Cultural Organization* (16 November 1945).

'Convention on the Protection and Promotion of the Diversity of Cultural Expressions will enter into force on 18 March 2007', press release 2006-155 (18 December 2006).

Convention on the Protection and Promotion of the Diversity of Cultural Expressions, CLT-2005/CONVENTION DIVERSITE-CULT REV (20 October 2005).

Culture, Trade and Globalization: Questions and Answers (Paris: UNESCO, 2000).

Decisions Adopted by the Executive Board at Its 166th Session, 166 EX/Decisions (14 May 2003).

Declaration of the Principles of International Cultural Co-operation, 14 C/Resolution 8 (4 November 1966).

Final Report: Intergovernmental Conference on Cultural Policies for Development, CLT-98/Conf.210 (31 August 1998).

First Session of the Intergovernmental Meeting of Experts on the Preliminary Draft Convention on the Protection of the Diversity of Cultural Contents and Artistic Expressions: Report by the Secretariat, CLT-2004/CONF.201/9 (November 2004).

'General Conference Adopts Convention on the Protection and Promotion of the Diversity of Cultural Expressions', press release 2005-128 (20 October 2005).

'General Conference Adopts Universal Declaration on Cultural Diversity', press release 2001-120 (2 November 2001).

Our Creative Diversity (1995).

Preliminary Draft Convention on the Protection of the Diversity of Cultural Contents and Artistic Expressions: Preliminary Report of the Director-General, CLT/CPD/2004/CONF.201/1 (July 2004).

Preliminary Draft Convention on the Protection of the Diversity of Cultural Contents and Artistic Expressions: Presentation of Comments and Amendments, CLT/CPD/2004/CONF.607/1, partie IV (December 2004).

Preliminary Draft Convention on the Protection of the Diversity of Cultural Contents and Artistic Expressions: Text Revised by the Drafting Committee, 14–17 December 2004, CLT/CPD/2004/CONF.607/6 (23 December 2004).

Preliminary Report of the Director-General Containing Two Preliminary Drafts of a Convention on the Protection of the Diversity of Cultural Contents and Artistic Expressions, CLT/CPD/2005/CONF.203/6 (3 March 2005).

Preliminary Study on the Technical and Legal Aspects Relating to the Desirability of a Standard-Setting Instrument on Cultural Diversity, 166 EX/28 (12 March 2003).

Recommendation Concerning the International Exchange of Cultural Property, 19 C/Resolutions, annex I, 16 (26 November 1976).
Recommendation for the Safeguarding and Preservation of Moving Images, 21 C/Resolutions, annex I, 156 (27 October 1980).
Recommendation on Participation by the People at Large in Cultural Life and Their Contribution to It, 19 C/Resolutions, annex I, 29 (26 November 1976).
Recommendation on the Safeguarding of Traditional Culture and Folklore, 25 C/Resolutions, annex I(B), 238 (15 November 1989).
Records of the General Conference, 16th Session, vol. I: *Resolutions* (14 November 1970).
Records of the General Conference, 31st Session, vol. I: *Resolutions* (15 October to 3 November 2001).
Report of the Third Meeting of Experts (Category VI) on the Preliminary Draft of the Convention on the Protection of the Diversity of Cultural Contents and Artistic Expressions, CLT/CPD/2004/603/5 (23 June 2004).
UNESCO and the Issue of Cultural Diversity: Review and Strategy, 1946–2004 (Revised version, September 2004).
(ed.), *World Culture Report: Cultural Diversity, Conflict and Pluralism* (Paris: UNESCO, 2000).
(ed.), *World Culture Report: Culture, Creativity and Markets* (Paris: UNESCO, 1998).
World Report on Culture and Development, 26 C/Resolution 3.4 (6 November 1991).
UNESCO, General Conference, *Preliminary Draft Convention on the Protection and Promotion of the Diversity of Cultural Expressions*, 33 C/23, annex V (4 August 2005).
Preliminary Report by the Director-General Setting out the Situation to be Regulated and the Possible Scope of the Regulating Action Proposed, Accompanied by the Preliminary Draft of a Convention on the Protection and of the Diversity of Cultural Contents and Artistic Expressions, 33 C/23 (4 August 2005).
Resolution 34 Adopted at the 32nd Session (29 September 2003–17 October 2003).
UNESCO, Third Intergovernmental Meeting of Experts, *Recommendation* (3 June 2005).
United Nations Development Programme, *Human Development Report 2004: Cultural Liberty in Today's Diverse World* (2004).
USA, WTO, *Second Submission to the Panel in Mexico – Tax Measures on Soft Drinks and Other Beverages* (21 January 2005).
USTR, 'Hills Announces Implementation of Special 301 and Title VII', press release (26 April 1991).
2002 National Trade Estimate Report on Foreign Trade Barriers (2002).
'USTR Announces Commercial Agreement in the U.S. – Canada Country Music Television Dispute', press release 96-22 (7 March 1996).
WTO, *Agreement on Telecommunications Services (Fourth Protocol to General Agreement on Trade in Services)*, 36 ILM 254 (1997).
Australia – Final List of Article II (MFN) Exemptions, GATS/EL/6 (15 April 1994).
Brazil – Final List of Article II (MFN) Exemptions, GATS/EL/13 (15 April 1994).
Canada – Final List of Article II (MFN) Exemptions, GATS/EL/16 (15 April 1994).
Canada – Schedule of Specific Commitments, GATS/SC/16 (15 April 1994).
Developing Countries and the Multilateral Trading System: Past and Present – Background Note by the Secretariat, WTO High Level Symposium (17–18 March 1999).

Egypt – *Final List of Article II (MFN) Exemptions*, GATS/EL/30 (15 April 1994).
European Communities and Their Member States – *Final List of Article II (MFN) Exemptions*, GATS/EL/31 (15 April 1994).
European Communities and Their Member States – *Schedule of Specific Commitments*, GATS/SC/31 (15 April 1994).
Fourth Protocol to the General Agreement on Trade in Services, S/L/20 (30 April 1996).
The Hashemite Kingdom of Jordan – *Final List of Article II MFN Exemptions*, GATS/EL/128 (15 December 2000).
Iceland – *Schedule of Specific Commitments*, GATS/SC/41 (15 April 1994).
India – *Final List of Article II (MFN) Exemptions*, GATS/EL/42 (15 April 1994).
India – *Schedule of Specific Commitments*, GATS/SC/42 (15 April 1994).
Information Note from the Director-General, WTO Public Symposium – 'WTO After 10 Years: Global Problems and Multilateral Solutions', 20 to 22 April 2005, WT/INF/87 (13 April 2005).
Israel – *Final List of Article II (MFN) Exemptions*, GATS/EL/44 (15 April 1994).
'Lamy: "We have resumed negotiations fully across the board"', news item (7 February 2007).
Malaysia – *Schedule of Specific Commitments*, GATS/SC/52 (15 April 1994).
Mexico – *Schedule of Specific Commitments*, GATS/SC/56 (15 April 1994).
New Zealand – *Final List of Article II (MFN) Exemptions*, GATS/EL/62 (15 April 1994).
Norway – *Final List of Article II (MFN) Exemptions*, GATS/EL/66 (15 April 1994).
The People's Republic of China – *Schedule of Specific Commitments*, GATS/SC/135 (14 February 2002).
Report by the Chairman of the Trade Negotiations Committee to the General Council, TN/C/5 (28 July 2005).
Services Database: Predefined Report – *All Countries' MFN Exemptions* (21 March 2005) at <http://tsdb.wto.org/wto/WTOHomepublic.htm> (accessed 4 August 2006).
Services Database: Predefined Report – *All Sectors in Each Country* (21 March 2005) at <http://tsdb.wto.org/wto/WTOHomepublic.htm> (accessed 4 August 2006).
Switzerland – *Final List of Article II (MFN) Exemptions*, GATS/EL/83 (15 April 1994).
'Talks suspended. "Today there are only losers"', news item (24 July 2006).
Thailand – *Schedule of Specific Commitments*, GATS/SC/85 (15 April 1994).
Work Programme on Electronic Commerce Adopted by the General Council on 25 September 1998, WT/L/274 (30 September 1998).
Work Programme on Electronic Commerce: Submission by the United States, WT/COMTD/17; WT/GC/16; G/C/2; S/C/7; IP/C/16 (12 February 1999).
World Trade Report 2004: Exploring the Linkage between the Domestic Policy Environment and International Trade (Geneva: WTO, 2004).
World Trade Report 2006: Exploring the Links between Subsidies, Trade and the WTO (Geneva: WTO, 2006).
WTO, Committee on Trade and Development, *Implementation of Special and Differential Treatment Provisions in WTO Agreements and Decisions: Note by the Secretariat*, WT/COMTD/W/77 (25 October 2000).
WTO, Committee on Trade and Environment, *Report (1996) of the Committee on Trade and Environment*, WT/CTE/1 (12 November 1996).

WTO, Consultative Board, *The Future of the WTO: Addressing Institutional Challenges in the New Millennium* (2004).
WTO, Council for Trade in Goods, *Work Programme on Electronic Commerce: Background Note by the Secretariat*, G/C/W/128 (5 November 1998).
WTO, Council for Trade in Services, *Audiovisual Services: Background Note by the Secretariat*, S/C/W/40 (15 June 1998).
Australia: Revised Services Offer, TN/S/O/AUS/Rev.1 (31 May 2005).
Canada: Revised Conditional Offer on Services, TN/S/O/CAN/Rev.1 (23 May 2005).
Chile: Conditional Revised Offer, TN/S/O/CHL/Rev.1 (5 July 2005).
Colombia: Initial Offer, TN/S/O/COL (18 September 2003).
Communication from Brazil – Audiovisual Services, S/CSS/W/99 (9 July 2001).
Communication from Canada: Initial Canadian Negotiating Proposal, S/CSS/W/46 and Corr.1 (14 March 2001).
Communication from the European Communities and Its Member States: Conditional Revised Offer, TN/S/O/EEC/Rev.1 (29 June 2005).
Communication from the European Communities and Their Member States: Electronic Commerce Work Programme, S/C/W/183 (30 November 2000).
Communication from Hong Kong China, Japan, Mexico, the Separate Customs Territory of Taiwan, Penghu, Kinmen and Matsu, and United States: Joint Statement on the Negotiations on Audiovisual Services, TN/S/W/49 (30 June 2005).
Communication from Israel – Review of Article II Exemptions: Replies to Questions Posed on Israel's MFN Exemptions in the Area of Audiovisual Services in the Course of the Review of MFN Exemptions, S/C/W/158 (10 July 2000).
Communication from Japan: The Negotiations on Trade in Services, S/CSS/W/42 (22 December 2000).
Communication from Norway: The Negotiations on Trade in Services, S/CSS/W/59 (21 March 2001).
Communication from Slovenia, Bulgaria, Czech Republic, Poland and Slovak Republic: Note on Assessment of Trade in Services in Certain Transition Economies, S/CSS/W/18 (5 December 2000).
Communication from Switzerland – GATS 2000: Audiovisual Services, S/CSS/W/74 (4 May 2001).
Communication from the United States – Audiovisual and Related Services, S/CSS/W/21 (18 December 2000).
Communication from the United States – Audiovisual Services, S/C/W/78 (8 December 1998).
Communication from the United States: Initial Offer, TN/S/O/USA (9 April 2003).
Decision on Negotiations on Emergency Safeguard Measures, S/L/43 (2 December 1997).
Fifth Decision on Negotiations on Emergency Safeguard Measures, S/L/159 (17 March 2004).
Fourth Decision on Negotiations on Emergency Safeguard Measures, S/L/102 (27 March 2002).
Guidelines and Procedures for the Negotiations on Trade in Services, S/L/93 (29 March 2001).
Guidelines for the Scheduling of Specific Commitments under the General Agreement on Trade in Services (GATS): Adopted by the Council for Trade in Services on 23 March 2001, S/L/92 (28 March 2001).

Iceland: Revised Offer on Services, TN/S/O/ISL/Rev.1 (14 June 2005).
Japan: Revised Offer, TN/S/O/JPN/Rev.1 (24 June 2005).
Liechtenstein: Revised Offer, TN/S/O/LIE/Rev.1 (20 July 2005).
Malaysia: Revised Offer, TN/S/O/MYS/Rev.1 (31 January 2006).
New Zealand: Revised Conditional Offer, TN/S/O/NZL/Rev.1 (17 June 2005).
Norway: Revised Offer, TN/S/O/NOR/Rev.1 (28 June 2005).
Oman: Initial Offer, TN/S/O/OMN (14 March 2006).
Pakistan: Conditional Initial Offer on Services, TN/S/O/PAK (30 May 2005).
Presence of Natural Persons (Mode 4): Background Note by the Secretariat, S/C/W/75 (8 December 1998).
Report of the Meeting Held on 25 February 2000: Note by the Secretariat, S/C/M/41 (3 April 2000).
Report of the Meeting Held on 19–22 March 2002: Note by the Secretariat, TN/S/M/1 (5 June 2002).
Report of the Meeting Held on 9 December 2002–13 January 2003: Note by the Secretariat, TN/S/M/5 (21 February 2003).
Report of the Meeting Held on 19–22 May 2003: Note by the Secretariat, TN/S/M/7 (30 June 2003).
Report of the Meeting Held on 23 September 2004: Note by the Secretariat, S/C/M/74 (10 November 2004).
Report of the Meeting Held on 30 November 2004: Note by the Secretariat, S/C/M/76 (4 February 2005).
Republic of Korea: Revised Offer on Services, TN/S/O/KOR/Rev.1 (14 June 2005).
Second Decision on Negotiations on Emergency Safeguard Measures, S/L/73 (5 July 1999).
Special Session – Report of the Meeting Held on 28, 29 and 30 March 2001: Note by the Secretariat, S/CSS/M/8 (14 May 2001).
Third Decision on Negotiations on Emergency Safeguard Measures, S/L/90 (8 December 2000).
The Work Programme on Electronic Commerce: Note by the Secretariat, S/C/W/68 (16 November 1998).
WTO, Council for Trade-Related Aspects of Intellectual Property Rights, *Article 27.3(b), Relationship between the TRIPS Agreement and the CBD and Protection of Traditional Knowledge and Folklore: Communication from Peru*, IP/C/W/447 (8 June 2005).
Minutes of Meeting held on 21 and 22 September 2000, IP/C/M/28 (23 November 2000).
The Protection of Traditional Knowledge and Folklore: Summary of Issues Raised and Points Made – Note by the Secretariat (Revision), P/C/W/370/Rev.1 (9 March 2006).
Taking Forward the Review of Article 27.3(b) of the TRIPS Agreement: Joint Communication from the African Group, IP/C/W/404 (26 June 2003).
WTO, DSB, *Canada – Continued Suspension of Obligations in the EC – Hormones Dispute: Request for the Establishment of a Panel by the European Communities*, WT/DS321/6 (14 January 2005).
Canada – Measures Affecting Film Distribution Services: Request for Consultations by the European Communities, WT/DS117/1, S/L/53 (22 January 1998).

BIBLIOGRAPHY 269

Japan – Measures Concerning Sound Recordings: Notification of a Mutually-Agreed Solution, WT/DS42/4, IP/D/4/Add.1 (17 November 1997).
Japan – Measures Concerning Sound Recordings: Request for Consultations from the European Communities, WT/DS42/1, IP/D/4 (4 June 1996).
Minutes of Meeting Held in the Centre William Rappard on 23 May 1997, WT/DSB/M/33 (25 June 1997).
Minutes of Meeting Held in the Centre William Rappard 25 September 1997, WT/DSB/M/37 (4 November 1997).
Minutes of Meeting Held in the Centre William Rappard on 16 January 1998, WT/DSB/M/40 (18 February 1998).
Minutes of Meeting Held in the Centre William Rappard on 6 November 1998, WT/DSB/M/50 (14 December 1998).
Minutes of Meeting Held in the Centre William Rappard on 19 June 2000, WT/DSB/M/84 (24 July 2000).
Minutes of Meeting Held in the Centre William Rappard on 5 November 2001, WT/DSB/M/112 (4 December 2001).
Minutes of Meeting Held in the Centre William Rappard on 23 October 2002, WT/DSB/M/134 (29 January 2003).
Minutes of Meeting Held in the Centre William Rappard on 27 January 2003, WT/DSB/M/142 (6 March 2003).
Minutes of Meeting Held in the Centre William Rappard on 19 May 2003, WT/DSB/M/150 (22 July 2003).
Minutes of Meeting Held in the Centre William Rappard on 20 April 2004, WT/DSB/M/167 (27 May 2004).
Minutes of Meeting Held in the Centre William Rappard on 24 March 2006, WT/DSB/M/208 (28 April 2006).
Turkey – Taxation of Foreign Film Revenues: Notification of Mutually Agreed Solution, WT/DS43/3, G/L/177 (24 July 1997).
Turkey – Taxation of Foreign Film Revenues: Request for Consultations by the United States, WT/DS43/1, G/L/85 (17 June 1996).
Turkey – Taxation of Foreign Film Revenues: Request for the Establishment of a Panel by the United States, WT/DS43/2 (10 January 1997).
United States – Continued Suspension of Obligations in the EC – Hormones Dispute: Request for the Establishment of a Panel by the European Communities, WT/DS320/6 (14 January 2005).
United States – Imposition of Anti-Dumping Duties on Imports of Colour Television Receivers from Korea: Communication from Korea, WT/DS89/9 (18 September 1998).
United States – Imposition of Anti-Dumping Duties on Imports of Colour Television Receivers from Korea: Request for the Establishment of a Panel by Korea, WT/DS89/7 (7 November 1997).
WTO, Economic Research and Analysis Division, *Market Access: Unfinished Business – Post-Uruguay Round Inventory and Issues (Special Study No. 6)*.
WTO, General Council, *Amendment of the TRIPS Agreement: Decision of 6 December 2005*, WT/L/641 (8 December 2005).
Annual Report 2004, WT/GC/86 (12 January 2005).

Decision Adopted by the General Council on 1 August 2004, WT/L/579 (2 August 2004).
Dedicated Discussions under the Auspices of the General Council on Cross-Cutting Issues related to Electronic Commerce: Report to the 24–25 July Meeting of the General Council, WT/GC/W/505 and Corr.1 (21 July 2003).
Minutes of Meeting Held on 15 and 16 February 1999, WT/GC/M/35 (30 March 1999).
Minutes of Meeting Held on 20 October 2004, WT/GC/M/88 (11 November 2004).
Minutes of Meeting Held on 27–28 July 2006, WT/GC/M/103 (10 October 2006).
Procedures for Amendment and Interpretation of the Dispute Settlement Understanding – Response to European Communities' Request for an Authoritative Interpretation of the Dispute Settlement Understanding pursuant to Article IX:2 of the WTO Agreement: Communication from the United States, WT/GC/W/144 (5 February 1999).
Request for an Authoritative Interpretation pursuant to Article IX:2 of the Marrakesh Agreement Establishing the World Trade Organization: Communication from the European Communities, WT/GC/W/143 (5 February 1999).
WTO, Ministerial Conference, *Agriculture – Framework Proposal: Joint Proposal by Argentina, Bolivia, Brazil, Chile, China, Colombia, Costa Rica, Cuba, Ecuador, El Salvador, Guatemala, India, Mexico, Pakistan, Paraguay, Peru, Philippines, South Africa, Thailand and Venezuela*, WT/MIN(03)/W/6 (4 September 2003).
Declaration on Global Electronic Commerce, Adopted on 20 May 1998, WT/MIN(98)/DEC/2 (25 May 1998).
Declaration on the TRIPS Agreement and Public Health, WT/MIN(01)/DEC/2 (20 November 2001).
Doha Work Programme: Ministerial Declaration Adopted on 18 December 2005, WT/MIN(05)/DEC (22 December 2005).
Ministerial Declaration Adopted on 14 November 2001, WT/MIN(01)/DEC/1 (20 November 2001).
Organisation internationale de la francophonie (OIF): Statement Circulated by HE Mr Abdou Diouf, Secretary General (As an Observer), WT/MIN(05)/ST/57 (15 December 2005).
Report of the Working Party on the Accession of Tonga, Addendum: Part II – Schedule of Specific Commitments in Services, List of Article II MFN Exemptions, WT/ACC/TON/17/Add.2, WT/MIN(05)/4/Add.2 (2 December 2005).
WTO Secretariat, *Fifth Dedicated Discussion on Electronic Commerce under the Auspices of the General Council on 16 May and 11 July 2003: Summary by the Secretariat of the Issues Raised*, WT/GC/W/509 (31 July 2003).
Guide to the GATS: An Overview of Issues for Further Liberalization of Trade in Services (The Hague: WTO/Kluwer, 2001).
A Handbook on the GATS Agreement (Cambridge: WTO/Cambridge University Press, 2005).
WTO, TPRB, *Trade Policy Review, Australia: Minutes of Meeting, 23 and 25 September 2002 – Addendum*, WT/TPR/M/104/Add.1 (3 December 2002).
Trade Policy Review, Australia: Report by the Secretariat, WT/TPR/S/104 (26 August 2002).
Trade Policy Review, Canada: Report by the Secretariat, WT/TPR/S/78 (15 November 2000).

Trade Policy Review, Canada: Report by the Secretariat, WT/TPR/S/112/Rev.1 (19 March 2003).
Trade Policy Review, Pakistan: Report by the Secretariat, WT/TPR/S/95 (21 December 2001).
Trade Policy Review of the Republic of Korea: Minutes of Meeting Held on 15 and 17 September 2004, WT/TPR/M/137 (19 November 2004).
Trade Policy Review of Switzerland and Liechtenstein: Minutes of Meeting held on 15 and 17 December 2004, WT/TPR/M/141 (16 February 2005).
Trade Policy Review, United States: Report by the Secretariat, WT/TPR/S/126 (17 December 2003).
WTO, Working Party on Domestic Regulation, *Necessity Tests in the WTO: Note by the Secretariat*, S/WPDR/W/27 (2 December 2003).
WTO, Working Party on GATS Rules, *Annual Report of the Working Party on GATS Rules to the Council for Trade in Services (2004)*, S/WPGR/14 (25 November 2004).
Communication from Argentina and Hong Kong, China: Development of Multilateral Disciplines Governing Trade Distortive Subsidies in Services, S/WPGR/W/31 (16 March 2000).
Communication from Chile: The Subsidies Issue, S/WPGR/W/10 (2 April 1996).
Communication from the United States: Desirability of a Safeguard Mechanism for Services: Promoting Liberalization of Trade in Services, S/WPGR/W/37 (2 October 2001).
Limitations in Members' Schedules Relating to Subsidies: Note by the Secretariat – Addendum, S/WPGR/W/13/Add.2 (30 August 2004).
Negotiations on Emergency Safeguard Measures: Report by the Chairperson of the Working Party on GATS Rules, S/WPGR/9 (14 March 2003).
Negotiations on Subsidies: Report by the Chairperson of the Working Party on GATS Rules, S/WPGR/10 (30 June 2003).
Subsidies and Trade in Services: Note by the Secretariat, S/WPGR/W/9 (6 March 1996).
Subsidies for Services Sectors: Information Contained in WTO Trade Policy Reviews – Background Note by the Secretariat, S/WPGR/W/25 (26 January 1998).

ARTICLES, BOOKS, CHAPTERS, AND PAPERS

Abbott, Frederick, 'The "Rule of Reason" and the Right to Health: Integrating Human Rights and Competition Principles in the Context of TRIPS' in Thomas Cottier, Joost Pauwelyn, and Elisabeth Bürgi (eds.), *Human Rights and International Trade* (Oxford: Oxford University Press, 2005) 279.
Abbott, Frederick, Breining-Kaufmann, Christine, and Cottier, Thomas (eds.), *International Trade and Human Rights: Foundations and Conceptual Issues* (Ann Arbor: University of Michigan Press, 2006).
Acheson, Keith, 'Globalization' in Ruth Towse (ed.), *A Handbook of Cultural Economics* (Cheltenham: Edward Elgar, 2003) 248.
Acheson, Keith, and Maule, Christopher, 'Canada – Audio-Visual Policies: Impact on Trade' in Paolo Guerrieri, Lelio Iapadre, and Georg Koopmann (eds.), *Cultural Diversity and International Economic Integration: The Global Governance of the Audiovisual Sector* (Cheltenham: Edward Elgar, 2005) 156.

'Canadian Magazine Policy: International Conflict and Domestic Stagnation' in Robert Stern (ed.), *Services in the International Economy* (Ann Arbor: University of Michigan Press, 2001) 395.
'Convention on Cultural Diversity' (2004) 28 *Journal of Cultural Economics* 243.
'Copyright, Contract, the Cultural Industries, and NAFTA' in Emile McAnany and Kenton Wilkinson (eds.), *Mass Media and Free Trade: NAFTA and the Cultural Industries* (Austin: University of Texas Press, 1996) 351.
Much Ado about Culture: North American Trade Disputes (Ann Arbor: University of Michigan Press, 1999).
Adalsteinsson, Ragnar, and Thórhallson, Páll, 'Article 27' in Gudmundur Alfredsson and Asbjørn Eide (eds.), *The Universal Declaration of Human Rights: A Common Standard of Achievement* (The Hague: Martinus Nijhoff, 1999) 575.
Adlung, Rudolf, 'GATS and Democratic Legitimacy' (2004) 59(2) *Aussenwirtschaft* 127.
'Public Services and the GATS' (2006) 9(2) *Journal of International Economic Law* 455.
Adlung, Rudolf, and Roy, Martin, 'Turning Hills into Mountains? Current Commitments under the General Agreement on Trade in Services and Prospects for Change' (2005) 39(6) *Journal of World Trade* 1161.
Adorno, Theodor, *The Culture Industry: Selected Essays on Mass Culture* (London: Routledge, 1991), edited with an introduction by J. M. Bernstein.
Adorno, Theodor, and Horkheimer, Max, *Dialectic of Enlightenment* (New York: Herder & Herder, 1972), translated by John Cumming (original publication 1944).
Albro, Robert, 'Managing Culture at Diversity's Expense? Thoughts on UNESCO's Newest Cultural Policy Instrument' (2005) 35(3) *Journal of Arts Management, Law, and Society* 247.
Alfredsson, Gudmundur, and Eide, Asbjørn (eds.), *The Universal Declaration of Human Rights: A Common Standard of Achievement* (The Hague: Martinus Nijhoff, 1999).
Alston, Philip, 'Resisting the Merger and Acquisition of Human Rights by Trade Law: A Reply to Petersmann' (2002) 13(4) *European Journal of International Law* 815.
Alston, Richard, *Additional Government Funding Guarantees Radio Australia Service*, press release, Minister for Communications, Information Technology and the Arts; Deputy Leader of the Government in the Senate Doc. 41/01 (28 March 2001).
Altinger, Laura, and Enders, Alice, 'The Scope and Depth of GATS Commitments' (1996) 19(3) *World Economy* 307.
Alvarez, Jose, 'How Not to Link: Institutional Conundrums of an Expanded Trade Regime' (2001) 7 *Widener Law Symposium Journal* 1.
Anderson, Kym, 'Setting the Trade Policy Agenda: What Roles for Economists?' (2005) 39(2) *Journal of World Trade* 341.
Appadurai, Arjun, *Modernity at Large: Cultural Dimensions of Globalization* (Minneapolis: University of Minnesota Press, 1996).

Atkey, Ronald, 'Canadian Cultural Industries Exemption from NAFTA – Its Parameters' (1997) 23 *Canada–United States Law Journal* 177.
Baker, Edwin, 'An Economic Critique of Free Trade in Media Products' (2000) 78 *North Carolina Law Review* 1357.
Baker, Stewart, and Shenk, Maury, 'Trade and Electronic Commerce' in Patrick Macrory, Arthur Appleton, and Michael Plummer (eds.), *The World Trade Organization: Legal, Economic and Political Analysis* (New York: Springer, 2005) (vol. II) 469.
Bartels, Lorand, 'Applicable Law in WTO Dispute Settlement Proceedings' (2001) 35(3) *Journal of World Trade* 499.
Barton, John, 'The Economics of TRIPS: International Trade in Information-Intensive Products' (2001) 33 *George Washington International Law Review* 473.
  'The International Video Industry: Principles for Vertical Agreements and Integration' (2004) 22 *Cardozo Arts and Entertainment Law Journal* 67.
Baumol, William, 'Applied Welfare Economics' in Ruth Towse (ed.), *A Handbook of Cultural Economics* (Cheltenham: Edward Elgar, 2003) 20.
Benhamou, Françoise, 'Comment' (2004) 28 *Journal of Cultural Economics* 263.
Bernier, Ivan, 'Cultural Diversity and International Trade Regulations' in UNESCO (ed.), *World Culture Report: Cultural Diversity, Conflict and Pluralism* (Paris: UNESCO, 2000) 70.
  'Cultural Goods and Services in International Trade Law' in Dennis Browne (ed.), *The Culture/Trade Quandary: Canada's Policy Options* (Ottawa: Centre for Trade Policy and Law, 1998) 108.
  'La dimension culturelle dans le commerce international: quelques réflexions en marge de l'accord de libre-échange Canada/Etats-Unis du 2 janvier 1988' (1987) 25 *Canadian Yearbook of International Law* 243.
  Mondialisation de l'économie et diversité culturelle: les enjeux pour le Québec (La Commission de la culture, Assemblée nationale, Québec, 2000).
  'Trade and Culture' in Patrick Macrory, Arthur Appleton, and Michael Plummer (eds.), *The World Trade Organization: Legal, Economic and Political Analysis* (New York: Springer, 2005) (vol. II) 747.
Bernier, Ivan, and Ruiz Fabri, Hélène, *Evaluation de la faisabilité juridique d'un instrument international sur la diversité culturelle* (2002).
Beviglia-Zampetti, Americo, 'WTO Rules in the Audio-Visual Sector' in Paolo Guerrieri, Lelio Iapadre, and Georg Koopmann (eds.), *Cultural Diversity and International Economic Integration: The Global Governance of the Audio-Visual Sector* (Cheltenham: Edward Elgar, 2005) 261.
Bhagwati, Jagdish, *The Wind of the Hundred Days: How Washington Mismanaged Globalization* (Cambridge, MA: MIT Press, 2000).
Bhagwati, Jagdish, and Hudec, Robert (eds.), *Fair Trade and Harmonization: Prerequisites for Free Trade?* (Cambridge, MA: MIT Press, 1996).
Bhala, Raj, 'The Myth About Stare Decisis and International Trade Law (Part One of a Trilogy)' (1999) 14 *American University International Law Review* 845.
  'The Power of the Past: Towards De Jure Stare Decisis in WTO Adjudication (Part Three of a Trilogy)' (2001) 33 *George Washington International Law Review* 873.

'The Precedent Setters: De Facto Stare Decisis in WTO Adjudication (Part Two of a Trilogy)' (1999) 9 *Journal of Transnational Law and Policy* 1.
Bosland, Jason, 'The Culture of Trade Marks: An Alternative Cultural Theory Perspective' (2005) 10(2) *Media & Arts Law Review* 99.
Bourgeois, Jacques, Berrod, Frédérique, and Fournier, Eric Gippini (eds.), *The Uruguay Round Results: A European Lawyers' Perspective* (Brussels: European Interuniversity Press, 1995).
Boven, Theo van, Flinterman, Cees, Grünfeld, Fred, and Hut, Rita (eds.), *SIM Special No. 20: The Maastricht Guidelines on Violations of Economic, Social and Cultural Rights* (Utrecht: Netherlands Institute of Human Rights, 1998).
Breining-Kaufmann, Christine, 'The Legal Matrix of Human Rights and Trade Law: State Obligations versus Private Rights and Obligations' in Thomas Cottier, Joost Pauwelyn, and Elisabeth Bürgi (eds.), *Human Rights and International Trade* (Oxford: Oxford University Press, 2005) 95.
Bronckers, Marco, and Larouche, Pierre, 'Telecommunications Services' in Patrick Macrory, Arthur Appleton, and Michael Plummer (eds.), *The World Trade Organization: Legal, Economic and Political Analysis* (New York: Springer, 2005) 989.
Broude, Tomer, 'Cultural Diversity and the WTO: A Diverse Relationship' (21 November 2005) *ASIL Insight*.
  International Governance in the WTO: Judicial Boundaries and Political Capitulation (London: Cameron May, 2004).
  'Taking "Trade and Culture" Seriously: Geographical Indications and Cultural Protection in WTO Law' (2005) 26(4) *University of Pennsylvania Journal of International Economic Law* 623.
Browne, Dennis (ed.), *The Culture/Trade Quandary: Canada's Policy Options* (Ottawa: Centre for Trade Policy and Law, 1998).
Buchsbaum, Jonathan, 'After GATT: Has the Revival of French Cinema Ended?' (2005) 23(3) *French Politics, Culture & Society* 34.
Búrca, Gráinne de, and Scott, Joanne (eds.), *The EU and the WTO: Legal and Constitutional Issues* (Oxford: Hart, 2001).
Burt, Tim, 'Quotas Fail to Save European Producers from an Influx of US Television Shows', *Financial Times* (Paris, 27 May 2005).
Button, Catherine, *The Power to Protect: Trade, Health and Uncertainty in the WTO* (Oxford: Hart, 2004).
Cameron, Sam, 'Cinema' in Ruth Towse (ed.), *A Handbook of Cultural Economics* (Cheltenham: Edward Elgar, 2003) 114.
Canoy, Marcel, van Ours, Jan, and van der Ploeg, Frederick, 'The Economics of Books' (Working Paper No. 1414, Center for Economic Studies and Institute for Economic Research, 2005).
Carlson, Andrew, 'The Country Music Television Dispute: An Illustration of the Tensions between Canadian Cultural Protectionism and American Entertainment Exports' (1997) 6 *Minnesota Journal of Global Trade* 585.
Carmody, Chi, 'When "Cultural Identity was Not at Issue": Thinking about Canada – Certain Measures Concerning Periodicals' (1999) 30 *Law and Policy in International Business* 231.

Carmody, Chios, 'WTO Obligations as Collective' (2006) 17(2) *European Journal of International Law* 419.
Carniaux, Anton, 'L'audiovisuel dans les accords internationaux favorisant le libre-échange: des problèmes économiques et culturels difficiles à négocier' (1995) 26 *Revue générale de droit* 455.
Cass, Ronald, and Boltuck, Richard, 'Antidumping and Countervailing-Duty Law: The Mirage of Equitable International Competition' in Jagdish Bhagwati and Robert Hudec (eds.), *Fair Trade and Harmonization: Prerequisites for Free Trade?* (Cambridge, MA: MIT Press, 1996) (vol. II) 351.
Cassese, Antonio, Clapham, Andrew, and Weiler, Joseph (eds.), *Human Rights and the European Community: The Substantive Law* (Baden-Baden: Nomos Verlagsgesellschaft, 1991).
Caves, Richard, *Creative Industries: Contracts between Art and Commerce* (Cambridge, MA: Harvard University Press, 2000).
  International Trade, International Investment and Imperfect Markets (Special Papers in International Economics No. 10, Princeton: Princeton University Press, November 1974).
Charnovitz, Steve, 'An Analysis of Pascal Lamy's Proposal on Collective Preferences' (2005) 8(2) *Journal of International Economic Law* 449.
  'Free Trade, Fair Trade, Green Trade: Defogging the Debate' (1994) 27 *Cornell International Law Journal* 459.
  'The Moral Exception in Trade Policy' (1998) 38 *Virginia Journal of International Law* 689.
  'The (Neglected) Employment Dimension of the World Trade Organization' in Virginia Leary and Daniel Warner (eds.), *Social Issues, Globalisation and International Institutions: Labour Rights and the EU, ILO, OECD and WTO* (Leiden: Martinus Nijhoff, 2006) 125.
  'The World Trade Organization and Social Issues' (1994) 28(5) *Journal of World Trade* 17.
Chen, Jim, 'A Sober Second Look at Appellations of Origin: How the United States Will Crash France's Wine and Cheese Party' (1996) 5 *Minnesota Journal of Global Trade* 29.
Chinkin, Christine, 'The Challenge of Soft Law: Development and Change in International Law' (1989) 38 *International & Comparative Law Quarterly* 850.
Choi, Byung-il, *Culture and Trade in the APEC: Case of Film Industry in Canada, Mexico and Korea*, APEC Study Series 02-01 (2002).
Choi, Won-Mog, *'Like Products' in International Trade Law: Towards a Consistent GATT/WTO Jurisprudence* (Oxford: Oxford University Press, 2003).
Clapham, Andrew, and Weiler, Joseph (eds.), *Human Rights and the European Community: The Substantive Law* (Baden-Baden: Nomos Verlagsgesellschaft, 1991).
Coburn, Cara, 'Out of the Petri Dish and Back to the People: A Cultural Approach to GMO Policy' (2005) 23(2) *Wisconsin International Law Journal* 283.
Cocq, Emmanuel, and Messerlin, Patrick, 'French Audio-Visual Policy: Impact and Compatibility with Trade Negotiations' in Paolo Guerrieri, Lelio

Iapadre, and Georg Koopmann (eds.), *Cultural Diversity and International Economic Integration: The Global Governance of the Audiovisual Sector* (Cheltenham: Edward Elgar, 2005) 21.

Coe, Neil, and Johns, Jennifer, 'Production Clusters: Towards a Critical Political Economy of Networks in the Film and Television Industries' in Dominic Power and Allen Scott (eds.), *Cultural Industries and the Production of Culture* (London: Routledge, 2004) 188.

Cohen, Elie, 'Globalization and cultural diversity' in UNESCO (ed.), *World Culture Report: Cultural Diversity, Conflict and Pluralism* (Paris: UNESCO, 2000) 66.

Condron, Anne Marie, 'Cinema' in Sheila Perry (ed.), *Aspects of Contemporary France* (London: Routledge, 1997).

Coombe, Rosemary, *The Cultural Life of Intellectual Properties: Authorship, Appropriation, and the Law* (Durham, NC: Duke University Press, 1998).

'Protecting Cultural Industries to Promote Cultural Diversity: Dilemmas for International Policymaking Posed by the Recognition of Traditional Knowledge' in Keith Maskus and Jerome Reichman (eds.), *International Public Goods and Transfer of Technology under a Globalized Intellectual Property Regime* (Cambridge: Cambridge University Press, 2005) 599.

Cossy, Mireille, WTO, *Determining 'Likeness' Under the GATS: Squaring the Circle?*, Staff Working Paper ERSD-2006-08 (September 2006).

Cottier, Thomas, 'The Agreement on Trade-Related Aspects of Intellectual Property Rights' in Patrick Macrory, Arthur Appleton, and Michael Plummer (eds.), *The World Trade Organization: Legal, Economic and Political Analysis* (New York: Springer, 2005) (vol. I) 1041.

'Trade and Human Rights: A Relationship to Discover' (2002) 5(1) *Journal of International Economic Law* 111.

Cottier, Thomas, and Mavroidis, Petros (eds.), *Regulatory Barriers and the Principle of Non-Discrimination in World Trade Law* (Ann Arbor: University of Michigan Press, 2000).

(eds.), *The Role of the Judge in International Trade Regulation: Experience and Lessons for the WTO* (Ann Arbor: University of Michigan Press, 2003).

Cottier, Thomas, Pauwelyn, Joost, and Bürgi, Elisabeth (eds.), *Human Rights and International Trade* (Oxford: Oxford University Press, 2005).

Cowen, Tyler, *Creative Destructions: How Globalization is Reshaping World Cultures* (Princeton: Princeton University Press, 2002).

Good and Plenty: The Creative Successes of American Arts Funding (Princeton: Princeton University Press, 2006).

In Praise of Commercial Culture (Cambridge, MA: Harvard University Press, 1998).

Crawford, James (ed.), *The Rights of Peoples* (New York: Oxford University Press, 1988).

Croome, John, *Reshaping the World Trading System: A History of the Uruguay Round* (The Hague: Kluwer, 2nd rev. edn, 1999).

Cunningham, Collette, 'In Defense of Member State Culture: The Unrealized Potential of Article 151(4) of the EC Treaty and the Consequences for EC Cultural Policy' (2001) 34 *Cornell International Law Journal* 119.

Curtis, Johnlee, 'Culture and the Digital Copyright Chimera: Assessing the International Regulatory System of the Music Industry in Relation to Cultural Diversity' (2006) 13(1) *International Journal of Cultural Property* 59, 80.

Czako, Judith, Human, Johann, and Miranda, Jorge, *A Handbook on Anti-Dumping Investigations* (Cambridge: WTO/Cambridge University Press, 2003).

Dallmeyer, Dorinda (ed.), *Joining Together, Standing Apart: National Identities after NAFTA* (The Hague: Kluwer, 1997).

Davey, William, and Pauwelyn, Joost, 'MFN Unconditionality: A Legal Analysis of the Concept in View of its Evolution in the GATT/WTO Jurisprudence with Particular Reference to the Issue of "Like Product"' in Thomas Cottier and Petros Mavroidis (eds.), *Regulatory Barriers and the Principle of Non-Discrimination in World Trade Law* (Ann Arbor: University of Michigan Press, 2000) 13.

Deardorff, Alan, 'What Might Globalization's Critics Believe?' (2003) 26(5) *World Economy* 639.

Dehesa, Guillermo de la, *Winners and Losers in Globalization* (Oxford: Blackwell Publishing, 2006).

Desurmont, Thierry, 'Réflexions sur les rapports entre la convention sur la protection et la promotion de la diversité des expressions culturelles et la protection du droit d'auteur' (2006) 208 *Revue internationale du droit d'auteur* 2.

Dorland, Michael (ed.), *The Cultural Industries in Canada: Problems, Policies and Prospects* (Toronto: Lorimer, 1996).

Doyle, Gillian, and Hibberd, Matthew, 'The Case of the UK Audio-Visual System' in Paolo Guerrieri, Lelio Iapadre, and Georg Koopmann (eds.), *Cultural Diversity and International Economic Integration: The Global Governance of the Audiovisual Sector* (Cheltenham: Edward Elgar, 2005) 131.

Drake, William, and Nicolaïdis, Kalypso, 'Global Electronic Commerce and GATS: The Millennium Round and Beyond' in Pierre Sauvé and Robert Stern (eds.), *GATS 2000: New Directions in Services Trade Liberalization* (Washington, DC: Brookings Institution Press/Harvard University Center for Business and Government, 2000) 399.

Dutfield, Graham, 'Protecting Traditional Knowledge: Pathways to the Future' (working paper, International Centre for Trade and Sustainable Development, 2006).

Echols, Marsha, 'Food Safety Regulation in the European Union and the United States: Different Cultures, Different Laws' (1998) 4 *Columbia Journal of European Law* 525.

  Food Safety and the WTO: The Interplay of Culture, Science and Technology (London: Kluwer, 2001).

Economist, The, 'Disney-in-the-Dales' (22 May 2003).

  'French Films' (24 February 2005) 30.

Ehlermann, Claus-Dieter, 'Six Years on the Bench of the "World Trade Court": Some Personal Experiences as Member of the Appellate Body of the World Trade Organization' (2002) 36(4) *Journal of World Trade* 605.

Ehlermann, Claus-Dieter, and Ehring, Lothar, 'The Authoritative Interpretation under Article IX:2 of the Agreement Establishing the World Trade

Organization: Current Law, Practice and Possible Improvements' (2005) 8(4) *Journal of International Economic Law* 803.

Ehring, Lothar, '*De Facto* Discrimination in World Trade Law: National and Most-Favoured-Nation Treatment – or Equal Treatment?' (2002) 36(5) *Journal of World Trade* 921.

Eide, Asbjørn, Alfredsson, Gudmundur, Melander, Göran, Rehof, Lars Adam, and Rosas, Allan (eds.), *The Universal Declaration of Human Rights: A Commentary* (Oslo: Scandinavian University Press, 1992).

Eide, Asbjørn, and Alfredsson, Gudmundur, 'Introduction' in Asbjørn Eide, Gudmundur Alfredsson, Göran Melander, Lars Adam Rehof and Allan Rosas (eds.), *The Universal Declaration of Human Rights: A Commentary* (Oslo: Scandinavian University Press, 1992) 5.

Elias, T., 'The Doctrine of Intertemporal Law' (1980) 74(2) *American Journal of International Law* 285.

Eröcal, Deniz, *Case Studies of Successful Companies in the Services Sector and Lessons for Public Policy*, DSTI/DOC(2005)7, OECD Directorate for Science, Technology and Industry Working Paper 2005/7 (15 June 2005).

Evans, G., and Blakeney, Michael, 'The Protection of Geographical Indications After Doha: Quo Vadis?' (2006) 9(3) *Journal of International Economic Law* 1.

Ezetah, Chinedu, 'Canadian Periodicals: Canada – Certain Measures Concerning Periodicals' (1998) 9(1) *European Journal of International Law* 182.

'Patterns of an Emergent World Trade Organization Legalism: What Implications for NAFTA Cultural Exemption?' (1998) 21(5) *World Competition* 93.

Falkenberg, Karl, 'The Audiovisual Sector' in Jacques Bourgeois, Frédérique Berrod, and Eric Gippini Fournier (eds.), *The Uruguay Round Results: A European Lawyers' Perspective* (Brussels: European Interuniversity Press, 1995) 429.

Feddersen, Christoph, 'Focusing on Substantive Law in International Economic Relations: The Public Morals of GATT's Article XX(a) and "Conventional" Rules of Interpretation' (1998) 7 *Minnesota Journal of Global Trade* 75.

Feketekuty, Geza, 'Assessing and Improving the Architecture of GATS' in Pierre Sauvé and Robert Stern (eds.), *GATS 2000: New Directions in Services Trade Liberalization* (Washington, DC: Brookings Institution Press/Harvard University Center for Business and Government, 2000) 85.

'Regulatory Reform and Trade Liberalization in Services' in Pierre Sauvé and Robert Stern (eds.), *GATS 2000: New Directions in Services Trade Liberalization* (Washington, DC: Brookings Institution Press/Harvard University Center for Business and Government, 2000) 225.

Feldthusen, Bruce, 'Awakening from the National Broadcasting Dream: Rethinking Television Regulation for National Cultural Goals' in David Flaherty and Frank Manning (eds.), *The Beaver Bites Back? American Popular Culture in Canada* (Montreal: McGill-Queen's University Press, 1993) 42.

Filipek, Jon, '"Culture Quotas": The Trade Controversy over the European Community's Broadcasting Directive' (1992) 28(2) *Stanford Journal of International Law* 323.

Finger, Michael, Ng, Francis, and Wangchuk, Sonam, *Antidumping as Safeguard Policy*, World Bank Policy Research Working Paper 2730 (2001).
Fitzmaurice, Gerald, 'The Law and Procedure of the International Court of Justice 1951–4: Treaty Interpretation and Other Treaty Points' (1957) 33 *British Yearbook of International Law* 203.
  'Some Problems Regarding the Formal Sources of International Law' (1958) *Symbolae Verzijl* 153.
Flaherty, David, and Manning, Frank (eds.), *The Beaver Bites Back? American Popular Culture in Canada* (Montreal: McGill-Queen's University Press, 1993).
Footer, Mary, 'European Communities – Measures Affecting Asbestos and Asbestos-Containing Products: The World Trade Organization on Trial for its Handling of Occupational Health and Safety Issues' (2002) 3 *Melbourne Journal of International Law* 120.
  'The Future for a Cultural Exception in the World Trade Organisation' (paper presented at the Meeting of the International Trade Law Committee of the International Law Association, Geneva, 22–3 June 1995).
Footer, Mary, and George, Carol, 'The General Agreement on Trade in Services' in Patrick Macrory, Arthur Appleton, and Michael Plummer (eds.), *The World Trade Organization: Legal, Economic and Political Analysis* (New York: Springer, 2005) (vol. I) 799.
Footer, Mary, and Graber, Christoph, 'Trade Liberalization and Cultural Policy' (2000) 3 *Journal of International Economic Law* 115.
'Foreign Investment: Investment Talks to Continue at OECD; MAI Now On Course for 1999 Completion' (1998) 15 *International Trade Reporter* 525.
Fox, Eleanor, 'Competition Law and the Millennium Round' (1999) *Journal of International Economic Law* 665.
François, Patrick, and van Ypersele, Tanguy, 'On the Protection of Cultural Goods' (2002) 56 *Journal of International Economics* 359.
Fraser, Stephen, 'Berne, CFTA, NAFTA and GATT: The Implications of Copyright Droit Moral and Cultural Exemptions in International Trade Law' (1996) 18 *Hastings Communications and Entertainment Law Journal* 287.
French, Duncan, 'Treaty Interpretation and the Incorporation of Extraneous Legal Rules' (2006) 55(2) *International & Comparative Law Quarterly* 281.
French, Shaun, Crewe, Louise, Leyshon, Andrew, Webb, Peter, and Thrift, Nigel, 'Putting E-commerce in Its Place: Reflections on the Impact of the Internet on the Cultural Industries' in Dominic Power and Allen Scott (eds.), *Cultural Industries and the Production of Culture* (London: Routledge, 2004) 54.
Frey, Bruno, 'Creativity, Government and the Arts' (2002) 150(4) *De Economist* 363.
  'Public support' in Ruth Towse (ed.), *A Handbook of Cultural Economics* (Cheltenham: Edward Elgar, 2003) 389.
Gagné, Gilbert, 'Une Convention internationale sur la diversité culturelle et le dilemme culture-commerce' in Gilbert Gagné (ed.), *La diversité culturelle: Vers une convention internationale effective?* (Saint-Laurent: Fides, 2005) 37.

(ed.), *La diversité culturelle: Vers une convention internationale effective?* (Saint-Laurent: Fides, 2005).

Galperin, Herman, 'Cultural Industries Policy in Regional Trade Agreements: The Cases of NAFTA, the European Union and MERCOSUR' (1999) 21(5) *Media, Culture & Society* 627.

Garrett, Lisa, 'Commerce versus Culture: The Battle Between the United States and the European Union Over Audiovisual Trade Policies' (1994) 19 *North Carolina Journal of International Law and Commercial Regulation* 553.

Geradin, Damien, and Luff, David (eds.), *The WTO and Global Convergence in Telecommunications and Audio-Visual Services* (Cambridge: Cambridge University Press, 2004).

Germann, Christophe, 'Content Industries and Cultural Diversity: The Case of Motion Pictures' (2002–3) special issue *Culturelink Review* 97.

'Culture in Times of Cholera: A Vision for a New Legal Framework Promoting Cultural Diversity' (2005) 1 *ERA – Forum* 109.

'Diversité culturelle à l'OMC et l'UNESCO à l'exemple du cinéma' (2004) 3 *Revue Internationale de Droit Economique* 325.

Gervais, Daniel, *The TRIPS Agreement: Drafting History and Analysis* (London: Sweet & Maxwell, 1998).

Ghertman, Michel, and Hadida, Allègre, 'Institutional Assets and Competitive Advantage of French over U.S. Cinema: 1895–1914' (2005) 35(30) *International Studies of Management and Organization* 50.

Ghoneim, Ahmed Farouk, 'The Audio-Visual Sector in Egypt' in Paolo Guerrieri, Lelio Iapadre, and Georg Koopmann (eds.), *Cultural Diversity and International Economic Integration: The Global Governance of the Audiovisual Sector* (Cheltenham: Edward Elgar, 2005) 192.

Gibson, Chris, and Connell, John, 'Cultural Industry Production in Remote Places: Indigenous Popular Music in Australia' in Dominic Power and Allen Scott (eds.), *Cultural Industries and the Production of Culture* (London: Routledge, 2004) 243.

Gibson, Johanna, *Community Resources: Intellectual Property, International Trade and Protection of Traditional Knowledge* (Aldershot: Ashgate, 2005).

Goode, Walter, *Dictionary of Trade Policy Terms* (Cambridge: Cambridge University Press, 4th edn, 2003).

Graber, Christoph, 'Audiovisual Media and the Law of the WTO' in Christoph Graber, Michael Girsburger, and Mira Nenova (eds.), *Free Trade versus Cultural Diversity: WTO Negotiations in the Field of Audiovisual Services* (Zurich: Schulthess, 2004) 15.

'Audio-Visual Policy: The Stumbling Block of Trade Liberalisation?' in Damien Geradin and David Luff (eds.), *The WTO and Global Convergence in Telecommunications and Audio-Visual Services* (Cambridge: Cambridge University Press, 2004) 165.

Handel und Kultur im Audiovisionsrecht der WTO: Völkerrechtliche, ökonomische und kulturpolitische Grundlagen einer globalen Medienordnung (Bern: Stämpfli Verlag, 2003).

'WTO: A Threat to European Films?' (paper presented at the Conference on European Culture, University of Navarra, Pamplona, 28–31 October 1991).

Graber, Christoph, Girsburger, Michael, and Nenova, Mira (eds.), *Free Trade versus Cultural Diversity: WTO Negotiations in the Field of Audiovisual Services* (Zurich: Schulthess, 2004).
Grant, Peter, and Wood, Chris, *Blockbusters and Trade Wars: Popular Culture in a Globalized World* (Vancouver: Douglas & McIntyre, 2004).
Griffiths, Jonathan, and Suthersanen, Uma (eds.), *Copyright and Free Speech: Comparative and International Analyses* (Oxford: Oxford University Press, 2005).
Guerrieri, Paolo, and Iapadre, Lelio, 'Introduction' in Paolo Guerrieri, Lelio Iapadre, and Georg Koopman (eds.), *Cultural Diversity and International Economic Integration: The Global Governance of the Audio-Visual Sector* (Cheltenham: Edward Elgar, 2005) 1.
Guerrieri, Paolo, Iapadre, Lelio, and Koopmann, Georg (eds.), *Cultural Diversity and International Economic Integration: The Global Governance of the Audio-Visual Sector* (Cheltenham: Edward Elgar, 2005).
Hakfoort, Jacco, 'Copyright in the Digital Age: The Economic Rationale Re-Examined' in Ruth Towse (ed.), *Copyright in the Cultural Industries* (Cheltenham: Edward Elgar, 2002) 63.
Hart, Michael, 'Canada' in Patrick Macrory, Arthur Appleton, and Michael Plummer (eds.), *The World Trade Organization: Legal, Economic and Political Analysis* (New York: Springer, 2005) (vol. III) 29.
Hartley, John (ed.), *Creative Industries* (Malden, MA: Blackwell, 2005).
Held, David, McGrew, Anthony, Goldblatt, David, and Perraton, Jonathan, *Global Transformations: Politics, Economics and Culture* (Cambridge: Polity Press, 1999).
Henderson, David, *The MAI Affair: A Story and Its Lessons* (London: Royal Institute of International Affairs, 1999).
Hesmondhalgh, David, *The Cultural Industries* (London: Sage, 2002).
Hoda, Anwarul, *Tariff Negotiations and Renegotiations under the GATT and the WTO: Procedures and Practices* (Cambridge: WTO/Cambridge University Press, 2001).
Hoekman, Bernard, *Tentative First Steps: An Assessment of the Uruguay Round Agreement on Services*, World Bank Policy Research Working Paper 1455 (1995).
  'Toward a More Balanced and Comprehensive Services Agreement' in Jeffrey Schott (ed.), *The WTO After Seattle* (Washington, DC: Institute for International Economics, 2000) 119.
Hoekman, Bernard, and Kostecki, Michel, *The Political Economy of the World Trading System: The WTO and Beyond* (New York: Oxford University Press, 2nd edn, 2001).
Hoekman, Bernard, and Messerlin, Patrick, 'Liberalizing Trade in Services: Reciprocal Negotiations and Regulatory Reform' in Pierre Sauvé and Robert Stern (eds.), *GATS 2000: New Directions in Services Trade Liberalization* (Washington, DC: Brookings Institution Press/Harvard University Center for Business and Government, 2000) 487.
Hoskins, Colin, Finn, Adam, and McFadyen, Stuart, 'Television and Film in a Freer International Trade Environment: US Dominance and Canadian Responses' in Emile McAnany and Kenton Wilkinson (eds.), *Mass Media and Free Trade: NAFTA and the Cultural Industries* (Austin: University of Texas Press, 1996) 63.

Howse, Robert, 'Adjudicative Legitimacy and Treaty Interpretation in
International Trade Law: The Early Years of WTO Jurisprudence' in Joseph
Weiler (ed.), *The EU, the WTO and the NAFTA: Towards a Common Law of
International Trade* (Oxford: Oxford University Press, 2000) 35.
 'Human Rights in the WTO: Whose Rights, What Humanity? Comment on
Petersmann' (2002) 13(3) *European Journal of International Law* 651.
 'Managing the Interface between International Trade Law and the Regulatory
State: What Lessons Should (and Should Not) Be Drawn from the
Jurisprudence of the United States Dormant Commerce Clause' in Thomas
Cottier and Petros Mavroidis (eds.), *Regulatory Barriers and the Principle of Non-
Discrimination in World Trade Law* (Ann Arbor: University of Michigan Press,
2000) 139.
 'The Most Dangerous Branch? WTO Appellate Body Jurisprudence on the
Nature and Limits of the Judicial Power' in Thomas Cottier and Petros
Mavroidis (eds.), *The Role of the Judge in International Trade Regulation:
Experience and Lessons for the WTO* (Ann Arbor: University of Michigan Press,
2003) 11.
Howse, Robert, and Esserman, Susan, 'The Appellate Body, the WTO Dispute
Settlement System, and the Politics of Multilateralism' in Giorgio Sacerdoti,
Alan Yanovich, and Jan Bohanes (eds.), *The WTO at Ten: The Contributions
of the Dispute Settlement System* (Cambridge: Cambridge University Press,
2006) 61.
Howse, Robert, Langille, Brian, and Burda, Julien, 'The World Trade Organization
and Labour Rights: Man Bites Dog' in Virginia Leary and Daniel Warner (eds.),
*Social Issues, Globalisation and International Institutions: Labour Rights and the EU,
ILO, OECD and WTO* (Leiden: Martinus Nijhoff, 2006) 157.
Howse, Robert, and Mutua, Makau, *Protecting Human Rights in a Global Economy:
Challenges for the World Trade Organization* (International Centre for Rights
and Democratic Development, 2000).
Howse, Robert, and Nicolaïdis, Kalypso, 'Enhancing WTO Legitimacy:
Constitutionalization or Global Subsidiarity?' (2003) 16(1) *Governance* 73.
Hudec, Robert (ed.), *Essays on the Nature of International Trade Law* (London:
Cameron May, 1999).
 'GATT/WTO Constraints on National Regulation: Requiem for an "Aim and
Effects" Test' (1998) 32 *International Lawyer* 619.
 '"Like Product": The Differences in Meaning in GATT Articles I and III' in
Thomas Cottier and Petros Mavroidis (eds.), *Regulatory Barriers and the
Principle of Non-Discrimination in World Trade Law* (Ann Arbor: University of
Michigan Press, 2000) 101.
 'Tiger, Tiger, in the House: A Critical Appraisal of the Case Against
Discriminatory Trade Measures' in Robert Hudec (ed.), *Essays on the Nature of
International Trade Law* (London: Cameron May, 1999) 281.
Hutter, Michael, and Rizzo, Ilde (eds.), *Perspectives on Cultural Heritage* (New York:
St Martin's Press, 1997).
Iapadre, Lelio, 'Comment' (2004) 28 *Journal of Cultural Economics* 267.

Irwin, Douglas, *Against the Tide: An Intellectual History of Free Trade* (Princeton: Princeton University Press, 1996).
Jackson, John, 'Reflections on the Possible Research Agenda for Exploring the Relationship between Human Rights Norms and International Trade Rules' in Frederick Abbott, Christine Breining-Kaufmann, and Thomas Cottier (eds.), *International Trade and Human Rights: Foundations and Conceptual Issues* (Ann Arbor: University of Michigan Press, 2006) 19.
  World Trade and the Law of the GATT (A Legal Analysis of the General Agreement on Tariffs and Trade) (Charlottesville: The Michie Company, 1969).
  The World Trading System: Law and Policy of International Economic Relations (Cambridge, MA: MIT Press, 2nd edn, 1997).
James, Christine, 'Trade, Culture and Technology: A Test of Canada's Cultural Mettle' (1997) 8(7) *Entertainment Law Review* 253.
Jasanoff, Sheila, 'Technological Risk and Cultures of Rationality' in National Research Council (ed.), *Incorporating Science, Economics, and Sociology in Developing Sanitary and Phytosanitary Standards in International Trade: Proceedings of a Conference* (Washington, DC: National Academy Press, 2000) 65.
Jennings, Robert, 'What is International Law and How Do We Tell It When We See It?' (1981) 37 *Schweitzerisches Jahrbuch für Internationales Recht* 59.
Jones, Eric, *Cultures Merging: A Historical and Economic Critique of Culture* (Princeton: Princeton University Press, 2006).
Kaul, Inge, Grunberg, Isabelle, and Stern, Marc (eds.), *Global Public Goods: International Cooperation in the 21st Century* (Oxford: Oxford University Press, 1999).
  'Defining Global Public Goods' in Inge Kaul, Isabelle Grunberg, and Marc Stern (eds.), *Global Public Goods: International Cooperation in the 21st Century* (Oxford: Oxford University Press, 1999) 2.
Kim, Joongi, 'The Viability of Screen Quotas in Korea: The Cultural Exception under the International Trade Regime' (1998) 26 *Korean Journal of International and Comparative Law* 199.
Kish, Karsie, 'Protectionism to Promote Culture: South Korea and Japan, A Case Study' (2001) 22 *University of Pennsylvania Journal of International Economic Law* 153.
Knight, Trevor, 'The Dual Nature of Cultural Products: An Analysis of the World Trade Organization's Decisions Regarding Canadian Periodicals' (1999) 57 *University of Toronto Faculty of Law Review* 165.
Kohona, Palitha, 'Reservations: Discussion of Recent Developments in the Practice of the Secretary-General of the United Nations as Depositary of Multilateral Treaties' (2005) 33(2) *Georgia Journal of International and Comparative Law* 415.
Kónya, István, 'Modeling Cultural Barriers in International Trade' (2006) 14(3) *Review of International Economics* 494.
Koskenniemi, Martti, 'Introduction' in Martti Koskenniemi (ed.), *Sources of International Law* (Aldershot: Ashgate, 2000) xi.

(ed.), *Sources of International Law* (Aldershot: Ashgate, 2000).
Koskenniemi, Martti, and Leino, Päivi, 'Fragmentation of International Law? Postmodern Anxieties' (2002) 15(3) *Leiden Journal of International Law* 553.
Krajewski, Markus, *National Regulation and Trade Liberalization in Services: The Legal Impact of the General Agreement on Trade in Services (GATS) on National Regulatory Autonomy* (The Hague: Kluwer, 2003).
 'Public Services and Trade Liberalization: Mapping the Legal Framework' (2003) 6(2) *Journal of International Economic Law* 341.
Kuijper, Pieter Jan, 'The Law of GATT as a Special Field of International Law' (1994) *Netherlands Yearbook of International Law* 227.
Leary, Virginia, and Warner, Daniel (eds.), *Social Issues, Globalisation and International Institutions: Labour Rights and the EU, ILO, OECD and WTO* (Leiden: Martinus Nijhoff, 2006).
Lee, Yong-Shik, 'Emergency Safeguard Measures under Article X in GATS: Applicability of the Concepts in the WTO Agreement on Safeguards' (1999) 33(4) *Journal of World Trade* 47.
 Safeguard Measures in World Trade: The Legal Analysis (The Hague: Kluwer, 2003).
Legrain, Philippe, *Open World: The Truth About Globalisation* (London: Abacus, 2002).
Lennard, Michael, 'Navigating by the Stars: Interpreting the WTO Agreements' (2002) 5(1) *Journal of International Economic Law* 17.
Leroux, Eric, 'What Is a "Service Supplied in the Exercise of Governmental Authority" under Article I:3(b) and (c) of the General Agreement on Trade in Services?' (2006) 40(3) *Journal of World Trade* 345.
Lorimer, Rowland, 'Book Publishing' in Michael Dorland (ed.), *The Cultural Industries in Canada: Problems, Policies and Prospects* (Toronto: Lorimer, 1996) 3.
Low, Patrick, and Mattoo, Aaditya, 'Is There a Better Way? Alternative Approaches to Liberalization under GATS' in Pierre Sauvé and Robert Stern (eds.), *GATS 2000: New Directions in Services Trade Liberalization* (Washington, DC: Brookings Institution Press/Harvard University Center for Business and Government, 2000) 449.
Luff, David, 'Telecommunications and Audio-Visual Services: Considerations for a Convergence Policy at the World Trade Organization Level' (2004) 38(6) *Journal of World Trade* 1059.
'The Maastricht Guidelines on Violations of Economic, Social and Cultural Rights' in Theo van Boven, Cees Flinterman, Fred Grünfeld, and Rita Hut (eds.), *SIM Special No. 20: The Maastricht Guidelines on Violations of Economic, Social and Cultural Rights* (Utrecht: Netherlands Institute of Human Rights, 1998) 1.
McAnany, Emile, and Wilkinson, Kenton (eds.), *Mass Media and Free Trade: NAFTA and the Cultural Industries* (Austin: University of Texas Press, 1996).
McDonald, Joe, 'China Shuts Door on New Foreign TV Channels', *The Guardian* (Beijing, 5 August 2005).
McGinnis, John, 'The Appropriate Hierarchy of Global Multilateralism and Customary International Law: The Example of the WTO' (2003) 44 *Virginia Journal of International Law* 229.

McLachlan, Campbell, 'The Principle of Systemic Integration and Article 31(3)(c) of the Vienna Convention' (2005) 54 *International & Comparative Law Quarterly* 279, 290.
Macmillan, Fiona, 'Commodification and Cultural Ownership' in Jonathan Griffiths and Uma Suthersanen (eds.), *Copyright and Free Speech: Comparative and International Analyses* (Oxford: Oxford University Press, 2005) 35.
  'International Economic Law and Public International Law: Strangers in the Night' (2004) 10(6) *International Trade Law & Regulation* 115.
McNair, Arnold, *The Law of Treaties* (Oxford: Clarendon Press, 1961).
Macrory, Patrick, Appleton, Arthur, and Plummer, Michael (eds.), *The World Trade Organization: Legal, Economic and Political Analysis* (New York: Springer, 2005).
Magder, Ted, 'Film and Video Production' in Michael Dorland (ed.), *The Cultural Industries in Canada: Problems, Policies and Prospects* (Toronto: Lorimer, 1996) 145.
Mann, Catherine, and Knight, Sarah, 'Electronic Commerce in the WTO' in Jeffrey Schott (ed.), *The WTO After Seattle* (Washington, DC: Institute for International Economics, 2000) 253.
Marceau, Gabrielle, 'A Call for Coherence in International Law – Praise for the Prohibition Against "Clinical Isolation" in WTO Dispute Settlement' (1999) 33(5) *Journal of World Trade* 87.
  'Conflicts of Norms and Conflicts of Jurisdictions: The Relationship between the WTO Agreement and MEAs and Other Treaties' (2001) 35(6) *Journal of World Trade* 1081.
  'La jurisprudence sur le principe de précaution dans le droit de l'OMC' (paper presented at the Leçon inaugurale, Faculté de Droit de l'Université de Genève, 19 May 2005).
  'WTO Dispute Settlement and Human Rights' (2002) 13(4) *European Journal of International Law* 753.
Martin, Lisa, 'The Political Economy of International Cooperation' in Inge Kaul, Isabelle Grunberg, and Marc Stern (eds.), *Global Public Goods: International Cooperation in the 21st Century* (Oxford: Oxford University Press, 1999) 51.
Martin, Robert, *Final Statement of the United States Delegation: Third Session of the Intergovernmental Meeting of Experts, UNESCO* (Paris, 3 June 2005).
Marwell, Jeremy, 'Trade and Morality: The WTO Public Morals Exception After Gambling' (2006) 81 *New York University Law Review* 802.
Mas-Colell, Andreu, 'Should Cultural Goods be Treated Differently?' (1999) 23(1) *Journal of Cultural Economics* 87.
Maskus, Keith, and Reichman, Jerome, 'The Globalization of Private Knowledge Goods and the Privatization of Global Public Goods' in Keith Maskus and Jerome Reichman (eds.), *International Public Goods and Transfer of Technology Under a Globalized Intellectual Property Regime* (2005) 3.
  (eds.), *International Public Goods and Transfer of Technology under a Globalized Intellectual Property Regime* (Cambridge: Cambridge University Press, 2005).
Mattera, A., '"L'Union européenne assure le respect des identités nationales, régionales et locales, en particulier par l'application et la mise en œuvre du

principe de la reconnaissance mutuelle" (Un article 12 A à introduire dans le future Traité?)' (2002) 2 *Revue du Droit de l'Union Européenne* 217.

Mattoo, Aaditya, 'MFN and the GATS' in Thomas Cottier and Petros Mavroidis (eds.), *Regulatory Barriers and the Principle of Non-Discrimination in World Trade Law* (Ann Arbor: University of Michigan Press, 2000) 51.

'National Treatment in the GATS: Corner-Stone or Pandora's Box?' (1997) 31(1) *Journal of World Trade* 107.

Mattoo, Aaditya, and Fink, Carsten, *Regional Agreements and Trade in Services: Policy Issues*, World Bank Policy Research Working Paper 2852 (2002).

Mattoo, Aaditya, and Schuknecht, Ludger, *Trade Policies for Electronic Commerce*, World Bank Policy Research Paper 2380 (2000).

Mattoo, Aaditya, and Subramanian, Arvind, 'Regulatory Autonomy and Multilateral Disciplines: The Dilemma and a Possible Resolution' (1998) 1 *Journal of International Economic Law* 303.

Mavroidis, Petros, '"Like Products": Some Thoughts at the Positive and Normative Level' in Thomas Cottier and Petros Mavroidis (eds.), *Regulatory Barriers and the Principle of Non-Discrimination in World Trade Law* (Ann Arbor: University of Michigan Press, 2000) 125.

Melander, Göran, 'Article 27' in Asbjørn Eide, Gudmundur Alfredsson, Göran Melander, Lars Adam Rehof, and Allan Rosas (eds.), *The Universal Declaration of Human Rights: A Commentary* (Oslo: Scandinavian University Press, 1992) 429.

Merkin, William, 'United States Trade Policy and Culture: Future Strategies' in UNESCO (ed.), *World Culture Report: Cultural Diversity, Conflict and Pluralism* (Paris: UNESCO, 2000) 68.

Merryman, John, 'Two Ways of Thinking About Cultural Property' (1986) 80(4) *Americal Journal of International Law* 831.

Messerlin, Patrick, 'France and Trade Policy: Is the "French Exception" Passé?' (1996) 72(2) *International Affairs* 293.

Measuring the Costs of Protection in Europe: European Commercial Policy in the 2000s (Washington, DC: Institute for International Economics, 2001).

'Regulating Culture: Has It "Gone with the Wind"?' (paper presented at the Productivity Commission and Australian National University (Joint Conference) on Achieving Better Regulation of Services, Canberra, 26–7 June 2000).

Messerlin, Patrick, and Cocq, Emmanuel, 'Preparing Negotiations in Services: EC Audiovisuals in the Millennium Round' (paper presented at the World Services Congress on Services: Generating Global Growth and Opportunity, Atlanta, 1–3 November 1999).

Mitchell, Andrew (ed.), *Challenges and Prospects for the WTO* (London: Cameron May, 2005).

Legal Principles in WTO Disputes (Cambridge: Cambridge University Press, forthcoming).

'Towards Compatibility: The Future of Electronic Commerce within the Global Trading System' (2001) 4(4) *Journal of International Economic Law* 683.

Morrison, Peter, 'WTO Dispute Settlement in Services: Procedural and Substantive Aspects' in Ernst-Ulrich Petersmann (ed.), *International Trade Law and the GATT/WTO Dispute Settlement System* (London: Kluwer, 1999) 377.

Mosoti, Victor, 'Institutional Cooperation and Norm Creation in International Organizations' in Thomas Cottier, Joost Pauwelyn, and Elisabeth Bürgi (eds.), *Human Rights and International Trade* (Oxford: Oxford University Press, 2005) 165.

Mukherjee, Arpita, 'Audio-Visual Policies and International Trade: The Case of India' in Paolo Guerrieri, Lelio Iapadre, and Georg Koopmann (eds.), *Cultural Diversity and International Economic Integration: The Global Governance of the Audiovisual Sector* (Cheltenham: Edward Elgar, 2005) 218.

Mulcahy, Kevin, 'Cultural Policy: Definitions and Theoretical Approaches' (2006) 35(4) *Journal of Arts Management, Law, and Society* 319.

Musungu, Sisule, 'The Right to Health, Intellectual Property, and Competition Principles' in Thomas Cottier, Joost Pauwelyn, and Elisabeth Bürgi (eds.), *Human Rights and International Trade* (Oxford: Oxford University Press, 2005) 301.

National Research Council (ed.), *Incorporating Science, Economics, and Sociology in Developing Sanitary and Phytosanitary Standards in International Trade: Proceedings of a Conference* (Washington, DC: National Academy Press, 2000).

Neuwirth, Rostam, 'The Cultural Industries and the Legacy of Article IV GATT: Rethinking the Relation of Culture and Trade in Light of the New WTO Round' (paper presented at the Conference on Cultural Traffic: Policy, Culture, and the New Technologies in the European Union and Canada, Carleton University, 2002).

Niec, Halina (ed.), *Cultural Rights and Wrongs* (Paris/Leicester: UNESCO Publishing and Institute of Art and Law, 1998).

Nielson, Julia, and Taglioni, Daria, *Services Trade Liberalisation: Identifying Opportunities and Gains*, OECD Trade Policy Working Paper No. 1 (2004).

'Nine Lives Takes Top Swiss award', *BBC News* (14 August 2005).

Norton, Joseph, Andenas, Mads, and Footer, Mary (eds.), *The Changing World of International Law in the Twenty-First Century: A Tribute to the Late Kenneth R. Simmonds* (The Hague: Kluwer, 1998).

Nottage, Hunter, and Sebastian, Thomas, 'Giving Legal Effect to the Results of the WTO Trade Negotiations: An Analysis of the Methods of Changing WTO Law' (2006) 9(4) *Journal of International Economic Law* 989.

Oberthür, Sebastian, and Gehring, Thomas, 'Institutional Interaction in Global Environmental Governance: The Case of the Cartagena Protocol and the World Trade Organization' (2006) 6(2) *Global Environmental Politics* 1.

O'Keefe, Roger, 'The "Right to Take Part in Cultural Life" under Article 15 of the ICESCR' (1998) 47 *International & Comparative Law Quarterly* 904.

Ortino, Federico, 'Treaty Interpretation and the WTO Appellate Body Report in *US – Gambling*: A Critique' (2006) 9(1) *Journal of International Economic Law* 117.

Panagariya, Arvind, 'Electronic Commerce, WTO and Developing Countries' (2000) 23(8) *World Economy* 959.

Paracuellos, Jean-Charles, 'Le paysage audiovisuel français' (1993) 191 *Regards sur l'actualité* 3.
Pauwelyn, Joost, 'Adding Sweeteners to Softwood Lumber: The WTO–NAFTA "Spaghetti Bowl" is Cooking' (2006) 9(1) *Journal of International Economic Law* 197.
  Conflict of Norms in Public International Law: How WTO Law Relates to Other Rules of International Law (Cambridge: Cambridge University Press, 2003).
  'Human Rights in WTO Dispute Settlement' in Thomas Cottier, Joost Pauwelyn and Elisabeth Bürgi (eds.), *Human Rights and International Trade* (Oxford: Oxford University Press, 2005) 205.
  'The Jurisdiction of the World Trade Organization' (2004) 98 *American Society of International Law Proceedings* 135.
  'The Puzzle of WTO Safeguards and Regional Trade Agreements' (2004) 7(1) *Journal of International Economic Law* 109.
  'The Role of Public International Law in the WTO: How Far Can We Go?' (2001) 95 *American Journal of International Law* 535.
  'The UNESCO Convention on Cultural Diversity, and the WTO: Diversity in International Law-Making?' (15 November 2005) *ASIL Insight*.
Peacock, Alan, and Rizzo, Ilde (eds.), *Cultural Economics and Cultural Policies* (Dordrecht: Kluwer, 1994).
Perino, Grischa, and Schulze, Günther, 'Competition, Cultural Autonomy and Global Governance: The Audio-Visual Sector in Germany' in Paolo Guerrieri, Lelio Iapadre, and Georg Koopmann (eds.), *Cultural Diversity and International Economic Integration: The Global Governance of the Audio-Visual Sector* (Cheltenham: Edward Elgar, 2005) 52.
Perry, Sheila (ed.), *Aspects of Contemporary France* (London: Routledge, 1997).
Petersmann, Ernst-Ulrich, 'Human Rights, Markets and Economic Welfare: Constitutional Functions of the Emerging UN Human Rights Constitution' in Frederick Abbott, Christine Breining-Kaufmann, and Thomas Cottier (eds.), *International Trade and Human Rights: Foundations and Conceptual Issues* (Ann Arbor: University of Michigan Press, 2006) 29.
  (ed.), *International Trade Law and the GATT/WTO Dispute Settlement System* (London: Kluwer, 1999).
  'Time for a United Nations "Global Compact" for Integrating Human Rights into the Law of Worldwide Organizations: Lessons from European Integration' (2002) 13(3) *European Journal of International Law* 621.
Pignataro, Giacomo, 'Imperfect Information and Cultural Goods: Producers' and Consumers' Inertia' in Alan Peacock and Ilde Rizzo (eds.), *Cultural Economics and Cultural Policies* (Dordrecht: Kluwer, 1994) 55.
Posner, Richard, *Economic Analysis of Law* (New York: Aspen, 2003).
Power, Dominic, and Hallencreutz, Daniel, 'Profiting from Creativity? The Music Industry in Stockholm, Sweden and Kingston, Jamaica' in Dominic Power and Allen Scott (eds.), *Cultural Industries and the Production of Culture* (London: Routledge, 2004) 224.
Power, Dominic, and Scott, Allen (eds.), *Cultural Industries and the Production of Culture* (London: Routledge, 2004).

Productivity Commission (ed.), *Achieving Better Regulation of Services* (2001). *Broadcasting*, Inquiry Report No. 11 (3 March 2000).
Prott, Lyndel, 'Cultural Rights as Peoples' Rights in International Law' in James Crawford (ed.), *The Rights of Peoples* (New York: Oxford University Press, 1988) 93.
  'International Standards for Cultural Heritage' in UNESCO (ed.), *World Culture Report: Culture, Creativity and Markets* (Paris: UNESCO, 1998) 222.
  'Understanding One Another on Cultural Rights' in Halina Niec (ed.), *Cultural Rights and Wrongs* (Paris/Leicester: UNESCO Publishing and Institute of Art and Law, 1998) 161.
Psychogiopoulou, Evangelia, 'EC State Aid Control and Cultural Justifications' (2006) 33(1) *Legal Issues of Economic Integration* 3.
Ragosta, John, 'The Cultural Industries Exemption from NAFTA – Its Parameters' (1997) 23 *Canada–United States Law Journal* 165.
Redner, Harry, *Conserving Cultures: Technology, Globalization, and the Future of Local Cultures* (Lanham: Rowman & Littlefield Publishers, 2004).
Regan, Donald, 'Further Thoughts on the Role of Regulatory Purpose under Article III of the General Agreement on Tariffs and Trade: A Tribute to Bob Hudec' (2003) 37(4) *Journal of World Trade* 737.
  'Regulatory Purpose and "Like Products" in Article III:4 of the GATT (With Additional Remarks on Article III:2)' (2002) 36(3) *Journal of World Trade* 443.
Richardson, Bonnie, 'Hollywood's Vision of a Clear, Predictable Trade Framework Consistent with Cultural Diversity' in Christoph Graber, Michael Girsburger, and Mira Nenova (eds.), *Free Trade versus Cultural Diversity: WTO Negotiations in the Field of Audiovisual Services* (Zurich: Schulthess, 2004) 111.
Rifkin, Jeremy, 'When Markets Give Way to Networks . . . Everything Is a Service' in John Hartley (ed.), *Creative Industries* (Malden, MA: Blackwell, 2005) 361.
Rivery, Eric Morgan de, 'Unresolved Issues in the Audiovisual Sector and the US/ EC Conflict' in Jacques Bourgeois, Frédérique Berrod, and Eric Gippini Fournier (eds.), *The Uruguay Round Results: A European Lawyers' Perspective* (Brussels: European Interuniversity Press, 1995) 435.
Roessler, Frieder, 'The Concept of Nullification and Impairment in the Legal System of the World Trade Organization' in Ernst-Ulrich Petersmann (ed.), *International Trade Law and the GATT/WTO Dispute Settlement System* (London: Kluwer, 1999) 124.
  'Diverging Domestic Policies and Multilateral Trade Integration' in Jagdish Bhagwati and Robert Hudec (eds.), *Fair Trade and Harmonization: Prerequisites for Free Trade?* (Cambridge, MA: MIT Press, 1996) (vol. II) 21.
Roessler, Frieder, and Gappah, Petina, 'A Re-Appraisal of Non-Violation Complaints under the WTO Dispute Settlement Procedures' in Patrick Macrory, Arthur Appleton, and Michael Plummer (eds.), *The World Trade Organization: Legal, Economic and Political Analysis* (New York: Springer, 2005) (vol. I) 1371.
Rothwell, Donald, 'Quasi-Incorporation of International Law in Australia: Broadcasting Standards, Cultural Sovereignty and International Trade' (1999) 27(3) *Federal Law Review* 527.

Roy, Martin, 'Audiovisual Services in the Doha Round: *"Dialogue de Sourds, The Sequel"*?' (2005) 6(6) *Journal of World Investment and Trade* 923.
Ruiz Fabri, Hélène, *Analyse et commentaire critique de l'avant-projet de convention sur la protection de la diversité des contenus culturels et des expressions artistiques dans la version soumise pour commentaires et observations aux gouvernements des Etats membres de l'UNESCO: Etude réalisée à la demande de l'Agence intergouvernementale de la Francophonie* (August 2004).
Runge, C. Ford, Bagnara, Gian-Luca, and Jackson, Lee Ann, 'Differing U.S. and European Perspectives on GMOs: Political, Economic and Cultural Issues' (2001) 2(2) *The Estey Centre Journal of International Law and Trade Policy* 221.
Sacerdoti, Giorgio, Yanovich, Alan, and Bohanes, Jan (eds.), *The WTO at Ten: The Contributions of the Dispute Settlement System* (Cambridge: Cambridge University Press, 2006).
Salée, Daniel, 'NAFTA, Quebec, and the Boundaries of Cultural Sovereignty: The Challenge of Identity in the Era of Globalization' in Dorinda Dallmeyer (ed.), *Joining Together, Standing Apart: National Identities after NAFTA* (The Hague: Kluwer, 1997) 73.
Salusinszky, Imre, 'A critique of cultural protectionism' (1999) 15(3) *Policy* 18.
Samuelson, Pamela, 'Implications of the Agreement on Trade Related Aspects of Intellectual Property Rights for the Cultural Dimension of National Copyright Laws' (1999) 23 *Journal of Cultural Economics* 95.
Sandler, Todd, 'Intergenerational Public Goods: Strategies, Efficiency and Institutions' in Inge Kaul, Isabelle Grunberg, and Marc Stern (eds.), *Global Public Goods: International Cooperation in the 21st Century* (Oxford: Oxford University Press, 1999) 20.
Sauvé, Pierre, 'Completing the GATS Framework: Addressing Uruguay Round Leftovers' (2002) 57(3) *Aussenwirtschaft* 301.
Sauvé, Pierre, and Steinfatt, Karsten, 'Towards Multilateral Rules on Trade and Culture: Protective Regulation or Efficient Protection?' in Productivity Commission (ed.), *Achieving Better Regulation of Services* (2001).
Sauvé, Pierre, and Stern, Robert (eds.), *GATS 2000: New Directions in Services Trade Liberalization* (Washington, DC: Brookings Institution Press/Harvard University Center for Business and Government, 2000).
Schott, Jeffrey (ed.), *The WTO After Seattle* (Washington, DC: Institute for International Economics, 2000).
Schott, Jeffrey, Bradford, Scott, and Moll, Thomas, *Negotiating the Korea–United States Free Trade Agreement*, Institute for International Economics, Policy Briefs in International Economics No. PB06-4 (June 2006).
Schulze, Günther, 'International Trade' in Ruth Towse (ed.), *A Handbook of Cultural Economics* (Cheltenham: Edward Elgar, 2003) 269.
 'International Trade in Art' (1999) 23(1) *Journal of Cultural Economics* 109.
Scott, Allen, and Power, Dominic, 'A Prelude to Cultural Industries and the Production of Culture' in Dominic Power and Allen Scott (eds.), *Cultural Industries and the Production of Culture* (London: Routledge, 2004) 3.

Sen, Amartya, 'Satyajit Ray and the Art of Universalism: Our Culture, Their Culture', *The New Republic* (Washington, DC, 1 April 1996) 32.
Serageldin, Ismail, 'Cultural Heritage as Public Good: Economic Analysis Applied to Historic Cities' in Inge Kaul, Isabelle Grunberg, and Marc Stern (eds.), *Global Public Goods: International Cooperation in the 21st Century* (Oxford: Oxford University Press, 1999) 240.
Shahabuddeen, Mohamed, *Precedent in the World Court* (Cambridge: Cambridge University Press, 1996).
Shany, Yuval, *The Competing Jurisdictions of International Courts and Tribunals* (Oxford: Oxford University Press, 2003).
Shaw, Malcolm, *International Law* (Cambridge: Cambridge University Press, 5th edn, 2003).
Shelton, Dinah, 'Normative Hierarchy in International Law' (2006) 1002(2) *American Journal of International Law*.
Siebenhaar, Hans-Peter, 'Européanisation ou américanisation? Option pour la promotion de la production audiovisuelle dans l'Union européenne' (1994) 379 *Revue du Marché Commun et de l'Union Européenne* 357.
Siegel, Deborah, 'Legal Aspects of the IMF/WTO Relationship: The Fund's Articles of Agreement and the WTO Agreements' (2002) 96 *American Journal of International Law* 561.
Silverglade, Bruce, 'International Harmonization under the SPS Agreement' in National Research Council (ed.), *Incorporating Science, Economics, and Sociology in Developing Sanitary and Phytosanitary Standards in International Trade: Proceedings of a Conference* (Washington, DC: National Academy Press, 2000) 210.
Sinclair, Ian, *The Vienna Convention on the Law of Treaties* (Manchester: Manchester University Press, 2nd edn, 1984).
Sinclair, John, 'Culture and Trade: Some Theoretical and Practical Considerations' in Emile McAnany and Kenton Wilkinson (eds.), *Mass Media and Free Trade: NAFTA and the Cultural Industries* (Austin: University of Texas Press, 1996) 30.
Smiers, Joost, *Artistic Expression in a Corporate World: Do We Need Monopolistic Control?* (Utrecht: Utrecht School of the Arts, 2004).
Smith, Clint, 'International Trade in Television Programming and GATT: An Analysis of Why the European Community's Local Program Requirement Violates the General Agreement on Tariffs and Trade' (1993) 10(2) *International Tax & Business Lawyer* 97.
Smith, Fiona, and Woods, Lorna, 'A Distinction Without a Difference: Exploring the Boundary Between Goods and Services in the World Trade Organization and the European Union' (2005) 12(1) *Columbia Journal of European Law* 1.
Steger, Debra, 'The Jurisdiction of the World Trade Organization' (2004) 98 *American Society of International Law Proceedings* 142.
Stern, Robert (ed.), *Services in the International Economy* (Ann Arbor: University of Michigan Press, 2001).
Stilwell, Matthew, and Bohanes, Jan, 'Trade and the Environment' in Patrick Macrory, Arthur Appleton, and Michael Plummer (eds.), *The World Trade*

Organization: Legal, Economic and Political Analysis (New York: Springer, 2005) (vol. II) 511.

Sykes, Alan, 'Comparative Advantage and the Normative Economics of International Trade Policy' (1998) 1(1) *Journal of International Economic Law* 49.

'The Least Restrictive Means' (2003) 70 *University of Chicago Law Review* 403.

'Subsidies and Countervailing Measures' in Patrick Macrory, Arthur Appleton, and Michael Plummer (eds.), *The World Trade Organization: Legal, Economic and Political Analysis* (New York: Springer, 2005) (vol. II) 81.

Tawfik, Myra, 'Competing Cultures: Canada and the World Trade Organization – The Lessons from Sports Illustrated' (1998) 36 *Canadian Yearbook of International Law* 279.

Throsby, David, 'Cultural Capital' (1999) 23 *Journal of Cultural Economics* 3.

Economics and Culture (Cambridge: Cambridge University Press, 2001).

'Seven Questions in the Economics of Cultural Heritage' in Michael Hutter and Ilde Rizzo (eds.), *Perspectives on Cultural Heritage* (New York: St Martin's Press, 1997) 13.

Towse, Ruth (ed.), *Copyright in the Cultural Industries* (Cheltenham: Edward Elgar, 2002).

'Cultural Industries' in Ruth Towse (ed.), *A Handbook of Cultural Economics* (Cheltenham: Edward Elgar, 2003) 170.

(ed.), *A Handbook of Cultural Economics* (Cheltenham: Edward Elgar, 2003).

Trachtman, Joel, 'The Domain of WTO Dispute Resolution' (1999) 40(2) *Harvard International Law Journal* 333.

'The Jurisdiction of the World Trade Organization' (2004) 98 *American Society of International Law Proceedings* 139.

'Review of Joost Pauwelyn, Conflict of Norms in Public International Law: How WTO Law Relates to Other Rules of International Law' (2004) 98 *American Journal of International Law* 855.

'Trade and ... Problems, Cost-Benefit Analysis and Subsidiarity' (1998) 9(1) *European Journal of International Law* 32.

Trebilcock, Michael, and Howse, Robert, *The Regulation of International Trade* (London: Routledge, 2nd edn, 1999).

The Regulation of International Trade (London: Routledge, 3rd edn, 2005).

Vabres, Renaud Donnedieu de, *Journées de la coopération internationale et du développement allocution du ministre de la Culture et de la Communication de France* (Paris, 19 July 2005).

Valenzuela, María Soledad Alvear (Chilean Minister of Foreign Relations), letter to Robert Zoellick (United States Trade Representative), 'Side Letter on Television' (6 June 2003).

Van den Bossche, Peter, *The Law and Policy of the World Trade Organization: Text, Cases and Materials* (Cambridge: Cambridge University Press, 2005).

Van der Staay, Adriaan, 'Public Opinion and Global Ethics: A Descriptive Study of Existing Survey Data' in UNESCO (ed.), *World Culture Report: Culture, Creativity and Markets* (Paris: UNESCO, 1998).

Venturelli, Shalini, 'Culture and the Creative Economy in the Information Age' in John Hartley (ed.), *Creative Industries* (Malden, MA: Blackwell, 2005) 391.
Verhoosel, Gaëtan, *National Treatment and WTO Dispute Settlement: Adjudicating the Boundaries of Regulatory Autonomy* (Oxford: Hart, 2002).
Voon, Tania, 'A New Approach to Audiovisual Products in the WTO: Rebalancing GATT and GATS' (2006) 14(1) *UCLA Entertainment Law Review* 1.
  'Sizing Up the WTO: Trade-Environment Conflict and the Kyoto Protocol' (2000) 10(1) *Journal of Transnational Law & Policy* 71.
  'State Support for Audiovisual Products in the WTO: Protectionism or Cultural Policy?' (2006) 13(2) *International Journal of Cultural Property* 129.
  'UNESCO and the WTO: A Clash of Cultures?' (2006) 55(3) *International & Comparative Law Quarterly* 635.
Vranes, Erich, 'The Definition of "Norm Conflict" in International Law and Legal Theory' (2006) 17(2) *European Journal of International Law* 395.
Wai, Robert, 'Countering, Branding, Dealing: Using Economic and Social Rights in and around the International Trade Regime' (2003) 14 *European Journal of International Law* 35.
Waincymer, Jeffrey, *WTO Litigation: Procedural Aspects of Formal Dispute Settlement* (London: Cameron May, 2002).
Weber, Rolf, Rossnagel, Alexander, Osterwalder, Simon, Scheuer, Alexander, and Wüst, Sonnia, *Kulturquoten im Rundfunk* (Zurich, Baden-Baden: Schulthess, Nomos, 2006).
Weiler, Joseph (ed.), *The EU, the WTO and the NAFTA: Towards a Common Law of International Trade* (Oxford: Oxford University Press, 2000).
  'The Rule of Lawyers and the Ethos of Diplomats: Reflections on the Internal and External Legitimacy of WTO Dispute Settlement' (2001) 35 *Journal of World Trade* 191.
Wille, Serena, 'Recapturing a Lost Opportunity: Article III:2 GATT 1994, Japan – Taxes on Alcoholic Beverages 1996' (1998) 9(1) *European Journal of International Law*, 'Current Developments', <www.ejil.org> (online only, accessed 4 August 2006).
Winickoff, David, Jasanoff, Sheila, Busch, Lawrence, Grove-White, Robin, and Wynne, Brian, 'Adjudicating the GM Food Wars: Science, Risk, and Democracy in World Trade Law' (2005) 30(1) *Yale Journal of International Law* 81.
Withers, Glenn, 'Broadcasting' in Ruth Towse (ed.), *A Handbook of Cultural Economics* (Cheltenham: Edward Elgar, 2003) 102.
Witte, Bruno de, 'Trade in Culture: International Legal Regimes and EU Constitutional Values' in Gráinne de Búrca and Joanne Scott (eds.), *The EU and the WTO: Legal and Constitutional Issues* (Oxford: Hart, 2001) 237.
Witte, Bruno de, and Post, Harry, 'Educational and Cultural Rights' in Antonio Cassese, Andrew Clapham, and Joseph Weiler (eds.), *Human Rights and the European Community: The Substantive Law* (Baden-Baden: Nomos Verlagsgesellschaft, 1991) 123.

Wouters, Jan, and De Meester, Bart, 'UNESCO's Convention on Cultural Diversity and WTO Law: Complementary or Contradictory?' (Working Paper No. 73, KU Leuven Faculty of Law, Institute for International Law, 2005).

Wright, Claire, 'Hollywood's Disappearing Act: International Trade Remedies to Bring Hollywood Home' (2006) 39 *Akron Law Review* 739.

Wunsch-Vincent, Sacha, 'The Digital Trade Agenda of the U.S.: Parallel Tracks of Bilateral, Regional and Multilateral Liberalization' (2003) 58 *Aussenwirtschaft* 7.

'The Internet, Cross-Border Trade in Services, and the GATS: Lessons from US – Gambling' (2006) 5(3) *World Trade Review* 319, 329–35.

United Nations Information and Communication Technologies Task Force, *WTO, E-commerce, and Information Technologies: From the Uruguay Round through the Doha Development Agenda* (19 November 2004).

The WTO, the Internet and Trade in Digital Products: EC–US Perspectives (Oxford: Hart, 2006).

Yanovich, Alan, and Voon, Tania, 'What is the Measure at Issue?' in Andrew Mitchell (ed.), *Challenges and Prospects for the WTO* (London: Cameron May, 2005) 115.

Yerkey, Gary, 'Foreign Investment: U.S. to Oppose EU Bid to Exempt "Culture" from OECD Investment Accord' (23 May 1995) *BNA International Business & Finance Daily*.

York, George, 'Global Foods, Local Tastes and Biotechnology: The New Legal Architecture of International Agriculture Trade' (2001) 7 *Columbia Journal of European Law* 423.

Yúdice, George, *The Expediency of Culture: Uses of Culture in the Global Era* (Durham, NC: Duke University Press, 2003).

Zdouc, Werner, 'WTO Dispute Settlement Practice Relating to the GATS' (1999) 2(2) *Journal of International Economic Law* 295.

Index

Acheson, Keith, 22, 49, 62, 194
Adlung, Rudolf, 210
Adorno, Theodor, 19, 40
African Group, 16-17
Agreement on Agriculture, 231
  agricultural subsidies, 231-2
Agreement on Government Procurement, expiry of, 235
Agreement on Trade in Civil Aircraft, expiry of, 235
agriculture, 5, 17-18, 218, 240, 248 *see also* Agreement on Agriculture
aims-and-effects test, 82-5, 87, 89, 103, 155
alcohol, 13, 14, 77
anti-competitive conduct, 242-6
anti-dumping, 8, 90, 240 *see also* Anti-Dumping Agreement, dumping
  absence of disciplines in GATS, 238
  measures against services trade, 237-9
Anti-Dumping Agreement, 8, 237 *see also* GATT 1994: Article VI
  Article 17.6(ii) (standard of review), 125
Appadurai, Arjun, 49
Appellate Body, 9, 26, 66-79, 170, 209
  Reports, 26
arbitrary or unjustifiable discrimination, *see* discrimination: arbitrary or unjustifiable
Argentina
  and International Monetary Fund, 206
  position in agriculture negotiations, 232
  submissions in *Argentina – Textiles and Apparel*, 206
art, arthouse, *see* films: art film
asbestos, 3, 79, 107, 162
audio tapes, *see* sound recording: audio tapes
audiovisual sector, 19, 23, 29, 32, 237-9
  see also films, broadcasting
  convergence with telecommunications, 72-3, 224

GATS classification, 71-3, 224
  industrial vs cultural, 221
  market access limitations, 111-12
  MFN exemptions, 25-6, 88, 114-16, 226
  negotiations under GATS, 27-9, 117-18, 194, 216, 238, 248
  special nature, 25, 31, 39, 50, 58, 105, 107, 164-5
  subsidies, 227-32
  Uruguay Round negotiations and outcome, 23-7, 32, 34, 70, 95, 98-9, 109-10, 201, 221, 248
  US dominance, 44-50
audiovisual services, *see* audiovisual sector
Australia
  audiovisual subsidies, 22
  Australian Broadcasting Corporation, 22
  Australia United States Free Trade Agreement, 33
  co-production arrangements, 116
  cultural exports, 46
  foreign ownership controls, 112
  indigenous culture, 163
  local content quotas, 20, 33, 118
  MFN exemption, 115
  position in negotiations under GATS, 28, 39, 249, 255
  position in Uruguay Round, 24
  position on UNESCO Convention, 185, 192-3
  Radio Australia, 22
authors' rights, *see* copyright: authors' rights

Baker, Edwin, 44-6, 48, 54-7
ballet, 41
Bartels, Lorand, 214
Beirut Agreement, 64
Benhamou, Françoise, 174
Bernier, Ivan, 31, 77, 175, 184, 221
Big Brother, 46

295

biodiversity, 52 *see also* Convention on Biological Diversity
Boltuck, Richard, 48
books, 53, 55, 61-2, 64, 71, 76-7, 110, 112, 163, 176, 179, 224, 232, 242, 244, 248 *see also* publishing
bottom-up approach, 225
broadcasting, 20-3, 27, 33, 49, 51-2, 59, 62, 72-3, 91, 94-5, 111-12, 118, 157, 176-7, 179, 223, 233, 242, 246 *see also* radio, sound recording, television
Broude, Tomer, 16, 61

cable, 72, 106, 112
Calendar Girls, 57
Canada, 47-8, 50, 63, 67, 82, 103, 118, 178, 181, 190, 221, 247 *see also* NAFTA
  Audio-Visual Certification Office, 21
  audiovisual subsidies, 22
  book publishing, 62
  Book Publishing Industry Development Program, 23
  Canada Post, 96-8
  Canada Revenue Agency, 21
  Canadian Broadcasting Corporation, 91
  co-production arrangements, 115-16
  Country Music Television dispute, 112-13
  CRTC, 20, 112
  Cultural Industries SAGIT, 175-6
    Draft International Agreement on Cultural Diversity, 176-81, 190
  cultural policy measures, 20-1, 23, 58, 62, 112
  CUSFTA, 31
  Department of Foreign Affairs and International Trade, 175-78, 190
  English-speaking and French-speaking, 49
  Federal Cultural Policy Review Committee, 51, 62
  GATS commitments, 111-12
  local content quotas, 58
  MFN exemptions, 114, 116
  Polygram dispute, 27
  position in negotiations under GATS, 29, 37, 249
  position in Uruguay Round, 24
  position on MAI, 32
  position on UNESCO Convention, 183, 216
  Québec, 49, 116
  Radio Canada, 91
  runaway film production, 50
  submissions in *Canada – Periodicals*, 26-7, 40, 81, 84-5, 167
  Vancouver, 50

Carmody, Chi, 215
Cartagena Protocol, 189
Cass, Ronald, 48
CDs, *see* sound recording
César awards, 58
chapeau, *see* GATT 1994: Article XX chapeau, GATS: Article XIV chapeau
Charnovitz, Steve, 105, 147
Chile, 118
  Canada-Chile Free Trade Agreement, 175
  Chile-United States Free Trade Agreement, 33
  position in Uruguay Round, 24
  position on UNESCO Convention, 193
China, 109
  co-production arrangements, 115-16
  GATS commitments, 25
Chinese Taipei, 42
  GATS commitments, 25
  position in negotiations under GATS, 28-9
  position on UNESCO Convention, 193
cigarettes, 4
cinemas, 20, 22, 62, 64, 72, 91, 153 *see also* films
cinematograph films, *see* GATT 1994: Article IV
cinematographic archives, 144-6, 148 *see also* films
Cineplex-Odeon, 62
Cocq, Emmanuel, 62-3, 227
commercial presence, 86, 111, 233 *see also* GATS: modes under
Committee on Economic, Social and Cultural Rights, 152-3
communication services, 71, 111 *see also* telecommunications
comparative advantage, 4, 11, 48
competition laws, 49, 245-6
consumer preferences, 77-9, 82, 88-9, 231
consumer tastes and habits, *see* consumer preferences
consumption abroad, 86 *see also* GATS: modes under
contemporaneous interpretation, *see* VCLT: contemporaneous or evolutionary interpretation
Convention Against Illicit Traffic in Narcotic Drugs and Psychotropic Substances, 133
Convention for the Protection of Cultural Heritage, 12, 143
Convention on Biological Diversity, 131-2 *see also* biodiversity
  Cartagena Protocol, 189
Convention on Cultural Property in Armed Conflict, 12, 143, 147
Convention on International Trade in Endangered Species of Wild Fauna and Flora, 131

Convention on Migratory Species, 131-2
co-production arrangements, 88-9, 114-17, 149, 163-4, 187, 212, 253
copyright, 166, 243
    authors' rights, 243
countervailing measures, 8, 228, 231 *see also* subsidies
Country Music Television dispute, 112-13
Cowen, Tyler, 45, 57, 184
CPC, 89, 111, 113
creativity, 34, 58-60, 65, 165, 185, 244
cross-border supply, 3, 74, 86, 111 *see also* GATS: modes under
cultural diversity, 23, 29-30, 37, 44, 47, 52, 54, 56, 60-1, 64, 66, 155, 165, 172-82, 190-1, 216, 243-4, 252-3 *see also* UNESCO Convention, Universal Declaration on Cultural Diversity
    as global public good, 53
    safeguards for, 239-43
cultural industries, 32-3, 40, 43, 53, 55-6, 58-9, 61, 71, 77, 85, 90, 98, 104-6, 118-19, 149, 163-4, 217-18, 221, 230, 232, 246, 248, 249, 255 *see also* culture: culture industry. Canada: Cultural Industries SAGIT
    definition of, 18-19, 27, 30-1
    origins of term, 19
    US dominance in, 44-50
cultural policy measures, 35-6, 42-3, 71, 73, 96, 101-4, 107-8, 117-19, 124, 127, 144, 155, 166, 169-71, 173, 179-82, 197-8, 201-2, 220, 222, 226, 232-3, 236, 242, 250, 252-3
    definition of, 19, 90
    discrimination in, 35, 37, 54-60, 67-70, 75, 79, 89-90, 92, 102, 105, 113-14, 149, 159, 172, 215, 227-32, 242-3, 246-7, 250, 255-6
    effectiveness of, 61-4
    examples of, 19-23, 110, 114, 116, 163
    impact on trade, 34, 37, 39, 54, 64-7, 69, 89-90, 113, 149, 159, 215-16, 218, 225, 247, 255
    motives for, 38, 49, 60-1, 69, 85, 106, 163-4, 172, 249, 251, 256
cultural premium, 46-7
cultural products, 9, 22-3, 27, 30-6 *see also* cultural policy measures, digital products
    as goods or services, 34, 71-3, 226, 251
    as public goods, 52-3
    as merit goods, 40-1, 51
    cultural value of, 11, 33, 41, 53, 63, 105, 244, 250
    definition of, 18-19, 144

distinctiveness of, 12, 25, 31, 37, 39, 50, 55-6, 58, 62, 84, 89, 105, 107, 160, 176-7, 185, 221, 242, 249, 251
    economic value of, 11, 41, 53, 185, 244
    likeness of, 75-89
    market failure, 33, 43-54
    promoting culture through, 41-3, 68, 227, 230
    quality of, 48, 57, 62, 76, 221
cultural property, 105 *see also* Convention for the Protection of Cultural Heritage, Convention on Cultural Property in Armed Conflict
    illicit transfers of, 144
cultural rights, 17, 107, 124, 142, 150-5, 157-9, 161-2, 183-4, 222, 243, 252-3 *see also* human rights
culture, 17-18, 34, 46-7, 50, 51-2, 55, 58, 92, 115-16, 147, 160, 165, 192, 226, 248 *see also* cultural diversity, cultural policy measures, cultural products
    as public good, 52-3
    culture industry, 19
    definition of, 12-13, 18, 41
    dialogic sense, 54-6, 59-60, 90
    exception for, 24
    international laws on, 12, 36, 66, 105, 124, 143, 146, 148, 156, 163, 167, 171-2, 179, 251
    museum sense, 56-7, 59-60
    threats to, 13, 47, 187-8, 244, 248-9
    trade and culture problem, 11-12, 23, 26, 29, 31, 33, 36, 67, 69, 119, 193, 199, 234-5, 243, 248, 255
    value of, 42-3
cultural services, *see* audiovisual sector, cultural products
customary international law, *see* international law: customary
customs duties, 5, 64, 74-5, 79-80, 223-5, 246 *see also* tariffs

developed countries, 146, 164-5, 187, 231-2, 239
developing countries, 7-8, 17, 131-2, 146, 149, 163-6, 187, 222, 225, 232-3, 239, 247, 254 *see also* Enabling Clause, least developed countries, special and differential treatment
development, 7-8, 10, 28, 132-3, 137, 163-5, 177, 189, 194, 217-18, 225
dictionaries, 105, 137
digital products, 73-5, 119, 223-6, 236, 244, 246, 253

directly competitive or substitutable products, 80-2
discrimination, 5-8, 13, 69, 75, 77, 79, 85-6, 99-104, 106, 222, 239 *see also* cultural policy measures: discrimination in, non-discrimination
   against foreign cultural products, 34, 37, 54-9, 60, 66, 68, 109, 218, 226, 229-30, 250, 255
   arbitrary or unjustifiable, 7, 101-4, 132 *see also* GATT 1994: Article XX chapeau
   between foreign cultural products, 34, 38, 59-60, 68, 116, 220, 230, 250
   de jure, 54-5, 57, 59-60, 68, 218, 220, 229-30, 250, 255
   de facto, 54, 57, 59-60, 68, 81, 109, 218, 229-30, 250, 255
disguised restriction on international trade, 7-8, 101-4 *see also* GATT 1994: Article XX chapeau
distortion of trade, 4-6, 30-1, 34, 44, 54, 79, 98, 116, 220, 223, 225, 227, 233, 239, 247, 250
Doha Development Agenda, *see* WTO: Doha Round
Doha Round, *see* WTO: Doha Round
Dominican Republic, 4
   GATS commitments, 25
DSB, *see* WTO: DSB
DSU, 9 *see also* GATT 1994: Article XXIII, WTO: dispute settlement
   application of international law under, 203-5
   Articles 1 and 2 (covered agreements under), 206-7
   Article 3.2 (purpose of dispute settlement system), 123, 125, 129
   Article 3.2 (rules of interpretation), 124-6, 130, 134, 140-2, 148, 171, 203-4, 251
   Article 3.2 (adding to or diminishing rights or obligations), 125, 204, 209, 214
   Article 3.7 (mutually agreed solutions), 197-8, 208
   Article 3.10 (obligation of good faith), 206-8
   Article 4.2 (consultations), 197
   Article 7 (Panel terms of reference), 204, 209
   Article 11 (objective assessment of the matter by Panel), 208-9
   Article 19.2 (adding to or diminishing rights or obligations), 204, 209, 214
   Article 23 (compulsory nature of), 183, 195-7, 209

   claims that may be heard under, 199, 201, 203
   comprehensive nature of, 180
   estoppel under, 208
   function of Panels and Appellate Body under, 9, 26, 170, 209
   no rule of *stare decisis* under, 128
dumping, 8, 141, 237-9 *see also* anti-dumping
DVDs, *see* films: DVDs

EC, 6, 29, 42, 67, 118, 155, 163-4, 196, 221, 247, 249
   attitude to risk, 14-15
   audiovisual subsidies, 22
   Council of the European Union, 30
   ECJ, 154
   EC Treaty, 146, 220
      Article 87(1), 30
      Article 87(3)(d), 30
   Eurocentrism, 49
   European Constitution, 29
   European Convention on Human Rights, 154
   European Parliament, 30
   GATS commitments, 113
   GSP scheme, 132-3
   Member States of, 22, 29-30, 49, 94-5, 115
   MFN exemptions, 115-16, 238
   Polygram dispute, 27
   position in *Mexico - Taxes on Soft Drinks*, 170
   position in negotiations under GATS, 73, 224
   position in Uruguay Round, 24-6
   position in *US - Cotton Yarn*, 141
   submissions in *EC - Export Subsidies on Sugar*, 208
   submissions in *EC - Poultry*, 206
   submissions in *EC - Tariff Preferences*, 134, 164
   Television Without Frontiers Directive, 21, 94-5, 115
Echols, Marsha, 14
economic integration agreements, *see* free trade agreements
Egypt
   Censorship Authority, 109
   film industry, 46, 91-2
   position in Uruguay Round, 24
   restrictions on foreign films, 21, 111
   Union of Radio and Television, 91
Ehlermann, Claus-Dieter, 211
electronic commerce, 73-5 *see also* digital products
Enabling Clause, 8

as exception, 8, 132, 222
paragraph 3(c), 133, 137
environment, 3, 7, 10, 17, 82, 130, 132, 136, 222
environmental law, 149, 189, 198, 205, 214
estoppel, 208
European Convention on Human Rights, 154
European Union, *see* EC
evolutionary interpretation, *see* VCLT: contemporaneous or evolutionary interpretation
exhaustible natural resources, 7, 10, 103, 130-2, 136-7, 143, 148
externalities, 50-4
Ezetah, Chinedu, 64

farming, 7
Feketekuty, Geza, 225-6
Fifth Element, The, 58
film festival, Locarno, 45
films, 11, 17, 19-22, 27, 41, 43, 45-50, 55-8, 61-5, 71-3, 88-9, 91-4, 109, 111-12, 114, 117, 159-61, 163-4, 176, 178, 219-20, 223, 230, 232-3, 238, 242, 244, 248 *see also* audiovisual sector, cinemas, cinematographic archives, screen quotas, video
  art film, arthouse film, 221, 242
  DVDs, 64, 71, 242
fisheries, 7
Fitzmaurice, Gerald, 134
Florence Agreement, 64, 184
  Nairobi Protocol, 65
folklore, *see* traditional knowledge and folklore
food, 14-15, 56, 240
fragmentation, *see* international law: fragmentation of
France, 55, 57, 216 *see also* Lang Plan
  audiovisual subsidies, 22, 58
  co-production arrangements, 115-16
  effect of subsidies, 62-3
  foreign ownership controls, 113, 116
  impact on Television Without Frontiers Directive, 95
  involvement in INCP, 178
  involvement in UNESCO Convention, 183
  local content quotas, 20-1
  position on MAI, 32
freedom of speech, 34, 58, 190
free-rider problem, 52
free speech, *see* freedom of speech
free trade agreements, 32, 220, 230, 233 *see also* NAFTA
  Australia-United States, 33
  Canada-Chile, 175

Chile-United States, 33
CUSFTA, 31
exception from MFN rule, 90, 117, 210-11, 227

gambling, 4, 108
game shows, 57
GATS, 35, 149 *see also* MFN, national treatment, market access, Scheduling Guidelines
  absence of anti-dumping disciplines, 238-9
  amending, 233-5, 253
  Annex on Air Transport Services, 219, 234
  Annex on Article II Exemptions, 114, 116, 226, 236, 242
  Annex on Financial Services, 219, 234
  Annex on Movement of Natural Persons Supplying Services under the Agreement, 86
  Annex on Telecommunications, 72, 219, 234
  Article I (coverage of), 70, 73, 88, 90-2, 95, 223-4, 236, 246, 253
  Article II (MFN), 86-9, 113-17, 182, 225-7, 238, 242, 246
  Article V (economic integration agreements), 117, 227
  Article VIII (monopolies and exclusive service suppliers), 91
  Article IX (business practices), 246
  Article X (safeguards), 240-2
  Article XIV (general exceptions), 42, 100, 104, 107, 163, 171, 173
  Article XIV chapeau, 104, 158, 162
  Article XIV(a) (public morals and public order), 90, 104, 107-8, 132, 142, 156-9, 252
  Article XIV(b) (health), 143, 162, 165
  Article XIV(c) (securing compliance), 132, 143, 166-7, 171
  Article XIV*bis* (national security), 8, 90
  Article XV (subsidies), 98-100, 228-31
  Article XVI (market access), 96, 110-11, 113, 182, 225-6
  Article XVII (national treatment), 66, 85, 87, 89, 99, 110, 157, 182, 225-7
  Article XIX (continued negotiations), 28, 70, 117, 194-5, 200, 216-19, 228-31, 235, 240-1, 248, 251, 254
  Article XXI (modifying schedules), 235, 240
  Article XXIII (dispute settlement), 199, 201
  Article XXVII (denial of benefits), 86
  Article XXVIII (definitions), 229
  Article XXIX (Annexes), 234

300　INDEX

GATS (cont.)
　bottom-up or positive list approach, 225
　classification under, 71-2
　flexibility under, 23, 70, 90, 109-10, 113, 159, 195, 203, 224, 239, 250-1
　horizontal commitments, 111-12
　modes under, 54, 86
　negotiations leading to, 23-4, 71, 74, 99-100, 201
　objectives in preamble, 69, 195, 200, 218-19, 224-5
　overlap and inconsistency with GATT 1994, 23, 34, 71, 73-4, 96, 98, 100, 105, 109, 118-19, 172, 218-19, 224-6, 246, 250-1
　potential conflict with UNESCO Convention, 186, 212
　reference paper, 227, 235, 242
　schedules under, 74, 99-100, 110-13, 118, 182, 235, 254
　top-down or negative list approach, 225
GATT 1947, 3-4, 95 *see also* GATT 1994, Uruguay Round
　application to television, 94
　core disciplines under, 5, 23
　drafting of, 92, 136
　expansion of, 23
　Director-General, 99
　Panel decisions under, 13, 80, 82
　Secretariat, 91, 99
GATT 1994, 15, 26, 69-70, 110, 127, 218-19, 244 *see also* GATT 1947, MFN, national treatment, quantitative restrictions, tariff bindings,
　Article I (MFN), 6, 75, 79-80, 85, 86, 87, 182, 212
　Article II (tariff bindings), 5, 114
　Article III (national treatment), 5-6, 27, 75-6, 78, 80-3, 85, 87-8, 103-4, 212, 225
　Article III:8(b) (subsidies), 93, 96-9, 119 *see also* SCM Agreement, subsidies
　Article IV (cinematograph films, screen quotas), 35, 42, 92-6, 109, 118, 142, 159-62, 177, 219-20, 222, 233-4, 242, 246, 250, 252-3
　Article VI (anti-dumping and countervailing measures), 8, 237 *see also* anti-dumping, Anti-Dumping Agreement, SCM Agreement
　Article XI (quantitative restrictions), 5, 13, 40, 67, 110, 113, 130, 225
　Article XVI (subsidies), 8, 96, 228, 231 *see also* SCM Agreement, subsidies
　Article XIX (safeguards), 239-40, 242 *see also* Safeguards Agreement
　Article XX (general exceptions), 7, 9, 35, 42, 66, 83, 90, 100-1, 104, 130, 132, 150, 163, 165, 171, 173, 222
　Article XX chapeau, 7-8, 101-4, 132, 139 *see also* discrimination: arbitrary or unjustifiable, disguised restriction on international trade
　Article XX(a) (public morals), 90, 101, 105-9, 142, 147, 156, 220, 250
　Article XX(b) (health), 7, 103, 143, 162, 164
　Article XX(d) (securing compliance), 107, 143, 166-71
　Article XX(f) (national treasures), 90, 101, 104-6, 109, 142-9, 220, 250, 252
　Article XX(g) (exhaustible natural resources), 7, 10, 103, 130-2, 136-7, 143, 148, 222
　Article XXI (national security), 8, 90
　Article XXIII (dispute settlement), 200-1 *see also* DSU
　Article XXIV (free-trade areas and customs unions), 117, 210-11
　core disciplines or obligations, 5-6, 75
　objectives in preamble, 218, 251
　overlap and inconsistency with GATS, 23, 34, 71, 73-4, 96, 98, 100, 105, 109, 118-19, 172, 218-19, 224-6, 246, 250-1
　potential conflict with UNESCO Convention, 186
　proposals for a new cultural exception under, 220-2, 253
general principles of law, *see* international law: general principles of law
genetic engineering, 14
genetic resources, 16-17
genetically modified food, 15
geographical indications, 15-16, 61
Germann, Christopher, 45, 245-6
Germany, 59
　co-production arrangements, 116
　involvement in UNESCO Convention, 183
　public broadcasters, 91
Gibson, Johanna, 16
globalisation, 176, 178, 181, 248
global public goods, 52-3
good faith, 98, 127, 139, 205-8
goods, 4-5, 11, 19, 23, 30, 33, 35, 39, 54, 70-1, 85, 92, 176, 181-3, 185-7, 218, 221, 227, 230-1, 237, 240, 243, 246, 248-9 *see also* public goods
　as distinct from services, 34, 71, 73-5, 94, 100, 118-19, 155, 223, 236, 238-9, 246, 250-1
　classification of, 76, 89, 224
　definition of, 71

INDEX

Graber, Christoph, 45, 47, 105, 154–5, 221, 242–3, 245–6
GSP, 134, 230 *see also* Enabling Clause

Hahn, Michael, 59, 221, 223
Harmonized System, 71, 73, 76, 223
health, 7, 79, 90, 107, 143, 162–6, 234, 245
Hoekman, Bernard, 241
Hollywood, 11, 47, 50, 58, 63
Honduras, position on UNESCO Convention, 185
Hong Kong, 28, 42
    GATS commitments, 25
    position in negotiations under GATS, 28–9, 249
    position on UNESCO Convention, 193
hormones, 3, 14
Howse, Robert, 11, 40, 56, 62, 125, 147
human rights, 142, 147, 186, 214, 227
    see also cultural rights
    in interpreting WTO provisions, 149–59, 165, 222
Human Rights Committee, 155, 161–2

ICCPR, 152 *see also* Human Rights Committee
    Article 19, 154–5
    Article 27, 161–2
ICESCR, 152–3, 157–8 *see also* Committee on Economic, Social and Cultural Rights
    Article 2(1), 152–3
    Article 15, 152–3, 161
    States parties to, 152, 157
ICJ,
    Statute of, 129, 137–41, 157
    as dispute settlement forum, 188
    decisions of, 108, 129, 135–6
ILC, Study Group on fragmentation, 134, 136, 138, 149, 203, 215
INCD, 176, 181, 193
    Proposed Convention on Cultural Diversity, 181–3, 191
INCP, 176, 178, 180–1
    draft International Convention on Cultural Diversity, 178–83, 190
India
    audiovisual subsidies, 22
    co-production arrangements, 88–9
    GATS commitments, 25, 110–11
    film and television industry, 45–6, 65, 232
    MFN exemption, 88–9
    position in Uruguay Round, 24
    Prasar Bharati, 91
    role in and arguments regarding *US – Shrimp*, 130, 136

submissions in and arguments regarding *EC – Tariff Preferences*, 132–4
Indigenous and Tribal Peoples Convention, 143, 154
intellectual property rights, 15, 23, 237, 243, 245 *see also* copyright, genetic resources, geographical indications, traditional knowledge and folklore, TRIPS Agreement
Inter-American Convention for the Protection and Conservation of Sea Turtles, 132
international law, 12, 34–6, 42, 66, 105, 129–30, 143–6, 148–9, 156, 158–9, 163, 166–7, 169–71, 175, 179, 184, 186, 202–5, 207–9, 213, 251
    conflicts in, 211–15
    customary, 126, 139–41, 151–2, 157, 161–2, 171, 204–5, 208
    customary rules of interpretation, 124–8, 130–42, 204 *see also* VCLT
    fragmentation of, 134, 138, 150, 203 *see also* ILC
    general principles of law, 138–40
    sources of, 137–8, 156 *see also* ICJ: Statute of
International Monetary Fund, 206
internet, 62, 63, 73, 223, 226
interpretation, *see* VCLT
Israel
    co-production arrangements, 114, 116
    GATS commitments, 25
    MFN exemption, 114
    position on UNESCO Convention, 185

Jackson, John, 94
Jamaica, music industry, 46, 50
Japan, 49
    GATS commitments, 25
    position in negotiations under GATS, 28–9
    position in Uruguay Round, 24
    position on UNESCO Convention, 193
    submissions in *Japan – Alcoholic Beverages II*, 13–14
    submissions in *Japan – Leather II (US)*, 13
jus cogens, 214

Knight, Sarah, 224, 226
Knight, Trevor, 82
Koskenniemi, Martti, 134, 213–14

Lang Plan, 63
League of Nations, 108
least developed countries, 7, 163, 232, 254
Leino, Päivi, 213–14
Lennard, Michael, 126, 139
lex posterior, 214

lex specialis, 214
liberalisation, *see* trade liberalisation
Liberia, position on UNESCO Convention, 185
likeness, 70, 75-80, 87-9, 154-5 *see also* aims-and-effects test, directly competitive or substitutable products
   like products, 6, 75-81, 85, 87, 96, 145
   like services and service suppliers, 85-9, 227
local content requirements, 20-1, 33, 58, 118, 157-60, 177, 212, 233, 246
Long Dimanche de Fiançailles, Un, 58
Low, Patrick, 225

Macmillan, Fiona, 243-4
magazines, 19, 26, 41, 81-2, 85, 176, 179, 248 *see also* publishing
MAI, 31-2, 221
Malaysia,
   GATS commitments, 25-6, 111
   role in *US – Shrimp*, 130
Mann, Catherine, 224, 226
Marceau, Gabrielle, 138, 196, 204, 214
market access, 5, 25, 116, 164, 201, 221, 244
   limitations, 110-13, 226
   commitments under GATS, 25-6, 35, 96, 109-13, 118, 182, 195, 225-7, 229, 242, 246-7, 251, 254
Marrakesh Agreement,
   Annex 1A (goods agreements), 70-1
   Article IX (authoritative interpretations of WTO law), 235-6
   Article X (amendments to WTO law), 234
   entry into force, 117
   general interpretative note to Annex 1A, 71
   objectives in preamble, 4, 6-7, 10, 163, 218
Mas-Colell, Andreu, 55-7
Mattoo, Aaditya, 66, 225-6
Maule, Christopher, 22, 49, 62, 175, 194-5
Mavroidis, Petros, 9, 108
McDonald's, 11
McNair, Arnold, 134
merit goods, 40-1, 51
Messerlin, Patrick, 58, 62-3, 221, 227
Mexico, *see also* NAFTA
   GATS commitments, 25-6, 112
   involvement in and position on UNESCO Convention, 183, 193
   local content quota, 20
   position in negotiations under GATS, 28-9, 249
   submissions in *Mexico – Taxes on Soft Drinks*, 167, 170-1, 208

MFN, 6, 8, 21, 25, 35, 59, 70, 75, 79-80, 86-9, 93, 113, 132, 159, 182, 187, 212, 219-20, 225, 227, 229-31, 237-9, 242, 250, 252-3 *see also* likeness
   exemptions under GATS, 25, 35, 70, 88-90, 113-17, 226-7, 236, 238, 246, 251, 255
minorities, 13, 55, 160-2, 164, 187 *see also* UN: Declaration on Minorities
moratorium, 74, 223, 225, 246
motion pictures, *see* films
multifunctionality, 17
music, 41, 43, 46, 53, 82, 163 *see also* sound recording
   Country Music Television dispute, 112-13

NAFTA, 6, 30-1, 112, 167, 220-1
   Country Music Television dispute, 112-13
Mexico – Taxes on Soft Drinks, 170, 208
Nairobi Protocol, 65
national identity, 112
national security, 4, 90 *see also* GATS: Article XIV*bis*, GATT 1994: Article XXI
national treasures, *see* GATT 1994: Article XX(f)
national treatment, 5-6, 21, 31, 49, 54, 56, 66, 70, 75-8, 80, 85-9, 92-3, 96, 99, 115, 159, 167, 182, 186-7, 200, 212, 219-20, 222, 225-8, 233-4, 250, 253-4 *see also* likeness
   commitments under GATS, 25-6, 35, 74, 100, 109-13, 118, 157, 195, 225, 229, 233, 242, 246-7, 251, 254
natural persons, presence of, 86, 88-9, 110, 113, 233 *see also* GATS: modes under
necessity, 7-9, 60, 66, 68, 90, 117, 103-7, 132, 158-9, 162-3, 165-71, 198, 220, 226, 240, 242 *see also* GATT 1994: Article XX, GATS: Article XIV
negative list approach, *see* top-down approach
negotiating history, 207-8 *see also* travaux préparatoires, Uruguay Round
Netherlands, television industry, 46
newsagency services, 116
newspapers, 179 *see also* publishing
New Zealand
   GATS commitments, 25-6
   position in Uruguay Round, 24
   renters' film quota, 93
NGOs, 184
Nigeria, position on UNESCO Convention, 185
Nine Lives, 45

non-discrimination, 38, 54, 67, 102–3, 232, 240, 242 *see also* discrimination, MFN, national treatment
non-tariff barriers, 9, 218
non-violation complaints, 200–1
Norway, MFN exemption, 115

OECD, 40
  Invisibles Code, 31
  MAI, 31–2

pacta sunt servanda, *see* VCLT: Article 26
Panels, 9, 26, 66–79, 170, 209
  Reports, 26
parallelism, *see* Safeguards Agreement: parallelism
Pather Panchali, 65
Pauwelyn, Joost, 132, 135, 138–9, 203–5, 211, 215
Perino, Grischa, 59
periodicals, 19, 27, 30, 73, 82, 84–5, 97–8, 110, 112, 226, 248 *see also* publishing
  split-run editions of, 40, 81, 84
piracy, 244
policy space, 34, 250
pollution, 162
Polygram dispute, 27
positive list approach, *see* bottom-up approach
precautionary principle, 205–6
printing, 19, 27, 29, 31–2, 40, 71, 97, 105, 110, 113, 116, 155, 233, 254 *see also* publishing
protectionism, 6, 9–10, 37–8, 49, 56, 61, 63, 68, 78, 84, 150, 159, 239 *see also* disguised restriction on international trade
disguised protectionism, 75, 194, 249, 255
public goods, 52, 54
  global public goods, 52–3
public interest, 154, 243, 245
public morals and public order, 90, 101, 104–9, 119, 142, 147, 155–9, 219–20, 227, 252
publishing, 19, 23, 29–30, 40, 61–2, 71, 77, 97, 105, 110, 112–13, 116, 176, 226, 233, 254 *see also* books, magazines, newspapers, periodicals, printing

quantitative restrictions, 4–5, 13, 20–1, 31, 33, 58, 62–4, 67, 110–11, 113, 145–6, 157–9, 182, 225–7, 239, 246–7 *see also* local content requirements, screen quotas
quarantine, 7, 11
quotas, *see* quantitative restrictions

radio, 19–20, 22, 72–3, 90–1, 94, 111–12, 153, 157, 223, 233, 246, 248 *see also* broadcasting
reference paper, *see* GATS: reference paper, telecommunications: reference paper
regional trade agreements, *see* free trade agreements
regulatory autonomy, 23, 38, 56 *see also* sovereignty
regulatory competence, 10, 176, 249
regulatory diversity, 10, 239
regulatory objectives or goals, 9, 11, 38, 41–4, 67, 83, 108
Richardson, Bonnie, 238
rights, *see* human rights
rollback, 220

safeguards, *see* GATS: Article X, cultural diversity: safeguards for, Safeguards Agreement
Safeguards Agreement, 210, 240, 242 *see also* GATT 1994: Article XIX
  Article 2.2 (application of safeguards on MFN basis), 210, 239–40
  Article 5.1 (limits on application of safeguards), 141
  parallelism, 211
SAGIT, *see* Canada: Cultural Industries SAGIT
satellite, 40, 62, 73, 112
Scheduling Guidelines,
  1993, 99, 100, 111
  2001, 74, 99, 100
Schuknecht, Ludger, 226
Schulze, Günther, 59
SCM Agreement, 96, 100, 229–30
  Article 1 (definition of subsidy), 229
  Article 3 (prohibited subsidies), 67
  Article 27 (special and differential treatment), 232
  Part II (prohibited subsidies), 230–1
  Part III (actionable subsidies), 231
  Part V (countervailing duties), 231
screen quotas, 32, 62, 64, 90, 92–6, 118–19, 142, 159–62, 177, 219–20, 233, 252–3 *see also* GATT 1994: Article IV
Sen, Amartya, 65
Senegal, 163
  involvement in UNESCO Convention, 183
services, 4, 11, 19, 21, 27–8, 33, 35, 39, 54, 95, 98–100, 108, 110–13, 116, 166, 176, 181, 185–7, 225, 229–31, 233–4, 238–40, 248–9, 256 *see also* audiovisual sector, likeness: like services and service suppliers

services (cont.)
    as distinct from goods, 34, 71, 73-5, 94, 100, 118-19, 155, 223, 236, 238-9, 246, 250-1
    classification of, 71-5, 89, 111, 113, 253
    definition of, 90
    government-supplied, 90-2
    trade in, 4, 23-4, 35, 98, 104, 117, 156, 183, 218-19, 225, 227-8, 236, 238, 241, 243, 246, 254
Shany, Yuval, 196
shrimp, 3, 130, 132
situation complaints, 200
soap opera, 40-1, 53
soft law, 171
sound recording, 19, 27, 40, 49, 50, 56, 64-5, 72-3, 100, 112, 118, 157, 176, 179, 223, 226, 232, 242, 248 *see also* music, radio
    audio tapes, 71
    CDs, 71, 177, 223, 242
sovereignty, 35, 83, 179, 181, 186, 199, 252 *see also* regulatory autonomy
special and differential treatment, 187, 222, 232, 246-7 *see also* developing countries
Sports Illustrated, 40
SPS Agreement, 9, 15
    Article 5.6 (trade-restrictiveness of SPS measures), 66
    Article 5.7 (reflection of precautionary principle), 206
    preamble, 7-8
standstill, 220, 233, 253
subsidies, 8, 22, 30-1, 35, 58, 62-4, 67, 88, 90, 118, 141, 177, 181, 219-20, 232-4, 242, 246, 247, 254 *see also* GATT 1994: Article III:8(b), GATT 1994: Article VI, GATT 1994: Article XVI, SCM Agreement, tax incentives, countervailing measures
    export subsidies, 230, 232
    GATS disciplines on, 98-100, 109, 118-19, 227-31, 241
    GATT 1994 disciplines on, 96-8, 109
    import substitution subsidies, 230-2
    regulation as, 28
Sutherland, Peter, 99
Sweden, 115
    co-production arrangements, 116
    music industry, 46
    position in Uruguay Round, 24
Sykes, Alan, 227

Taiwan, *see* Chinese Taipei
tariff preferences, 132-3, 181
tariffication, 5

tariffs, 4, 67, 92, 220, 231, 238-9 *see also* customs duties
    applied, 114
    bound, 5, 114
    bindings, 5, 8, 237, 239
    classification of, 76, 78, 82
    reductions, 5, 218
tax incentives, 21-2, 62, 177, 181, 191, 228
technology, 13-14, 48, 50, 63, 72, 178, 223-4, 232-3, 244-5
telecommunications, 72-3, 235
    convergence with audiovisual services, 72-3, 224
    GATS Annex on, 72, 219, 234
    reference paper, 242
    universal service clause, 242
television, 19-21, 33, 40, 43, 45-7, 55, 58-9, 62, 64, 72-3, 88, 91, 94-5, 111-12, 114-15, 117, 163, 223, 226, 232-3, 238, 246, 248 *see also* broadcasting, Country Music Television dispute, Television Without Frontiers Directive
Television Without Frontiers Directive, 21, 94-5, 115
Thailand, 4
    foreign ownership controls, 112
    GATS commitments, 25-6
theatre, 41, 72, 89, 93 *see also* cinemas
Throsby, David, 12-13, 41, 53, 184
Tonga, accession to WTO, 25-6
top-down approach, 225
TPRB, *see* WTO: TPRB
Trachtman, Joel, 3, 7, 204, 214
trade distortion, *see* distortion of trade
trade liberalisation, 3-4, 6-7, 10-12, 24, 28, 34-5, 43, 60, 64-5, 69-70, 74, 93, 114, 116, 117, 119, 123, 149, 155-6, 172, 178, 180, 193, 195, 216, 219, 221-2, 225-7, 229, 243, 246-8, 251, 253-4
trade-off devices, 7
trade remedies, 8 *see also* anti-dumping, countervailing measures, safeguards
traditional knowledge and folklore, 16, 17, 43, 245
travaux préparatoires, 135 *see also* negotiating history
Trebilcock, Michael, 40, 62, 147
TRIPS Agreement, 16, 70, 244 *see also* intellectual property rights
    competition principles and, 245
    impact of digitalisation, 244
    potential conflict with UNESCO Convention, 186
    public health and, 234, 245
    relevance to culture, 15, 243

Turkey,
  film tax dispute, 27
turtles, 3, 130-2, 148

UDHR, 150-4, 157-8
  Article, 22, 151
  Article 27(1), 151-2, 161
UK,
  British culture, 57
  co-production arrangements, 115-16
  cultural policy measures, 21, 92
  music industry, 50
UN, 133, 150 *see also* UDHR
  Charter, 151, 179, 186
  Commission on Human Rights, 44, 151, 160
    Special Rapporteurs, 149
  Declaration on Minorities, 161
  High Commissioner for Human Rights, 149, 156, 158, 160, 222
  Member States of, 151-2, 158
  Rio Declaration on Environment and Development, 132
  United Nations Convention on the Law of the Sea, 131
  United Nations Development Programme, 164
UNCTAD, 163-5, 185
UNESCO, 36, 44, 65-6, 165, 252-3, 255
    see also UNESCO Convention, UNESCO Convention on Cultural Property, UNESCO Recommendation on Participation in Cultural Life
  Action Plan on Cultural Policies for Development, 165
  Declaration of the Principles of International Cultural Co-operation, 65
  definition of cultural industries, 19
  General Conference, 147, 184-5, 193-4
  Intergovernmental Conference on Cultural and Media Policies for Development, 12, 165
  membership of, 42, 189, 193
  Our Creative Diversity, 12, 165
  purpose and role of, 42, 174, 178, 180-1
  Recommendation for the Safeguarding and Preservation of Moving Images, 43
  Recommendation on the Safeguarding of Traditional Culture and Folklore, 43
  Universal Declaration on Cultural Diversity, 12, 39, 65
  World Commission on Culture and Development, 165
UNESCO Convention, 29, 34-5, 174-5, 191, 217, 252, 256
  as defence to WTO violation, 169-70, 202-15
  dispute settlement mechanism, 187-8
  entry into force, 185, 250, 253
  guiding principles, 186, 216
  negotiations leading to, 175, 178, 180-1, 183-5, 188, 216
  potential conflicts with WTO law, 180, 183, 187-9, 211-15
  potential impact on WTO disputes, 175, 195-202, 216
  potential impact on WTO negotiations, 175, 194-5, 216, 253
  preamble, 185
  rights and obligations, 186-7
  scope of, 185-6
  votes on, 185
  WTO Members' views on, 189, 192-4, 248
UNESCO Convention on Cultural Property, 144
  potential conflict with WTO law, 145-8
  States parties, 144
UNESCO Recommendation on Participation in Cultural Life, 41, 43, 65, 153
UNIDROIT Convention on Cultural Objects, 145
United Kingdom, *see* UK
United States of America, *see* USA
Universal Declaration on Cultural Diversity, 12, 39, 65
universal service clause, 242
Uruguay Round, 4-5, 10, 23-7, 32, 34-7, 69-70, 89, 91, 95, 98-9, 111, 174, 201, 217, 221, 235, 238, 248-9, 252, 254-6
USA, 14, 17, 136 *see also* NAFTA
  audiovisual sector dominance, 44-50, 85, 239
  Australia-United States Free Trade Agreement, 33
  Chile-United States Free Trade Agreement, 33
  co-production arrangements, 163
  Country Music Television dispute, 112-13
  CUSFTA, 31
  film tax dispute, 27
  foreign ownership controls, 112
  free trade agreements, 32-3, 230, 233
  GATS commitments, 25-6
  position in negotiations under GATS, 28-9, 37, 39, 72, 74, 105, 107, 118, 224, 247, 249
  position in Uruguay Round, 24-5, 221
  position on aims-and-effects test, 82-3
  position on DSU Article 3.2, 126
  position on GATT Article IV, 94
  position on MAI, 32

USA (cont.)
  position on obligation of good faith, 207
  position on UNESCO Convention, 185, 193–4
  'Special 301', 95
  submissions in *Canada – Periodicals*, 97
  submissions in *Mexico – Taxes on Soft Drinks*, 167
  Television Without Frontiers dispute, 95
United States Trade Representative, 95

VCLT,
  and DSU Article 3.2, 124–6
  Article 26 (*pacta sunt servanda*), 206–7 *see also* good faith
  Article 28 (non-retroactivity), 139–40
  Article 30 (successive treaties), 213, 215
  Articles 31 and 32 (rules of interpretation), 124–8, 140, 155, 171
  Article 31(1) (ordinary meaning, context, object and purpose), 126–8, 130–7, 139, 142–3, 148, 158, 161–2, 167, 171
  Article 31(3)(b) (subsequent practice), 100
  Article 31(3)(c) (relevant rules of international law), 123, 128, 131, 137–42, 154, 161–2, 171
  Article 41 (modifying multilateral treaties), 214–15
  contemporaneous or evolutionary interpretation, 134–7, 143, 156, 162
  customary rules of interpretation, 124–8, 130–42, 204
  general rule of interpretation, 127
  negotiating history of, 207
  supplementary means of interpretation, 99–100, 128, 135
Verhoosel, Gaëtan, 38

video, 19, 21, 111–12, 114, 176, 179 *see also* films
video tapes, 71–2, 111
Viet Nam, accession to WTO, 25–6
violation complaints, 199, 201

Wai, Robert, 150
Waiver, 89, 214–15, 236
Waincymer, Jeffrey, 140
Warner Brothers, 58
Willis, Bruce, 58
Wood, Chris, 50
World Intellectual Property Organization, 185
WTO, 3–4, 29, 33, 36
  accession to, 25–6, 110, 254
  core disciplines, 5–6, 38, 67
  Council for Trade in Services, 28, 117, 241
  Council for TRIPS, 16
  Director-General, 192
  dispute settlement, 9, 34–6, 66, 96, 123–6, 129, 143, 149–50, 155, 159–60, 172–3, 177, 180, 194–9, 203, 207–9, 217, 228, 231, 250–1, 253, 256 *see also* DSU
  Doha Round, 28, 35–6, 194, 217–18, 234, 238–9, 241, 247, 248, 251–6
  DSB, 9, 124–6, 129, 133, 136, 156, 170, 177, 197–8, 204–5, 207, 210
  General Council, 99, 235
  Members, 42, 144
  Ministerial Conference, 16, 28, 99, 235–6
  Secretariat, 22, 72, 74, 113, 192, 238
  TPRB, 20
  Working Party on GATS Rules, 241
Wunsch-Vincent, Sacha, 72, 224, 226

For EU product safety concerns, contact us at Calle de José Abascal, 56–1°,
28003 Madrid, Spain or eugpsr@cambridge.org.

www.ingramcontent.com/pod-product-compliance
Ingram Content Group UK Ltd.
Pitfield, Milton Keynes, MK11 3LW, UK
UKHW020156060825
461487UK00017B/1428